Encyclopedia
of
NEW JERSEY

Encyclopedia
of
NEW JERSEY

—a volume of
ENCYCLOPEDIA OF THE UNITED STATES

SOMERSET PUBLISHERS

FOREWORD

Information on this state is available from many other sources. Histories and geographies abound; there are place-name books, guidebooks and biographical references; many excellent atlases provide map detail; government registers contain in-depth coverage of the political organization.

It is the existence of so many varied sources of information that makes a systematic, encyclopedic reference necessary - a single source for the most useful information about New Jersey.

A secondary purpose of this volume is to play a part in a national reference on all of the states, a systematic approach to referencing the entire nation - an *Encyclopedia of the United States* with each volume following a planned outline that matches each other volume in the series - with exceptions in the format made only when necessary.

This goal was partly achieved during the Great Depression years with the publication of the WPA Federal Writers' Project State and City Guidebooks, which we are proud to have republished in recent years in their original form. While containing a wealth of interesting and still useful information they are outdated for most of the reference needs of today. And they were essentially *tour-guides* rather than general reference books. They were, however, very useful in the planning of this new work.

By providing consistency in format throughout the series of volumes in this Encyclopedia, researchers, whether they are academic scholars or occasional public library users, will be aided in knowing that a source exists for information on any of the states.

It is our hope that this Encyclopedia series will have a permanence through the issuance of revised editions at intervals to be determined by a careful watch on the availability of new material. Undoubtedly changes in the concept will be reflected in later editions as a result of feed back from users and the observations and introspection of our editors.

We wish to acknowledge with great appreciation the cooperation of the many state and local government offices that have furnished or reviewed material.

We are further grateful to the many librarians who have made their facilities so available during the years that this project has been in process.

Frank H. Gille

EDITOR AND PUBLISHER
Frank H. Gille

MANAGING EDITOR
Beth Blenz

ASSOCIATE EDITOR
Timothy F. Gille

CAMERA GRAPHICS
Thomas F. Gille

PRODUCTION
Bryan D. Loy

INDEXING
Margaret Regis

MECHANICAL ART
Susan E. B. Paruolo

TABLE OF CONTENTS

INTRODUCTION

NEW JERSEY: The Garden State

F ar from living completely in the shadow of New York City, New Jersey has demonstrated, especially in recent years, that it has a life of its own. Below the booming industrial cities facing Manhattan are surprisingly vast areas of near-wilderness, small towns with histories as long as the United States', and glamorous resorts that compete with the world's other playgrounds for big money.

New Jersey, like many other states, boasts of its diversity. But what makes it different from other states is that its contrasts can be observed within a tiny area of 7,800 square miles. Twenty miles south of the factories and overcrowding of Elizabeth are the gently rolling hills where blueberries and dairy products are the main industries. Travelers may see the state as merely a passageway between New York City and Philadelphia. Off the Jersey Turnpike, however, along the side roads between Victorian Cape May and the Appalachian heights of the Kittatinny Mountains, something more of the state may be discovered.

State Symbols

THE NAME

The province, now the state, of New Jersey, was so named in 1664 in the grant to the proprieters, Lord Berkeley and Sir George Carteret, after the Island of Jersey, upon which Sir George had sheltered the Duke of York from Puritan England in 1650. Carteret was a native of the Isle of Jersey, in the English Channel. The formal name was the Latin *Nuova Caesarea* .

The province was formerly called New Canary and its Indian name was *Scheyichlie* .

Philip Falle, basing his statement on Camden's *De Insulis Brittanicis*, gives the derivation of the term "Jersey" as a corruption of the term Caesarea. He says that in the language of the northern nations who overran England about 700 A.D., *ey*, the suffix of the word Jersey, meant "island," and that *jer* or *ger* is a contraction of "Caeser", or "Caeser's Island." Other forms of the name of the island are Gersey, Gearsey, Jarsey, Jarsy, Jarzie and Jerseye.

"New" simply indicates the novelty of this colonial territory.

THE NICKNAME

People call New Jersey the "Camden and Amboy State," or the "State of Camden and Amboy," the "Clam State," the "Foreigner State," the "Garden State," the "Jersey Blue State," the "Mosquito State," "New Spain," and "State of Spain," as well as the "Switzerland of America."

New Jersey was designated as the "State of Camden and Amboy" during the time when the Camden and Amboy Railroad influence held a dominating power in the state.

The immense quantities of clams, taken from the Atlantic Ocean and the Delaware Bay in New Jersey and shipped out, give rise to the use of the nickname, "The Clam State."

This state is sometimes called the "Foreigner State," "New Spain," and the "State of Spain" because when the fortunes of the Bonaparte family fell, Joseph Bonaparte, then King of Spain, fled to New Jersey about 1812 and bought 1,400 acres of land at Bordentown, upon which he built a palatial mansion, "where he dwelt until 1832, entertaining many illustrious Frenchmen." Historian King says in this connection that the "Philadelphians were rather jealous of the good luck of New Jersey in securing such distinguished residents, and called the state Spain with good-humored raillery reading it out of the Union. Hence arose the gibe that this domain is in some sense a foreign land; and the people were called foreigners and Spaniards, since their social leader was the King of Spain."

New Jersey has many large truck farms producing agricultural and floral products, especially in the valley of the Delaware River, catering particularly to the New York and Philadelphia metropolitan areas; consequently she is called the "Garden State," and this appears on motorists' automobile licenses today.

The "Jersey Blue State," given as a sobriquet to New Jersey, commemorates the fact that the Revolutionary Militia of the colony wore blue uniforms, or probably the name goes back for its origin to the Blue Laws of the state.

"We get the scornful title, the "Mosquito State," one state librarian said, "because we seem to have our share of these industrious and bloodthirsty insects. As a matter of fact, however, a considerable number of other states have as many, if not more, of the pests."

New Jersey has been called the "Switzerland of America," probably because of its mountain scenery in the northwestern part of the state, occasioned by the Kittatinny Range of mountains and by the ranges of the Watchung, Sourland and the Pickle mountains to the southeast. "The most famous of these is the Palisades, a line of wonderful basaltic precipices extending along the Hudson River from Staten Island Sound to Ladentown, New York, and looking down the crowded streets of New York," according to Moses King.

New Jerseyans are designated as "Clam-Catchers," "Clams," "Foreigners," "Jersey Blues," and "Spaniards." The nicknames mentioned above originated in the same sources as those given in the previous discussion of the nicknames of the state.

THE FLAG

By legislative action the state flag of New Jersey was approved March 26, 1896. The law provides that it "shall be of buff color, having in the center thereof the arms of the state properly emblazoned thereon."

The official colors of New Jersey for use on the state flags were established in 1965 as "buff" and "Jersey blue."

MOTTO

The state motto of New Jersey is "Liberty and Prosperity," and it appears on the state seal. It was informally adopted in 1821 as the best of several suggested mottos. A variety of mottos occur; but among the earliest is that used in the Joseph Justice edition of the laws (1821) where the words "liberty and prosperity" are found. This is now the recognized motto of New Jersey, when such is used.

THE STATE SEAL

New Jersey's state seal was designed by Pierre Eugene du Simitiere and presented in May 1777 to the legislature, which was then meeting in the Indian King Tavern in Haddonfield.

The three plows in the shield honor the state's agricultural tradition. The helmet above the shield faces forward, an attitude denoting sovereignty and thus particularly fitting for one of the first governments created under the notion that the state itself is the sovereign. The crest above the helmet is a horse's head.

The supporting female figures are Liberty and Ceres, the Roman goddess of grain, symbolizing abundance. Liberty, on the viewer's left, carries the liberty cap on her staff. Ceres holds a cornucopia filled with harvested produce.

Although the seal's major elements have kept their relative positions for more than 200 years, there have been a number of lesser changes. The staff that Liberty now holds with her right hand she once held in the crook of her left arm. While the female figures now face straight ahead they at one time looked away from the shield. The cornucopia that Ceres now holds upright was once inverted, its open end upon the ground. The changes were made when the seal was redesigned in accordance with Joint Resolution 8 of the Laws of 1928. It was then that the year, 1776, first appeared in Arabic figures.

THE STATE FLOWER

The state flower of New Jersey is the violet, as officially declared in as concurrent resolution of 1913 that passed the assembly and the senate on March 28 and April 2, respectively, of that year.

Later, in 1971, the legislature adopted a bill officially designating the violet, *Viola sororia* , as the state flower. Garden clubs claimed the early concurrent resolution had no permanence in law.

An earlier and unofficial effort to have a state flower designated was made through an appeal to the schools for an expression of choice, but there was only a limited response and this was not regarded as determinative. Most of the responses favored the sunflower.

THE STATE TREES

The official state tree is the Red Oak, *Quercus borealis maxima* . The Red Oak was authorized by a joint resolution of the legislature signed by Gov. Alfred E. Driscoll in 1950. The state Memorial Tree is the Dogwood, authorized by Assembly Concurrent Resolution No. 12 of 1951.

THE STATE BIRD

The Eastern Goldfinch is the New Jersey State Bird, having been so declared by Chapter 283 of the Laws of 1935.

THE STATE BUG

The honey bee, *apis mellifera* , is the state bug, having been so designated by Chapter 42 of the Laws of 1974. The legislature enacted the bill, A-671, and Gov. Brendan T. Byrne signed it June 20, 1974. They were encouraged by a group of children from the Sunnybrae School in Hamilton Township, who came to the State House with a presentation that included a song and a poem.

Despite the official designation, scientists do not classify the bee as a bug. The bee is listed in the order Hymenoptera, which means "membranous wings," while true bugs are listed in the order Hemiptera.

THE STATE ANIMAL

The state animal is the horse, *Equus Caballus* , so designated in Chapter 173 of the Laws of 1977. Gov. Brendan T. Byrne signed the law August 14, 1977, while attending the farm and horse show at Augusta, Sussex County. The senate bill, which eventually became the law, had been introduced December 13, 1976. A statement attached to the bill said the state had more than 38,000 horses and 4,654 horse farms, of which 888 were involved in developing race horses. The fifth grade class of Our Lady of Victoria School, Harrington Park, took a special interest in the legislation. One of the class's members, Michael J. McCarthy, solicited the signatures of many of the 24 senators who sponsored the bill.

THE STATE SONG

New Jersey does not have an official state song despite attempts to find one.

As the result of a 1939 contest, a report was submitted on December 9, 1940, in favor of the "New Jersey Loyalty Song," by Samuel Monroe, but the legislature never acted upon the recommendation.

Similar action taken by the 1954 legislature resulted in the State Department of Education, on May 18, 1956, submitting a report to the effect "that no song had been found...of sufficient worth to recommend as the official state song."

In 1964 the New Jersey Tercentenary Commission sponsored a state song contest but did not endeavor to establish an official state song.

On November 20, 1972, the general assembly approved, 48-6, a senate bill declaring "I'm from New Jersey" as the official state song.

Before the passage of the measure, the composer, Joseph Rocco "Red" Mascara of Phillipsburg, sang the lyrics from the assembly gallery, accompanied by a six-piece group. Mr. Mascara had lobbied 11 years to secure passage of the bill. The bill was not signed into law, however.

On June 12, 1980, the assembly by voice vote passed ACR-121, designating the song "Born to Run" as the state's unofficial rock anthem. The song had been commercially performed by Bruce Springsteen, who was born in Freehold on September 23, 1949. There were protests that the song lacked the inspirational quality appropriate for a state anthem. The resolution was referred to the senate's State Government Committee, which did not immediately move to release it.

STATE CAPITOL

The New Jersey capitol at Trenton, completed in 1889, has been several times enlarged by additional buildings. The original structure is 160 feet long, 67 feet wide, and 145 feet high to the top of the dome. L.H. Broome of Jersey City was the designer. It represents the Classical style of Renaissance architecture. The walls are constructed of solid, fireproof brick masonry, faced with a light-colored stone from Indiana, known as Salem oolitic, with foundations and trimmings of New Jersey free stone, from the Prallsville quarries, in Hunterdon County. The cost of this original capitol was $275,000.

The main entrance corridor is hung with portraits of early Jersey statesmen and patriots; portraits of various governors hang in the executive chambers. Against the walls of the small rotunda are musty cabinets of Civil War regimental flags. The second and thir floors are labyrinths of corridors and passageways weaving in and out of erractically placed offices.

In 1891 an assembly chamber was added to this structure. James Moylan of Jersey City designed this new part, which is 120 feet long, and 75 feet wide. The foundation is built of brown stone, from the Stockton quarries, and the trimmings of light Indiana stone.

. A senate chamber was erected in 1903 with Arnold Moses of Merchantville as the architect.

In 1907 another building, representing the Classical style of architecture, was added. George E. Poole, the state architect, designed this structure which is built of brick. In 1911 and 1912, $130,000 was appropriated for constructing the east and west wings. The completed edifice stands upon a nineteen-acre tract of land, the total cost of all buildings and improvements amounting to about $400,000.

Further down State Street is the State Capitol annex, built in 1931 from designs of J. Osborne Hunt and Colonel Hugh Kelly. The four story Indiana limestone building is a well-planned H-shaped structure housing a number of state departments, and a state museum (See also **Trenton**).

Annual Events in New Jersey

February

    Pee Wee Russell Memorial Stomp, Martinsville

March

    Bergen County Festival, Hackensack

April

    Festival of Fine Arts, Long Branch
    Antiques Fair and Sale, Morristown
    Teen Arts Festival, West Long Branch

May

    Showcase, West Long Branch

June

    Arts and Crafts Festival, Cape May
    Garden State Arts Gala (through Sept.), Holmdel
    Irish, Italian, Polish and Ukranian Festivals,
      Holmdel
    Jewish Festival of Arts, Holmdel
    Folk Festival, Middletown
    Spring Festival, Seaside Heights
    Waterloo Village Music Festival (through Aug.),
      Stanhope
    June Days Folk Festival, West Orange

July

    Hydrangea Festival, Atlantic City
    Black Heritage Festival, Holmdel
    Maurice Podell Outdoor Art Festival, Long Branch
    Festival of Art, Willingboro

August

    Boardwalk Art Show, Ocean City

September

      German-American Festival, Holmdel
      Grecian Arts Festival, Holmdel
      Puerto Rican Heritage Festival, Holmdel
      Scottish Heritage Festival, Holmdel
      Great Falls Festival, Paterson
      New Jersey State Fair, Trenton
      Art Show, West Orange

October

      Columbus Day Landing Pageant, Asbury Park
      Victorian Weekend: Tours, Cape May
      Half-Marathon at Music Pier, Ocean City
      Assunpink Creek Folk Festival, Trenton
      Oktoberfest, Waterville

November

      Waterfowl Week, Brigantine National Wildlife
        Refuge
      Art Show, West Orange

PREHISTORY
AND
ARCHEOLOGY

A rcheologists concerned with New Jersey usually center their interest on two main problems: (1) remains of the Lenni-Lenape Indians and their ancestors or predecessors, and (2) traces of an ancient, glacial age man. About the Indians there is much conclusive information, but evidence of ancient man has been the crux of New Jersey's archeological dispute.

About 7,000 years ago. the first humans reached the Atlantic region now known as New Jersey. They had come to North America thousands of years before, from Siberia and across the Bering Strait on a land-bridge that rose above the waters at that time. From these early people arose the Lenni-Lenape, or "Original People" in the New Jersey region.

The theory of an ancient man in New Jersey was first advanced with evidence by Dr. Charles C. Abbott, a Trenton physician, who discovered crude argillite blades, which he assigned to the glacial period. The spot where these remains were found in gravel along the Delaware River bluff, one mile south of Trenton, consequently became one of the most important archeological sites in the eastern United States. An article concerning his finds, written by Dr. Abbott in 1872, raised a storm of argument.

Late in 1887, Henry C. Mercer. curator of the Museum of American and Prehistoric Archeology at the University of Pennsylvania, investigated the site. He reported, "No token of an antecedent race was discovered." Beginning in 1894 and continuing for nearly twenty years, the Abbott farm was excavated by Ernest Volk, under the direction of F.W. Putnam of Harvard University. Volk, agreeing with Dr. Abbott, wrote that "the conclusive evidence ... asserts the antiquity of man on this continent at least as far back as the time of these glacial deposits in the Delaware Valley." Dr. Leslie Spier dug several trenches on the Abbott farm in 1914 and 1915. He found large stone blades, arrowheads and other artifacts of a simple culture differing widely from that of the historic Lenni-Lenape Indians, but he did not attempt to answer the question of its being a possible Paleolithic, or Stone Age, culture.

In April 1936 the Indian Site Survey, a Works Progress Administration project sponsored by the state museum and directed by Dr. Dorothy Cross, began excavations at the Abbott farm and later at other sites. Nothing has been discovered yet that may be attributed to an ancient or glacial man. On the contrary, what evidence has been uncovered tends to disprove Dr. Abbott's interpretation of his findings; as an instance, designs on unearthed pottery indicate that the earlier people responsible for them were not of the glacial age, but lived shortly before the Lenape.

Before the modern archeologists, however, the Lenni-Lenape themselves had a record of their own "prehistory." Their *Walum Olum* , or "painted records" tell of ancestors who struggled over terrible terrain to reach their gentle land near the ocean. *Walum Olum* was translated into English in the 1830s by Constantine S. Rafinesque and possibly inspired Abbott, Mercer, Cross and others to find evidence of the earliest New Jerseyans.

The scantiness of evidence of these earlier people is in direct contrast to the great number and variety of recent Indian artifacts found by members of the Survey and by other investigators. From the tools, implements decorative or ceremonial items, weapons, skeletons, and household units discovered, much progress has been made in determining the life and customs of these people. Of importance are the remains of their homes mere darkened spots in the ground. The sunken posts around which the bark and grass houses of the Indians were built have left their marks, and these, when plotted out, serve as a basis for reconstructing the actual living quarters.

The tools and agricultural and household implements afford an especially good indication of the cultural level. Made primarily of stone and clay, they demonstrate an appreciable ingenuity. Knives, drills, scrapers hoes and spades were chipped into shape from the harder stones. Some of the uses to which the tools were put can be determined. For example, the edges of the knives sometimes have one or more notches where they have been used for shaping rounded objects, such as reeds for arrow shafts. Some hoes and spades show signs of having been fitted into handles. Another method of shaping tools was by grinding and polishing. Most of the cutting implements—axes, hatchets, adzes and gouges—were made in this way.

Mortars and pestles show one method for preparing food. Clay pots and stone hearths also tell the story of cooking methods. (Pots and baskets were frequently sunk in the ground, and the food cooked by placing hot stones in the vessels.) Food was sometimes stored in large pots of thin clay, buried so that the rim was flush with the surface of the house floor. Some of these pots, most of them cracked, have been recently excavated. They are decorated with impressions of fiber or bark.

Other smaller pieces of pottery and fragments that can be reconstructed bear elaborate incised designs extremely important in tracing tribal distribution. Each group of Indians used definite patterns in decorating its pottery, and, where given designs are found, the work is almost certainly that of some particular group. Certain mixtures of designs show relations between the tribes.

Among the most interesting items are ornaments made of the rarer stones — banded slate, rose quartz, steatite, serpentine, mica, schist, and clay marl — highly polished. These include pendants, beads of tubular and disk shapes, gorgets more elaborately designed than pendants and with more than one perforation and banner stones. There has been much speculation about the banner stones — usually highly polished stones in the shape of butterfly wings, which were centrally drilled or notched. Early historical accounts suggest that they were mounted on shafts and carried as scepters, but there is disagreement on this point. Among the rarest ornaments are the bird stones, shaped like birds; these were made only from the finer stones, such as slate, steatite and serpentine. Boat stones, resembling canoes and sometimes perforated to be worn as pendants, are also among the rare items.

Many thousands of implements have been found to date in various excavations. Judging by the artifacts found, the Abbott farm site must have been a favorite place for hunting, fishing and farming. Numerous arrowheads, spearheads and other implements of the chase have been found here, together with sinew stones, used for making animal gut pliable, and semi-lunar knives, used for scraping flesh from hides or for chopping meat.

The innumerable net sinkers, usually mere notched pebbles, show that fishing was popular. Hoes, mortars and pestles, found in surprising quantities, indicated that the land was cultivated even more extensively than was formerly supposed. Axes and gouges prove that the felling of trees and wood working were common practices.

The People the White Man Met

The Indians who inhabited New Jersey when the white man came called their country *Scheyechbi* and themselves *Lenni-Lenape*, meaning "Original People." The colonists named them *Delawares* because most of them lived along the Delaware River.

The Delawares belonged to the general group of Algonkian Indians in northeastern United States and eastern Canada. The larger tribe was divided into three sub-tribes. Each sub-tribe was further divided into family groups, each having an individual totem or guardian spirit. The Minsi (or Munsee) sub-tribe lived in the north and used the wolf as a totem; the Unami, in the central part of the state, adopted the turtle; and the Unalachtigo, in the south, were known by the wild turkey.

With an aboriginal population variously estimated from between 10,000 and 40,000 persons, the traditional Delawaran homeland extended throughout the Middle Atlantic coastal plain and adjacent highland interior of southwestern Connecticut, southeastern New York, western Long Island, all of New Jersey, southeastern Pennsylvania and the state of Delaware.

Known among their Eastern Algonkian (Algonquin) brethren as "grandfathers," their Iroquoian-speaking neighbors to the north and west called the Delaware "nephews." The Algonquin and Souian peoples who shared their long westward exile knew them as *Wapanachki*, "easterners, or people of the dawn." The Delawarans on their part knew European colonists that streamed upon their lands as *Swannekens,* "salt water, or bitter people." Long years of struggle led the Delaware to name the American successors to the Europeans *Kwun-nah-she-kun* "long knives."

Never politically united, the Delawarans did share a common tongue. The Algonquian linguist Ives Goddard has identified two closely related Delaware languages, *Munsee* and *Unami*. Goddard has stated that Munsee was spoken by the lower Hudson and upper Delaware River valley groups while Unami was used by the Delawarans of the lower Delaware River watershed. Each language was further divided into a presently unknown number of dialects. Most closely related to *Mahican* and the *Southern New England Algonquian* languages to the north and the *Nanticoke* to the south, the relationship between Delaware and other Algonquian languages is poorly understood.

The Dutch merchant-explorers that first visited the Delawaran homeland during the seventeenth century came upon a neolithic farming, fishing, hunting and gathering people whose settlements thickly lined the watercourses, lagoons and beaches of their territories. Those who lived near the coast drew their lives from the sea. They hooked, speared, netted and trapped cod, salmon, herring, sturgeon and many other kinds of fish. Hard clams, oysters, mussels, crabs, lobsters and other forms of shellfish were also very important parts of the coastal Delaware diet. Sharp fishbones were used as needles and awls while the cracked shells of molluscs provided keen cutting edges. The shells of hard clams and periwinkles were ground into tubular white and purple beads. These became a species of currency known as *sewan* or *wampum* . The flesh and eggs of seabirds, a galaxy of berries, many forms of seaweed and the meat and oil from seals and stranded whales were other major coastal Lenni-Lenapean food sources. Wetlands supported luxuriant stands of tall grasses that provided the raw material for the mats that served as floor, wall and roof for the coastal Delaware roundhouses and longhouses. Grasses were also woven into the bags and baskets that served as the furniture for their dwellings and the luggage for their journeys. Rimless conical pottery, bark and skin containers, and hollowed logs furnished their homes and lined their cooking fires. Low sleek dugout canoes expertly plied the waterways of their territories, bringing people and resources together. White tailed deer, bear and smaller mammals were hunted and trapped for their flesh and fur. Corn, beans and squash were cultivated in small garden plots. These crops, however, made only a modest contribution to coastal Delawaran subsistence.

The coastal Delawares made their homes in large villages located in sheltered bays and sounds during the blustery winter months. These settlements broke up during the spring and the villagers moved to small fishing, shellfishing and hunting camps during the warmer months. Large numbers of coastal people periodically joined their relations in the interior at this time. Many inland people were hosted in their turn by their coastal relatives from the late spring through the fall.

The Delawares of the highland interior made their livelihood from the upland fields, forests and streams. Large gardens yielded abundant harvests of corn, beans, squash, sunflowers and other crops. Spawning anadramous fish like shad, salmon and herring added to the substantial catch of pike, bass, pickerel, catfish, carp and other lake and river fish. Individual and group hunts brought in an abundance of meat and skins from white tailed deer, elk, black and brown bear, forest bison, beaver and many other forest animals. Extensive rock groups of argillite, jasper and quartz furnished the raw materials for a wide range of cutting and piercing tools. An extensive selection of tubers, greens, fruits and berries were available during the warmer months. The flesh, feathers and eggs of passenger pigeons, ducks, geese, turkey and other birds rounded out the interior Delawaran diet. The bark of elm, hickory and birch trees provided building materials for longhouses, canoes and cooking utensils. The deep pine and oak forests furnished fuel as well as house frames, tool handles and many other necessary utensils. Clays gathered from riverbeds and lakebottoms were transformed by Delaware craftswomen into globular pots with high elaborately decorated castelated rims.

The interior Delawaran groups inhabited small scattered hunting camps located in sheltered upland valleys during the winter months. The families gathered by the falls and rapids of the rivers and their major tributaries to harvest the massive anadramous fish runs of the early spring. The matriclan segments then moved into the large agricultural villages located along the fertile river bottoms during the late spring and early summer. Lower Delawaran villages were strung out along sections of large river valleys. Upper Delawaran agricultural villages were far more concentrated, with many of the larger settlements fortified with timber palisade walls during periods of hostility.

Inland and coastal Delaware people exchanged visits to each others' settlements following the spring planting and fishing harvests. Summer was the time for trading and raiding, and the able bodied accordingly roved widely throughout the region while the very young and very old tended the fields and gathered wild plants.

The people rejoined their families in the agricultural villages for the fall harvest and its attendant festival. They then returned into their forests for the annual communal hunt. Parties numbering from several score to several hundred individuals surrounded a section of woodland, set it afire, and then drove whatever game contained within the circle of flame and people into an enclosure located at the section's center. The game slaughtered in this trap was preserved and used during the coming winter months. The families then returned to their hunting camps until the spring.

Little is known about aboriginal Delawaran religion. Early European observers noted the Delawaran groups followed an extensive round of religious dances and feasts. Guardian spirits obtained through dreams and visions played an important part in Delaware life. Medicine people of both sexes were active in the society.

Delaware men and women were lightly clad during the warmer months. Men generally only wore skin breechclothes, while the women dressed in skin kilts. Both sexes wore moccasins made from tanned deer hide. The people normally applied clarified bear grease mixed with onion grass to protect their bodies from sun and insects. Both sexes adorned themselves with paint, ear and nose ornaments and tattoos. Successful warriors and gifted medicine persons sported particularly elaborate tattoos located all over their bodies. Men and women usually wore their hair long in a wide variety of styles. Warriors shaved their heads and wore a small scalp lock decorated with feathers, wampum and fur. Both sexes wore leggings, loosely fitted shirts, and bearskin robes during the colder months.

The longhouse was the predominant Delawaran house type. Ranging in length from 30 to 60 feet and from 10 to 15 feet wide, the longhouse was constructed of thick saplings joined together to form a series of arches. These arches were connected by supporting branches and the frame was covered with grass mats or bark. Fireplaces were located along the central corridor and families occupied cubicles on their side of the hearths. The center portion of the roof was left open to let the smoke from the fires out, and access to and from the structure was made possible by doors located at either end of the long central corridor. Goods were stored in baskets below the family sleeping compartments, and matrilineage possessions were kept in storage rooms located at the ends of the longhouse. Dried foodstuffs and other perishables were either hung from the ceiling, kept in caches above ground, or buried in pits near the settlements.

The Delawarans reckoned descent through their women. Groups of related women and their male kinsmen made up a matriclan segment. These segments were parts of a larger matriclan whose members resided at various locations throughout the Delaware homeland. Later sources suggested th.

existence of three Delaware matriclans, identified by the wolf, the turtle and the turkey. Such a division of lineages has not been confirmed in the seventeenth century record, and aboriginal Delaware society was probably organized into a larger number of matriclans.

The Delawares required people to select marriage partners from other lineages. The rule of matrilocal residence saw to it that Delaware husbands moved into their wives' households. Important or wealthy men were permitted more than one wite, but these were usually from the same matriclan. When wives were of different lineages, the man either lived with the senior wife, a favorite, or divided his time among the households of his various spouses.

The seventeenth century Delaware never acted as a distinct political entity. Though they shared significant linguistic, kinship and ethnic ties, locality was always the single most compelling aspect of Delawaran political life. Family ties claimed the strongest allegiance in aboriginal Delaware society. Organization above the clan level was flexible and largely voluntaristic.

Each level of Delaware society was led by a civil chief, known as a *sachem* or *sagamore* during peacetime and a war captain in times of war. Both chiefs were further supported by their respective councils. The office of civil chief was transmitted hereditarily and descended through the matriclan. War captains achieved their rank through battlefield successes. Councils were constituted of chiefs of the same approximate rank, and council leaders were very much "first among equals." War captains could compel absolute obedience during military operations. Sachems, however, were not permitted to arbitrarily order any action. All civil decisions were made by a consensus, and a leader's authority depended upon diplomatic ability rather than coercive power.

The End of an Era

From the time the first white explorer Verrazano anchored off the shores of New Jersey in 1524 until the last group of Indians left the state in 1802, the relationship between aborigines and white intruders was often peaceful and friendly, but mostly destructive to the natives.

Massive smallpox and measles epidemics combined with warfare against the Dutch, the interior groups and each other killed over 90 percent of the Delawaran people. Exhausted by their losses, the Delawarans eagerly allied themselves with English following the fall of New Netherland to a British fleet in 1664. The Delaware groups slowly withdrew into the upper reaches of their river valley domains as the English acquired the more desirable lowland tracts. Population losses coupled with land sales caused most of the Delawaran groups to merge in their upriver retreats scattered throughout the traditional Delaware homeland during the last decades of the seventeenth century.

The eighteenth century Delawarans had undergone profound changes during the preceding century. They had fully adapted to an interior woodland settlement-subsistence pattern and had further been fully incorporated into the European economy. They lived in large permanent villages, and their menfolk were absent throughout the winter tending their traplines. Furs and military service provided the European trade goods that the Delawaran groups had become dependent upon. Relocation onto heavily forested lands favored hunting and trapping and discouraged farming. Agriculture had furnished the greater part of the traditional Delawaran diet, and the deemphasis on cultivation forced them to increasingly depend upon white foodstuffs. Sociopolitical power was fast moving from the matriclans into the hands of powerful chiefs. The steady centralization of Delawaran society further saw the rising importance of confederacies throughout their territories.

Extensive land sales, including the notorious fraudulent "Walking Purchase" of 1737 that alienated most of the upper Delaware River valley forced most of the Delawaran people to relocate in the Susquehanna and Allegheny valleys under the sponsorship of the Five Nations during the 1730s and 1740s. These groups swiftly affiliated with and absorbed elements of the Mahican, Nanticoke, Conoy and other Algonquin refugees settling under Iroquoian auspices. These communities, located at Shamokin, Wyoming, Otsiningo, Chugnut and Kenestio in Pennsylvania, were governed by representatives of the Five Nations, who gradually sold these lands from under them, forcing them to move into the upper Ohio River valley by the 1750s.

Numerous treaties were formulated, the Indian interest being taken care of by native chieftains and sympathetic white statesmen. Perhaps the most notable chief of the Delawares was Teedyuscung, who represented his people at the five councils of Easton between 1756 and 1761. In treaty making, the Indians of New Jersey were usually affiliated with their kinsmen on the western shores of Delaware River because they "drank the same water." Teedyuscung represented the entire group. He had a remarkable career as a bold warrior, opportunist Christian, eloquent speaker and able counselor for his tribe. Born near Trenton shortly after the turn of the century, he became chief in 1754 and continued to rule until 1763, when he died in his burning house.

Teedyuscung was mainly interested in restoring the prestige lost by the Delawares in 1725, when they became subservient to the Iroquois after refusing to fight against the English. During this association, the Iroquois addressed the Delawares as "women" because the women in the Iroquois council were the ones who had the right to ask for peace, and the Delawares had often shown peace-loving tendencies. They were frequently called upon as mediators during the colonial period.

Another great leader was Oratam, chief of the Hackensacks during the middle part of the seventeenth century, who represented his people at numerous peace treaties and land transfers in the northern part of the state.

The rapid decline of the Indian population after the coming of the white men was due principally to the sale of their lands, to disease and to liquor. By 1758 there were but a few hundred scattered over the entire colony. In that year the colony purchased 3,000 acres of land for a reservation at the present village of Indian Mills in Burlington County. Here were collected almost 100 Indians, mainly Unamis, who agreed to surrender their title to all unsold lands, and attempted to form a self-supporting community. Governor Bernard appropriately named the community Brotherton. The colony erected private homes, a meeting house, a general store and a sawmill. The Indians kept their rights to unrestricted hunting and fishing. Stephen Calvin, a native interpreter, was the local schoolmaster. This Utopia did not last long, and in 1762 the group petitioned the assembly to pay bills for provisions, clothing and nails.

The bulk of the Delaware groups relocated in the upper Ohio drainage after the War of 1812, and many of these people fought against the English during the Pontiac War of 1762-64.

An uneasy peace followed the end of the Pontiac War, and the Delaware prepared for future conflicts by establishing strong ties with their Miami, Shawnee, Chippewa, Ottawa, and Wyandot neighbors. The Delawaran groups largely attempted neutrality when the War of Independence against England broke out in 1775. By 1778 the Delawares were promised entry into the Union as a separate Indian State in return for their continued noninvolvement in the conflict. The Delaware were strongly divided by the struggle, however, and the pro-English faction finally won the support of the Delawaran villages following the American massacre of the Delaware-Mahican mission community of Gnadenhutten in 1782.

Most Delawarans withdrew deeper into Ohio after the end of the War of Independence. Other Delaware groups settled the upper White River valley of Indiana during the 1780s. The Delawarans fought in the resistance against the American armies during the 1780s and 1790s and large Delaware contingents were present during the defeats of the armies of Generals Harmar and St. Clair in the Indiana country. The defeat of the Native Coalition at Fallen Timbers in 1794 finally forced them to abandon the Ohio, and most of the Delawarans withdrew into Indiana. The English continued to support the Delawarans and their allies against the Americans during the next decades, and many Delaware followed Tecumseh and his brother, the Shawnee prophet during the first decade of the nineteenth century. Defeat during the War of 1812 caused many Delaware to move to Ontario, Canada, where their descendants continue to reside at Munceytown, Newfairfield and Grand River.

In 1801 the Indians living at New Stockbridge, New York invited their kinsmen at Brotherton to join them. The Lenape petitioned the legislature again, and a law was passed in that year appointing three commissioners to dispose of the Brotherton tract at public sale. The land brought from $2 to $5 an acre, enough to pay the Indians' fare to their new home, allow a donation to the New Stockbridge treasury, and leave a remainder that was invested in United States securities.

In 1822 the Stockbridge group moved to Green Bay, Wisconsin. Ten years later the New Jersey contingent appealed to Bartholomew Calvin, son of their old schoolmaster, for further monetary aid in exchange for the relinquishment of hunting and fishing rights not mentioned in the 1801 settlement. Calvin obtained a legislative grant of $2,000. In a stirring speech of acceptance he said:

"Not a drop of our blood have you spilled in battle; not an acre of our land have you taken but by our consent. These facts speak for themselves, and need no comment. They place the character of New Jersey in bold relief and example to those states within whose territorial limits our brethren still remain. Nothing save benisons can fall upon her from the lips of the Lenni-Lenape."

The descendants of these people still live in the Stockbridge-Munsee Reservation today.

The main body of the Delaware gradually removed from

the Indiana country to southern Missouri in 1815. Continual pressure for their lands forced them to move to a reservation in eastern Kansas in 1829. This reservation was liquidated by 1854, and the bulk of the Delaware Nation settled among the Cherokee and Creek in northeastern Oklahoma, where their descendants live to the present day.

The long century of westward exile worked profound changes upon Delawaran society. Repeated removals and continual military reversals at the heads of the white armies and hostile native groups impoverished the Delawaran people. The termination of the fur trade and the end of their utility as allies for the contending European forces forced them to depend upon the annuities they received in payment for their lands by the federal government. Prophets rose among them, and the rise of the Big House religion allowed the Delaware to continue their traditional cultural life while making drastic adjustments to changing economic conditions. The men gradually turned to farming, ranching and wage labor for the whites. The clans lost their importance, and the Delaware languages began to disappear. Participation in the white economy devalued women, and the shift to patrilineal-neolocal kinship organization was virtually completed by the end of the nineteenth century. Most Delaware were sent to white schools, at least nominally adopted the white religion, wore white dress and spoke English. The last Big House ceremonies were "brought in" during the 1920s.

The modern Delawares have largely assimilated into white culture. Only a few very old people still speak the language or follow the old ways. Most Delawarans in the U.S. and Canada still live in reservations, however. The Oklahoma Delaware have been the recipients of the $12,000,000 from the Indian Lands Claims Commission for lands taken from them during their westward exile. The economic success of the Stockbridge-Munsee and the relative success of the Ontario Delawarans clearly demonstrate that the Delaware show every sign of cultural persistence in the face of the most damaging attempts to eradicate them as a cultural entity.

New Jersey—
A HISTORY

ew Jersey's position as a main corridor of eastern United States has broadly affected her political, social, economic and cultural history. Lying between two metropolises, New York and Philadelphia, the state from early times has been the highway and often the stopping place for hordes of people of many races, religions and cultures.

This location has brought both embarrassment and blessing. Governor Woodrow Wilson, who thought of New Jersey as "a sort of laboratory in which the best blood is prepared for other communities to thrive upon," gave the key to the state's history when he remarked in 1911 that "we have always been inconvenienced by New York on the one hand and Philadelphia on the other..." He called the state "the fighting center of the most important social questions of our time" and explained that "the whole suburban question...the whole question of the regulation of corporations and the right attitude of all trades, their formation and conduct...center in New Jersey more than any other single state of the Union."

Early European Claims

The first white man to see, and possibly to land on, New Jersey's shores is believed to have been the Florentine navigator Giovanni da Verrazano, sailing in the employ of the French Crown. In 1524 he is said to have anchored his vessel off Sandy Hook and with a small boat explored upper New York Bay as far as, or almost as far as, the New Jersey shore.

Almost a century later, in 1609, Henry Hudson, employed by Holland, sailed the *Half Moon* into New York Bay, dispatched a sounding party as far as Newark Bay and then sailed up the Hudson River. Within a few years the Dutch sent out trading expeditions and established a post at Manhattan, the base for the invasion of New Jersey. The first known outpost west of the Hudson River was the trading station of Bergen, founded in 1618 by colonists from the island. Five years later Captain Cornelius

Jacobsen Mey, who had sailed into the Delaware River in 1614, set up Fort Nassau on the east bank of the river, near the present site of Gloucester. Mey's name survives in Cape May.

Actual settlement of the unnamed New Jersey section of New Netherland was slow. Accordingly, the West India Company offered the federal title of patroon and a grant of land to any member who would establish a specific number of settlers. In 1629 the company granted to the Burgomaster of Amsterdam, Michael Pauw (Pauww) a tract on the shore opposite Manhattan where his agent, Cornelius Van Vorst, began to develop an estate called Pavonia. At the same time two other patroons, Godyn and Blommaert, shared a grant on both sides of Delaware Bay. Both attempts were futile, and Indian raids in 1643 drove all whites across to Manhattan from the Jersey side. By 1645 the only Dutch survival was the Van Vorst estate in Pavonia which had become the farm of the West India Company.

The Swedes came to New Jersey shortly after the New Sweden Company had built a fort and trading post in 1638 on the western shore of Delaware River. A vast tract of land between Cape May and Raccoon Creek was purchased from the Indians in 1640; small trading posts were peopled mostly with Flemings, Walloons and Finns. The enterprise was poorly managed however, and failed to attract many settlers.

The Dutch, who had reoccupied Fort Nassau after the Swedish arrival, were for a time friendly enough with the Swedes on the Delaware to unite with them against the encroaching English, whose claim was based upon John Cabot's discovery of North America in 1497. However, the Dutch unwisely considered Swedish competition in furs more dangerous than England's territorial ambitions. During the autumn of 1655 Peter Stuyvesant, Governor of New Netherland, peacefully took over the Swedish forts on the Delaware basin, thus ending the Swedish phase of the colony's history.

With the problems of its Rebellion and stormy Protectorate behind it, England seriously went into the business of colonization. In 1664, Charles II granted to his brother James, Duke of York, the Dutch domain, which included the area now New Jersey. In the same year the English took over New Netherland with a naval expedition. Having been treated by the mother country as less important than the fur-bearing animals they trapped, the few hundred Dutch and Swedish colonials in the New Jersey section of the grant indifferently took the oath of allegiance to England.

The change of sovereigns was far more significant than the inhabitants of Bergen, the largest settlement, could have sensed. From its experience in Virginia and Massachusetts Bay, England was learning that permanent settlements were commercially sounder than the trading posts established by the Dutch and Swedes as a short cut to riches. As an indication that colonization was to be the English policy, the Duke of York's Deputy Governor in New York, Richard Nicolls, immediately issued the so-called Elizabethtown and Monmouth patents, providing for the founding of New Jersey towns on the New England model.

New Jersey Becomes a Province

While Nicolls was still at sea, the Duke of York in June 1664 created New Jersey with a stroke of his quill. He granted the area between the Hudson and Delaware Rivers to two of his favorites, John, Lord Berkeley and Sir George Carteret. The area was to be known as *Nova Caesarea* or New Jersey in memory of the island where in 1650 Carteret as governor had sheltered the Duke from Puritan England. The new proprietors commissioned 26-year-old Philip Carteret a cousin of Sir George, as New Jersey's first English Governor.

York's simple act not only created New Jersey but also perplexities for the Colony for the next forty years. Unaware of the Duke's grant, Governor Nicolls in New York encouraged settlements at the sites of contemporary Elizabeth, Shrewsbury and Middletown. These settlements, as well as that of Newark in 1666, were made chiefly by religious dissenters from New England and by adventurous Long Islanders. Confusion began when Philip Carteret arrived at Elizabethtown in 1665 and was surprised to find four families under the Nicolls grant. Some of the colonists brought by Nicolls compromised temporarily by taking the oath of allegiance required by Berkeley and Carteret.

When the Governor's first assembly met at Elizabethtown in 1668 with delegates from that village and from Bergen, Newark, Middletown and Shrewsbury, it became clear that New England Puritanism was dominant in the settled part of the colony. Swearing, drunkenness and fornication were made penal offenses and the child over 16 who cursed or smote at his parents might incur the death penalty. The government operated under the "Concessions and Agreements of the Lords Proprietors," which Carteret had brought from England in 1665. This document, which may be termed New Jersey's first constitution, contained a particularly emphatic guarantee of religious liberty, no doubt motivated by the Proprietors' desire to promote rapid settlement.

The smoldering controversy of the dual land grants broke out in the assembly. Many settlers held that their grants from Nicolls and deeds of purchase from the Indians gave valid titles to their land, and that the Proprietors did not have the right of government. Barred from the assembly for this stand, a number of delegates formed the basis of an Anti-Proprietary party, which in 1670 refused to pay quitrents to the Proprietors. The revolt spread and in 1672 five of the seven settlements — Newark, Elizabethtown, Woodbridge, Piscatawqua and Bergen — held a revolutionary assembly at Elizabethtown. They deposed Philip Carteret as Governor and elected as "president" James Carteret, dissolute son of Sir George. With the settlers insisting that the Duke's lease to the Proprietors did not convey governing power, Philip Carteret hastened to England to lay the matter before the Proprietors, that they might be able to present their case. The King upheld the rights of Berkeley and Carteret against the grants of Nicolls.

A sudden attack by Holland temporarily swept aside these technical wrangles. In 1673 a Dutch fleet arrived at Staten Island and regained a portion of Holland's New World holdings, including New Jersey — but only until 1674, when the territory was restored to England by the Treaty of Westminster. Legally the province had thus reverted to the Crown, and Charles II regranted it to the Duke of York who in turn reconveyed the eastern part to Sir George Carteret. Philip Carteret returned as Governor in November 1674; four counties (Bergen, Essex, Middlesex and Monmouth) were created, and a system of courts and grand juries was established.

If eastern New Jersey seemed on the point of extricating itself from the snarls of conflicting claims, western New Jersey was just beginning an even more confused career. Before the King issued the charter of renewal to York, Berkeley in 1674 turned over his proprietary rights to John Fenwick in trust for Edward Byllynge. Immediately these two Quakers quarreled over their shares, and in 1676 William Penn arbitrated the case by awarding nine-tenths to Byllynge and one-tenth to Fenwick. Byllynge, however, became insolvent, and Penn, Gawen Lawrie, and Nicholas Lucas were appointed trustees for his creditors. Because this action involved New Jersey lands, it happened indirectly that William Penn's first Quaker colony was West Jersey.

In 1675 Fenwick settled Salem with his family and a few friends. Like Byllynge, he was soon in financial trouble; ultimately Penn and the other trustees acquired control of part of his land. On July 1, 1676, Byllynge and three trustees entered into a "quintipartite deed" with Sir George Carteret. This agreement officially clarified the previous haphazard division of the province into West and East Jersey by drawing a line northwest from Little Egg Harbor to a point on Delaware River just north of Delaware Water Gap, Carteret retaining East Jersey and West Jersey passing into the hands of the Quakers.

The choice of the boundary itself represented more logic than almost any previous act in the management of the colony. The line cut through what is still the least populous part of the state. Across that wasteland there was neither commercial, political nor religious unity. East Jersey, the section northeast of the boundary line, has always been dependent upon New York, while West Jersey has been linked to Pennsylvania and Delaware. Not even modern superhighways nor radio have been able entirely to controvert the astuteness of the men who divided the colony.

The "Concessions and Agreements" for the government of West Jersey, adopted in 1677 and largely devised by Penn himself, provided a liberal and surprisingly modern frame of government, although the constitution was never put into full effect and it was not until 1681 that the first assembly met. Meanwhile, the present town of Burlington had been settled by Quakers in 1677 and other colonists were arriving in considerable numbers.

New Jersey was faced with a struggle for independence in 1674 when the Duke of York sent Edmund Andros to New York with authority to govern New Jersey as well, even though Governor Philip Carteret had returned on the same boat with Andros. No man to waste prerogative, Andros in 1676 dispatched soldiers to the Salem district and jailed Fenwick as a usurper, although he (Fenwick) was shortly released. The death of Sir George Carteret in 1679 gave Andros an opportunity to employ high-handed methods in East Jersey. Philip Carteret was warned to relinquish the governorship; when he refused, Andros jailed him. . Insisting that all New Jersey trade should clear through New York, Andros aroused so much popular disapproval that he was summoned to England to answer charges, leaving Carteret master of east Jersey. A strongly worded remonstrance, probably the work of Penn and his Quaker associates, induced the Duke of York to accept New Jersey's independence of New York.

The elimination of Andros failed to bring harmony to East Jersey and in 1682 the province was put up at public auction. For the sum of £3,400, Penn and eleven associates obtained the land; their shares were divided into innumerable fragments, many of which were purchased by Scots and other non-Quakers. Perth Amboy, which had already attained the dignity of port of East Jersey, was selected as the capital in 1686.

While the population of the two Jerseys grew to an estimated 15,000 in 1702, the Proprietors became, as one historian phrases it, "mere rent-chargers." Their position was no happier than the traditional one of any landlord. Finally after riots and interference with government dignified by the name of "revolution," the Proprietors of both East Jersey and West Jersey surrendered their governing power to the Crown in 1702 and New Jersey became a united Royal Colony under the administration of Lord Cornbury, the Governor of New York.

Despite the merging of the two Jerseys, separate capitals were maintained at Perth Amboy and Burlington, the legislature meeting alternately in the two cities until after the Revolution. And although New Jersey was to remain under New York's governor until 1738, the governor held a separate commission that recognized the political independence of the colony.

The Proprietors, it must be noted, relinquished only their civil authority. Their land rights were retained and proved a troublesome influence on political affairs in the colony. To this day the successors of Penn and his associates maintain small offices in Perth Amboy and Burlington, where they meet regularly and exercise jurisdiction over any unlocated or new lands, such as fluvial islands.

Lord Cornbury's instructions provided for a council and an assembly, guaranteed some personal rights, and in effect formed a constitution for the united province. New Jersey retained its own legislature and officials, who found many causes for disagreement with the new governor.

Cornbury was removed after five years. His successors encountered Proprietary disputes and continual complaints against absentee government from New York. Finally Lewis Morris of Monmouth County was named in 1738 as the first Governor of New Jersey alone.

Morris had frequently complained against previous governors; but now, as legal representative of the King, he faced the same difficulties that formerly he had fostered. He found it hard to get troops for King George's War, and there was frequent trouble in managing the currency. When Morris died in 1746 his salary had been unpaid for two years, and was never collected by his widow.

Increased population on many small farms developing throughout the Province resulted in new rebellion against the territorial claims of the Proprietors. Disputes over the old Nicolls grants were kept alive, and squatters in the western part of the colony stood their ground. The doctrine of man's natural right to land frequently appeared. Riots against the Proprietors broke out at Newark in 1745 and soon spread to other sections, continuing under Governor Belcher until the outbreak of the French and Indian war in 1754.

Economic Growth: Agriculture and Industry

As a Royal Province, New Jersey made notable economic progress, although it did not rank as one of the most valuable Crown possessions. The farms yielded a variety of fruit, vegetables, poultry and cattle, and the grain crop was important enough to make New Jersey one of the "bread colonies." Hunterdon County was known as the "bread basket," producing more wheat than any other county in the colonies. Cider and apple brandy were then, as now, well known products. By 1775 the Colony was an important source for iron, leather and lumber, while some glass and paper were produced. On the whole, however, economic development suffered from the proximity of New York and Philadelphia.

Agricultural development was the chief economic interest of New Jersey from the early period of its existence as a colony. Small farms were intensively cultivated in the eastern section and large plantations, operated mainly by slaves, flourished in the west. Although the isolation of farm people contributed to the establishment of home industry, it likewise stunted commercial manufacturing.

The self-supporting farm was the standard unit of the colony's economy for the two earliest generations at least. Even the small towns clustered at the head of tidewater regions on the eastern shore or along the Delaware were largely devoted to agriculture. Soap, candles, textiles, even tools were manufactured in the home by the pioneer women and children.

Trade, however, began to flourish almost as soon as the colonists sighted the Indians. Furs, skins and tobacco found a ready market in England; oil and fish in Spain, Portugal, and the Canary Islands; and agricultural products in neighboring colonies and the West Indies.

Gradually manufacture spread from the home to the community. The miller, almost invariably first on the scene, was soon joined by the weaver, fuller, tanner, shoemaker and carpenter. Newark had a commercial gristmill in 1671 and the earliest sawmill was established in Woodbridge in 1682. Tanning, which had been started as a business in Elizabeth in 1664 by the Ogden family, quickly led to saddlery and harness making.

The fine forests in southern New Jersey yielded their lumber to ship carpenters of Burlington, Salem, Newton and Cape May, where shipbuilding became a leading industry. Equally significant was the development of whaling from Cape May and Tuckerton; in many respects these towns rivaled the more celebrated New England ports of the colonial period. Tar and terpentine were also important exports from the southern part of the colony.

Toward the close of the seventeenth century and the opening of the eighteenth centuries, several industries were founded in New Jersey that were destined to become not only leading sources of wealth but traditional occupations as well. An abundant supply of beaver, raccoon and sheep furnished the materials for hat manufacturing, which attained its greatest strength in the southern area. At the same time, the colony was rapidly becoming distinguished for its brewing skill. Hoboken, still identified with beer drinking, had the first brewery in 1642. Beer was a major interest in Burlington in 1698. Two years later, Newark made more than 1,000 barrels of cider, and Jersey applejack seems to have been as renowned among the colonies as it was throughout the East during the Prohibition era.

In several spurs of the Appalachian range, running through the northern and central sections of the state, lay mineral deposits unusual for their richness and variety. The state's earliest iron works were established at Shrewsbury in 1676 by Colonel Lewis Morris, a merchant of the Barbadoes. Forges, furnaces and bloomeries began to appear all over the northern part of the state, with a concentration of Boonton, the center of several rich mines in Morris County which supplied most of the nation's iron. These mines were a mainstay to Washington's army during the Revolution.

At the same time, swamps throughout southern New Jersey were utilized as an important source of iron deposits. Iron-laden water impregnated the marshy soil; the Indians had long used the ore, mixed with bear grease, to make an excellent war paint. The ore was hauled to charcoal-heated furnaces built on the banks of streams, which provided power for the bellows and an easy means of shipping the finished product. Weymouth, Batsto and Atsion were typical iron centers — thriving little communities a century or more ago but ghost towns today. The bog iron industry lasted until the middle of the nineteenth century, when competition from the iron mines and coal-burning smelters gradually smothered it. (*See also* "The Pine Barrens.")

Copper mines were worked in New Brunswick, and in 1768 the discovery that the marl of Monmouth County could be used as fertilizer led to the establishment of another new industry. Steel manufacture at this time was concentrated principally in Trenton.

Another famous early industry in New Jersey was glass making. The first glass factory was founded at Allowaystown in 1740 by Caspar Wistar, a German immigrant. The sand of the southern part of the state proved especially suitable for the manufacture of glass, and within a few decades Salem County was a leading producer of bottles, jugs, pitchers and other glassware.

Growth as a People — Culture and Politics

Despite the late start in settlement, population grew with fair rapidity. By 1726 the total was 32,442 (including 2,550 slaves); 47,402 (3,981 slaves) by 1737; 61,383 (4,605 slaves) in 1745. At the outbreak of the Revolution the population was estimated at 138,000.

Several important cultural contributions were made by the colony. In architecture some of the finest examples of the Dutch Colonial were built in New Jersey — comfortable stone houses, modest in scale and design, and in harmony with their surroundings. From the early Swedish settlements came the pattern for the typical log cabin of the American frontier. The founding of the College of New Jersey (later Princeton University) and of Queen's college (later Rutgers University) made this the only colony with more than one college. New Jersey was the center of the humanistic work of John Woolman, the Quaker preacher of Mount Holly. Other sects developed notable strength, the Baptists having been established at Middletown in 1668, and the Presbyterians at Freehold in 1692.

Continual disagreements between the royally appointed Governors and the popularly elected assemblies, combined with unwise commercial restrictions put in force by the British Government, ranged New Jersey in 1774 on the side of Massachusetts against the British. In February of that year the assembly had already followed the lead of Virginia by appointing nine men as a Committee of Correspondence; similar township and county committees sprang up during the summer. On July 21, county committees met at New Brunswick as the First Provincial Congress and chose Stephen Crane, John de Hart, James Kinsey, William Livingston and Richard Smith as delegates to the proposed Continental Congress at Philadelphia.

In spite of strong Tory sentiment — later proved by the organization of six battalions of Loyalists — anti-British feeling swept New Jersey. In November 1774, at Greenwich on Cohansey River, a band of young men disguised themselves as Indians and burned a shipload of tea. Indignant citizens of Newark branded a New York printer a "vile ministerial hireling" and boycotted the paper. Rejection of other Loyalist papers from New York and Philadelphia later resulted in the founding of a local and patriotic press. As the Royal agents desperately tried to stem the tide of the Revolution, volunteers began drilling on village greens in the summer of 1775, and official after official yielded his authority to the aroused colonists. Finally, in June 1776, the Provincial Congress arrested Governor William Franklin, natural son of Benjamin, when he attempted to revive the defunct assembly.

The strategy of the Revolutionary generals showed that New Jersey's position on the Hudson and Delaware Rivers rendered the state dependent upon the fortunes of New York and Philadelphia in war as well as in peace. To the discomfort of the patriots of 1776 and the delight of local patriots ever after, Washington spent one-quarter of his career as commander in chief in New Jersey, moving his army across the state four times. Within its boundaries were fought four major battles and at least ninety minor engagements.

Toward the close of 1776 Washington retreated across the northern part of the state and into Pennsylvania, seizing every boat for miles along the Delaware to prevent British pursuit. On Christmas night he recrossed the river and captured the Hessian garrison at Trenton in a surprise attack that did much to rebuild the waning morale of the Revolutionaries. A few days later, after outwitting Cornwallis at Trenton, he marched by night to Princeton and there on January 3, 1777, defeated three British regiments. The exhausted American Army then went into winter quarters at Morristown.

Coming by water route from New York, the British seized Philadelphia in September 1777, but in June 1778, they evacuated Philadelphia and retreated across the state, harassed by Jersey troops. Washington hurried with his main army to intercept the British Army of General Howe in the indecisive Battle wer-Monmouth on June 28. That winter, parts of the Continental Army encamped at Somerville, and in the winter of 1779-80 Washington again made his headquarters at Morristown. From New Brunswick in 1781 the American Army started its march southward to the final victory at Yorktown. In 1783 Washington delivered his farewell address to part of the Army at Rocky Hill, near Princeton.

The war proved a stimulus to agriculture, industry and commerce in New Jersey. The state's farmers, sometimes involuntarily but mostly with the shrewdness of non-combatants, turned a handsome profit supplying provisions to both sides. Ironworks, gristmills, sawmills, fulling mills, tanyards and salt works operated at capacity. Goods brought in by privateers and smugglers were advertised in the newspapers, indicating the luxury possible to those who could afford it. Prices rose and labor was scarce. In the rapid shift of values, due partly to monetary inflation, fortunes were made and lost. The end of the war found the debtor a problem for the first time since 1776. The lure of the West was soon to prove an attraction too strong for tax-burdened farmers on worn-out lands to resist.

Early Statehood

In June 1776 the fourth Provincial Congress of New Jersey had transformed itself into a constitutional convention and on July 2 adopted a combined declaration of independence and constitution. The hastily drawn document provided for its nullification "if a reconciliation between Great Britain and the colonies should take place..." Nevertheless, this constitution was retained for sixty-eight years. The colony's long struggle with Proprietary and Royal governors inspired a provision for annual election of the governor by the legislature. This arrangement, at first adopted by several other states, obviously violated the prevailing theory of separation of powers (executive, legislative and judicial) in a free government. New Jersey's first state governor, William Livingston, was elected August 27, 1776, for one year.

In the two-house legislature, the upper chamber (the council) was composed of one representative from each county, a precedent for equal county representation in the senate under the present constitution. The lower house (the assembly) was apportioned among the counties roughly by population.

The franchise was limited to "all inhabitants of this colony, of full age, who are worth £50 proclamation money..." Under laws passed in 1790 and 1797, women were permitted to vote. In 1807, however, the women were disenfranchised by a statute justified as "highly necessary to the safety, quiet, good order and dignity of the state." This harsh stricture came from a legislature beset with charges of fraudulent voting by women, notably in an exciting referendum on the location of the Essex County courthouse. Another 1807 statute reduced voting qualifications by giving the franchise to any taxpayer.

For brief periods, two New Jersey towns had the honor of being the national capital — at least the temporary capital. When, in June 1783, Congress in session at Philadelphia was confronted by mutinous troops, demanding what it could not give, the session was adjourned to meet again on June 30, at Princeton. There, in somewhat cramped quarters, the national government remained seated until November 4. A year later, November 1, 1784, Congress convened at Trenton. It was even thought that a "Federal Town" — a permanent national capital — would be built near Trenton. The plan however never materialized — New York and Philadelphia were too powerful — and the Congressional session at Trenton was very brief. Congress adjourned on Christmas Eve of 1784 to meet again a fortnight later in New York City.

New Jersey in the days after the Revolution was grimly compared to a keg tapped at both ends. The state's economy was seriously hampered by commercial restrictions imposed by New York, through which most of the state's goods had to pass. Her representatives demanded that Congress be given power over interstate commerce and the exclusive right to lay duties on imports. When New York and other states failed to meet their fiscal obligations to the weak Congress, New Jersey also withheld payments to the Federal Treasury, hoping to force more cooperative action. Finally, New Jersey was one of the five states that participated in the Annapolis Conference of 1786 which led to the Constitutional Convention at Philadelphia in 1787.

At the Philadelphia convention New Jersey, long conditioned to fear New York and Pennsylvania, became the chief spokesman for the small states in their struggle against the

Virginia or "large state" plan for a powerful national government with a Congress based on population. Although the Virginia plan was adopted for the House of Representatives, the New Jersey plan of equal representation matured into the provision for the balancing Senate. The small states' victory was the greater one, since Congress could not act without the consent of a majority of the states, regardless of population.

A further New Jersey contribution to the Constitution was the all-important clause which declares that the Constitution, laws and treaties of the United States shall be the supreme law of the land. From this clause, together with the provision for a national judiciary empowered to determine all legal questions involving the Constitution, the United States Supreme Court later derived the power to harmonize federal and state laws with the Constitution by the process called judicial review.

Satisfaction with the document itself and with the opportunity for protection against New York and other neighboring states resulted in prompt ratification. On December 18, 1787, New Jersey became the third state to approve the Constitution.

Between 1790 and 1840 the foundations of the state's present industrial system were laid. In 1791 Alexander Hamilton founded the Society for Establishing Useful Manufactures, selecting the Great Falls of Passaic River as the site for an industrial city, Paterson. The first factory built at Paterson began to operate in 1794, printing calico goods. As Newark's leather and Trenton's pottery industries grew, businessmen developed important branches of commerce. Banks were chartered at Newark, Trenton and New Brunswick during the first decade of the nineteenth century, and insurance began in the same period.

At Trenton, which had become the state capital in 1790, the legislature sensed the power of trade. Many turnpike companies were chartered even before the need for good roads was emphasized by the War of 1812. Scientists and inventors — John Fitch and Colonel John Stevens with their steamboats and, later, Seth Boyden with malleable iron and patent leather — accelerated the trend toward industrialization.

The first census of manufactures taken in New Jersey in 1810 placed the total industrial wealth at $4,816,288, listing textiles, hides, leather, iron products and liquor as the most important goods. Cotton manufacture and cotton machinery so completely dominated Paterson at this time that it earned the title of "The Cotton City." Twenty-five forges indicated the growth of mining, while items like 36,000 packs of playing cards and 300,000 pounds of chocolate candy illustrated the diversity of industry.

On this groundwork there rose, following the short depression at the end of the Napoleonic wars in 1815, a twenty-year prosperity. By 1828, the state had about 550 miles of gravel and dirt roads under 54 charters. Between 1810 and 1840 New Jersey ranked third as a iron producer in the nation. The value of iron products in 1830 was about $657,000; glass and pottery, $490,000; and cotton products, $1,733,000. Encouraged by the protective tariff of 1816, investors developed water power and mill sites for textiles and flour. By 1830 Paterson had fulfilled its early promise and had become a busy mill town, rich with profits and scarred with labor exploitation.

The invention of new processes in the manufacture of iron, notably Seth Boyden's discovery of a method for making malleable iron in Newark in 1826, brought increased prosperity to this flourishing business. In 1830 the East Jersey Iron Manufacturing Company established a $283,000 plant at Boonton, capable of producing 1,000 tons of malleable iron annually.

Boyden also contributed to the growth of the leather industry with his process for making patent leather. Moses Combs had earlier founded the shoe industry in Newark, and by the end of the eighteenth century a majority of the city's industrial population was engaged in the leather trade. Combs was also famous as the first slave owner in local history to teach his slaves a trade in order to raise their economic and social level.

Shortly after the rise of leather Newark developed another manufacture which has remained one of its leaders. In 1801 Epaphras Hinsdale opened on Broad Street a jewelry factory which soon became a fashionable gathering place for the ladies of the town. By 1836 the industry numbered four establishments, with an annual output of $225,000 and 800 workers employed. Many years, however, had to pass before the general public would accept articles known to have been made in America. Believed to be products of Paris or London, Newark jewelry, remarkable for its workmanship, found a market in the largest cities here and abroad.

To weld the expanding sections of the state as well as to modernize the New York-Philadelphia highway, the industrial barons of the day hurried across-state transportation lines. Colonel John Stevens of Hoboken had proved in 1824 that his "steam waggon" could run 12 miles per hour. Six years later his son Robert got a charter for the Camden and Amboy Railroad, and by 1834 the line was finished. The railroad soon absorbed the new Delaware and Raritan Canal, which it paralleled. In 1831 the Morris Canal between Newark and Phillipsburg opened a water route to a rich mining district. Newark, because of its key position on the canal and rail routes and on the Passaic River, strengthened its grip as the leading city of the state. With the stage set for even greater economic progress, the speculative bubble of industrial prosperity burst in the panic of 1837.

Industrial Age Brings Social Advances

During the 1830s New Jersey was affected by the spirit of reform that was sweeping the country, partly as a result of the industrial revolution. The legislature began to allot money for public schools; hospitals were built; and a start was made toward guarding the public health. In 1844 Dorothea Dix presented to the legislature a memorial describing the disgraceful conditions in jails and poorhouses and the medieval treatment of the mentally retarded, epileptics and the insane. Public indignation resulted in prison reform and the establishment of an insane asylum. Reform was a leading topic in public meetings and in newspaper columns. With an increase of almost 200,000 in population since 1790, the citizens of the state were demanding democratization of their political structure.

It came in 1844. A constitutional convention swept away property qualifications for voters, provided for separation of powers among the three governmental departments and included a formal bill of rights and a clause permitting amendment (the latter had been omitted from the 1776 document). The 1844 constitution was amended only a few times, and wasn't completely changed until 1947.

The influx of European immigrants in the 1840s supplied needed manpower to the state's growing industries. Paterson gradually shifted from cotton to silk manufacture after 1840, when John Ryle devised a way of winding silk on a spool. A decade later New Jersey ranked second only to Connecticut in the national production of spool silk, and Paterson was already known as the "Silk City."

When the business cycle swung toward good times in 1845, the Camden and Amboy Railroad emerged as a monopoly, since the charter, after merger with two terminal roads, prohibited any other line between New York and Philadelphia. So complete was the railroad's grasp of the state's economic and political life that New Jersey was for a generation bitterly referred to as "the State of Camden and Amboy."

In the same period, potteries were founded at Trenton, brick works expanded enormously at Perth Amboy, and in 1852 Edward Balback established America's first smelting and refining plant, on the Passaic River near Newark, where he refined the floor sweepings from local jewelry factories. Woolen mills, formerly situated chiefly in the south at Mount Holly and Bridgeton, began to move north to Passaic.

Old industries yielded to this amazing variety of new occupations. Between 1840 and 1850 Newark alone had been producing more than 2,000,000 pairs of shoes annually. On the eve of the Civil War, however, the industry there as well as in Orange and Burlington revealed the strain of New England competition. Similarly the discovery of rich iron deposits in Michigan and Minnesota began to reduce the state's mining importance.

New Jersey During the Civil War

Rising anti-slavery feeling together with pro-tariff and anti-immigrant sentiment turned the state Republican in 1857, at its first opportunity to elect a Republican governor. But, in the crucial election of 1860, the conflict between industrial and agricultural interests and anti-slavery men and unionists-at-any-cost split New Jersey's electoral vote for the only time. Lincoln received four votes and Douglas three.

In 1863 copperhead opposition to the Civil War, partly created by the New York bankers' mistrust of Lincoln, caused New Jersey to revert to political type and elect Joel Parker, a Democrat, as governor. Yet New Jersey provided 88,000 troops and $23,000,000 for the war.

After 1865 profits from war supplies and a favorable location as the nexus of the most populous and prosperous sections of the nation contributed to an intense industrial activity. Paterson was processing two-thirds of the country's silk imports; Newark could proudly hold an impressive trade exhibition of its varied manufactures in 1872; kerosene and other oil products were being refined in Bayonne; and agriculture was passing into its present form of lucrative truck farming. While real estate companies plot chimerical developments, the legislature recklessly issued charters for any kind of money-making enterprise. The great economic spree which lasted until the panic of 1873 fastened New York's hold upon New Jersey more securely than ever.

The hold that the Camden and Amboy had upon the state had been considerably weakened by 1867. In that year its opponents, seeking a charter for a competing line across the state, had turned the legislature into a roundhouse battleground. When the Camden and Amboy sensed that public opinion would ultimately spell defeat, the company prudently leased its lines to the Pennsylvania Railroad. The Pennsylvania took up in 1871 where its predecessors had left off and brought about a Republican victory in the legislature. The railroad retained a majority in 1873, but this time it was the legislators who felt the popular wrath. They passed a bill opening the state to all lines.

Although the Pennsylvania lost the battle, the state's history shows that it won the war. The act giving any company the right to put down rails in New Jersey was much less objectionable to the Pennsylvania than the alternative of a special charter to a single competing line. Like its predecessor, the new company succeeded during the next generation in maintaining a powerful hold on state government.

As far back as 1871, however, public opinion had caused the legislature to attempt checks on railroad domination. In that year the railroads were denied free loading space along the Hudson. In 1883 Leon Abbett was elected governor on a platform calling for railroad franchise taxes. Although the subservient legislature compromised on a plan for assessment and taxation of railroad property, this action resulted in investigation of the Lackawanna Railroad. A state audit of the company's books yielded New Jersey several hundred thousand dollars.

Nevertheless, for more than a quarter of a century the railroads generally enjoyed an extraordinary privilege to profiteer. This license illustrates the beginning of a gradual blurring of party labels between 1870 and 1900, for even on the few occasions when the Democrats won complete control of the state government, their efforts to curb the railroad were feeble. Shut out of the governorship since 1869, the Republicans had to bid for power by such trivial stratagems as seeking the Prohibition vote through the passing of a county option law in 1888. Such schemes failed to elect a governor, but the Democrats' own corruption finally lost them the legislature in 1893. Even then the Republican victory was delayed while eight hold-over Democratic senators attempted to steal the senate back from the Republicans simply by organizing themselves into a rump senate, which prevented the seating of any new members. This bold bid was thwarted by the courts.

Except for the electoral split in 1860 and a shift to Grant in 1872, New Jersey gave a majority to every Democratic Presidential candidate between 1852 and 1896. In the latter year Mark Hanna himself was astounded when New Jersey gave McKinley a plurality of 87,692 over Bryan, and elected John W. Griggs as its first Republican governor in 30 years.

Several factors were responsible for the Republican ascendancy. As the psuedo-agricultural party, the Democrats lost relative strength because the number of farms decreased after 1880. At the same time, the commuter vote, composed largely of Republicans from New York and Philadelphia, increased. Finally, the economic eye of the state was becoming more and more sensitive to the high-tariff button eternally pinned on the Republican lapel.

In that era of seemingly limitless national expansion — when the value of manufactured products in New Jersey rose from $1,69,237,000 in 1870 to $611,748,000 in 1900 — the state began to assume its present leadership in industry. To man the prospering factories and mills, thousands of immigrants, chiefly from southern and eastern Europe, poured into the industrial cities where they quickly established lasting foreign quarters. In the brick and terra cotta works around Perth Amboy, in the heavy industries of Newark, in the woolen mills of Passaic, in the shipyards of Camden, and in the ceramic plants of Trenton, European skills joined with native enterprise to further New Jersey industry.

Turn of the Century

Following the panic of 1873, the state entered another period of expansion in which the gains began to fit into New Jersey's industrial pattern as it appears today. Bayonne started on its way to becoming one of the great oil refining centers of the world in 1875 when the Prentice Refining Company established a still there. John D. Rockefeller came next, and within a decade three other companies followed Standard Oil to the site so close to the huge oil and kerosene market in New York City. The steel cable industry was established in Trenton by the Roebling family, and that city became known as a center of supply for suspension bridge construction after the Roeblings built Brooklyn Bridge.

The work of Thomas A. Edison at Menlo Park and Edward Weston at Newark established New Jersey as a vast electrical industry, especially in light bulbs and phonograph records, dynamos, and power plant supplies. John Wesley Hyatt's invention of the roller bearing and celluloid and Hannibal Goodwin's perfection of photographic film introduced important new manufacturing activities into Newark and its environs. As electricity replaced steam in industry, the state's manufacturing continued to grow even in the face of depression.

The state, which had grown from a population of 373,306 in 1840 to 1,883,669 in 1900, was becoming a more integral part of the economic and cultural life of the Atlantic seaboard. Much of the spirit of speed and efficiency of New York and Philadelphia business life flowed across the Hudson and Delaware, quickening the tempo of New Jersey's cities and suburbs. In the same way, important cultural threads of the two metropolises were spun across, drawing up New Jersey in the wave.

The state's educational facilities were strengthened by the founding of Rutgers Scientific School in 1863 and by the opening of the Stevens Institute of Technology in 1871. In the latter year a free school system was established and in 1874 a compulsory education law was passed. To Princeton College many of the well-to-do families of New York and Philadelphia sent their sons.

As early as the 1840s Cape May was a summer social capital, and after the Civil War Long Branch became the vacation choice of Presidents — as well as the playground for the Astors and Fishes of New York, the Biddles and Drexels of Philadelphia. A quarter of a century later Atlantic City and Asbury Park were performing the same service for many thousands of Philadelphia and New York vacationers. New Jersey's oyster and cranberry industries catered to the national appetite, while its truck gardens and dairy farms supplied a large portion of the produce sold in metropolitan markets.

For New York and Pennsylvania financiers and for corporation builders generally New Jersey offered a special attraction. From the 1870s on the state's lax incorporation laws invited the formation of trusts and monopolies in hastily rented offices in Newark or Jersey City. When Lincoln Steffens and other "muckrakers" began to investigate "big business" they contemptuously labeled New Jersey "The Mother of Trusts."

New Jersey's role as a green pasture for foaling corporations illustrates several important characteristics of the state at the turn of the century. Maker Sullivan, in *Our Times*, raised the question of why New Jersey "voluntarily assumed a role which made it a subject of jeering for twenty years," after New York and Ohio court decisions had killed the trusts in those states. He cites the theory of Steffens that New Jersey's position as the terminal of many great railroad systems made the state responsive to corporate influence, and he suggests that nearness to Wall Street may also have been a factor.

Another probable reason, Sullivan points out, was the fact that many of the ablest New Jersey citizens were commuters who took little interest in the state in which they merely slept. "In such a community," he concludes, "it would be easy for politicians and lawyers representing financial interests to take possession of the machinery of the state and to use it to the advantage of the interests they represented. The revenue accruing to the state from the fees it received for providing a home for outside corporations lightened the burden of taxes on New Jersey voters and their property. Many New Jersey voters people frankly and publicly justified the laws favoring trusts on that ground."

The nineteenth century revolt against railroad domination was soon paralleled by an early twentieth century attack on the trusts and machine politics. George L. Record, who had broken with the Hudson County Democratic machine, was the leader of the "New Idea" movement that carried the assault. Closely associated with him were Mark Fagan, who repudiated his boss after being elected the first Republican mayor of Jersey City in many years; Austin Colgate, Frank Sommer, Everett Colby and others. Their program called for election reforms, equal taxation of railroads and utilities, and regulation of public utilities. Although the New Idea men accomplished little during the terms of Governors Stokes and Fort, they had their chance with Governor Woodrow Wilson.

Paradoxically, Wilson was nominated in 1910 by the Democratic leaders against the opposition of the young progressives in his party. Colonel George Harvey was looking for a 1912 Presidential candidate. He induced James Smith, Jr., titular Democratic chief, to select Wilson as a man who would impart a respectable tone to the gubernatorial campaign. When the "safe" professor from Princeton University repudiated the bosses during the campaign, they did not take him seriously. When, however, after the election, Wilson successfully supported James E. Martine against Smith for United States Senator, the machine politicians realized that they had unwittingly elected a champion of the progressives.

Upon the strength of this victory, Wilson was able to push through his bewildered legislature bills for direct primaries, regulation of public utilities, employers' liability, and other reforms, which were in part inspired and supported by some of the New Idea Republicans, notable George L. Record. Thus

Wilson sought to justify his belief in the mission of New Jersey as a "mediating" state, destined to inspire and lead her neighbors into better ways. His courageous and successful fight for reform made him President in 1912, in spite of the bitter opposition of the very men who had deliberately started him on the road to that office.

Wilson held his post in Trenton until March 1, 1913, completing his program by passage of the "Seven Sisters" acts. With these laws he hoped to restrain monopolies and to impose penalties against individual officers of offending corporations. Other states promptly invited the business which New Jersey turned away; while New Jersey "mediated," they would take the cash. With Wilson safely in Washington, the "Seven Sisters" acts were gradually repealed until by 1920 there was hardly a vestige left, but New Jersey never recaptured her former preeminence as the favorite home of new corporations.

Ironically, at the time when the state was first perceiving the danger of corporation control, there arose a new industrial power. In 1903 the Public Service Corporation was formed and started on its way toward virtual control of gas and electric power, trolley and bus transportaion.

Under Governor Fielder the reform movement continued at a slower pace until it was interrupted by World War I. New Jersey's geography and its industrial resources gave it a strategic part in the conflict. Camp Dix and Wrightstown was an important training center, and Camp Merritt (new Dumont) and Hoboken became known to a majority of the men who went overseas as their last points of contact with the homeland. New Jersey shipyards were unceasingly busy and New Jersey factories supplied a large proportion of the nation's chemicals and munitions.

World War I and Industry

The guns of Europe, however, shattered the opportunity for normal growth by plunging the state into the most intense industrialization in its history. The production of high explosives, textiles, steel and ships rocketed to new heights. The Bureau of Statistics reported that expansion in manufacturing was 400 percent greater in 1916 than in any preceding year. Chief among the cities that benefited from the industrial resurgence were

Newark, Perth Amboy, Jersey City and New Brunswick. The chemical industry in New Jersey sprang up almost overnight. Six factories for the production of aniline, formerly imported from Germany, were set up within the state, the most important at Kearny. Other towns that became chemical centers were Carteret, Chrome, Maywood and Perth Amboy.

The success of aircraft in the war made aeronautical manufacture in New Jersey a leading industry, chiefly represented by the Wright Aeronautical Corporation of Paterson, one of the world's largest airplane engine factories.

Governor Walter E. Edge declared, however, that the outstanding features of his wartime term were "the inauguration of the state highway system, the Delaware River Bridge and the Hudson River Tunnels," and the establishment of the state department of institutions and agencies.

The state's post war improvement of transportation facilities attests Edge's perspicacity. When the automobile required another modernization of the New York-Philadelphia highways, New Jersey responded with a splendid and expensive highway system, a proud bid for the praise of millions of travelers who annually cross its borders. Another post war development was a widespread popular campaign against the utilities, featured by the attacks on the gas and electric rates and a spreading though scattered demand for public ownership.

To understand New Jersey in the early twentieth century, it is necessary to visualize the progressive transformation of the state from an agricultural to a primarily industrial and urban region. In 1890 the urban population was about 60 percent; by 1900 it was bout 70 percent, and by 1930 it was 82.6 percent.

The tide of war prosperity, except for recurrent dips such as that of 1921, continued to rise until 1929. The value of manufactures from 1919 to 1929 increased $165,091,000, whereas workers' wages for the same period rose only $10,000,000, and in the same decade, through technological improvements, there was a decrease of 60,000 workers. Production in chemical factories was 450 percent greater in 1929 than than in 1914. Electrical supplies multiplied by 700 percent in the same period, foundry products by 300 percent, and petroleum products by 300 percent.

Building in the middle 1920s prospered to such an extent that the appearance of many New Jersey cities was transformed by the construction of new skyscrapers, factories, apartment houses, small home developments and public parks.

While wealth and industry continued to increase, agriculture declined in relative importance. The amount of improved farming land dropped from 1,977,042 acres in 1899 to 1,305,528 acres in 1924, although the total value of industrial output multiplied sixfold from $611,748,000 in 1900 to $3,937,157,000 in 1930, and the number of wage earners rose from 241,582 to 442,328.

The total population more than doubled between 1900 and 1930, rising from 1,883,669 to 4,041,334. The most spectacular growth was in the five counties of the New York metropolitan area which reached a total of 2,496,558, about three-fifths of the state's population.

A large volume of immigration helped to push census figures upward and to increase the diversification of population that began in colonial times. To the colonial settlers — Dutch, English, Scotch and smaller numbers of French, Germans, Swedes, Blacks and others — thousands of Irish and Germans had been added by the middle of the nineteenth century. In the latter part of the century large numbers of immigrants from southern and eastern Europe poured into New Jersey via New York.

The state's immigration population was further increased between 1920 and 1930 (after the influx from Europe had been stemmed by federal legislation) through migration from other states. Although the foreign-born white population of the entire nation increased by only 11,013 in that decade and most states showed a decline, the figure for New Jersey rose by 106,014 to a total of 844,442 — almost double the number of foreign-born whites in 1900.

The most rapid increase in the Black population occurred in the large cities, beginning when World War I industries mustered manpower. Many hundreds of Blacks were also imported for work as servants in the homes of wealthy residents of Montclair and other suburban communities. By 1930 the Black population was 208,828, almost treble the figure in 1900.

Twentieth Century Politics and The Depression

The twentieth century politics of New Jersey has continued to be dominated — after interruption of Woodrow Wilson's term as governor — by the natural conservatism of the industrial and business interests. The conservative forces have helped to defeat movements toward municipal ownership of utilities, to hamper organization of labor, and to delay modernization of the archaic property tax system.

In the political field, the blurring of party labels in the 1880s became almost a total effacement by the 1920s. Although New Jersey remained Republican in national politics from 1896 to 1932, except when Wilson won in 1912, it has been much more inclined to elect Democratic governors. In 1934, however, Harold Hoffman, a Republican, was elected. His term was a stormy one, especially amid the New Deal sentiments of the time. Later Hoffman was connected with political patronage in his administration, and a large scale embezzlement scheme while he held office.

Both Hoffman and Hague made official efforts to check the growth of the Congress of Industrial Organizations in mass industries. Although locally the Democratic Party had for years advocated legislation to curb injunctions in labor disputes, it reversed its position in 1937. Mayor Hague explained that he felt the shift was necessary to avoid frightening employers or prospective employers from the state.

The responsibility for piloting the state through the depression fell on both the Democratic and Republican parties. The administration of relief was handled by the state until 1936, when the legislature turned it back to the municipalities. Although the change was hailed by some as a step toward economy and common sense, searching and severe criticism soon came from experts of the state and federal governments. In 1937 a study for the Social Science Research Council showed that the average New Jersey family on relief lived 40 percent below the minimum subsistence standard, and that it was practically impossible for many of the smaller communities to give adequate aid.

In New Jersey as elsewhere the prosperity of the 1920s vanished with the crash of 1929. The state, which had been increasing its industrialization at a terrific rate since 1900 suddenly halted and backslid so that by 1932 its formerly busy industrial sections became silent witnesses of reckless spending and general lack of planning. Shantytowns built of galvanized iron, packing boxes and other materials salvaged from dumps sprang up in front of idle factories, and relief became the real industrial problem of the state.

The situation gradually improved. By 1934 recovery slowly began to make itself felt throughout the paralyzed industrial structure. Production in 1937 reached pre-depression levels in some fields, greatest gains being made in the electrical, iron, steel and aircraft industries. Widespread layoffs in the latter part of the year, characterized as a "recession," interrupted the period of the "little prosperity."

In the 1937 gubernatorial campaign the Democratic candidate, Senator A. Harry Moore, defeated the Reverend Lester H. Clee by the slender margin of 43,600 votes, as compared with a Moore plurality of 230,053 in the 1931 election. Dissatisfied with the results of the election of 1937, representatives of a large portion of the 425,000 New Jersey members of the Committee for Industrial Organization and the American Federation of Labor held a preliminary convention in the fall of 1937, looking toward the formation of an independent Labor Party in New Jersey.

New Jersey Enters World War II

European immigrants in the state's larger cities grew tense as the conflict in the Old Country increased. Although some German-Americans believed Hitler was a great man, other Eastern Europeans were outraged at the Nazi advance; clearly the Jews grieved over the infrequent stories about Hitler's pogroms.

When the U.S. entered the War, New Jersey again became a crucial armaments-producing region. Employment reached pre-Depression levels and the value of products nearly regained their 1919 height and then soared above it as the war progressed. But the times were not joyous for everyone; 560,000 men and 10,000 women from New Jersey joined the armed services, one-eighth of the total state population. Of those, 13,172 died in war. Still, this "Arsenal of Democracy" learned how to make better airplanes, ships, radios and telephone systems, which were usable long after the War. Wages rose from an average of $26 per week before the War to $52 per week in 1944.

This prosperity appeared short-lived once the War was over and less armaments were needed. But once the soldiers had settled at home again, the demand for products, especially household appliances, rose steadily, putting many people back to work. The soldiers were marrying and beginning families as well, and Veteran's Administration loans made it possible to buy a small tract house in the suburbs, away from the soot and crime of Jersey's industrial cities. After 1945, the population in the state boomed, as it did elsewhere in the nation. Agricultural acreage declined as the farmers found big profits from land developers.

In 1947, the government leaders and the voters decided it was time to bring the state's 1844 constitution into the modern world. A new taxation system was needed, as were laws that would reflect a drastically changed and enlarged society. The court system was reorganized and simplified, and racial, sexual and religious equality were guaranteed in the new 10,000 word document.

Racial equality was indeed a question in modern New Jersey, with its melting pot of cultures. In the 1950s, '60s and on into the '70s, the Czech, German, Irish and Jewish immigrants who had come to New Jersey in the early part of the century were supplemented by the Cubans, Puerto Ricans and Blacks from the South. The more settled white immigrants moved out to "Suburbia" while the newcomers filled the decaying cities. Blacks especially found little opportunity in Jersey City, Newark, Elizabeth, Paterson and the others, and were forced to live in poorly heated, ill-lit tenements. Hundreds of thousands of former farm laborers from the South could not find work in the offices and factories where specific skills were necessary. Newark, for example, was nearly 50 percent black in the 1960s, and yet this large minority had little power in city affairs. One observer noted that Newark "had become a racial ghetto." In 1967, pent-up anger over this situation erupted in one of the nation's worst race riots. After four days of chaos, twenty-three people were dead and $10 million in property was lost. It appeared that nothing was gained by the outburst, but blacks soon found more power in the city, and in the 1970s a black engineer named Kenneth Gibson was elected mayor of Newark.

Jersey City had severe problems as well, but not so much racial as generally corrupt. John V. Kenny ran the city much as Hague had, with an unstoppable political machine. Unstoppable, that is, until 1969 when a new federal prosecutor, Frederic Lacey, investigated and indicted Kenny's ring of corrupt leaders.

The '70s, '80s, and the Future

The political climate in New Jersey has been volatile in recent years as well. Republicans as well as Democrats have taken over, as voters are not so concerned about party line as the honesty and popular appeal of a candidate. Both Paterson and Jersey City have seen an end to the "Boss" style of government, and both a Republican and a Democrat have served as chief ex- ecutive of the state during the 1970s.

Business in New Jersey has not returned to that of World War II. Unemployment reached 13 percent in 1975 in some cities, and remained at that level in much of the state throughout the 1970s and early 1980s. As the new decade began, city leaders worried about the rising conservatism in federal government policy, especially about the effects President Reagan's economic program would have on welfare and other urban aid. But the state remains a main transportation corridor between the megalopolis New York City and Philadelphia, as well as a major industrial center for a dizzying variety of goods, an agricultural leader, and a center for tourism and sports, with the development of Atlantic City and the new multi-million dollar sports complex at Hackensack Meadowlands. The history of this tiny state, which many people pass through without really seeing, is a microcosm for the history of the nation.

CHRONOLOGY
OF
NEW JERSEY

150,000 B.C.—
(approx.) Ice masses moved down from the Arctic to cover New Jersey, creating lakes Passaic and Hackensack.

23,000 to
18,000 B.C.— Ice sheet retreated; New Jersey shoreline reached present levels.

5,000 B.C.— First men reached New Jersey, ancestors of the Lenni-Lenape.

1524 A.D.— Giovanni da Verrazano, commissioned by Francis I, King of France, coasted along the New Jersey shore and possibly landed on the Jersey side of upper New York Bay.

1609— Henry Hudson sailed along the New Jersey coast, and ascended the Hudson River to the head of navigation.

1610— Captain Samuel Argall, an English navigator, sighted Delaware Bay and named it for Lord De La Warr, governor of Virginia.

1616-20— Cornelius Mey tried to claim Delaware Bay and River for the United Netherland Company, naming all land nearby for himself (Cape May is the only remnant of this naming)

1618 circa—Dutch trading post established at Bergen (Jersey City).

1623— Fort Nassau built by Dutch on Delaware River, near Gloucester, New Jersey.

1626—   Peter Minuit purchased Man-a-hat-ta Island from the Indians for a few trinkets worth $25.

1629—   Michael Pauw obtained grant of present-day Jersey City, first recorded land transfer, and named it Pavonia, or "Land of the Peacock."

1633—   Two houses built at Pavonia.

1636-37—   Pauw surrendered land grant.

1638—   Swedish settlers entered Delaware Bay.

1640—   Swedes purchased land from Cape May to Raccoon Creek from the Indians.
            Aert Van Putten and family began farm at present Hoboken.

1642—   Van Putten opened first brewery at Hoboken.

1643—   Dutch murdered a group of Indians after months of raids on settlers' farms in Hudson River area.

1647—   Peter Stuyvesant became director-general of New Amsterdam, which included New Jersey side of the river.

1649—   Stuyvesant argued against revenge for Indian killing of a Pavonia farmer.

1651—   Copper discovered by Dutch in Kittatinny Mountains.
            Stuyvesant challenged Swedish leaders for Delaware River area of New Jersey.

1653—   Johan Printz, Swedish leader, returned to Sweden, abandoning his country's claim to New Jersey.

1655—   Dutch under Stuyvesant overthrew Swedish rule on the Delaware.

1660—   Bergen established — New Jersey's first village — by Stuyvesant, who wanted to band settlers togethr to protect them from Indian raids.

1661—   Dutch court opened at Bergen, and first sheriff appointed.
         At Communipaw section, a ferry began to run across the Hudson River.

1662—   First school and church established at Bergen.

1664—   Dutch surrendered New Netherland (New York and New Jersey) to English. Colonel Richard Nicolls took possession for the Duke of York. Duke of York granted the New Jersey area to Lord Berkeley and Sir George Carteret, and named it for Sir George's work in the Isle of Jersey, "New Caesarea" or New Jersey.

1666—   Newark settled by 30 families from Connecticut.
         Governor Carteret sold part of Elizabethtown to Puritans who created Woodbridge and Piscataway.

1668—   First meeting of assembly took place at Elizabethtown. Bergen chartered. Grant of 276 acres issued for Hoboken.

1670—   Colonists refused to pay rents to Carteret.

1672—   Colonists called unauthorized assembly and fired Carteret as governor, replacing him with a son of Sir George.
         First Quaker meeting house built at Shrewsbury.

1673-74— Dutch naval force reestablished Dutch rule, but forced to vacate in 1674.

1674—   Lord Berkeley sold his half of New Jersey to John Fenwick in trust for fellow Quaker Edward Byllynge.
         Philip Carteret returned to New Jersey, in power again.
         Iron works opened at Elizabethtown.

1675—   John Fenwick founded Salem on Delaware Bay, first Quaker settlement in West Jersey.

1676—   Byllynge interest placed in trust with William Penn and others.
         Boundary between East and West Jersey defined by deed.

Earliest recorded New Jersey iron works founded at Shrewsbury.

1677— Quakers signed "Concessions and Agreements of the Province of New Jersey," a liberal document written by Penn and Byllynge.
Byllynge continued as governor of West Jersey, though he never left London.
Burlington settled by Quakers from Yorkshire and London; named West Jersey capital in 1681.

1678— Mahlon Stacy founded a town at "ye falls of ye De La Warr," at present-day Trenton.

1679— First settlement in vicinity of Trenton.

1680— Sir George Carteret died, and Philip Carteret arrested and jailed by New York Governor Andros.

1680-82— Richard Arnold and William Cooper settled at Cooper's Ferry (Camden).

1682— Philip Carteret died.
Mark Newbie opened colonies' first bank of issue at Gloucester, distributing Irish halfpence.
William Penn, and eleven associates, bought East Jersey from the Carteret heirs.

1683— Perth Town (Perth Amboy) platted, to become East Jersey's capital.
First tavern in New Jersey opened at Woodbridge.

1684— East New Jersey Board of Proprietors organized, locating its capital at Ambo Point on the Raritan River.

1685— George Scot wrote of New Jersey's natural resources for East New Jersey Proprietors.

1686— Scots emigrated to colony.

1687— Edward Byllynge, chief proprietor of West Jersey, died; his proprietary interest acquired by Dr. Daniel Coxe, who moved to New Jersey from London.

1688— Sir Edmund Andros claimed "Dominion of New England" included New York and New Jersey, with Boston as the capital. New Jerseyans were happy that power was taken from Proprietors.
First pottery works established by Dr. Coxe at Burlington.

1689— King James deposed in England's "Glorious Revolution," and Governor Andros was arrested in Boston. Proprietors regained control of New Jersey.

1690— Robert Barclay, Proprietor and life governor of East Jersey, died.

1692— Thirteen houses at Cape May constructed for whalers. Alexander Hamilton became governor of both East and West Jersey.

1698— "Vast quantities" of whale oil and bones produced at Cape May.

1699— Proprietors of New Jersey secretly offered to give up their powers in the colony, amid growing unrest.

1700— Violence erupted in New Jersey against any authority other than the settlers'. Ouster of Hamilton demanded.

1701— Colonists threatened Governor Hamilton's life if an imprisoned rioter was harmed; he was not.

1702— Proprietors of East and West Jersey officially surrendered civil government to the English Crown. Both Jerseys were merged. Lord Cornbury, governor of New York, separately commissioned as governor of New Jersey as well.

1707— Assembly wrote Bill of Complaints against Cornbury for ignoring Quakers' authority in New Jersey.

1708— Cornbury returned to England.

1710— Proprietors railroaded a Middlesex election in their favor.
Governor Robert Hunter arrived, allying with Scotch Proprietors.

1711—   Quakers regained rights under the new governor.

1719—   Governor Hunter fell ill, and returned to England at the height of his popularity.

1723—   New Governor William Burnett opened first loan office in colony, setting up much-needed paper currency system.

1725—   Voting laws were reformed.

1728—   New Jersey assembly petitioned for a separate government from New York.

1732—   Governor William Cosby promised to visit New Jersey half of his time, but only met assembly once in next four years.

1734—   Lewis Morris traveled to England to ask for a separate New Jersey government, to no avail.

1737—   Population: 47,402.
            "Walking" Purchase outraged Delaware Indians.

1738—   New Jersey finally separated from New York, and Lewis Morris was appointed governor.
            First election for colonial offices held in eight years.

1739—   Weekly mail route, by post boys, established between New York and Philadelphia.
            Four Rotterdam glassblowers emigrated to Salem County to begin first successful glass factory in America.

1740—   Caspar Wistar built factory for Rotterdam glassblowers near Salem.
            Rev. George Whitefield preached at New Brunswick and Elizabethtown.
            Stage wagons ran between South Amboy and Bordentown on the Delaware River.

1743—   First pig iron made in New Jersey—from a furnace at Oxford, Warren County.

1745—   Population: 61,383.
               Improved road between New York and Philadelphia
               completed through New Jersey.
               Squatters arrested in Essex County, but other settlers
               broke open jail to release them; Proprietors couldn't
               control growing land rebellion.

1746—   Governor Lewis Morris died at Kingsbury, near Tren-
               ton.
               College of New Jersey (Princeton University)
               chartered.

1747—   Riot broke out among farm tenants in Morris County.

1751—   Governor Belcher, under the King's order, set up a
               commission to study land rebellion and to restore the
               peace.

1753—   First steam engine imported from England was
               delivered at Schuyler copper mine, in New Barbados
               Neck, now North Arlington, September 25 (first
               operated in 1755).
               New Jerseyans refused to join English army as
               French and Indian War began.

1755—   Delaware Indians joined French in War.
               500 militia men raised for battle, as war reached
               Sussex County.

1756—   Swartout family murdered by Delaware braves at
               Swartzwood Lake.

1757—   New Jersey regiment under Peter Schuyler captured
               by French and Indians at Oswego, New York.
               Funds to build barracks at Elizabethtown, New
               Brunswick, Perth Amboy, Burlington and Trenton ap-
               propriated by the assembly.

1758—   Delaware Indians signed a separate peace with the
               English.
               Brotherton, first Indian Reservation in America,
               created at Indian Mills — 3,000 acres in Burlington
               County. In October, Governor Bernard acquired from
               New Jersey tribes, for 1,000 pounds, a release of all In-
               dian titles to the colony's land.

1760—   8,000 Black slaves in colony.

1763—   Sandy Hook Lighthouse (now oldest remaining in America) erected.
          William Franklin became governor of colony, last English-controlled governor of New Jersey. He was Benjamin Franklin's son.

1766—   New Jersey Medical Society incorporated at New Brunswick, and Queen's College (Rutgers University) chartered there.

1768—   Townshend Acts burdened New Jerseyans.

1769—   Present boundary between New Jersey and New York established.
          Riots over land titles erupted in Newark.

1770—   Two-thirds of New Jersey described as debtors "who do not know how to extricate themselves" because of taxation and ban on letters of credit.

1771—   Rutgers University opened to students.

1774—   July 21: First Provincial Congress met at Trenton.
          November 22: Cargo of tea burned at Greenwich.

1775—   April: Newark leaders resolved to "risk lives and fortunes for American liberty.
          May: Provincial Congress met again at Trenton.
          November-December: Provincial Assembly held last session.
          New Jersey Quakers denounced revolutionary movement as against the Gospel.

1776—   William Franklin arrested as a Loyalist.
          July 2: Provincial Congress adopted state constitution, proclaiming independence.
          August 2: New Jersey's delegates to Continental Congress signed the national Declaration of Independence.
          August 31: First general assembly at Princeton elected William Livingston as first governor of state.
          November: General Washington skillfully retreated

across New Jersey after abandoning Fort Lee.
December 8: Washington crossed the Delaware River into Pennsylvania.
December 25-26: Washington crossed the Delaware again, and defeated enemy forces at Trenton.

1777—
January 3: Battle of Princeton; army retired to winter quarters at Morristown.
Washington and army quartered at Camp Middlebrook in Somerset County.
June: General Howe evacuated New Jersey. Went by water to Delaware River and occupied Philadelphia.
December 15: Isaac Collins published the New Jersey *Gazette*.
Battle of Red Bank occurred.
William Livingston met with his Council of Safety 400 times in 18 months beginning this year.
Loyalists were arrested, many hanged, until Gov. Livingston secured an Act of Indemnity for them.

1778—
June 28: Battle of Monmouth.
Privateers looted British ships that tried to pass by New Jersey shoreline.

1779—
Washington and army wintered at Morristown (until 1780).
American forces, under Major Henry Lee, surprised British at Paulus Hook.
New Jersey *Journal* published at Chatham by Shepard Kollock to aid Revolutionists.

1780—
Benedict Arnold court martialed at Morristown.

1781—
Soldiers at Morristown left camp to demand better provisions from Congress in Philadelphia.
Washington's troops traversed New Jersey to get to Battle of Yorktown.

1783—
Residents of Bergen and Elizabethtown watched British evacuate New York City across the Hudson.
June 30: Princeton became national capital. Continental Congress held session there.
Washington wrote farewell address to army at Rocky Hill.

1784—   New Brunswick incorporated as a city.

1785—   New Jersey declared independence from Congress until New York would agree to pay import taxes like the other states were required to.

1786—   John Fitch's steamboat chugged in New Jersey waters — first in America.
Philadelphia established as national capital.

1787—   New Jersey delegates to Constitutional Convention in Philadelphia argued state should pay taxes only in proportion to their influence in national affairs.

1790—   Population: 184,139.
Trenton named state capital.
William Livingston died.
Federalists gained control of state politics.

1791—   Alexander Hamilton incorporated a Society for Establishing Useful Manufactures and founded Paterson.

1794—   First Paterson factory — calico prints — went into operation.
Moses Combs, Newark founder of shoe industry, opened first free vocational school.

1797—   Paterson mill failed.

1800—   Population: 211,149.

1801—   Morris Turnpike — Elizabethtown to the Delaware River — chartered, state's first toll road.
Cape May became first summer resort to advertise for guests.
Anti-Federalist governor elected.

1804—   Act passed in February making free all persons born in the state after July 4, 1804.
First bank chartered, the Newark Banking and Insurance Company.
Alexander Hamilton and others formed the Associates of New Jersey to create a town at present Jersey City, but hopes were dashed when Aaron Burr killed Hamilton in a duel at Weekhawken.

1806— New Jersey Turnpike approved to go between New Brunswick and Phillipsburg. Trenton Bridge built.

1807— Franchise extended to every white male taxpayer; women voted illegally in Essex County election, but votes were counted anyway.

1810— Population: 245,562.
1811— First steam ferry operated between New York and Hoboken.

1812— New Jersey voters backed peace as war began.
British blockaded New Jersey coastline, but state legislature condemned war as "inexpedient" and militia refused to fight outside of the state.

1815— As many as 50 families per day left state for lands westward.
America's first railroad charter was given to John Stevens at Trenton.

1817— Legislature permitted townships to raise money for free schools.

1818— First patent leather produced at Newark by Seth Boyden.
Vail Works at Speedwell (Morris County) built machinery for the *Savannah*, first steamship to cross the Atlantic.

1820— Population: 277,575.
Jersey City chartered.

1822— George P. Macculoch made plans for Morris Canal while fishing on Lake Hopatcong.

1825— Stevens' "Steam Waggon" ran over 630 feet on a circular track at Hoboken, the first locomotive built in America.
Morris Canal excavation began, from Newark to Phillipsburg.

1826— Seth Boyden produced first malleable cast iron in U.S.

1828—   Legislature first allocated taxes in support of education.
           Paterson mechanics joined millworkers in first recorded sympathy strike.

1830—   Population: 320,823.
           Camden and Amboy Railroad chartered to Stevens the same day the Delaware and Raritan Canal was chartered.

1831—   Morris Canal opened.
           Stevens joined with D&R Railroad to form the "Joint Companies."

1832—   New York-Philadelphia traffic was given solely to Camden and Amboy Railroad.
           Legislature gave Indians $2,000 to end all remaining titles to their New Jersey land.

1833-34—   New Jersey's first railroad, the Camden and Amboy, began operation with the English *John Bull* locomotive.

1834—   Delaware and Raritan Canal between New Brunswick and Bordentown opened.
           Boundary dispute between New York and New Jersey settled.
           America's first hot blast furnace opened at Oxford, New Jersey.

1835—   Morris and Essex Railroad, to traverse the Orange Mountains, chartered.

1836—   First Colt revolver made in Paterson by Samuel Colt.
           Legislature rejected offer to buy the "Joint Companies."

1837—   Locomotive industry at Paterson founded.
           Financial panic.

1838—   Samuel F.B. Morse demonstrated his magnetic telegraph at Morristown with Alfred Vail.
           Morris and Essex Railroad opened a commuter service between New Jersey and New York City.
           First high school opened at Newark.

1839— State's first rubber factory opened at New Bruswick.
1840— Population: 373,306.
Silk winding spools, devised by John Ryle, built Paterson industry.
Nearly one-third of nation's glass was made in New Jersey during the next twenty years.
Forty newspapers operated in state.

1843— North American Phalanx, a self-sufficient commune, was founded in Monmouth County, and lasted ten years.
Dorothea Dix found atrocious treatment of the insane and mentally retarded in state's institutions.

1844— New state constitution abolished property qualification for voters. Convention in session May 14 to June 29, and constitution was ratified by the voters in August.
Miss Dix inspired legislature to appropriate funds for a state mental asylum.

1845— New Jersey Historical Society organized at Trenton.

1846— First professional baseball game in world played at Hoboken between Knickerbocker Giants and a New York team.

1848— Representative (later Governor) William Newell began successful campaign for Federal aid to a lifesaving service.
John Roebling moved his wire rope factory to Trenton.
Joseph Dixon developed the first high-grade steel.
State mental hospital built in Ewing Township near Trenton.

1850— Population: 489,555.
Camden and Amboy Railroad carried as many as 450,000 passengers per year in the next decade.
Atlantic City placed on the map when rail lines were planned to reach it.

1851— Clara Barton established free school at Bordentown.

1852— Camden and Atlantic Railroad chartered to traverse southern New Jersey.

1854—   First wrought-iron beams for building rolled at Peter
           Cooper's Iron Works in Trenton.
           Morris and Essex Railroad reached Phillipsburg.
           First travelers rode train from Camden to Atlantic Ci-
           ty.

1855—   First New Jersey Normal School established.

1857—   Thousands of unemployed men met in Newark to de-
           mand work from large companies.

1858—   First transatlantic cable message (sent to President
           Buchanan from Queen Victoria) forwarded from New-
           foundland, received by John Wright at Trenton.
           Steel pen factory established at Camden by Richard
           Esterbrook.
           Dr. Edward R. Squibb opened a pharmaceutical plant
           at New Brunswick, beginning of a massive industry.

1860—   Population: 672,035.
           25,318 free blacks in state and 18 slaves, although the
           difference in their status was slight in reality.
           State divided between Republicans and Democrats.

1861—   April 30: State legislature appropriated $2 million for
           Civil War purposes.
           May 3: Four regiments of New Jersey volunteers left
           for Annapolis.
           Major General Philip Kearny, commanding New
           Jersey volunteers, slain in Battle of Chantilly.
           Secession flag flown at Hackensack.

1862—   Democrats won most state elections, and many pro-
           tested war effort.

1863—   Emancipation Proclamation was not popular in New
           Jersey. Of 30,000 men enlisted in Union Army from
           New Jersey, over 6,000 died in war. Anti-war pro-
           testers rioted in Newark.

1864—   Lincoln failed to win New Jersey votes.
           State College of Agriculture opened at Rutgers Col-
           lege.

1865— Governor Parker and legislature opposed to the Thirteenth Amendment abolishing slavery.
April: Civil War ended. Total New Jersey involvement was 76,814 men, including re-enlistment; reduced to three years' standing, 57,908.
September: Rutgers Scientific School opened at New Brunswick.

1866— New legislature created a state Board of Education and passed the Thirteenth Amendment.

1867— Conflict over blacks' right to vote.

1869— Celluloid patented by John Wesley Hyatt of Newark.
Rutgers defeated Princeton in first intercollegiate football game.
Joseph Campbell began tomato packing and canning business at Camden.

1870— Population: 906,096.
First boardwalk completed at Atlantic City.
Jersey City became the "Gateway to the West," as three major rail lines had terminals there.

1871— Free public schools system established throughout state.
Pennsylvania Railroad entered New Jersey with a lease of Camden and Amboy lines.
Stevens Institute of Technology founded at Hoboken.

1872— Dr. Charles Abbot discovered important artifacts in Trenton gravels.
Industrial Exhibition held at Newark.

1873— Pennsylvania Railroad monopoly between New York and Philadelphia ended with law opening the state to all railroads.
Isaac Singer opened a huge sewing machine factory at Elizabethport.
Financial panic slowed industrial growth.

1874— Act making school attendance compulsory passed.

1875—   Elizabeth Cady Stanton tried to vote in Terrafly, but was prevented from doing so.
           Twenty-eight amendments to the state constitution were ratified by the voters, among them, restrictions on state power in cities and eligibility to vote in state elections for black men.

1876—   Jersey City gained right to govern itself without state interference.
           Standard Oil Company established a refinery at Bayonne.

1877—   Socialist Labor Party of America held its first national convention at Newark.
           State Board of Health created.
           Prudential Insurance Company founded at Newark.
           Edison invented the first phonograph at Menlo Park.
           New Jersey was fifth in manufacturing output in U.S.
           Cheap train route from Philadelphia to Atlantic City began operation.
           Edward Weston began first dynamo factory at Newark.

1878—   Board of Labor Statistics created.
           John Holland launched first submarine in Passaic River.

1879—   World's first practical incandescent lamp lit by Edison at Menlo Park.

1880—   Population: 1,131,116.
           American Society of Mechanical Engineers founded at Hoboken.
           Passaic woolen mill founded by German immigrants.

1881—   Alliance, a communal farming town, was settled in Salem County.

1882—   Roselle became the first town in U.S. to be fully lit by electricity.

1883—   Agricultural Experiment Station established at New Brunswick.
           Newark *Evening News* founded.

1884— Election of Grover Cleveland, only president born in New Jersey.

1885— General George McClellan died at Orange.
Johnson brothers opened a bandage factory at New Brunswick.

1886— Glassworkers strikes were unsuccessful.

1887— Standard Oil took advantage of New Jersey's liberal trust and "holding company" laws.

1890— Population: 1,444,933.
Streetcars replaced horse carriages in Newark.
New York City millionaires began to move estates to hills near Morristown.

1891— World's first smokeless powder, developed at Hudson Maxim's plant at Maxim, was first used in America at Sandy Hook in an eight inch rifled gun.

1892— Walt Whitman died at Camden.

1894— Women founded Morris County Golf Club, the first country club run by women in the United States.
New Jersey Federation of Women's Clubs founded.

1895— First woman (Mary Philbrook) admitted to New Jersey Bar.
Highest temperature (109 degrees) reported at Somerville.

1896— Corporation laws revised to facilitate formation of trusts.

1897— State constitution amended again.

1898— Three regiments of infantry mustered in at Sea Girt for Spanish-American War.

1899— Thomas A. Edison, Jr. and Edward Hewitt bought steam-powered autos, the first in New Jersey.
Hewitt and his wife drove from Ringwood to New York City in one day.

1900—   Population: 1,883,669.
           Hoboken steamship and wharf fire; 145 lives lost.

1901—   Stricter child labor laws passed.

1902—   Paterson silk dyers struck, led by anarchists.

1903—   Public Service Corporation formed.
           Official ballots, regular registration, and election
           boards enacted.

1904—   Lowest temperature (34 degrees below zero) recorded
           at Riverdale.

1908—   Hudson and Manhattan Railroad Company opened
           first tunnel under Hudson River between Jersey City
           and New York.

1910—   Population: 2,537,167.
           Woodrow Wilson elected governor.

1911—   Legislature passed direct primaries act and corrupt
           practices act among other reforms urged by Governor
           Wilson.

1912—   Woodrow Wilson elected President.

1913—   John Reed and other radical organizers led Paterson
           textile strike.
           "Seven Sisters Act" passed, limiting corporate
           privileges in New Jersey.

1915—   Strike guards fired into pickets at Carteret fertilizer
           factory; six killed and twenty-eight wounded.
           "Boss" leaders tried to stop women's suffrage move-
           ment by buying votes against it.
           Czarist agents tested explosives at Lakehurst range.

1916—   Black Tom gunpowder depot exploded at Jersey City;
           three people were killed and a large amount of muni-
           tions for World War I were destroyed.
           Standard Oil workers in Bayonne struck; eight killed
           and seventeen wounded in conflict.

1917—   U.S. entered World War I and Hoboken became the embarkation port for the war. Camps Dix and Merritt established for mobilization and training. Over 150,000 served in the war, and of these, 3,836 died.
             German agents arrested at Hoboken and German ships were seized at their New Jersey docks.

1918—   State had six factories making bombshells.
             New Jersey College for Women opened at New Brunswick.
             Severe influenza epidemic struck 300,000 in state.
             Town of Morgan damaged by explosion at a TNT plant.

1919—   Newark led American cities in shipbuilding.

1920—   Population: 3,155,900.
             Women gained suffrage.

1921—   WJZ, world's second radio station, opened at Newark.

1924—   *Shenandoah*, a dirigible, made firs transcontinental flight from Lakehurst to California.

1925—   Industrial production nearly reached World War I levels.

1926—   Camden-Philadelphia suspension bridge opened.
             15,000 Passaic textile workers struck for a year.

1927—   Holland vehicular tunnel between New York and Jersey City opened.
             Charles Lindbergh flew across the Atlantic in a plane containing a Wright Whirlwind engine, built in Paterson.
             State constitution amended.

1928—   Goethals Bridge and Outerbridge Crossing, connecting New Jersey and Staten Island, opened.

1929—   Air mail service began at Newark airport.
             Graf Zeppelin started and finished a 21 day around the world trip at Lakehurst.
             Stock market crash in New York City halted industrial boom in New Jersey; 50,000 on relief by end of year.

1930—   Population: 4,041,334.
Bergen hired unemployed men to build public roads.

1931—   George Washington Bridge between Fort Lee and Manhattan opened.
Bayonne Bridge between Bayonne and Staten Island opened.

1932—   Lindbergh baby kidnapped at Hopewell.
Amelia Earhart flew from Los Angeles to Newark; firs transcontinental nonstop flight by a woman.

1933—   *Akron*, a Navy dirigible, crashed off Barnegat; Admiral Moffett and 73 others lost.
Morristown National Historical Park established.
Pulaski Skyway between Jersey City and Newark dedicated.
Banks closed for one week.
Average yearly income in state was only $433.
Albert Einstein, exiled from his native Germany, took a professorship at Princeton University.

1934—   Ward Line steamship *Morro Castle* burned off Asbury Park; 134 died.
Dr. Harold Urey of Leonia received Nobel Prize in physics.

1935—   University of Newark organized.
Legislature ratified national child labor amendment.
Lindbergh kidnapping trial held in Hunterdon County.

1936—   Unemployed marchers occupied state capitol for nine days.
Bruno Richard Hauptmann executed at Trenton for murder of the Lindbergh baby.
American newspaper guild members on Newark *Ledger* won nation's first important strike of editorial workers.

1937—   German dirigible *Hindenberg* destroyed by fire at Lakehurst. Thirty-six passengers died.
Perth Amboy pottery workers won first sit-down strike.
First tube of Lincoln Tunnel between Weehawken and New York opened.

1938— A. Harry Moore inaugurated as first third-term governor under 1844 constitution.
Swedes celebrated 300th anniversary of coming to Delaware Valley.
Census showed 287,530 employed in state.

1939— Senate passed bill to bar employment or unionizing of illegal aliens.
State industry began to reach World War I levels again.

1940— Alien registration began.
Works Progress Administration planned many new highways in New Jersey.
Population: 4,160,165.

1941— Legislators considered a constitutional convention.
U.S. entered World War II, and state geared up its industrial plants.

1942— Over 560,000 men and 10,000 women from New Jersey would serve in the War.

1943— Former Governor Hoffman admitted political patronage system in his civil service commission, and defended the practice of providing jobs for friends.
Court upheld the right of a Cherokee Indian to vote.
Federal shipyards at Kearny produced ships faster than any other in U.S.

1944— Proposed constitutional amendments failed in November vote.
A state council was formed to plan for postwar problems.
Governor Edge donated his Princeton estate, "Morven," to the state as a governor's mansion and historic site.
Navy established military government school at Princeton.

1945— Bill signed to permit persons in armed services to vote by absentee ballots in all elections.

1946— Coal strike prompted Governor Edge to declare a state of emergency.

1947— Constitutional convention held in New Brunswick, and a new document was approved by the voters to change the 1844 Constitution. New laws were set on gambling, lotteries and taxes, and blacks were integrated with whites in the National Guard for the first time.

1948— Researchers at Princeton developed a glass cloth laminate to lower fire hazards.

1949— Loyalty "oath of allegiance" to the U.S. government required of all candidates for state office.

1950— Population: 4,835,329.
Cities population was declining as suburbia grew.
Cost of living dropped by almost one percent in state.
State supreme court ovverruled 1949 oath of allegiance requirements of state officials.

1953— New Jersey Turnpike opened.
Puerto Ricans received first resettlement and educational aid from Rutgers University program at Perth Amboy.
Governor Driscoll reported a balanced budget.

1954— Ex-Governor Hoffman revealed he had been involved in a large-scale embezzlement scheme of state funds.
Garden State Parkway opened.

1957— New Jersey Supreme Court ruled state had same rights as New York to lower New York Bay.
Vice President Richard Nixon supported a Republican candidate for state governor.

1958— Economic situation looked gloomy, but a Rutgers University study held that the growth potential outweighed drawbacks because of state's many resources.
Princeton U. dining clubs issued membership quotas on Jewish persons and other religious and ethnic groups; students protested.

1959— "Games of Chance" allowed by legislature and voters at amusement parks and beach boardwalks.
State budget in "worst crisis since before the Civil War," according to budget officials.

1960—   Population: 6,066,782.
             New Jersey Tercentennial plans begun.
             Superior Court held New Jersey's right to lease
             tidelands.

1961—   Governor Meyner feared air pollution controls would
             stunt industrial growth and ordered increased public
             building. Later in year, he asked for an increased
             budget and more taxes to prevent program and
             building cuts.
             $35 million donated anonymously to Princeton Univer-
             sity for a public service program — highest donation
             ever given to a U.S. university or college.

1962—   Economic upswing reported by bankers.
             State aimed to make public buildings more accessible
             to the handicapped.

1963—   Republicans took control of the legislature.

1964—   Tercentenary celebrated and astronaut L. Gordon
             Cooper was given a special medal. Delaware Indians'
             descendants participated as well.
             Legislature reapportioned districts according to one-
             man-one-vote principle.
             First woman speaker of the assembly elected,
             Republican Marion W. Higgins.

1965—   Democrats regained power in state, first time for both
             houses since 1913.
             Commission on Equal Opportunity created.
             New $7 million cultural center completed at Trenton.

1966—   Assemblyman David Friedland asked that catfish be
             named the state fish, and the swallow the state bird
             because these animals were among the few that could
             withstand New Jersey's pollution.
             State supreme court ruled new apportionment of the
             legislature was unconstitutional. Assembly was
             enlarged from sixty to eighty members and the senate
             from twenty-nine to forty members.
             Mildred B. Hughes elected as first female state
             senator.

1967—   Republicans regained control of both houses of the
           legislature.
           Major race riot left twenty-three dead in Newrk.

1968—   Faculty commission at Princeton urged admission of
           women to the university.
           NAACP charged state Civil Rights Division was racist
           and slow to enforce equality laws.
           State faced financial difficulties, and asked for more
           taxes to avoid becoming a "third rate state."

1969—   Urban Industrial Act recommended to deal with civil
           disorders and deteriorating cities in state.
           Hackensack Meadowlands reclaimed and open for
           development.
           Governor Cahill urged attack on corruption after a
           report that Mafia members offered bribes to obtain
           lucrative state contracts.
           170 women entered Princeton University for first
           time.
           State lottery begun to raise funds for education.

1970—   Population: 7,168,164.
           Internal Revenue Service investigated state officials
           thought to be involved in corruption.
           Thirteen largest cities in New Jersey showed popula-
           tion decreases, though total state population increased
           by seventeen percent since 1960.
           Princeton students held strike against U.S. involve-
           ment in Cambodia.
           Newark population was over 50 percent black, but
           whites still controlled most of the government.

1971—   Governor Cahill asked for new federal aid to New
           Jersey cities to prevent financial collapse.
           Several county officials charged for involvement with
           organized crime.
           Large sports complex approved for the Hackensack
           Meadowlands.

1972—   Several top New Jersey state officials, including the
           Secretary of State, charged with extortion, bribery,
           and accepting kickbacks for political favors.

1973—   State supreme court ruled public schools could no longer be funded by property taxes.

1975—   Economists showed how New Jersey faced worse problems during the recession than the rest of the nation. Unemployment increased by 241,000 persons in one year, with 13 percent rate total.
         Governor Byrne announced a "rock bottom" state budget of $2.8 million, and asked for heavy new taxes. A small income tax was initiated for first time.

1976—   New Jersey legalized casino gambling at Atlantic City.
         Falls area of Passaic River declared a national historic site, encouraging redevelopment of rundown area of Paterson.

1978—   First casino, Chalfonte-Haddon Hall, opened at Atlantic City's boardwalk.

1980—   Five southern counties voted to secede from New Jersey and form new state, but vote was nonbinding and not seriously considered.
         New Jersey Senator Harrison Williams indicted in ABSCAM bribery case.
         Spanish-speaking residents numbered more than 700,000 and although blacks and Hispanics accounted for twenty-six percent of the state's population, only five members of the legislature were from minority groups.
         State Capitol underwent interior redecorating.
         Population: 7,364,158.
         Many New Jerseyans moved to the Sun Belt during 1970s.

1981—   Plans made to move governor's mansion from "Morven" to "Drumthwacket," an 1833 house at Princeton.
         State officials worried about the effects of President Reagan's cutbacks in New Jersey's troubled cities.

1982—   Anti-Republican sentiment felt in November elections; political newcomer Frank Lautenberg won 93 percent of the vote against popular Rep. Millicent Fenwick in the U.S. Senator race.

GEOGRAPHY OF NEW JERSEY

A Description of the Natural Landscape

by
John P. Snyder

New Jersey, frequently considered a small, crowded place nestled between New York City and Philadelphia, has been called an "historical accident." It was given its official name in 1664 when the southern limb of a large grant of land to the Duke of York was broken off as a gift to his court friends. New Jersey has become well known, however, in its own right for prominence in fields ranging from great inventions and model progressive legislation to political corruption and organized crime.

Its variety is not confined to its political and economic flavoring. For a state fifth smallest in area, 7,836 sq. mi., it is heterogeneous, with substantial numbers of several racial, religious and national groups, and it has a variety of natural scenery ranging from mountains to plains, from lakes to seashores. Little more than its urban and commercial landscapes are visible along the heavily traveled corridor between New York and Philadelphia, but to the south are the extensive, nearly flat Pine Barrens of the Coastal Plain leading to the Atlantic Ocean with its almost continuous recreational beaches from Sandy Hook to Cape May. To the north of the corridor are the Kittatinny Mountains extending from the Delaware Water Gap to High Point (New Jersey's "summit" at 1,803 feet above sea level) and other ridges characterizing the Highlands between the Kittatinnies and urban New Jersey.

John P. Snyder is author of **The Story of New Jersey's Civil Boundaries, 1606-1968** *and* **The Mapping of New Jersey: The Men and the Art**

New Jersey's population is larger than that of many independent nations. The average density of the New Jersey population is greater than that of any other state. The average density by county varies nearly 100-fold when Sussex County in the northwest is compared with Hudson County bordering New York City. There are municipalities with fewer than ten inhabitants per square mile and others with more than 30,000.

The latitude of New Jersey ranges from 38°56'to 41°21' North; the longitude from 73°54' to 75°34' West. The greatest length of the state is only 166 miles. Borders consist of natural features on three sides. The percentage of water boundaries (90 percent) is the highest of any state except Hawaii. The entire western boundary is the Delaware River; on the south it is Delaware Bay and on the east, the Hudson River, Arthur Kill and the Atlantic Ocean. Only the northern boundary is an artificial line across land; intended to be straight, the line surveyed in 1774 veered one-half mile south at the center because the surveyors did not compensate properly for compass deviations caused by the magnetic iron ore in the Highlands.

The Delaware River is shared by New Jersey and Pennsylvania except for its islands, which are governed by the nearest state. Exact state lines along the other rivers and through Delaware Bay have been carefully delineated as a series of artificial lines roughly down the middle of each. One exception is the boundary of the state of Delaware along Delaware Bay near Salem. It follows the original low water line on the Jersey side, placing in Delaware some landfill areas attached to the Salem County shore. It was unsuccessfully contested in the U.S. Supreme Court by New Jersey; the court ruled in favor of Delaware in 1934.

Terrain

New Jersey is geographically divided into four distinctive "physiographic provinces," with lines of demarcation running almost parallel from northeast to southwest (Figure 1). these can be identified by changes in elevations or by geological variation. Farthest northwest is the Appalachian Ridge and Valley, comprising most of Sussex and Warren Counties. The Highlands of Morris and western Passaic Counties are next, followed by the Piedmont Plateau and finally the Coastal Plain, the latter including all of the state south of Trenton and Perth Amboy, or more than half the total area.

The Appalachian Ridge is marked by the Kittatinny Mountains, bridging the Blue Mountains in eastern Pennsylvania with the Shawangunk Mountains of southern New York state. A relatively narrow ridge from one to five miles wide, like these neighboring ranges, the Kittatinnies extend northeastward from the Delaware Water Gap, rising from 287 feet above sea level at the Delaware River to 1,500 feet in about five miles and continuing for some thirty miles at a similar elevation with moderate gaps until leaving the state just beyond High Point. The Appalachian Trail enters New Jersey from the south at the Water Gap and follows the ridge to High Point, although north of there it breaks east to the New York line near Greenwood Lake and does not follow the Shawangunk Mountains.

The Delaware Water Gap is one of New Jersey's most beautiful natural features, with mountains parting for the Delaware River, which has gradually eroded the gap after the crustal upheavals which formed the Appalachians millions of years ago.

The Kittatinnies divide two valleys which lead to the Delaware River on the northwest and to the Highlands on the southeast. Both valleys show considerable undulation, containing river valleys as low as 400 feet above sea level and surrounding low-lying ranges of hills and individual peaks as high as 800-900 feet. Like the mountain range, the valleys are but part of a larger system extending for hundreds of miles in the Eastern United States.

The Highlands extend northeast from the Phillipsburg area at the Delaware River to a 20 mile-wide swath centered on Greenwood Lake at the New York border. The elevation ranges from 500 feet in some of the valleys to nearly 1,500 feet at some peaks. Rivers draining the region generally flow parallel to the ranges, but there are some flowing transversely. Numerous ranges within the Highlands are identified as individual mountains such as Schooleys, Green Pond and Bearfort.

The Piedmont Plateau, literally meaning "foot of the mountains," varies from sea level to 400 feet in elevation but is generally 100 to 200 feet high., It is most noted for containing the bulk of the densely crowded population of northeastern New Jersey, since it includes the area from the Hudson River to Bernardsville, Morristown and Pompton Lakes, but also reaches Trenton. It has several low ridges separating wide valleys. The most notable ridges are the Palisades along the Hudson River, the First and Second Watchung Mountains just west of Newark, and the Sourland Mountains north of Trenton. Some of New

Jersey's most attractive forested county parks are located in the
Watchung Mountains: the Watchung Reservation (Union County), South Mountain and Eagle Rock Reservations (Essex County), and Garret Mountain Reservation (Passaic County).

The large Coastal Plain is often subdivided into the Inner
and Outer regions. While there is some undulation over the area,
the changes in elevation are so gradual that hills are seldom
recognizable as such. One significant exception is near Sandy
Hook: the Navesink Hills sighted by Henry Hudson's crew in 1609
are among the highest promontories along the Atlantic seacoast,
although only 276 feet high. The flatness of most of the coast itself
has led to the blessing of excellent recreational beaches joined
with the cruise of vulnerability to a number of damaging ocean
storms. Except for the dense population along portions of the
coast and especially along the Delaware River valley from Trenton south through Camden County, the Coastal Plain is noted for
the truck gardening of southwest Jersey and the almost un-
populated Pine Barrens.

Geology

Relatively young geological upheavals of sandstone and
conglomerate formed the Kittatinny Mountain Range some 400
million years ago, but the adjacent valleys lie on limestones and
shales emanating from 500-600 million years ago, all of these formations occurring during the Paleozoic era according to the
adopted geological timetable.

The Highlands contain the oldest rocks in New Jersey,
dating from the Precambrian era, more than 600 million years
ago. Most are highly compacted metamorphic rocks containing
most of the mineral wealth which led to New Jersey's important
role as a mining area during the eighteenth and nineteenth centuries. Iron, marble and zinc were the more noted products, but
also important were the limestone and shale folded into the
valleys.

All of the Piedmont formations occurred during the
Triassic and Jurassic periods of the Mesozoic era, some 200
million years ago. The sedimentary rock formations of the Piedmont are dominated by red shale and by a brown sandstone often
used as the building material "brownstone." The Watchung
Mountains, the Palisades and the Sourland Mountains consist of
the much more resistant basalt which erupted as lava through
the sandstone strata.

During the Pleistocene or Ice Age, beginning a million years ago, the Piedmont region was affected by several ice advances. The most recent, the "Wisconsin Ice," receded little more than 10,000 years ago after advancing as far south as a line of terminal moraine extending from Belvidere through Netcong, Morristown and Summit south to Perth Amboy and across Staten Island. The ice sheet reached a thickness of up to a half mile. Glacial lakes Passaic and Hackensack were formed during the recession of this ice in the regions of the rivers now bearing these names. After the lakes drained, the still-existing Great Swamp, Troy Meadows, Hatfield Swamp and Hackensack Meadows remained.

Both the Inner and Outer Coastal Plain areas consist of underpinnings of older Precambrian, Paleozoic and Triassic rocks, upon which lie varieties of Cretaceous or Tertiary sand, gravel and clay of 100 million years ago. Not only do the thickness of layers vary, but the outcroppings produce contrasts between the Inner and Outer regions — clay in the former and porous sand in the latter, leading to marked differences in fertility and population density. Along the shores of both the ocean and Delaware Bay, the drainage is poorer and swamps are extensive.

Drainage

The dominant drainage pattern for most of the Outer Coastal Plain is southeast to the Atlantic Ocean, especially via the Metedeconk, Toms, Mullica and Great Egg Harbor River basins. The Maurice River and its tributaries drain a small portion south into Delaware Bay, and the Rancocas and Crosswicks Creeks carry another small portion northwest into the Delaware River. The Inner Coastal Plain below Trenton drains northwesterly into the Delaware.

North Jersey drainage follows a much different pattern. With the generally northeast-southwest pattern of mountain ranges, the rivers for the most part flow southwest, whether to the Delaware' River on the west, or eventually to the Hudson River or Raritan Bay on the east. There are important exceptions to this pattern: the Wallkill River flows northeasterly into New York State; about half the length of the Passaic River flows northeast (although the remainder flows southerly), the Millstone flows northwest and north, and the Raritan River cuts easterly across Somerset and Middlesex Counties. There are also lesser rivers like the Pequannock and Rockaway flowing east or southeast across the Highlands. Beautiful falls and cascades are sprinkled through northern New Jersey; the most significant is the Great Falls of the Passaic in the heart of Paterson. Seventy feet high, its volume and grandeur attract many tourists and as a source of power inspired Alexander Hamilton to locate Paterson on the site in 1791.

During its past geologic history, however, the river patterns in the New Jersey area have differed substantially from those of the present — flowing northwesterly into Paleozoic oceans covering much of Sussex County but also southeasterly, during the Ice Age, across the future Coastal Plain.

Minerals

New Jersey has produced usable minerals for over 300 years. Since the middle-nineteenth century, when extensive iron ore deposits became unprofitable because of the vast ore discoveries and exploitation in the Mesabi range of Minnesota, minerals have taken a back seat to most other New Jersey industries (some of which process ores from other parts of the world).

Copper was mined near Belleville during much of the eighteenth century, but this work had ended by the time of the Revolution. Other copper mines were still less successful. The first ironworks were built on the Shrewsbury River in 1674. Eventually, ironworks dotted the Highlands, beginning in 1710 at Succasunna in the future Morris County. Oxford, High Bridge and Andover were examples farther west, and Charlotteburg, Ringwood and Long Pond (Greenwood Lake) were a few of the many works in and near the Ramapo Mountains opened just before the Revolution. While north Jersey yielded magnetite and hematite ores blasted and dug out from shafts and pits which are often still visible from the surface, south central Jersey yielded bog ore formed as deposits from the seepage of cedar swamp water through rock-containing iron. Revivals of north Jersey iron mining occurred after both the Revolution and the Civil War. Peak production of over 900,000 tons of iron ore occurred in 1882, to be closely approached again only in 1956.

The other major metallic product of New Jersey mines has been zinc. The two principal deposits were in Sussex County at Franklin and Ogdensburg. Commercial mining began about 1850 and has continued on a reduced scale to the present, with a short lapse during the 1950s.

Non-metallic quarrying has been an almost continuous industry from the time of the first production of earthenware pottery in Burlington in 1685. Clay, sand and gravel are found in many areas of the state and are used for a variety of commercial products, including important glass industries in south Jersey.

Climate

New Jersey naturally varies in weather from its northern to its southern limits, but its weather is affected perhaps more by its topographic variety ranging from Appalachian mountain terrain to seashore. Cold air masses from Canada vie with warm air fronts from the southeastern United States and a variety of fronts from the ocean. Thus New Jersey readily qualifies for the trite expression used in numerous states, that if the current weather is considered unsuitable, one need only wait awhile. Recorded temperatures have ranged from -7°C (-34°F) at River Vale in northeastern Bergen County to 43°C (110°F) at Runyon in Middlesex County. Temperatures averaged over a month's time are as low as -3° to +2°C (27° to 36°F) in January, and as high as 22° to 24°C (71° to 76°F) in July, depending on the location.

Rainfall in New Jersey has generally been unusually stable in both quantity and even distribution throughout the year, although droughts in 1965 and again in 1980 are recent exceptions to this generalization. The water shortages resulting from these droughts are accentuated by the rapid growth in population in northern Jersey, where the problem has been most acute. The existence of many water reservoirs in that area, developed over many decades, is proof of the inability of the relatively uniform rainfall alone to satisfy requirements even in the past.

The average annual rainfall varies from 48 inches at some locations in Essex, Passaic and Atlantic Counties to 34 inches at Cape May, with an allover average of 44. The monthly averages vary up to thirty percent.

The growing season for vegetation is taken as the period during which the temperature averages at least 6°C (43°F) every day. It begins as early as March 15 near Salem and as late as April 5 near High Point. The season lasts until November 10 at High Point and November 30 at Cape May, a length of 220 and 255 days, respectively, the extremes of the state. The normal frost-free period, relating to 0°C (32°F) instead of 6°C, extends from May 10 to September 30, or 140 days, at High Point, and from April 10 to October 30, or 200 days, at Cape May. This is a much wider range than expected for a state this size. It has been related to other inland temperatures by pointing out that the average January temperatures at High Point and Cape May are comparable to those of northern Ohio and southern Virginia, respectively.

Snowfall varies much more widely than rainfall (which includes equivalent snow). Over 40 inches per year may be expected in Sussex county and under 10 in Cape May. Sleet and ice are all too common a form of the precipitation in the Garden State.

Soils

The soils of New Jersey have in recent years been grouped into twenty-eight major types with subdivisions based on slope or drainage. The soil types follow zone boundaries similar to those of the physiographic zones, but also change as the line of terminal moraine is crossed in north-central New Jersey.

Thin, infertile acid soils predominate on the ridges of the Kittatinnies. More fertile soils derived from limestone and shale, thickly augmented in some areas with peat and other organic decay, lie in the valleys. The Highlands contain predominantly well-drained acid soils on steep terrain. Here the slope and drainage affect vegetation more than the soil chemistry. In southern Warren County, near the Musconetcong River, is a deep, well-drained, slightly acid silt which is among the best soil in North Jersey.

The types of soil in the Piedmont vary too widely for simple categorizing, but include sandy, loamy and silty soils varying from well to poorly drained. On the Inner Coastal Plain, the region of the most active farming in the state, the soils are generally excellent and well drained. The outer Coastal Plain is famous for sandy soil almost throughout, except for tidal marshes close to the shore and along Delaware Bay. In Cumberland and Gloucester Counties, sand covers fertile subsoil suitable for commercial farming.

Vegetation

The extensive forestation of a densely populated New Jersey is a tribute in part to the victory of natural reproduction and action by conservationists over the consumption of resources by humans, fire and insects. Until the mid-nineteenth century, wood was the only source of fuel. It was used for heating houses, for the extensive manufacture of iron, charcoal and glass, for steam-powered transportation, and for building. The shift to coal led to stabilization of the forests, so that in spite of over a ten-fold increase in population between 1850 and the present, the total estimated forest area has varied little from 46 percent of the state in 1860, 1900 or 1970. This incongruity has resulted from the tendency of the population to gain the most numbers in the areas with minimal forestation, as well as from the decrease of farmlands and the increase of conservation practices.

The largest single concentration of forests is largely coniferous, but includes substantial stands of oaks and occurs in the Pine Barrens of the Outer Coastal Plain, while the second largest is deciduous (broad-leaved) and is found in the mountainous areas of northern New Jersey — the Kittatinnies and the Highlands. Chestnut trees once dominated the deciduous forests, but a blight brought from Asia in 1904 destroyed all established chestnut trees in New Jersey within fifty years. Oaks, maples, birches and dogwoods are typical of the present northern forests.

The lowlands of New Jersey again provide examples of the variety to be found in such a small state. Salt marshes lie near the tidal waters of the coast, especially in protected areas such as the Hackensack Meadows, in Hudson County and the shores of Barnegat Bay on the east and of Delaware Bay on the south. Freshwater marshes are more sporadic, occurring especially in the basin of Glacial Lake Passaic in Morris and Essex Counties.

Bogs do not receive the regular flooding so characteristic of marshes, but instead are highly acid, poorly drained repositories of partially decayed plants or peat. Although bogs are found in north Jersey, those in south Jersey are best known because of the cranberries and blueberries which are produced in them.

Swamps and floodplains are better drained than bogs, and are therefore less acidic and have less peat accumulation. The Great Swamp of southern Morris County is an example which was almost forgotten until a 1959 proposal to build a jet port in the area melded opposition into a successful effort to have it set aside as a national wildlife refuge. While the marshlands are almost exclusively grassy, the drier portions of bogs and swamps have many of the types of trees seen elsewhere. Best-drained areas are the sand dunes, found along the ocean from Sandy Hook to Cape May. Dune vegetation varies from grassland to holly, cherry, maple and pine trees.

Population

By the time New Jersey received its name in 1664, American Indians had inhabited the region for at least 6,000 years. The Lenni-Lenape Indian population in 1648 was estimated at "2,000 warriors," but it had dwindled to almost none by the beginning of the eighteenth century, due largely to smallpox, alcohol, emigration and murder by whites. In 1758, "Brotherton," an Indian reservation of about five square miles, was established in Burlington County to contain all the remaining Indians, about 100 families. This was used until 1802, when the Indians left New Jersey completely as a separate ethnic group. Descendants of other tribes as well as those resulting from intermarriage still live in the state. The number reported by the U.S. Census rose from 63 in 1900 to about 4,700 in 1970.

Early white settlements grew sporadically. The colony of New Sweden along Delaware Bay was short-lived, 1641-1655 on the east shore, and reached a maximum population of 368. Jersey-area Dutch settlements of New Netherland primarily were concentrated near the village of Bergen, which began in 1660 within the present bounds of Jersey City as the first settlement continuing to the present. After English seizure in 1664, Elizabeth-Town (now Elizabeth) became the first permanent English settlement in the province. It was followed by Middletown, Shrewsbury, Woodbridge and especially Newark in 1666. Salem, in 1675, was the first of the permanent settlements at the other end of the province.

In 1726, the year of the first census, the total population had reached over 32,000. Monmouth was the most populous county, with 4,900, although it contained nearly all of the present Ocean County until 1850. The population of the province nearly doubled by 1745, and reached 184,000 for the first federal census in 1790. It took another 50 years for the population to double again, but with the emigration from Europe in the late nineteenth century, there were almost four times as many people in New jersey in 1890 as there were in 1840. The population almost trebled again between 1890 and 1940, but the rate slowed somewhat thereafter, to increase about 75 percent from 1940 to 1980, when the total was reported as 7,364,158. It has nearly leveled off at 13 percent less than an official state prediction of the early 1960s.

This growth was still sufficient to bring New Jersey past Rhode Island in the 1970 census to qualify as the most densely-populated state in the country, averaging 950 persons per square mile. As stated earlier, this density varies widely throughout the state. The U.S. Census Bureau considers only 12 percent of the 1970 population to be rural. Essex County passed Hudson in 1920 as the most populous county, only to lose this rank to Bergen County in the 1980 Census.

New Jersey's population relative to other states is indicated by the number of members of the House of Representatives allocated since 1912, when total membership was stabilized at 435. At that time New Jersey had twelve Congressmen. In 1931 this was increased to fourteen and in 1961 to fifteen. With the 1980 Census, New Jersey was once again allowed only fourteen, ranking ninth in population.

As the most identifiable minority, blacks in New Jersey as elsewhere have borne extensive discrimination because of race from the seventeenth century to the present, alleviated only gradually until the civil rights struggles of the 1960s. At first discrimination in Jersey was legal. Later the laws were rescinded, but practices remained. Since the 1940s, New Jersey has been a leader in passage of state laws to remove many of the tacit barriers in housing and employment. In the early censuses of 1726, 1737 and 1745, all blacks were listed as slaves, about eight percent of the total population. In 1790 the census listed about 11,400 slaves and 2,800 "free" blacks. After a peak of 12,400 slaves in 1800, the number declined as a result of a law of 1804 providing for gradual emancipation. By 1830 there were about 2,300 slaves and 18,300 free blacks. In 1860, the last census before the Civil War and the Emancipation Proclamation, there were still eighteen "slaves," actually aged apprentices, all in northern New Jersey, and 25,300 free blacks. The number of blacks continued to rise with the general population to a 1970 total of 770,000. The percentage of blacks, however, dropped from 9.0 in 1800 to 3.3 in 1890, but gradually rose again to 10.8 in 1970. The heaviest concentration is in Essex County (30 percent); the lightest in Sussex County (0.4 percent).

Among the white inhabitants of New Jersey, there has been a marked change in national origin over the years. Estimates for 1790 indicate that about half the total population was of English and Welsh stock, one-sixth Scot and Irish, one-sixth Dutch, and one-tenth German. While the U.S. census reports national origin differently, the intensive immigration of the mid- to late-nineteenth century led to a 1900 census which listed 24 percent of the total as foreign-born, of which 28 percent was German, 22 percent Irish, 11 percent English and Welsh, and 10 percent Italian. In 1960, 35 percent of the total population was of foreign stock, meaning foreign-born or having at least one foreign-born parent.

Of the 35 percent, 25 percent was Italian, 12 percent was German, 11 percent Polish and 10 percent was from the United Kingdom. The remaining stocks in each case were individually under 10 percent. Direct comparisons of national origin over the years cannot be made from these figures because of their different bases, but they can be qualitatively related to show, with the statistics of black population a heterogeneous society in continual flux. The population of races other than white and black, primarily from China and Japan, total less than one percent.

With the changes in immigration patterns have also come changes in religious affiliation. The earliest white settlers brought with them preferences for Dutch Reformed, Congregational and Presbyterian churches in northeastern New Jersey, and Quaker meetings along the lower Delaware River. In 1786 it was estimated that the population was 24 percent Presbyterian, 16 percent Quaker 16 percent Dutch Reformed, 10 percent Calvinist and 10 percent with no affiliation. Most of the remainder were Lutheran, Baptist and Episcopalian. Roman Catholics were estimated at 0.1 percent, but Catholic churches were illegal.

By 1906, 19 percent of the total population was Catholic, 24 percent Protestant, 0.2 percent Jewish and the rest unaffiliated. In 1960, the Catholic population well outnumbered Protestants, 40 percent to 23 percent, while Jewish population was estimated at slightly over 5 percent. Of the Protestants, about two-thirds were almost evenly divided among Presbyterians, Methodists and Episcopalians, in that order.

Civil Division

New Jersey is divided into 21 counties and 567 civil subdivisions. The state is different from most states to the south and west in that each of these subdivisions is a municipality with its own mayor and government independent of the others. Pennsylvania, New York and most of New England are similar in this respect, although Pennsylvania and New Jersey use the term "township" for the basic division, while the others use "town." The only portion of New Jersey not within the boundaries of a municipality is Sandy Hook, entirely state or federal land since 1846.

Of all the municipalities, about 45 percent are boroughs, 40 percent are townships and 10 percent are cities. The other 5 percent are either towns or villages. While New Jersey's categories formerly denoted roughly whether a municipality was urban or rural, they mean little now. Townships such as Weehawken, Shrewsbury and Winfield are among the smallest in area and most dense in population of any municipalities in the state. Several optional forms of local government authorized in 1911, 1923 and 1950 are open to each of the five municipal categories, so there is now little incentive to switch from one of the five to another, although such changes frequently happened before 1930. Recently however, some municipalities made such a change solely to become eligible for added federal subsidies.

Aside from the scores of annexations and a handful of consolidations of two or more municipalities, the dominant pattern from the seventeenth century until 1957 was the creation of new municipalities. Since then there have been no new municipalities — in fact, one consolidation. By 1700 there were nine vaguely bounded counties containing some thirty-five townships. Five of these counties were in East New Jersey, the other four in West New Jersey. These were the two proprietary colonies into which New Jersey was officially split in 1676 by a line not surveyed until 1743. An effective division occurred with the 1687 survey of a straight line running from Little Egg Harbor to the South Branch of the Raritan River. It was extended the next year by a meandering boundary along the North Branch of the Raritan, the Passaic River and the Pequannock River to the New York line.

While these two colonies were united as a royal province in 1702, the division continued culturally until after the Revolution and affected economic differences persisting to the present. New Jersey had two capitals, Burlington and Perth Amboy, until 1790 when Trenton replaced both. By then the nine counties had become 13 (Figure 2), with 90 townships, three cities (Burlington, Perth Amboy and New Brunswick), and the borough of Elizabeth. Newark was still a township comprising most of present-day Essex County.

New Jersey created all eight of its remaining counties by 1857, when the number of municipalities had more than doubled to 194. The latter number almost trebled, however, during the following century. The greatest surge occurred between 1890 and 1910, when 134 new boroughs were formed following the passage of laws facilitating local secession to escape existing tax obligations.

Home rule, as evidenced by the number of civil divisions, has been a fiercely defended banner of New Jersey residents, another of the many ironies within the small state, in spite of, or perhaps partly because of, the close proximity among the crowded communities of the urban area.

For Further Reading

Kelland, Frank S. and Marylin. *New Jersey: Garden or Suburb.*
    Dubuque, Iowa, 1978. Kennedy, Steele Mason, ed. *The New
Jersey Almanac.* Cedar Grove,
    N.J. 1966.
Robichaud, Beryl, and Buell, Murray F. *Vegetation of New
Jersey.*
    New Brunswick, N.J., 1973.
Snyder, John P. *The Story of New Jersey's Civil Boundaries,
    1606-1968* . Trenton, 1969.
Vecoli, Rudolph J. *The People of New Jersey.* Princeton, 1965.
Wacker, Peter O. *Land and People. A Cultural Geography of
    Preindustrial New Jersey: Origins and Settlement Patterns.*
    New Brunswick, N.J. 1975.
Widmer, Kemble. *The Geology and Geography of New Jersey* .
    Princeton, 1964.
Wolfe, Peter E. *The Geology and Landscapes of New Jersey.*
    New York, 1977.

THE PINE BARRENS

"Hope and the future for me are not in lawns and cultivated fields, not in towns and cities, but in the impervious and quaking swamps."

With the megalopolis of New York City and Philadelphia as its neighbors, and the teeming New Jersey Turnpike not ten miles past its westernmost borders, the flat, swampy area known as the "Pine Barrens" has somehow escaped the industrial fate of the rest of New Jersey. With the village of Chatsworth at its rough center, a 1,000 square mile chunk of New Jersey is a virtual wilderness. However, this oasis of nature may give way to increasing development in the next few years, as almost 500,000 acres are privately owned and uncontrolled.

The deep scrub forest and wetlands are criss-crossed by hundreds of sandy roads, unmarked, and dating perhaps to colonial times when "bog iron" was mined and molded into cannonballs, nails, flagstones and even tombstones. Atsion Forge was the first recorded forge, established in 1765 by Charles Read, who built another in Batsto a few years later. The Batsto works eventually supplied armaments to the Revolutionary Army. Charcoal was also made from the pines of the forest, and even when these industries declined in the 1850s, paper milling and glass blowing brought trade here for a few years.

However, by the end of the nineteenth century, the industrial boom of the Pines had ended, and the few who remained learned to live off the woods and swamplands. These people, isolated from the developing cities around them, came to be known as "pineys," returning as author John McPhee has described it, to a "pre-Colonial desolation, becoming as they have remained, a distinct and separate world." The pineys gathered sphagnum moss, cord and pulpwood, blueberries (or huckleberries, as they are called here), and pinecones for sale to the outside world. They made charcoal, and began developing the cranberry bogs that have made this region third in the nation in cranberry production.

In 1913, sociologist Elizabeth Kite of the Vineland School visited the Pines and reported in her *Survey* on the people who inhabited them. She reported on unusual marriage (or non-marriage) customs and living conditions, which shocked outsiders who lived but twenty miles away in comfortable suburbia. Many called them "feebleminded" and "a serious menace to the state of New Jersey" because of their apparent lawlessness and lack of conventional morality. However, Dr. Kite was impressed by the majority of the people in the pines. In 1940, she told a reporter, "I think it a most terrible calamity that the newspapers publicly took the term (pineys) and gave it a degenerative sting...I have no language in which I can express my admiration for the Pines and the people who live there." All of the bad publicity has made some of the pineys mistrustful of outsiders, but they have become less inbred as more roads reach through the wilderness and industrial towns have seeped further along its borders. A few still gain their living from the forest and bogs, and others work for the state forestry department. Most have outside jobs, however.

Underlying all of this is a deep layer of sandy soil, which drinks the area's heavy rainfall so efficiently that there is enough clear, potable water underground to quench New York City's thirst. In fact, all of the Pine Barrens water is potable, even when it is clouded by naturally-occurring iron oxides or cedar tannins from time to time. None of the streams here originate anywhere else; no harmful pollutants from nearby cities can wash into the area's water supply. But the absorbent soil leaves the forest dry.

Often, fires ravage the vulnerable pines. Some of the blazes are started by lightning, but many are begun by arsonists, angry at the pineys for some reason or another, or by an angry piney himself. In some cases, stolen automobiles from the cities are taken to the wilderness here, stripped, and set afire, which in turn sets the woods ablaze. Forest rangers sit on observation towers during the dry season for hours, looking for signs of smoke. A 1971 fire burned nearly 30,000 acres.

But fires are not the worst threat to the pines; the woods recuperate beautifully after a blaze. Developers of mobile home parks, retirement centers and major roadways may change the forest forever, disturbing its delicate ecological balance. A proposed supersonic jet port and 250,000 population community would surely end the overall quiet that now pervades the Pine Barrens. Some of the pineys welcome the money such changes would bring, but others claim that nothing but pollutants and noise would come to them. "It'd be the end of the woods, I can tell you that," as resident Bill Wasovwitch puts it."

Directory of
State Services

AERONAUTICS, DIVISION OF
Transportation Bldg., 1035 Parkway Ave., Trenton, 08625.

AGING, DIVISION ON
363 W. State Street, P.O. Box 2768, Trenton, 08625.

AGRICULTURE, DEPARTMENT OF
John Fitch Plaza, P.O. Box 1888, Trenton, 08625.

AIR POLLUTION CONTROL, BUREAU OF
1110 Labor and Industry Bldg., John Fitch Plaza,
C.N. 027, Trenton, 08625.

ALCOHOLIC BEVERAGE CONTROL, DIVISION OF
N. International Plaza, U.S. Rte. 1-9, P.O. Box
2039, Newark, 07114.

ALCOHOLISM, DIVISION OF
129 E. Hanover Street, Trenton, 08625.

ARCHIVES AND HISTORY, BUREAU OF
185 W. State Street, Trenton, 08625.

ARTS, STATE COUNCIL ON THE
109 W. State Street, Trenton, 08608.

ASSEMBLY, CLERK OF
State House, Trenton, 08625.

ATTORNEY-GENERAL
State House Annex, Trenton, 08625.

AUDITING, DIVISION OF, STATE
232 State House, Trenton, 08625.

BANKING, DEPARTMENT OF
36 W. State Street, C.N. 040, Trenton. 08625.

BUDGET AND ACCOUNTING, DIVISION OF
State House, P.O. Box 2447, Trenton, 08625.

BUILDING AND CONSTRUCTION
Taxation Bldg., W. State and Willow Streets,
Trenton, 08646.

CIVIL RIGHTS DIVISION
1100 Raymond Blvd., Newark, 07102.

CIVIL SERVICE DEPARTMENT — PERSONNEL
Arnold Constable Bldg., 215 E. State Street, Trenton 08625.

COMMUNITY AFFAIRS, DEPARTMENT OF
363 W. State Street, Trenton, 08625.

COMMUNITY HEALTH SERVICES
1911 Princeton Avenue, Trenton, 08648.

COMPTROLLER AND BUDGET DIRECTOR
State House, P.O. Box 1447, Trenton, 08625.

CONSUMER AFFAIRS, DIVISION OF
1100 Raymond Blvd., Newark, 07102.

CORRECTIONS DEPARTMENT
Whittlesey Road, P.O. Box 7387, Trenton, 08628.

COURTS, ADMINISTRATIVE OFFICE OF
State House Annex, C.N. 037, Trenton, 08625.

DATA PROCESSING AND TELECOMMUNICATIONS DIVISION
28 W. State Street, Trenton, 08625.

DEFENSE, DEPARTMENT OF
P.O. Box 979, Trenton, 08625.

DISPUTE SETTLEMENT, DIVISION OF
428 E. State Street, P.O. Box 141, Trenton, 08625.

DRUG ABUSE COMMISSION
Department of Health, 129 E. Hanover Street, Trenton, 08608.

ECONOMIC DEVELOPMENT DIVISION
John Fitch Plaza, P.O. Box 1766, Trenton, 08625.

EDUCATION, HIGHER, DEPARTMENT OF
225 W. State Street, Trenton, 08625.

EDUCATION, GENERAL, DEPARTMENT OF
225 W. State Street, P.O. Box 2019, Trenton, 08625.

ELECTIONS SECTION
State House, Trenton, 08625.

ENERGY, DEPARTMENT OF
101 Commerce Street, Newark, 07102.

ENVIRONMENTAL PROTECTION
John Fitch Plaza, P.O. Box 1390, Trenton, 08625.

ETHICAL STANDARDS COMMISSION
122 W. State Street, Trenton, 08625.

FEDERAL RELATIONS OFFICE
363 W. State Street, P.O. Box 1768, Trenton, 08625.

FISH, GAME AND WILDLIFE DIVISION
363 Pennington Avenue, P.O. Box 1809, Trenton, 08625.

FORESTRY SERVICES
John Fitch Plaza, C.N. 028, Trenton, 08625.

GEOLOGIST, STATE — BUREAU OF GEOLOGY AND TOPOGRAPHY
Wallach Bldg., 88 E. State Street, P.O. Box 1390, Trenton, 08625.

HEALTH DEPARTMENT
Health Agriculture Bldg., John Fitch Plaza, P.O. Box 1540, Trenton, 08625.

HIGHWAY SAFETY, OFFICE OF
Stuyvesant Avenue, C.N. 048, Trenton, 08625.

HISTORIC PRESERVATION, OFFICE OF
109 W. State Street, Trenton, 08625.

HOUSING DIVISION
363 W. State Street, Trenton, 08625.

HUMAN RESOURCES, DIVISION OF
363 W. State Street, Trenton, 08625.

HUMAN SERVICES DEPARTMENT
Capitol Place One, 22 S. Warren Street, P.O. Box 1237,
Trenton, 08625.

INSURANCE DEPARTMENT OF
201 E. State Street, Trenton, 08625.

LAW, DIVISION OF
State House Annex, Trenton, 08625.

LABOR AND INDUSTRY, DEPARTMENT OF
John Fitch Plaza, P.O. Box V, Trenton, 08625.

LEGISLATIVE SERVICES AGENCY
128 State House, C.N. 042, Trenton, 08625.

LIBRARY, STATE (ARCHIVES AND HISTORY DIVISION)
185 W. State Street, P.O. Box 1898, Trenton, 08625.

LOCAL GOVERNMENT SERVICES, DIVISION OF
363 W. State Street, Trenton, 08625.

LOTTERY, DIVISION OF THE STATE
Taxation Bldg., W State and Willow Streets, C.N. 041,
Trenton, 08625.

MENTAL HEALTH AND HOSPITALS DIVISION
Capitol Place One, 222 S. Warren Street, Trenton, 08625.

MOTOR VEHICLES, DIVISION OF
25 S. Montgomery Street, Trenton, 08666.

PARKS AND FORESTRY, DIVISION OF
John Fitch Plaza, P.O. Box 1420, Trenton, 08625.

PAROLE, BUREAU OF
Edge Bldg., Whittlesey Road, P.O. Box 7387, Trenton, 08628.

PENSIONS, DIVISION OF
20 W. Front Street, Trenton, 08625.

PLANNING DIVISION
329 W. State Street, P.O. Box 2768, Trenton, 08625.

POLICE, DIVISION OF STATE
P.O. Box 7068, West Trenton, 08625.

PUBLIC DEFENDER, OFFICE OF THE
520 E. State Street, Trenton, 08625.

PUBLIC UTILITIES, BOARD OF
101 Commerce Street, Newark, 07102.

PUBLICATIONS SECTION
State House, Trenton, 08625.

PURCHASING AND PROPERTY DIVISION
135 W. Hanover Street, Trenton, 08625.

RAIL OPERATIONS CHIEF — NEW JERSEY TRANSIT CORPORATION
1100 Raymond Blvd., Newark, 07102.

SECRETARY OF STATE, DEPARTMENT OF STATE
State House, P.O. Box 1330, Trenton, 08625.

SECURITIES BUREAU
80 Mulberry Street, Newark, 07102.

SENATE, SECRETARY OF THE
State House, Trenton, 08625.

SOLID WASTE ADMINISTRATION
32 E. Hanover Street, Trenton, 08625.

SURPLUS PROPERTY PROGRAM (FEDERAL)
P.O. Box 7068, West Trenton, 08625.

TAXATION, DIVISION OF
Taxation Bldg., W. State and Willow Streets, Trenton, 08646.

TRANSPORTATION, DEPARTMENT OF
Transportation Bldg., 1035 Parkway Ave., Trenton, 08625.

TRAVEL AND TOURISM, DIVISION OF
Labor and Industry Bldg., John Fitch Plaza, Trenton, 08625.

TREASURY, DEPARTMENT OF
State House, First Floor, Trenton, 08625.

VETERANS' PROGRAMS AND SPECIAL SERVICES
143 E. State Street, Trenton, 08608.

VITAL STATISTICS, BUREAU OF
John Fitch Plaza, P.O. Box 1540, Trenton, 08625.

VOCATIONAL REHABILITATION, OFFICE OF
Labor and Industry Bldg., John Fitch Plaza, Trenton, 08625.

WATER RESOURCES DIVISION
1474 Prospect Street, C.N. 029, Trenton, 08625.

WEIGHTS AND MEASURES, OFFICE OF
187 W. Hanover Street, Trenton, 08625.

WELFARE DIVISION
3525 Quakerbridge Road, P.O. Box 1627, Trenton, 08625.

WORK PLACE STANDARDS COMMISSION
Labor and Industry Bldg., John Fitch Plaza, Trenton, 08625.

YOUTH AND FAMILY SERVICES DIVISION
1 South Montgomery Street, Trenton, 08625.

New Jersey
United States Senators

Elmer, Jonathan	1789-91
Paterson, William	1789-90
Dickinson, Philemon	1790-93
Rutherford, John	1791-99
Frelinghuysen, Frederick	1793-96
Stockton, Richard	1796-99
Schureman, James	1799-1801
Dayton, Jonathan	1799-1805
Ogden, Aaron	1801-03
Condit, John	1803-09, 1809-17
Kitchell, Aaron	1805-09
Lambert, John	1809-15
Wilson, James	1815-21
Dickerson, Mahlon	1817-29, 1829-33
Southard, Samuel	1821-23, 1833-42
McIlvaine, Joseph	1823-26
Bateman, Ephraim	1826-29
Frelinghuysen, Theodore	1829-35
Wall, Garret	1835-41
Miller, Jacob	1841-51
Dayton, William	1842-51
Stockton, Robert	1851-53
Thompson, John	1853-62
Wright, William	1853-59, 1863-66
Ten Eyck, John	1859-65
Field, Richard S.	1862-63
Wall, James W.	1863
Stockton, John P.	1865-66, 1869-75
Frelinghuysen, Frederick T.	1866-69, 1871-77
Cattell, Alexander	1866-71
Randolph, Theodore	1875-81
McPherson, John	1877-95
Sewell, William	1881-87, 1895-1902
Blodgett, Rufus	1887-93
Smith, John Jr.	1893-99
Kean, John	1899-1911
Dryden, John	1902-07

Briggs, Frank	1907-13
Martine, James	1911-17
Hughes, William	1913-18
Frelinghuysen, Joseph	1917-23
Baird, David	1918-19, 1929-31
Edge, Walter	1919-29
Edwards, Edward	1923-29
Kean, Hamilton	1929-35
Morrow, Dwight	1931-33
Barbour, William	1933-37, 1939-43
Moore, A. Harry	1935-38
Milton, John	1938-39
Smathers, William	1937-43
Walsh, Arthur	1943-44
Hawkes, Albert	1943-49
Smith, Alexander	1944-59
Hendrickson, Robert	1949-55
Case, Clifford	1955-79
Williams, Harrison, Jr.	1959-82
Bradley, Bill	1979-
Lautenberg, Frank	1982-

GOVERNORS
OF
NEW JERSEY

LIVINGSTON, WILLIAM— (1723-90), first governor of the state
of New Jersey (1776-90), was born in Albany, New York, the son
of Phillip and Catherine Van Brugh Livingston. He lived with his
grandmother and then with an English missionary to the
Mohawk Indians before entering Yale University, where he
graduated at the head of his class in 1741. He studied law with
James Alexander and soon afterwards began practicing law in
New York. He married Susanna French in 1745, and began his
family of 13 children. He was counsel for the defendants in the
suit between the proprietors of East Jersey and some of the settlers in that region. The theological controversies of the
Episcopalian Church led him to write philosophical and often wit-
ty treatises for a number of publications. As early as 1747 he
published an original poem of 700 lines, which afterwards was
reprinted several times, entitled "Philosophic Solitude." He
served on the New York provincial legislature, but in 1760 moved
to New Jersey, where he had purchased 120 acres near
Elizabethtown. He grew fruit trees there and built a house called
"Liberty Hall." He was appointed to the Continental Congress in
1774, and again in 1775. When the Revolution was declared, Livingston was made brigadier-general, and took command of the
New Jersey militia in June 1776. War was not appealing to Livingston, however, and he returned to his home to be elected the
first governor of the new state of New Jersey later in the year. He
was reelected for 14 years, with only slight opposition in a few of
the election years. Governor Livingston strongly supported the
American revolutionaries, and his first years in office were hec-
tic as the state legislature was forced to meet first at one place
and then another. The British Loyalists referred to him as "the
spurious governor," and called him the "Don Quixote of the
Jerseys." As soon as the war was over, Livingston left Trenton,
and returned to his house near Elizabethtown. He was a member
of a society to promote the emancipation of slaves and freed his
own slaves while governor. He was also a member of the delega-

tion that framed the U.S. Constitution in 1787, and was a strong supporter of quick passage of the document in his home state. Livingston remained governor of New Jersey until his death at home. He was the author of "A Funeral Eulogium on Reverend Aaron Burr," (1757), and a "Digest of the Laws of New York From 1691-1762."

PATERSON, WILLIAM— (1745-1806), second governor of New Jersey (1790-93), was the son of Richard and Mary Paterson of Ireland. He was born at sea on the way to America. He graduated from the College of New Jersey (Princeton) in 1763 and then studied law with Richard Stockton. In 1766 he received a Masters of Arts Degree from the College of New Jersey. When he was admitted to the bar in 1768, Paterson set up a practice in Bromley which lasted until his move back to Princeton, New Jersey in 1776, where he continued his law practice and operated a general store. In 1775-76, he was a member of the provincial congress, and when the Revolution began he was made New Jersey Attorney General as well as a member of the Minute Men Battalion. Paterson was also elected to the new state's senate in 1776 and 1777. After the war, he continued to serve as the state attorney general, until 1783. For a time, he practiced law, and then in 1787 he was made a delegate to the U.S. Constitutional Convention. He was a leader among those who preferred a weak rather than a strong central government, a difference that gave rise to one of the great compromises of the constitution. In 1789, he was again a member of the state senate, and in 1790, he was elected governor by the state legislature to replace the deceased Livingston. He won three consecutive one-year terms, in which he worked to codify the New Jersey legal system and allow for more manufacturing in the state. When he resigned in 1793, he had been appointed to the U.S. Supreme Court, and he continued as an associate justice until his death at Albany. He is buried at the Van Rensselaer Manor House Vault near Albany, New York.

HENDERSON, THOMAS—(1743-1824), acting governor of New Jersey (1793), was born in Monmouth (now Freehold), New Jersey. His parents were John and Ann Stevens Henderson, farmers. He graduated from the present Princeton University in 1761 and then studied medicine with a private doctor. He moved to Freneau, New Jersey and practiced as a physician there, meanwhile becoming a member of the first New Jersey Medical

Society. He married the former Mary Hendricks in 1767, and became involved in the Revolutionary movement. He was a lieutenant in the army, and was made a major in the Minute Men under General Stewart in 1776. He was a major in Heard's Battalion, and then lieutenant colonel in Heard's Brigade. In 1777 he was appointed lieutenant-colonel of Forman's Additional Continental Regiment, and served as brigade-major at the Battle of Monmouth in 1778. Henderson saw General Lee's retreat at the end of the war, and then became active in the formation of the new American government. He was in the New Jersey state assembly in 1780-84, while serving on a committee of retaliation. He was a judge of common pleas in 1783 and 1799, and master of the Chancery Court in 1790. As he was elected vice president of the New Jersey Council in 1793, he was chosen to fill the governor's seat in March through June 1793 when Governor Paterson resigned to become a Supreme Court justice. He served until governor-elect Richard Howell could take over. His short term was uneventful, and he returned to the New Jersey Council (he was elected to that body again in 1812-13). In 1795-97, he was also a U.S. Congressman. He retired in Freehold, New Jersey, where he died.

HOWELL, RICHARD—(1754-1803), third governor of New Jersey (1793-1801) was born in Newark, Delaware, the son of Ebenezer and Sarah Bond Howell, farmers. With his twin brother, Lewis, he was educated at Newcastle, and when about 15 years old his father settled in Cumberland county, N.J., leaving his two boys in Delaware until their education was completed. They joined him about 1774, when Lewis studied medicine, and Richard law. In November, 1774, Howell was one of a party who broke into a storehouse at Newcastle, N.J., and took out the boxes of tea which had been stored there, being a recent importation from the brig *Greyhound* , and burned them. Although the rooters were disguised as Indians they were recognized and were sued by the owners of the tea; but the case was never brought to trial, owing to the general favor in which the act was held by the people of that section. Early in 1775 Richard Howell was appointed an officer in a company of infantry, and in December of that year was commissioned captain of the 2d regiment of continental troops of New Jersey. The regiment in which he was a captain was ordered to Canada, and he served at Ticonderoga, and also at Quebec. In the following winter his brother Lewis was appointed surgeon of the regiment of which Richard was major. Lewis died from an attack of fever during the progress of the battle of Monmouth in June, 1778. Richard remained in the army until 1778, when he resigned and was licensed to practice law in Cumberland county, where he continued to live for several years. He married, in November of that year, Keziah, a daughter of Joseph Burr of Burlington county. His reason for resigning from the army is said to have been a special appointment by Gen. Washington to transact certain important private duties, which he could not perform while holding a military commission from Congress. At the time strong suspicions of his patriotism were aroused in the minds of those who were not aware of his authority for his acts, and this to such an extent that he was arrested in his father's house for high treason. At the supreme court of New Jersey, he produced his orders from Washington; whereupon he was not only discharged, but the judge ordered every proceeding in the case to be erased from the minutes of the court. He had been a special intelligence agent for Washington at British posts. In 1788 Howell was elected clerk of the supreme court of New Jersey. In 1793 he was elected governor of the state, and continued to be elected annually until 1801. At the time of the whiskey insurrection in 1794 Gov. Howell commanded the troops sent from New Jersey, and was assigned to the command of the right wing of the army by Gen. Washington. The victory, however, over the insurrectionists proved to be a bloodless one. In 1801, he declined to run for another term, but returned to his law practice. Gov. Howell died at his residence near Trenton, N.J., May 5, 1803. He had nine children.

BLOOMFIELD, JOSEPH—(1753-1823), fourth governor of New Jersey (1801-02 and 1803-12), was born in Woodbridge, New Jersey, the son of Dr. Moses and Sarah Ogden Bloomfield. While a boy, Joseph went to a classical school at Deerfield, Cumberland county. On leaving there he studied law with Cortlandt Skinner, who was an eminent lawyer, and attorney-general of New Jersey. In 1775 he was licensed to practice law in New Jersey, and settled at Bridgeton. In February, 1776, he was commissioned a captain in the 3d New Jersey regiment, commanded by Col. Elias Dayton. His company was ordered to Canada, but the news of the retreat from Quebec caused a change, and for a time they were at Fort Stanwix and later at Ticonderoga. Here Capt. Bloomfield was appointed judge-advocate of the northern army, and soon after was promoted to be major of his regiment. He fought in the battle of Brandywine and at Monmouth, and in one of these engagements was wounded. In 1778 he resigned from the army, and was chosen clerk of the assembly, and was afterward for several years register of the court of admiralty. He joined the Society of the Cincinnati, and was chosen vice-president, and in 1808 president of the society. In 1783, upon the resignation of William Paterson, he was elected attorney general of the state, and reelected in 1788. In 1793 he was chosen one of the trustees of Princeton college. He was also a general of militia, and in 1784 commanded a brigade during the whiskey insurrection. In 1792 he was one of the presidential electors. He was an active member, and for a time president of the New Jersey society for the abolition of slavery. In 1801 Gen. Bloomfield supported Jefferson for the presidency—an act which was considered a change of politics on his part, and he was alleged to have deserted his party. In the autumn of that year he received 30 votes from the legislature for governor against 20 cast for Richard Stockton, and from that time until 1812 was constantly re-elected. In the 1802 election, however, Bloomfield almost lost his seat because of a temporary Federalist conflict in the state assembly. He retook the governorship in October, 1803. On the declaration of the war of 1812, Bloomfield was appointed by President Madison a brigadier-general, and assigned to the army for the invasion of Canada. He was present in the attack on Fort George. He returned to Burlington after the war, and in 1818 lost his wife, whom he had married about 1779. She was Mary McIlvaine of Burlington, N.J. He was again married a few years later to Isabella(?), who survived him. In 1816 he was elected by the Democrats a member of Congress, and continued to serve until March 4, 1821. He died in Burlington, N.J.

LAMBERT, JOHN—(1746-1823), acting governor of New Jersey (1802-03), was born in Amwell Township, New Jersey to Gershom and Sarah Merriam Lambert, wealthy plantation owners. He received a public school education and was a voracious reader, so that he was largely self-taught. His parents died while he was still young, and he took over the family farm, which was extensive. He was a member of the state senate, and was chosen vice president of the body in 1795-1800. When Joseph Bloomfield's reelection was stalled in 1802, and he resigned the governorship until the deadlocked vote could be broken between his Republican party and the Federalists, Lambert was chosen interim governor, which lasted almost one year. Lambert spent much of his time working to keep the Republicans afloat, and in 1803, his fellow party member Bloomfield was elected. Lambert was a Congressman in 1805-09, and then was elected to the U.S. Senate for a six year term. Lambert died at his Amwell estate, leaving his wife and 13 children.

OGDEN, AARON—(1756-1839), fifth governor of New Jersey (1812-13), was born in Elizabethtown, New Jersey, the son of Robert, an Essex County Council Member and Speaker of the House, and Phoebe Hatfield Ogden. Aaron was carefully educated and sent to Princeton College, graduating in 1773 before he had attained the age of 17. After leaving college, he was assistant in a celebrated grammar school where Brockholst Livingston and Alexander Hamilton were pupils. In the winter of 1777 he entered the 1st New Jersey regiment, and continued in service until the end of the war. At that time Col. Lord Stirling, who was commanding a regiment of militia in that district, organized an expedition to capture a British vessel, the Blue Mountain Valley, lying in New York harbor, which was loaded with coal, flour, and livestock, designed for the British troops at Boston. The expedition embarked in small crafts, and succeeded in boarding the ship and capturing her. Capt. Ogden was present at the battle of Brandywine, where he acted under the special orders of Washington. He was an active participant in the battle of Monmouth, as aide to Lord Stirling, was the bearer of important despatches from the commander-in-chief, and was included in the officers who received from Congress a vote of thanks. The following winter, while in quarters in Elizabethtown, his regiment was surprised, and Ogden found himself in the camp of the enemy. He tried to escape but received a bayonet wound which nearly proved fatal. In 1779 Ogden commanded a company of light infantry under Maj. Gen. the Marquis Lafayette in Virginia, and was present at the siege of Yorktown. At the close of the war he became one of the members of the New Jersey branch of the Society of the Cincinnati. This order was organized in May, 1783, the following being the constitution then adopted: "It having pleased the Supreme Governor of the universe, in the disposition of human affairs to cause the separation of the colonies of North America from the dominion of Great Britain; and after a bloody conflict of eight years, to establish them free and independent and sovereign states, connected by alliances, founded on reciprocal advantages, with some of the great princes and powers of the earth. To perpetuate , therefore, as well the remembrance of this vast event, as the mutual friendships which have been formed under the pressure of common danger, and in many instances cemented by the blood of the parties, the officers of the American army do hereby, in the most solemn manner, associate, constitute, and combine themselves into one body of friends, to endure as long as they shall endure, or any of their eldest male posterity, and, in failure thereof, to the collateral branches who may be judged worthy of becoming its supporters and members. The officers of the American army, having generally been taken from the citizens of America, possess high veneration for the character of that illustrious Roman, Lucius Quintius Cincinnatus, and having resolved to follow his example by returning to their citizenship, they think they may, with propriety, denominate themselves the Society of the Cincinnati. The following principles shall be immutable, and form the basis of the society: An incessant attention to preserve inviolate those exalted rights and liberties of human nature, for which they have fought and bled, and without which the high rank of a rational being is a curse instead of a blessing: An unalterable determination to promote and cherish between the respective states that union and national honor so essentially necessary to their happiness and the future dignity of the American empire: To render permanent the cordial affection subsisting among the officers, this spirit will dictate brotherly kindness in all things and particularly extend to the most substantial acts of beneficence, according to the ability of the society, toward those officers and their families who unfortunately may be under the necessity of receiving it. The general society will, for the sake of frequent communications, be divided into state societies, and these again into such districts as shall be directed by the state society." The group met on the fourth of July for many years, but many people opposed the hereditary principle carried out by it. Six states had chapters of this organization, which boasted George Washington, Alexander Hamilton and Thomas Pinckney as members. Col. Ogden was elected President of the Cincinnatus in 1829.

Ogden was licensed as an attorney in 1784, and began practice at Elizabethtown. In October, 1787, he married Elizabeth Chetwood. In 1799 he was appointed to the command of the 11th regiment of the United States and a deputy quartermaster-general in that army. In 1803 he was elected trustee of Princeton College, from which institution he received in 1816 the honorary degree of LL.D. In 1801 he was chosen by the legislature of New Jersey senator of the United States for an unexpired term; he was also clerk of the county of Essex. In 1812 Ogden was elected governor of New Jersey, serving for one year. In 1813, he was appointed by President Madison a major general in the army of the

United States, which appointment he declined as he was already commander in chief of the militia of New Jersey. In the latter part of his life Gov. Ogden attempted to run a steamboat between Elizabethtown and New York, and came into conflict with the Livingstons and Fulton, who had the exclusive right to navigate the waters of New York state by steamboat for a term of years. The result was a state controversy, as the legislature of New Jersey had granted Ogden and another exclusive privileges in the waters of that state. Other litigation in regard to his steamboat speculations ensued until Ogden had sunk his entire fortune, which he never recovered. During the latter part of his life he lived on his pension mainly. In 1829 he settled in Jersey City, where he held a government position in the custom house up to the time of his death.

PENNINGTON, WILLIAM S.—(1757-1826), sixth governor of New Jersey (1813-15), was born in Newark, New Jersey. His parents were Samuel and Mary Sanford Pennington, farmers. Pennington was apprenticed to his mother's brother, a farmer, with whom he remained until the breaking out of the revolutionary war, on the generally understood promise that he was to be the heir of his employer. But his uncle was a Loyalist, and when his nephew joined the patriots he canceled his indentures and they parted. Young Pennington served as a non-commissioned officer in a company of artillery, and during an engagement he attracted the attention of Gen. Knox, while actively loading and firing a piece of artillery, quite alone and under fire. It was not, however, until 1780 that he received his commission as lieutenant. He was present at the execution of Major Andre, and on one occasion, had the honor of dining with Gen. Washington. Pennington kept a diary, in which he wrote an account of the mutiny of the Pennsylvania troops at Morristown in January, 1781, after which two of the ringleaders were executed. He was wounded during the siege of Yorktown, and on retiring from the army had the rank of captain. After the war he, for a time, engaged in the business of a hatter, and afterward in some employment in Newark. In 1797, and for three years following, he was a member of the assembly for the county of Essex, and in 1801 member of the council. He then entered the office of Elias Boudinot as a student of law, and in 1802 was licensed as an attorney. Two years later he was elected an associate justice of the supreme court. In 1813 and 1814 he was elected governor of the state of New Jersey. Pennington worried about New Jersey's vulnerability to the British naval forces, and studied the coastline for defense plans. He was opposed to the Hartford Convention as "hostile to the constitution and government of the Union." In 1815 he succeeded Robert Morris as judge of the U.S. district court for New Jersey, being appointed by President Madison. He died in Newark, N.J.

DICKERSON, MAHLON-(1770-1853), seventh governor of New Jersey (1815-17), was born in Hanover, New Jersey to Jonathan, an iron mine operator, and Mary Coe Dickerson. He studied at Princeton, where he was graduated in 1789, and was licensed as an attorney in 1793. The outbreak of the Whiskey Rebellion in the following year took him into Pennsylvania as a volunteer. Afterward he studied law for a time in the office of James Milnor of Philadelphia, and was admitted to the Pennsylvania bar in 1797. He was something of a writer and contributed to the *Aurora* newspaper, which was edited by William Duane. In 1799, Dickerson was chosen a member of the common council of Philadelphia and in 1802 was appointed by President Jefferson a commissioner of bankruptcy. In 1805 he was made adjutant-general and in 1808 resigned that office to become recorder of the city. Dickerson's father died, leaving valuable property in Morris County, New Jersey, and his son went there to reside. This was in 1810, and in 1812 he was elected a member of the state assembly from that county. In the following year he was made a justice of the supreme court. In 1815 he was chosen governor without opposition, and again in 1816. Governor Dickerson was known as an "ultra protectionist" of New Jersey businesses. He passed the first protective tariff in the state and authorized the construction of the Delaware and Raritan Canal. In 1817 he was made U.S. senator and reelected six years later, being succeeded in 1829 by Theodore Frelinghuysen. He was, however, elected to fill a vacancy and altogether was U.S. Senator for sixteen years. In 1834, he received the appointment of minister to Russia, which he declined because he had been appointed by General Jackson as secretary of the navy. He held this last position for four years, after which he resigned. He was then a judge of the District Court of New Jersey. During the latter part of his life he was interested in mining and the manufacture of iron in Morris County. He published *Speeches in Congress, 1826-1846*, and died in Morris County.

WILLIAMSON, ISAAC H.-(1767-1844), eighth governor of New Jersey (1817-29), was born in Elizabethtown, New Jersey, the son of General Matthias and Susannah Halsted Williamson, landowners. He received only a grammar school education; studied law with his brother; was licensed to practice in 1791; in 1796 was made a counselor, and in 1804 a sergeant-at-law. He took a high rank at the bar of the state, his practice extending into several adjoining counties besides his own. He was made deputy attorney-general of Morris County, and was considered one of the most satisfactory advisers on intricate wquestions of law in the state. In 1817 he was elected governor of New Jersey, and was afterward reelected every year until 1829. He was also chancellor of the state. Most of his governorship took place in the "Era of Good Feelings" in New Jersey politics. Governor Williamson enjoyed his position, but made little changes in state government except to increase the Chancery Court's jurisdiction. After the election of President Jackson in 1829 a violent contest occurred in New Jersey and that year Williamson lost his position. He then returned to the bar and was soon in full practice. In 1831 he was elected a member of the council for Essex County. In 1844 he was a member of the convention which framed the new constitution of the state, and unanimously elected president of that body. He died in Elizabeth.

VROOM, PETER D.-(1791-1873), ninth and twelfth governor of New Jersey (1829-32 and 1833-36), was born in Hillsborough Township, New Jersey, the son of Col. Peter D. Vroom Sr. and Elsie Bogart Vroom, landowners. He studied at the Somerville Academy and in 1806 entered Columbia College in New York. After his 1808 graduation, Vroom studied law with George McDonald of Somerville and was admitted to the bar in 1813. In 1816 he became a counselor, and a sergeant in 1828. His first office was in Morris County where he remained for 18 months. He continued an active practice in several New Jersey towns, meanwhile marrying the daughter (name unknown) of Peter Dumont, whose uncle made him a prosecutor of the pleas. In 1920 he settled in Somerville, where he remained for more than twenty years. Up to this time he had not interested himself in politics, and it was not until 1824, when he supported General Jackson, that he began to turn his attention in that direction. He represented Somerset County in the house of assembly in 1826, 1827 and 1829. In the latter year he was elected governor of New Jersey and was reelected in the next two years and again in 1833. His major action as governor was to incorporate the Delaware and Raritan

Canal Company in 1830. Upon retiring from office he resumed his practice in Somerville, and in 1837 was appointed by President Van Buren one of the three commissioners designated to adjust claims to reserves of land under the treaty made with the Choctaw Indians. This appointment carried him into Mississippi for several months. In 1838 he was elected member of Congress by the Democrats, and continued to hold that position until 1841. On leaving Washington he settled in Trenton, New Jersey. In 1844 he was elected a delegate to the constitutional convention from his native county. In 1846, with others, he engaged in a thorough revision of the statutes of the state. He afterward declined the office of chief justice of the supreme court of the state, which was offered him. In 1852, Governor Vroom was a presidential elector and cast his vote for Pierce. The following year he was appointed minister to Prussia, and remained in Berlin until 1857, when he asked to be recalled so that he could return to this law practice. As a diplomat, Vroom devoted himself particularly to the claims of Prussians who had become citizens of the United States through emigration, and who were afterward required to perform military duty in Prussia. In 1860, Governor Vroom was prominent as a candidate of the Southern Democrats for the Vice Presidency. In 1862 he was one of the representatives of New Jersey in a commission including delegates from twenty states, which met at Washington to adjust a sectional controversy, but which was unable to accomplish anything. During the Civil War, Vroom was prominent as a civilian in efforts to sustain the Union. He was an earnest supporter of General McClellan for the Presidency in the election of 1864. In 1868 he was again one of the presidential electors , his state casting votes for Horatio Seymour. Vroom had an LL.D. degree conferred on him by Columbia University and Princeton. He published *Reports of the Supreme Court of New Jersey* (6 vols., Trenton, 1866-73). The governor had two sons, one of whom became a mayor of Trenton. He died in that city.

SOUTHARD, SAMUEL LEWIS-(1787-1842), tenth governor of New Jersey (1832-33), was born in Baskingridge, New Jersey to Henry, a state legislator, and Sarah Lewis Southard. When about twelve years old, young Samuel began his education at a classical academy in his native village, and became interested in teaching, to which for some years he devoted himself. In September 1802, he entered the junior class at Princeton, and was graduated with honors two years later. Soon after leaving college he taught for a time in Morris County and then obtained a tutorship in the family of Colonel John Taliaferro, a member of Congress from Virginia, at his plantation in King George's County, near Fredericksburg. Here he remained for five years, instructing the children of the Colonel and his relatives. He also began the study of law, and in 1809 was admitted to practice. By his pupils in Virginia he was held in high esteem, and many remembered him after they reached manhood. While in Virginia Southard made the acquaintance of Monroe, Jefferson and Madison. He married Rebecca Harrow, a ward of his patron. In 1811, Southard settled in Flemington, New Jersey and devoted himself to law. He soon acquired a good business, besides being appointed prosecuting attorney of Hunterdon County. In 1814 Southard was elected a member of the state assembly and immediately after, one of the justices of the supreme court. He sat on the bench for five years, being, at the same time, the reporter of the decisions of the court. In 1820 he was a presidential elector, and in the same year was elected one of the U.S. Senators from New Jersey, in which body he took his seat in February 1821. Southard was the originator of the Missouri Compromise resolutions, which were presented by Henry Clay. In 1823 Southard was appointed secretary of the Navy, in which position he remained until March 1829; during some of that period being both secretary of the treasury and secretary of war, besides fulfilling the duties of his own office. During the period of the election of James Monroe to the presidency, in 1816, and that of the election of Jackson, in 1828, the party conditions assumed new shape. The old Federalists became disorganized and ceased to act as a party, and in 1824 the old party organizations were practically powerless, while the new ones had not become sufficiently well-formed to be influential. It happened, therefore, that both Jackson and Adams were voted for by Democrats and Federalists. After the inauguration of Adams considerable hostility toward him was shown in Congress and throughout the country. Southard was one of his supporters, and New Jersey gave Adams a decided majority. Jackson, however, was elected, and was the first chief magistrate after Washington who was really elected by the people. In 1829 Southard tried for senatorship in New Jersey, but failed. He was soon after chosen attorney-general of the state, however, and settled in Trenton. In the meantime, in 1822, he had been chosen one of the trustees of Princeton, and in 1832 received an LL.D. degree from the University of Pennsylvania. In the latter year he was elected governor of New Jersey; but in 1833, having been elected U.S. Senator, he assumed that office, which he held until 1842, when he resigned, being president of the senate in 1841. His short term as governor saw the beginning of the great canal and railroad boom of the nineteenth century. After he left politics, Southard continued his role as a public figure, giving many speeches and acting as a Princeton trustee. He died in Fredericksburg, New Jersey.

SEELEY, ELIAS P.-(1791-1846), eleventh governor of New Jersey (1833), was born in Fairfield Township, New Jersey to descendants of the Puritan settlers of New England; his father held many prominent positions in the county and was a state representative. He received a common school education, studied law with Daniel Elmer of Bridgston, New Jersey, and was admitted to the bar in 1815. In 1829 he was elected to the state legislative council and was reelected four times, serving as vice president of the body in 1832. He became governor of New Jersey in 1833 when Governor Southard was elected U.S. Senator, and only held the position for seven months, until Vroom took over again. Governor Seeley is known for his "Quaker Case" speech to the Chancery Court, which dealt with the various disputes in that sect. After Seeley's loss in October 1833, he was frequently elected to the legislature, and was active until his death.

DICKERSON, PHILEMON-(1788-1862), thirteenth governor of New Jersey (1836-37), was born in Morris County, New Jersey to Jonathan and Mary Coe Dickerson. His older brother was former governor Mahlon Dickerson. He received a liberal education, devoted himself to the study of law, and in 1813 was licensed as an attorney; in 1817 was made a counselor, and in 1834 a sergeant-at-law. This last degree, which was peculiar to New Jersey and one or two other states, was originally of some importance, as only sergeants could pass a common recovery in the supreme court, which followed in that respect the practice of the English court of common pleas. As for a time the examiners of students were appointed exclusively from sergeants, the distinction was continued until 1839, since which date no sergeants have been designated. Dickerson moved from Philadelphia, where he had been residing, to Paterson, New Jersey, in 1812, and there married and began the practice of law, which he continued until his election to the state assembly in 1821. He was a U.S. Representative in 1833-36. In 1836, he was elected governor of the state by the Jackson party. He held office, however, only one year. In 1839 the Democrats nominated him for Congress, and he was probably elected, but owing to irregularities in the returns he failed to obtain a certificate. In 1841 President Van Buren appointed him judge of the district court, an office which he held until his death. He is said to have exhibited in the few opinions he delivered while a chancellor, a discriminating mind, and a good knowledge of law and equity. He had a good practice as a lawyer, and as a U.S. judge was held in high esteem. A humorous story is told of him regarding an incident which occurred just after the beginning of the Civil War. A zealous Republican, who was acting as foreman of the grand jury, proposed that all the jurymen present should take the oath to support the constitution of the United States. Judge Dickerson remarked, in a quiet, businesslike manner, that if any persons in the court were so distrustful of themselves as to think the oath necessary, he was quite ready to administer it. No one responded, and the business of the court proceeded as usual. Dickerson died in Paterson, New Jersey.

PENNINGTON, WILLIAM JR.-(1796-1862), fourteenth governor of New Jersey (1837-43), was born in Newark, the son of Governor William S. and Phoebe Wheeler Pennington. He received his rudimentary education in the schools of Newark and entered Princeton college, where he was graduated in 1813. He studied law with Theodore Frelinghuysen; received his license as an attorney in 1817, a counselor in 1820, and in 1834 as a sergeant-at-law. He settled in Newark, married, and having interested himself in politics, represented Essex County in the state assembly, and in 1837 was elected by the Whigs governor of the state. He continued to be reelected governor every year until 1843. As chancellor and judge of the prerogative court — positions he held ex-officio as governor of the state — his decisions gave general satisfaction, and only one of his decrees was overruled by the court of appeals. At the time when he received the appointment of governor Pennington had excellent practice as a lawyer; when he ceased to be governor he resumed his business and was soon fully occupied, being especially relied upon for the argument of causes at the bar of the supreme court and in the court of errors. One of the most remarkable of his cases was an issue which grew out of William Jauncey's will, which was exceedingly complicated, and yet, as it covered the distribution of millions of dollars, raised great interest—so much so that while Pennington was selected in New Jersey as a counsel for the appellees, he was joined by the celebrated Charles O'Conor of New York. It goes without saying that these two distinguished advocates won their case. While Gov. Pennington earned the reputation of being a lawyer of remarkable ability, he also became known as the best leader the Whig party had ever had in New Jersey. An important incident during Pennington's governorship was marred by what was known as the "broad seal war." This arose out of the congressional election of 1838. Six congressmen were to be elected in New Jersey by a general ticket, and a discussion of the validity of the election of five of these arose. As the governor and council had to decide the question, it became necessary for Gov. Pennington to commission those persons who should properly represent the state in the house of representatives. Not being allowed by law to go behind the returns, Gov. Pennington commissioned all the Whig candidates who appeared to have the greatest number of votes. This caused considerable commotion in Congress because the five new Whigs determined the majority party of the House, and so the validity of the governor's appointments became suspect. John Quincy Adams was made temporary chairman, and an excited debate occurred on the question of the speakership, which resulted in the decision that only members whose seats were uncontested should vote as to that question. The result was that Robert Hunter of Virginia, afterward to become celebrated during the Civil War, was chosen speaker, and the five Democratic members from New Jersey were admitted to seats in the house of representatives. These were later reported, by the committee taking testimony concerning the controversy, to have been duly elected. The testimony filled a volume of nearly 700 pages. Considerable controversy was stirred by the fact that seats were refused to candidates to hold their commission under the "broad seal" of a sovereign state of the United States. In 1858 Gov. Pennington was elected a member of the thirty-sixth Congress. A virulent contest for the speakership of the house continued for nearly two months, with the result that William Pennington was selected as speaker. He remained in Congress until 1861, and on leaving Washington returned to Newark, where he died. His death was said to have been hastened by an overdose of morphine administered through the mistake of a druggist.

HAINES, DANIEL-(1801-1877), fifteenth and seventeenth governor of New Jersey (1843-45 and 1848-51), was born in New York City, the son of Elias, a successful merchant, and Mary Ogden Haines. He received his earlier education in a private school in New York, at an academy in Elizabethtown, and entered Princeton where he graduated in 1820. He then studied law at

Newton with his uncle, Judge Thomas Ryerson; was licensed as an attorney in 1823, as a counselor in 1826 and was made a sergeant-at-law in 1837. In 1824 he settled at Hamburg, Sussex County, where he continued to reside for many years. Haines was active in what was known as the "broad seal war" in 1839, being a member of the council, and one of the board of canvassers who resisted the governor in giving certificates of election to the Whig candidates. In 1843 he was elected Governor of the state. In that position he devoted himself to advancing the cause of education and to the proposed changes in the constitution of the state, and while in office proclaimed the new constitution. He continued in office one year; was again nominated in 1847 and elected by a respectable majority, although the legislature was of the opposite political party. When his constitutional term ended in 1851, Gov. Haines returned to the practice of law. He was involved with the celebrated Goodyear patents for vulcanizing india-rubber, in which case he was associated with Daniel Webster in the defense. In 1852 he was chosen a judge of the supreme court of the state, being a member ex-officio of the court of errors and appeals. For several years he presided in the Newark circuit, considered the most difficult and important in the state, and he left the bench in 1861 greatly respected by the bar. From 1870 to 1876 he was a member of several judicial commissions relating to state boundaries. He was a very religious man; a member of the Presbyterian church and for many years a ruling elder. He was one of the committee on the reunion of the branches of the church, North and South. He was also prominent in the American Bible Society. In 1845 he was appointed one of the commissioners to select the site for the state lunatic asylum, established near Trenton, and was a member of the first board of managers of that institution. Later he was one of the managers of the local home for disabled soldiers and a trustee of the state reform school for juvenile delinquents. He was greatly interested in prison reform and frequently acted on commissions relating to it, such as the National prison reform congress in 1870. He was vice-president of the national prison reform association, and one of the committee that met in London in 1872 to organize an international congress on prison discipline. At the time of his death he was the oldest trustee of Princeton. Haines died in Hamburg, New Jersey.

STRATTON, CHARLES C.— (1796-1859), sixteenth governor of New Jersey (1844-48), was born in Swedesboro, New Jersey, son of unnamed immigrants from England. He studied at the public school in his hometown, and received a degree from Rutgers College in 1814. He was a farmer, and soon became involved in Whig politics. After serving four terms in the legislature of New Jersey, he was elected a representative in the twenty-fifth Congress as a Whig, serving from September 1837 to March 1839. He was elected to the twenty-sixth Congress as well, and received his credentials bearing the "Broad Seal" of New Jersey, but was not admitted. He was elected to the next Congress, serving from May 1841 to March 1843, when he was chosen a member of the convention which revised the state constitution, and the following year was the first governor of New Jersey to be elected by the people (formerly, governors had been elected by the legislature). He concentrated on implementing the new constitution during his term. Upon leaving office, Governor Stratton retired to his farm in Gloucester County, near the historic village of Swedesboro, his birthplace, where he died.

FORT, GEORGE F.— (1809-1872), eighteenth governor of New Jersey (1851-54), was born in Pemberton, New Jersey, the son of unknown Methodists. After receiving an ordinary school education at his home and in that neighborhood, he entered the University of Pennsylvania, where he studied medicine, graduating in 1830. He began practice, in which he was successful, but, becoming interested in politics, was elected a member of the state assembly from Monmouth County. In 1844 he was a member of the convention organized to frame a new state constitution and soon after was elected to the state senate. In 1850 he became governor of New Jersey, which office he continued to hold until 1854. Governor Fort approved surveys for New Jersey's road system during his term. He was then appointed judge of the court of errors and appeals and held other important public offices. He was interested in the subject of Masonry. A work by him was published in 1875, in Philadelphia, entitled *Early History and Antiquities of Freemasonry* . He died in Egypt, Ocean County, New Jersey.

PRICE, RODMAN MCCAULEY— (1816-1894), nineteenth governor of New Jersey (1854-57), was born in Sussex County, New Jersey to Francis and Anne McCauley Price, wealthy landowners. After a preliminary education at New York City and Lawrenceville, New Jersey schools, he passed the examinations of Princeton College, but on account of ill health was unable to continue the courses. He afterward studied law for a time, but gave it up in 1840 upon the appointment as purser in the U.S. Navy. His first service was on the steamer *Fulton* in gun practice in New York harbor, and his second on the *Missouri*, the first U.S. steam vessel of war that crossed the Atlantic, and which, carrying the heaviest guns then afloat, was the wonder of the European navy. He then joined Commander Sloat's squadron at Monterey, California on the *Cyane*, and helped gain the *presidio* there for the United States. He was prefect and alcalde for Monterey in 1846-48. He was also a member of the convention that framed the constitution of California. Upon his appointment as navy agent in 1848, he was active in organizing the city government of San Francisco, advancing the first money to build a wharf in that city. Returning east in 1850 he met disaster by the burning of the steamer *Orleans St. John* on the Alabama River, in which he lost large sums of money, papers, vouchers and accounts, which subsequently gave him trouble in settling with the government. During the same year, he was elected a member of congress from New Jersey and in 1854 governor of the state. although the youngest man ever thus honored, he proved to be one of the best of New Jersey's governors in many opinions. Under his administration the public school system was established, including the common schools, Normal school, Teachers' institute and Model school. He canvassed the state in behalf of this system, laid the cornerstones of the Normal schools at Trenton and the Farnum Institute at Beverly, and was recognized as the father of public education in New Jersey. He also recommended and instituted the geological survey which aided greatly in the development of the mineral resources of the state. He urged the revision of the militia system and increased its efficiency. The first life-saving stations on the New Jersey coast were established through the enterprise of Governor Price. A system of working public roads was accomplished during his administration as well. He showed his appreciation of the importance of non-partisan judiciary by appointing judges of the supreme court from both parties. One of his greatest gubernatorial services was in determining the exclusive monopoly rights and privileges that had been granted in 1830 to the Camden and Amboy railroad company. The original charter of that company prohibited the state from granting the right to any other railroad company to build any other road across the state. The consequent excessive charges in passenger and freight rates that obtained created great controversy and some threatened violence to the company. The legislature granted the company present increase of power, but at the same time fixing a not distant date to end the exclusive monopoly. In December 1860, Governor Price was sent by his state as a delegate to the Peace conference, held at Washington, D.C., which was an attempt to stop secession and prevent war. At the expiration of his term of office, Governor Price established the ferry from Weehawken, New Jersey, to Forty-second Street in New York City. He also owned a quarry and sponsored land reclamation on the Hackensack River and English Creek. Vegetable farms were established on the once-soggy lands. All the ferry property and nearly 200 acres of land fell into his hands under foreclosure proceedings, and subsequently Samuel J. Tilden purchased the property. Governor Price always believed that the larger portion of New York's commerce would one day be done on the New Jersey shore of the Hudson, the termination of the continental railway system, thus giving it the advantage. He therefore was financially interested in various railroad and ferry boat enterprises. He died in Weehawken, New Jersey.

NEWELL, WILLIAM— (1817-1901), twentieth governor of New Jersey (1857-60), was born in Franklin, Ohio, to James W. and Eliza Hankinson Newell, who moved to Monmouth, New Jersey in 1820. He was educated at Rutgers College, New Brunswick, and was graduate from there in 1836. He afterwards studied medicine and was graduated as an M.D. from the Medical department of the University of Pennsylvania in 1841. Dr. Newell first practiced his profession at Manahawkin, New Jersey, but afterwards went to Imlaystown, and finally settled at Allentown, New Jersey, where he lived for many years and built up a large and successful practice both as a physician and surgeon, having distinguished himself by operations in the latter branch. He was a Whig in politics and was elected to Congress in 1846, reelected in 1848 and served until 1851. During this time he secured from Congress an appropriation of $10,000 to establish lifesaving stations on the coast. The first trial was made on the New Jersey coast between Sandy Hook and Tom's River, and resulted in such a saving of human life that the system was adopted for the entire sea and lake coast of the United States, and by other countries. In 1856 he was elected governor of the state of New Jersey, by the Republican and American parties. Although Governor Newell was strongly opposed by the Democratic-dominated state assembly, he was able to lead the Republicans to prominence in statewide politics. In 1861 among the first acts of President Lincoln was the appointment of Newell (with whom he had served in

Congress) as superintendent of the lifesaving service of New Jersey, which position he filled for the next two years. He was again elected to Congress in 1864 and the same year was sent as a delegate to the National Republican Convention at Baltimore. He always took a great interest in the welfare of his state, and was for several years president of the New Jersey state board of agriculture. In 1877 he was again a candidate for governor, but was defeated by General McClellan. In 1880 he was appointed governor of Washington territory by President Hayes, and four years later was made Indian commissioner for that territory. After the expiration of his term of office he made Olympia, Washington his home, but returned to New Jersey in 1898. He died at Allentown.

OLDEN, CHARLES S.— (1799-1876), twenty-first governor of New Jersey (1860-63), was born in Princeton, the son of Hart and Temperance Smith Olden. He received his early education at Lawrenceville, New Jersey, and after leaving school worked in a country store kept by his father for a time. In 1823, he took a clerkship in a business in Philadelphia, where he remained for three years. In 1826 he went to New Orleans and started in business, which he conducted with such success that eight years later he was able to retire. He returned to Princeton, which he afterwards made his home. He was appointed treasurer of Princeton College, and in 1844 was elected a member of the state senate, where he represented his county until 1850. In 1859 the Republicans elected him Governor of New Jersey, and at the outbreak of the Civil War he used his influence in obtaining the state's quota of troops to be sent to the front. The state legislature authorized a loan of $2 million to pay the volunteers and their families. After he left the chair of state in 1863, Governor Olden was judge of the court of errors and appeals, member of the court of pardons, riparian commissioner and presidential elector. He died in Princeton.

PARKER, JOEL — (1816-1888), twenty-second and twenty-fifth governor of New Jersey (1860-63 and 1872-75), was born in Freehold, New Jersey to Charles, a state treasurer and librarian and Sarah Coward Parker. The family moved to Princeton, where Joel received his early instruction, and having entered Princeton, was graduated in 1839. He had the good fortune to study law in the office of Henry W. Green, chief justice of the state supreme court. Having settled in Freehold, he soon entered politics, both as a speaker and worker on the Democratic side, and having made a good impression, was elected in 1847 to the state assembly, where he remained during the next four years. In 1852, and from that year until 1857, he was prosecuting attorney. In 1860 he was a presidential elector, and cast his vote for Stephen A. Douglas. That same year, he was elected governor of New Jersey. Having received the commission of brigadier-general of the state militia in 1857, he was made major-general in 1861. He opposed the Civil War in its inception, but as soon as it became an established fact, and during its continuance, he worked for the Union cause. He used his influence to keep the quota of New Jersey for the army up and successfully managed the finances of the state so that at the end of 1865 there was a surplus of $200,000 in the state treasury. Governor Parker favored an amnesty toward the Confederates, but was a consistent war Democrat throughout the conflict. At the National Democratic Convention of 1868, which was held in New York City, he was nominated for the Presidency, but was unsuccessful. In 1872 he was again elected governor of the state of New Jersey, and at the conclusion of his term became attorney-general. In 1880 he was made o judge of the supreme court and reelected in 1887. In 1883 the nomination for governor was again offered to him, but he declined it. Governor Parker received the degree of LL.D. from Rutgers College in 1872. He died in Philadelphia.

WARD, MARCUS— (1812-1884), twenty-third governor of New Jersey (1866-69), was born in Newark to Marcus, a manufacturer, and Fanny Brown Ward. He was a descendant of John Ward, who was one of the first settlers of Newark, in the year 1666. He received an education in the schools of the town, and after completing his studies began a mercantile career, which was a success. Although a Whig politically, he took no active part in politics, until the breaking up of that party in 1855, when he allied himself with the Republicans. He was a delegate to the national Republican conventions which were held at Chicago in 1860 and in Baltimore in 1864. At the outbreak of the Civil War, Ward abandoned business to give his time and means to the soldiers on the field, and their families at home. He visited the camps and battlefield in order to help the Union soldiers, and promoted a pension plan for War veterans. he was also instrumental in establishing a soldier's hospital at Newark, which he equipped and which the U.S. government in recognition of his patriotic conduct, named the "Ward" U.S. General Hospital. After the war this hospital became the New Jersey home for disabled soldiers, in which Ward maintained an active interest until his death. Ward was a candidate for the governorship of New Jersey in 1862, but was defeated. He was elected, however, in 1865 and served three years. Governor Ward was interested in reforms in the state; he supported a public school and depoliticized the state prison administration. In 1866 he was chairman of the National Republican Committee. He was elected a member of Congress in 1873 and served until 1875. Throughout his life he was recognized as a philanthropist and a patron of the arts, besides being interested in public institutions. He was a member of the New Jersey historical society, the Newark library association and the New Jersey Art Union. He died in Newark.

RANDOLPH, THEODORE P.— (1816-1883), twenty-fourth governor of New Jersey (1869-72), was born in New Brunswick, New Jersey, to James Fitz Randolph and an unknown mother. His father was a Congressman and publisher of the New Brunswick *Freedonian*. His early education was received at Rutgers grammar school and while still a boy, he entered business life as a clerk. In 1840 he went south to live in Vicksburg, Mississippi, where he engaged in mercantile pursuits for about ten years. In 1851 he married Fanny F. Colman of Kentucky, a grandniece, on her mother's side, of Chief Justice Marshall. Soon after his marriage he returned to New Jersey and lived in Jersey City, investing in coal mining and the transportation of iron and ores. He was also for many years the president of the Morris and Essex Railroad. He was elected a member of the New Jersey assembly in 1859, was reelected in 1860, and was a member of a special session of 1860, convened by a call of the governor on account of the outbreak of the Civil War. He was prominent on many of the committees, including that on federal relations. In 1861 he was elected state senator from Hudson County to fill a vacancy, and in 1862 was reelected for the full term of three years. he was energetic and efficient and served on the committees of education, civil service reform, Centennial Exposition and others. He moved to Morristown, where he afterward resided, and was elected governor of New Jersey in the fall of 1868. His administration was vigorous, with the establishment of the state riparian commission, which resulted in a large income to the state school fund; the passage of a system of general laws by which special legislation was avoided, and the repeal of the Camden and Amboy monopoly tax, which had so long burdened railroad users. He also originated the plan on which the Morris Plains lunatic asylum, one of the largest in the world at the time, was constructed. He called out the state police when rioting threatened the peace in Jersey City in March 1871, the anniversary of the Battle of the Boyne. No serious injuries occurred in New Jersey, although on the New York side of the Hudson River many lives were lost on the same day because of similar striking. He was elected U.S. Senator from New Jersey in 1875, and served until 1881. He was a member of the committees on mines and mining, military affairs and commerce, for all of which he was particularly well qualified. Governor Randolph was prominent in the councils of his party, both in the state and nationally. He was for several years chairman of the National Democratic Committee as well as a trustee of Rutgers College, and director of many corporations and institutions. By the time of his death, he had given away over one-tenth of his income in charity. He died in Morristown.

BEDLE, JOSEPH DORSETT— (1831-1894), twenty-sixth governor of New Jersey (1875-78), was born in Middletown Point (present Matawan), New Jersey, the son of Thomas I., a merchant, and Hanna Dorsett Bedle. His early education was obtained at the academy in Middletown Point, which was famous in that part of the state. He read law five years, chiefly in the office of William L. Dayton, at Trenton, but during that period attended the law school at Ballston Spa, New York, one winter, and also studied a short time with Henry S. Little in his native town. While engaged in studying law, he devoted much of his time to acquiring historical and literary knowledge, particularly connected with the profession of law. He was admitted to the bar in 1853, and immediately settled in Middletown Point, where he soon acquired a good practice and reputation. In 1855, he moved to Freehold. His advance at the bar was so rapid that in March 1865 when only 34 years old, he was appointed as a justice of the state supreme court to succeed Elias B. Ogden, one of New Jersey's most distinguished judges, who had died. The circuits of Judge Ogden were in the northern part of the state, embracing Hudson, Bergen and Passaic Counties, and to these Judge Bedle succeeded, and so he moved to Jersey City. The judicial career of Judge Bedle covered about ten years and during that time in the supreme court and court of errors and appeals he gained a high reputation. His prominence on the bench drew public attention to him. The country was very much depressed at the time; times were hard and there was a tendency in the minds of people to select a governor who had never entered the political arena. Although Judge Bedle had always been a Democrat, no partisanship had been shown on the bench, and he was looked upon as able to satisfy their demands. The Democratic convention nominated him for governor in the fall of 1874, and he was elected over a very popular competitor. Previous to his nomination he publicly announced he was not a candidate; he would take the seat if nominated, but would not campaign for office. This enamored him to the public even more, and he was inaugurated January 19, 1875, serving a constitutional term of three years. A writer in a biography of the governor said, "His administration from the first was marked by ability, prudence and a patriotism inspired by an earnest desire for the public welfare." He took an active part in behalf of the state in promoting the Centennial Exhibition in 1876. During his term the riots of 1877 occurred. As governor, he fought fraud in the state government and pushed for a reduction in state employees' salaries. Upon his retirement from office in 1878, he resumed his law practice in Jersey City. He declined to return to the supreme court, preferring to pursue his profession while in health. Princeton College conferred an honorary LL.D. degree in 1875. He died in New York City.

MCCLELLAN, GEORGE B. — (1826-1885), twenty-seventh governor of New Jersey (1878-81), was born in Philadelphia to George, a doctor, and Elizabeth Brinton McClellan. He attended public schools and the University of Pennsylvania in 1840 to 1842, and then went to the U.S. Military Academy at West Point as a cadet, from which he graduated second in his class in 1846. He joined the efforts in the war with Mexico, and was promoted to first lieutenant and then for his work at Contreras, Chapultepec, and the battle of Cerro Gordo. At the close of the war, Captain McClellan returned to West Point, where he acted as an instructor of practical engineering until 1851, and then took charge of the construction of Fort Delaware. In 1852 he published a *Manual of Bayonet Exercise*, adapted from the French. In the same year he was a member of an expedition under Captain Randolph B. Marcy, which explored the region of the Red River between Texas and the Indian territory; subsequently he had charge of explorations and surveys in Texas in 1853-54 was on engineer duty in Washington and Oregon territories, and began a topographical survey for the Western division of the Northern Pacific railroad.

On March 3, 1855, McClellan was appointed a captain in the first cavalry, and in the same year was sent to visit the scene of the Crimean War and to study the condition of the armies of Europe. His individual report on arms, equipment and organization was published in 1861, with the title *The Armies of Europe* . In 1857, McClellan resigned from the army and became chief engineer of the Illinois Central Railroad; in 1858 he was made its vice president and in 1859 was elected president of the eastern division of the Ohio and Mississippi Railroad Company, with headquarters in Cincinnati. In 1859-61 he was president of the St. Louis, Missouri and Cincinnati Railroad. As the Civil War broke out, he was called by the governor of Ohio to organize the volunteers. On April 23 he was commissioned major-general of Ohio volunteers and on May 14th, was appointed major-general of the U.S. Army, and placed in command of the department of the Ohio. He marched into western Virginia on May 26, occupying Parkersburg; at Carrick's Ford, on a Branch of the Cheat River, routed a Confederate force under General Garnett, and on July 12 received the surrender of Lieutenant Colonel Pegram, with 560 men and 33 officers. An attempt by General Lee to retrieve these disasters failed, and the Confederates retired from western Virginia, whose inhabitants, the majority of whom had opposed secession, were now encouraged to proceed with their efforts to form a separate state. In late 1861 and early 1862, McClellan fell ill, but he soon recovered to lead the Union as Commanding General of the Army. In late 1864, he was ordered to resign his command because of his lack of activity, and for awhile there was confusion about his loyalty to the Union. He ran unsuccessfully for President as a Democrat in 1864. Immediately afterwards, McClellan went to Europe, where he remained until 1868. Upon his return he settled in New York City, and for a year (1868-69) was employed in completing the Stevens ironclad floating battery for harbor defense. Declining the presidency of the University of California and of Union College, he became engineer-in-chief of the department of docks of the city of New York (1870-72), and subsequently president of the New York Underground Railroad Company, the U.S. Rolling Stock Company and the Atlantic and Great Western Railroad Company. Later he settled in West Orange, New Jersey, near the home of his father-in-law. In 1878, McClellan was elected governor of New Jersey on the Democratic ticket. While governor, McClellan approved new industrial schools and supported new tax laws and a system to govern unincorporated cities. The Constitution of 1844 prohibited him from seeking reelection and in 1881 he was appointed by congress as one of the board of managers of the National Home for Disabled Soldiers. The rest of his career was spent mainly giving speeches, dedicating monuments, and writing of his experiences in various magazines. His *Government Reports of Pacific Railways* was published in 1854; *Report on the Organization and Campaigns of the Army of the Potomac* in 1864; *McClellan's Own Story* in 1886, which is made up of extracts from letters to his wife. McClellan was abroad during his later life, but he died at home in New Jersey. He is buried at Trenton.

LUDLOW, GEORGE C.— (1830-1900), twenty-eighth governor of New Jersey (1881-84), was born in Milford, New Jersey, to Protestant parents. His early education was in the schools of his neighborhood, and he entered Rutgers College at the age of sixteen, graduating in 1850. He then began to study law, was admitted to the bar three years later and started a practice at New Brunswick. He soon established a reputation in his profession and won favor. Always an intense Democrat, he was wont to take a conspicuous part in politics, but never held office until 1876, when he was elected to the state senate. During his term of membership, he served on some of the most important committees, and throughout one session occupied the president's chair. He declined a renomination. In 1880 he became the Democratic nominee for the governorship of New Jersey, was elected the same year, and came into office the next. Child labor was limited, public libraries were established and women were made eligible to sit on school boards during Ludlow's term. He also created a Board of State Charities and Correction. His term expired in 1884, and he returned to his law practice.

ABBET, LEON— (1836-1894), twenty-ninth and thirty-first governor of New Jersey (1884-87 and 1890-93), was a native of Philadelphia, Pennsylvania. His parents were Ezekiel and Sarah Howell Abbett. Leon was graduated from the Central High School of Philadelphia in 1853, the valedictorian of his class. he began to study law in the office of John W. Ashmead of Philadelphia and about a year later moved to Hoboken, New Jersey and gained admission to the bars of that state and New York. In New Jersey he was retained in many important cases, and became a recognized authority in all cases involving municipal and constitutional law. In 1862 he married Mary Briggs of Philadelphia and in the following year entered public life as corporation attorney of Hoboken.

In 1864 he was elected as a Democrat to represent Hoboken in the legislature and was reelected in the following year. During both terms he was chairman of the Democratic assembly caucus. In 1866 he moved to Jersey City, and represented the first assembly district of that city in the legislature from 1868 to 1870, being speaker of the house in 1869-70. In 1869 Abbett was president of the board of education of Jersey City, and in 1872 a delegate at large to the Democratic National Convention in Baltimore. In 1876 he was again a delegate at the convention in St. Louis. During this time he was also corporate counsel for the cities of Bayonne and Union, and later Jersey City until 1883. He was nominated for state senator while on a trip to Europe in 1874, and upon his return was elected to a three year term. In 1878 he was appointed by Governor McClellan to the commission drafting a charter of city government, and later Governor Ludlow selected him a commission member to revise the tax laws. In 1883 he was nominated and elected governor of New Jersey. Between his two terms, he was an unsuccessful candidate for U.S. Senator. In his first inaugural address, Abbett called attention to the tax system of New Jersey by which the railroads of the state were practically exempt from taxation, and demanded immediate reform. The legislature then passed a series of tax laws imposing taxes on railroads and other corporations, to a large extent equalizing the burden of taxation. Governor Abbett then forced from the Morris and Essex Railroad Company the surrender of an alleged irreparable contract with the state, exempting the road from taxation, even compelling it to pay into the state treasury $235,000 in back taxes. At the same time he induced other railroads to relinquish their claims to exemption under alleged irreparable contracts. During his first term the labor laws of the state were also amended at his suggestion and a series of acts for better city government passed. In his second inaugural message of 1890, Abbett urged the passage of a ballot reform law, and his recommendations were promptly adopted by the legislature. He was chairman of the New Jersey delegation to the Democratic National Convention in 1880. After his second term, Abbett was appointed a justice of the New Jersey supreme court, where he served until his death at Jersey City the next year.

GREEN, ROBERT S.— (1831-1895), thirtieth governor of New Jersey (1887-90), was born in Princeton, the son of James S. Green and grandson of Rev. Ashbel Green, president of the College of New Jersey (Princeton). Robert Stockton Green, after a preliminary training, entered Nassau Hall, from which he graduated in 1850. He studied law, and was admitted to the bar in 1853, and became a counselor in 1856. That year he moved to Elizabeth. In 1862 he was elected surrogate of Union County and in 1868 was appointed presiding judge of the county courts. In 1873 he was chosen a member of the commission to suggest amendments to the constitution of the state, which were for the most part adopted by two successive legislatures and ratified by the voters. He was a delegate to the National Democratic convention at Baltimore in 1860, which nominated Stephen A. Douglas for the presidency, to the Cincinnati convention in 1880 and the St. Louis convention in 1888. In 1884 he was elected to Congress, and in 1886 elected governor of new Jersey, a trying position at the time, as the legislature was mostly Republican for the first two years of his term. A Democratic senate and assembly were elected in 1889, and his party was firmly established in its control of state affairs. His administration was characterized by an effort to reduce government expenses; to maintain a non-partisan judiciary; to preserve the rights of the state as to its submerged lands; to settled the disputed boundary line between New Jersey and New York and to enforce the collection of taxes from corporations. He also gained passage of a ballot reform law and established an intermediary prison. Representing the state he participated in the Centennial celebrations at Philadelphia in 1887, and in New York in 1889. In 1890 he was appointed a vice-chancellor of the state. He was honored by Princeton College in 1887, with the degree if LL.D. On June 26, 1894, he was appointed by Governor Werts a judge of the court of errors and appeals. He died at home in Elizabeth, New Jersey.

WERTS, GEORGE T.— (1846-1910), thirty-second governor of New Jersey (1893-96), was born in Hackettstown, New Jersey, the son of Peter Werts and a mother whose maiden name was Vanatta. In 1849 young Werts moved with his parents to Bordentown, where he attended the high school, with a subsequent course at the state model school at Trenton. At the age of seventeen, he went to Morristown, and studied law with his uncle, Mr. Vanatta. He was admitted to the bar in 1867 and began a practice. From May 1883 to May 1885, he was recorder of that town, and from 1886 until his resignation in 1892 he was mayor. He served six years in the state legislature, where for some time he was president of the senate. While a member of the senate, he drafted the liquor and ballot reform laws. He left the legislature in 1892 to accept the office of justice of the supreme court, appointed by Governor Abbett. In 1892 Judge Werts was elected governor of New Jersey, although he didn't actively campaign. His term was fraught with squabbling between the Democrats and Republicans, and for awhile there were two separate seats along party lines. The governor, a Democrat, supported his party's senate, but the state supreme court held the Republicans were the rightful senators. Werts authorized bills for constructing railways on turnpikes, revising of election registration procedures and constructing more free public libraries in small cities. He resumed his law practice after his term, and died in Jersey City.

GRIGGS, JOHN W.— (1849-1927), thirty-third governor of New Jersey (1896-98), was born in Newton, New Jersey, to Daniel and Emeline Johnson Griggs, farmers. He was educated at the Collegiate Institute, Newton, and at Lafayette College, Easton, Pennsylvania, where he graduated in 1868 and then took up the study with Robert Hamilton at Newton. Later he studied with Socrates Tuttle in Paterson, and in 1872, the year after his admission to the bar, formed a partnership with him which continued for eight years. His appointment to the office of city counsel soon followed; later he became president of the Paterson National Bank and the Paterson Safe Deposit Company. In 1875 Griggs was elected to the state assembly, and the next year was reelected. In 1882, he became a state senator, representing Passaic County, and in 1886 as president of that body, presided at the Laverty impeachment trial. The law for the taxation of miscellaneous corporations was drawn by him, and he was concerned with framing the railroad tax act. He led the Republicans in 1887 in the contest for the senatorship which ended in Governor Abbett's defeat. In 1888 he was a delegate to the Republican National Convention and presented William Phelps as a candidate for the vice presidency. In 1895, Griggs was elected governor of New Jersey, being the first Republican for thirty years to hold that office. His plurality over Alexander McGill was 26,900. A constitutional amendment prohibiting gambling was passed during his administration, and Governor Griggs appointed a commission to revise the general statutes. On the resignation of Joseph McKenna to become associate justice of the supreme court, he succeeded him as attorney general of the United States, taking the oath of office in 1898. In 1901 he resigned to resume a private law practice in Trenton. In late 1901, he went to The Hague to serve on the Permanent Court of Arbitration, until 1912. He was later involved in radio, telephone, steel and railroad corporations until his death.

VOORHEES, FOSTER MACGOWAN— (1856-1927), thirty-fourth and thirty-sixth governor of New Jersey (1898, 1899-1902), was born in Clinton, New Jersey to Nathaniel W. and Naomi Leigh Voorhees. Never married. He attended private schools and was graduated at Rutgers College in 1876, receiving the degrees of M.A. in 1879 and LL.D. in 1898. He also received the LL.D. degree from Princeton University in 1902. He was admitted to the New Jersey bar in 1880 and resided in Elizabeth afterwards. For several years he was a member of the Elizabeth Board of Education and during 1888-90 was a member of the state legislature. He was state senator from 1894 until 1898 and served as president of the senate during the last year. Upon the resignation of Governor Griggs in 1898 to become attorney-general in McKinley's cabinet, Voorhees became acting governor. He resigned ten months later to try to be elected in his own right. He took his seat again in January 1899, and held a three year term. While he was governor, the voting laws were made uniform, and a road improvement system was improvised. Voorhees also supported the construction of an armory at Trenton. After the expiration of his term of office he entered active practice of his profession and was associated with many of the financial and business enterprises of Elizabeth. He died at High Bridge, New Jersey.

WATKINS, DAVID O.— (1862-1938), thirty-fifth governor of New Jersey (1898-99), was born in Woodbury, New Jersey, the son of William and Honor Thomkin Watkins. He attended public schools and worked on the family farm until, at the age of eighteen, he became a private secretary to George G. Green. In 1886, he was elected mayor of Woodbury as a Republican, serving until 1890. Meanwhile, he studied law in town, and in 1891, traveled to Montana, where he completed his studies with Elbert Weed. In 1893, he returned to New Jersey to practice his profession in Woodbury, specializing in banking and corporation law. He was solicitor for the City of Woodbury and advised the Gloucester County Board of Freeholders before winning a seat in the New Jersey assembly. When Acting Governor Voorhees resigned in 1898, Watkins was called from his post as president of the state senate to assume the executive seat. He held the post for three months until Governor-elect Voorhees resumed it. In February 1899, he was named U.S. District Attorney for New Jersey by President McKinley. Watkins resigned his post in 1903 when he became commissioner of banking and insurance for New Jersey. After 1909, he resumed his private practice and interests in the

Woodbury Trust Company and the Farmers and Mechanics National Bank. From 1935 until his death he was a member of the state banking advisory commission.

MURPHY, FRANKLIN— (1846-1920), thirty-seventh governor of New Jersey (1902-05), was born in Jersey City to William H. and Abby Hagar Murphy. He was educated at public schools and at the Newark Academy, until 1862 when he joined the Union's Company A of New Jersey volunteers. He saw battle at Antietam, Chancellorsville and Gettysburg, and was with General Sherman's Western Army in the march through Georgia. At war's end, he was a first lieutenant. In 1866, his father and Thompson Price formed the Murphy Varnish Company, and young Franklin joined in the enterprise. He was a member of the Newark Common Council in 1883-86, while serving in the state assembly during its 1885 session. Active in the Republican national committee, Murphy led the state in electing McKinley as President. He was trustee for the boy's reform school at Jamesburg, New Jersey in 1886-89. In 1900 he was commissioner to the Paris Exposition, which took place the following year. In 1901 he received an honorary LL.B. degree from Lafayette University; the following year Princeton gave him the honor as well. He was elected governor of New Jersey in 1901, and his term was concerned with election and child labor laws. Fees were abolished for state and county services and banks were required to pay interest on state money. When he left office, Murphy was a prominent . Republican, engaging in several businesses until his death at Palm Beach, Florida.

STOKES, EDWARD— (1860-1942), thirty-eighth governor of New Jersey (1905-08), was born in Philadelphia, the son of Edward, a banker, and Matilda Kemble Stokes. He attended public schools in Millville, New Jersey, and the Friends' School in Providence, Rhode Island. He graduated from Brown University in 1883, and then joined his father at the Millville National Bank. Banking was not his interest, however, and in 1889 he was superintendant of the Millville public schools. Thereafter, he concentrated on his political career, first as an assemblyman (1891) and then as a state senator (1892-98). He was a clerk at the Court of Chancery in 1900-04, meanwhile becoming active in the Republican Party. In 1904, he beat the Democratic nominee for governor and began a term that was known for its openness and informality. Governor

Stokes was impatient with frivolity in state government and helped push through a tax increase on railroads that had been postponed for many years because of transportation companies' pressure. When his term was up, he returned to Trenton to manage the First Mechanics National Bank. He tried for a U.S. Senate seat unsuccessfully in 1902 and 1928, as well as for a second term as governor in 1913. He was chair of the Republican state convention in 1936. Afterwards, he lived quietly until his death at Trenton.

FORT, JOHN F.— (1852-1920), Thirty-ninth governor of New Jersey (1908-11), was born in Pemberton, New Jersey, the son of Andrew H. and Hannah A. Brown Fort. He received his early education at the Pennington Seminary in New Jersey and studied law first with Edward M. Paxson, and afterwards with Garrit S. Cannon and Ewan Merritt. Being graduated at the Albany Law School in 1872 with the degree of LL.B. he was admitted to the bar in the following year and began the practice of his profession in Newark, after serving one year as journal clerk of the New Jersey assembly. He was so successful and showed such marked ability that Governor McClellan appointed him judge of the first district court of the city of Newark for five years (1878), and at the expiration of his term he was reappointed by Governor Ludlow. He resigned in 1883. He was a delegate-at-large from New Jersey to the Republican national convention at Chicago which nominated James G. Blaine for the presidency. He served a chairman of the New Jersey Republican conventions of 1889 and 1895. In 1894 he was a member of the constitutional commission, subsequently becoming one of the three New Jersey members on uniform laws for all the states. Governor Griggs appointed Fort judge of the Essex court of common pleas in 1896, to fill a vacancy caused by the resignation of Andrew Kirkpatrick. Judge Fort was later appointed judge of Essex common pleas for the full term. In 1900, Governor Voorhees appointed him a justice of the supreme court for the full term of seven years. On November 5, 1908, Judge Fort was elected governor of New Jersey by a plurality of more than 8,000 votes over his Democratic opponent Frank S. Katzenbach. Governor Fort made a special study of prisons and criminal reformation and in 1902 was instrumental in closing the gambling houses in Long Branch. Before his judgeship he was president of several banks and trust companies. He was married in 1876 to Charlotte Stainsby of Newark, and had three children. He returned to his family and banking interests after the governorship, and was a delegate to the Progressive Convention of 1912. In 1919, he was a special member of the Federal Trade Commission. He died in South Orange, New Jersey.

WILSON, THOMAS WOODROW— (1856-1924), fortieth governor of New Jersey (1911-13), and twenty-eighth President of the U.S. (1913-21), was born in Staunton, Virginia, the son of the Reverend Joseph Ruggels and Janet Woodrow Wilson. He was educated in private Presbyterian schools and entered Davidson College, North Carolina in 1874, but was forced by ill health to leave before the end of his freshman year. In 1875 he matriculated at Princeton, where his personality made him one of the most respected and popular members of the student body. In his senior year he was president of the athletic committee, the baseball association, and managing editor of the *Princetonian*. The chance reading of an article in the *Gentlemen's Magazine* on the customs and procedure of the British parliament, soon after entering college, directed his attention to the field of politics. It led him to take a deep interest in the political life of his own country. He became a profound student of government, almost to the exclusion of other college subjects, specializing in the political history of the United States and England. He joined the Princeton debating society and later organized the Liberal Debating Club, modeling it after British parliament. During his senior year he wrote an article entitled "CABINET Government in the United States," contrasting the American and British systems of government, which was published in the *International Review* of August 1879, and attracted much attention. He was graduated A.B. from Princeton in 1879, and in the fall entered the University of Virginia to study law. He became one of the best debaters at the university and as a representative of the Jefferson Society won the prize for oratory. But his health again failed, and he completed his law studies at his father's home in wilmington, North Carolina, receiving the degree of LL.B. in 1881. He began to practice law in Atlanta, Georgia, in 1882, in partnership with Edward I. Renick, but clients were few and his leisure time was spent in outlining a comprehensive dissertation on "Congressional Government." He virtually abandoned the law when, in 1883, he began a post-graduate course in history and political science at Johns Hopkins University. Here, with his thesis on "Congressional Government," he won a fellowship in history, and in 1886 the degree of Ph.D. He was associate professor of history and political economy at Bryn Mawr College during 1885-88, and in 1887 he also delivered weekly lectures on political economy at

Johns Hopkins. In 1888 he became a professor at Wesleyan University, and two years later he was called to the chair of jurisprudence and political economy at Princeton College, his alma mater, to spend the next twenty years of his life. In 1897 he was advanced to the McCormick professorship of his field. Upon resignation of President Francis L. Patton in 1902, Wilson was appointed to succeed him, being the first layman to serve as president of Princeton. Gradually, he became more active in liberal and Democratic politics both in New Jersey and the nation. In 1910 many signs of dissension in the Republican party made the Democratic leaders believe that the right Democratic candidate could carry the country in 1912. It was also believed that Wilson's chances would be greatly increased if he could be elected governor of New Jersey before the national campaign. The state had been dominated by corporate interests for years and strong factions in both parties were determined to overthrow that domination. Wilson at first declined nomination because he feared he would be told what to do by the Democratic party "bosses," but he was able to write his own platform for the state convention, and even though he was considered part of the "old guard," he was able to win the support of enough progressives to be elected by a substantial majority over the Republican candidate. As governor he applied himself to carrying out the reforms promised in his platform, and through his efforts a program of progressive economic and social legislation was enacted. During the first year of his term the Republicans had a majority in the senate but in his second year the voters expressed approval of his efforts by electing a legislature that was overwhelmingly Democratic. His most notable political reform was in the regulation of trusts. The leniency of New Jersey's corporation laws had led many of the largest companies in the country to incorporate in that state, which was frequently called the "home of trusts." Shortly before the close of his term Wilson secured the passage of seven bills, known as the "Seven Sisters' Acts," which declared illegal all monopolies, holding corporations and agreements to fix prices, limit production, or prevent free competition in making, transporting or dealing in merchandise. His other reform measures adopted were the direct primary, limitation of campaign expenditures, commission form of government for cities and towns, regulation of public utilities, employers' liability and workmen's compensation, safety and sanitation for women and children in industry and regulation of their hours of labor. Wilson's struggle for popular government in New Jersey, his successive victories over corporate interests and "machine rule,"

and his extraordinary grasp of political problems convinced
Democratic leaders throughout the country that he was destined
to become a strong force in American political life. Among his
supporters was his experienced campaign manager, who convinced William Jennings Bryan not to run against Wilson for
governor. He was elected President in 1912 over Roosevelt and
Taft, and his inauguration ushered in a new era in American
history. Although most of his platforms during the campaign had
dealt with domestic issues, Wilson soon had to face bewildering
problems of international importance. Early in his administration, Wilson found prevalent in Latin America a growing resentment towards what was considered the patronizing attitude of the
U.S. government, and the exploitation of the Monroe Doctrine by
the United States as a pretext for assuming a position of
superiority in Latin American affairs. His conciliatory policy
was shown in his speech at the Southern Commercial Congress,
October 1913, when he sought to make amends to Colombia for
America's intervention in Panama during the Roosevelt administration. A treaty between the two countries was signed in
1914, and Wilson continued his conciliatory interest in Latin
America throughout his term. He tried to avoid war with Mexico
in 1914-15, when the government there was especially volatile,
and even when American citizens were killed at Santa Ysabel
and Columbus, New Mexico, he tried to reach a peaceful agreement with President Carranza instead of declaring war. Soon
afterwards, Wilson's attention was turned to the events in
Europe, especially the actions of the Germans. Wilson publicly
stated he would not get the U.S. into the conflict, and offered to
act as a mediator between the warring countries. However,
United States political and business interests were deeply involved in Europe and he declared war after the Germans sank
several neutral merchant ships that carried many Americans.
His historic speech to Congress declared the U.S. a "belligerent"
against Germany, and he said, "I advise the Congress declare
the recent course of the Imperial German government to be in
fact nothing less than war against the government of the United
States,...and that it take immediate steps not only to put the country in a more thorough state of defense, but also to exert all its
power and employee all its resources to bring the government of
the German Empire to terms and end the war...The world must
be made safe for democracy..." He continued to work on peace
negotiations, however, and through his League of Nations, which
led to the passage of his famous "Fourteen Points," and and end
to World War I. In 1918, he was the first President to visit a

foreign country when he went for diplomatic talks in Paris. In 1920, he received the Nobel Peace Prize for his efforts. When he left office, Wilson worked in a law firm with Bainbridge Colby. He died a few years later and was buried at the National Cathedral, Washington, D.C.

FIELDER, JAMES F.— (1867-1954), forty-first governor of New Jersey (1913 and 1914-17), was born in Jersey City, the son of George B., a congressman, and Eleanor A. Brinkerhoff Fielder. Fielder was educated in the public and high schools of Jersey City, at Selleck School, Norwalk, Connecticut, and was graduated at Columbia University Law School with the degree of LL.B. in 1887. After graduation he entered the office of his uncle, former Sen. William Brinkerhoff, and was admitted to the bar in 1888. He was a member of the assembly from Hudson County, in 1903 and 1904, was elected to the state senate in 1907 and was reelected in 1910 by the largest majority ever given to a state senator from his county. In 1913 he was elected president of the senate, and when Gov. Wilson became President of the U.S., Sen. Fielder became acting governor according to the state constitution. At the primary election held in September, 1913, James Fielder was nominated as a candidate for governor over Frank S. Katzenback by a majority of 45,000. He resigned in October 1913 and waited until he was formally elected governor in the November balloting. In January 1914 he took the seat again and served a term that saw many new reforms in the state, such as the Pure Food Law and health insurance for industrial workers. Fielder returned to his wife, the former Mabel Miller, and his law profession. In 1920, he was made vice chancellor of the state court of chancery. He died many years later in Montclair, New Jersey.

TAYLOR, LEON R.— (1883-1924), acting governor of New Jersey (1913-14), was born in Asbury Park, New Jersey. His parents were Reverent Thomas Taylor and an unknown wife. He studied in common and Baptist schools and then attended Denison University in Ohio. He studied law in his home state and began practice before being elected to the state assembly. The Democrat was Speaker of the Assembly in 1913, when he was appointed interim governor. James Fielder had resigned to gain the governorship by election in 1914. Governor Taylor hardly had time to accomplish anything in his three month term, which filled the vacancy left originally by Woodrow Wilson. Afterwards,

Taylor returned to law and during World War I he was a captain
in the Red Cross. He moved to colorado to improve his health and
died in Denver several years later.

EDGE, WALTER E.— (1873-1956), forty-second and fifty-second
governor of New Jersey (1917-19 and 1944-47), was born in
Philadelphia to William and Mary E. Evans Edge. After attending the public school at Pleasantville, New Jersey, where the
family had moved in 1876 following his mother's death, he went to
atlantic City to begin a career in publishing and advertising as a
printer's boy in the office of the *Review* . Later he represented
the New York *Tribune* as one of its local correspondents and
advertising agents and also as a member of its business staff in
Florida and Cuba. Returning to Atlantic city he joined an advertising agency which specialized in hotel and resort publicity,
afterwards purchasing it. His first publication venture was the
Atlantic City *Daily guest* (1895), a daily hotel newspaper. This
experiment in journalism was so successful that the next year he
started a similar paper in Jacksonville, Florida, *The Guest* . His
advertising activities in Atlantic City were conducted alternately
with legislative work in Trenton, where he early acquired an in-
sight into public affairs as journal clerk to the state senate during
the 1897-99 sessions. He was also secretary to that body in 1901
through 1904, in which year he was also a presidential elector
from New Jersey. Meantime he had renamed his hotel sheet in
Atlantic City the *Press* and issued it as a regular morning
newspaper. He originated a plan of cooperative advertising in
association with other newspapers throughout the country and
abroad to make Atlantic City better known. Active branches of
his agency were established in New York City, London, Paris,
Berlin, Rome and Buenos Aires. Conservative in tone and
Republican in politics, the *Press* advanced the growth of Atlantic City as an all-year resort more than any other single local influence. In 1905 he purchased the *Daily Union* , the resort's only
evening newspaper and conducted it as a night edition of the
Press . In 1908 he was an alternate delegate-at-large to the
Republican national convention in Chicago. A year later he was
elected to the New Jersey assembly and had the distinction of
becoming house leader the first year of his membership. He went
to the state senate in 1910 and was its Republican leader while
Woodrow Wilson was governor. After a careful study of the problems of employers' liability, especially the measures taken
toward its solution in other countries, while he was abroad in 1910

and 1911, he secured the passage of the New Jersey workmen's compensation law in 1911. It was the first American statute holding employers responsible for injuries and included all hazards; it survived constitutional litigation and served as a model for similar legislation in other states. He was reelected to the state senate in 1913, serving as its president in 1915 and was also acting governor for a few weeks. As chairman of the New Jersey economy and efficiency commission he helped to initiate the passage of measures which eliminated a number of superfluous bodies in the state government, consolidated various boards and departments, and established a state budget and central purchasing bureau. Under the new budget system the governor was required to base the appropriations recommended by him on the estimates submitted by the departments, while the buying of all supplies for departments was undertaken by the purchasing agency. In 1916 Edge ran for governor and defeated his Democratic opponent, Otto Wittpen, by the largest plurality ever obtained by a gubernatorial candidate in New Jersey. During his administration all state departmental functions were coordinated, becoming centralized under a single managing head — the executive. New legislation included important war emergency measures; local option and corrupt practices bills; bills authorizing and financing the Hudson River vehicular tunnel; the Delaware River bridge and a state highway system. He served only until May, 1919, of a three year term, having been elected in 1918 for the U.s. Senate to succeed David Baird. In his first term in the senate (1919-25), he was assigned to the committee on interoceanic canals (of which he became chairman), banking and currency, privileges and elections, commerce, District of Columbia, post offices and post roads, and the budget. His first measure was an enabling act sanctioning the cooperation of New Jersey and New York to construct a vehicular tunnel under the Hudson River. He took a prominent part with other fiscal reformers in Congress in laying ground for instituting a federal budgetary system, which had features in common with the budget he helped to establish in New Jersey. A third measure, the Edge Export Finance Act, aimed a expanding American banking, commerce and shipping to the world's markets, by enabling manufacturers to giving long term credit to responsible foreign traders in American products. He was a delegate at large at the national conventions of 1920 and 1924. In 1924 he was reelected to the senate by a 65,000 majority in the primaries and a majority over all his opponents (six) of 232,865. Edge resigned the senate in 1929 when he was appointed ambassador to France. He returned home four years later, and led a private life until 1943, when he ran successfully for governor again. His second term was in a completely different era than the first. He authorized a $25 million post-war surplus fund and an end to all public borrowing. Also, the legislature created a new anti-discrimination division within the Department of Education. Edge advocated the constitutional convention to revise the archaic 1844 document. He resumed his business interests in Atlantic City, and died in New York City.

RUNYON, WILLIAM N.— (1871-1931), forty-third governor of New Jersey (1919-20), was born to Nelson and Wilhelmina F. Trow Runyon at Plainfield, New Jersey. He studied in public schools and then yale University, from which he gained an A.B. in 1892. In 1894, he completed his studies at the New York Law School and began a practice in Plainfield. He was a member of the city's Common Council in 1897-98, and was city judge for eleven years afterward. In 1915-17, he was a member of the New Jersey assembly, and the senate in 1918-22. He was president of the state senate in 1919 when Governor Walter Edge stepped down to take a seat in the U.S. Senate, so he was appointed to fill out the term. He left the seat when his term as leader of the senate ended the next year. In 1922, he tried to be elected governor, but lost to George Silzer. He was made a judge of the U.S. District Court in New Jersey in 1923, where he sat until his death. He is buried in Plainfield, New Jersey.

CASE, CLARENCE— (1877-1961), acting governor of New Jersey (1920), was born in Jersey city to Phillip and Amanda Case. He studied at Rutgers University, receiving his A.B. degree in 1900. He then studied law in New York and received his LL.B. in 1902. After beginning a practice in his home state, Case was named clerk of the New Jersey Senate Judiciary Committee ion 1908, which helped him gain enough experience to run for the state senate in 1918. He became Senate President in 1920, when William Runyon's term expired and so was immediately promoted to the governorship, which was still vacant since Walter Edge had resigned in 1919. Case's term only lasted from January 13 to January 20, when governor-elect Edwards was inaugurated. After his short term, Case returned to his law practice and also worked on a legislative committee that investigated corrupt practices among Democrats in Hudson County. In 1929, he was appointed a justice of the state supreme court, and was promoted to chief of that court in 1945. Three years later he was renamed

Senior Associate Justice under the new constitution. He left the
bench in 1952 to pursue his private practice until his death in
Somerville, New Jersey.

EDWARDS, EDWARD I.— (1863-1931), forty-fourth governor of
New Jersey (1920-23), was born in Jersey City to William and
Emma Nation Edwards. He entered New York University with
the class of 1884 but left at the end of his junior year to take up the
study of law in the office of his brother, William. This, too, was
soon given up for a position as messenger boy with the First National Bank of Jersey City in 1882. He left the bank to engage in a
contracting and construction business with his brother and they
obtained some important contracts from the city government.
Returning to the First national Bank as assistant to the president
in 1903 he advanced to cashier in 1911, president in 1916 and chairman of the board in 1925. He was also vice president of the Merchant's National Bank and a director of a paper company, a
railroad and a motor company. Becoming active in politics, he
was chosen a member of the Hudson County Democratic committee and in 1911 was elected comptroller of New jersey. In that
position, he showed unusual vigor, inaugurating a "pay as you
go" policy and compelling strict compliance with the requisition
act which called for rigid accounting for every state expenditure.
He was reelected in 1914. In 1918-19 he was a member of the state
senate. In the latter year he was elected governor of New Jersey.
In his inaugural address he spoke out with a boldness that attracted national attention. He denounced the 18th Amendment as
an invasion of the liberties of the people, and asked the attorney
general of the state to institute proceedings to have the constitu-
tionality of the law tested. He called for a decrease in the personnel of the public utilities board from five to three members with a
salary increase, so that they might be elected by the people and
condemned the board for allowing increased traffic tariffs which
he denounced as an invasion of the law authorizing a physical
valuation of the transportation systems. He pushed for more good
roads and for an issue of short term bonds for the construction of
the Hudson vehicle tunnel and the Philadelphia-Camden Interstate bridge, and urged tax reform on the legislature. His victory at the polls had been large enough to carry the legislature
with him and he was successful in having his recommendations
enacted into laws. He received the support of the New Jersey
delegation to the Democratic convention for the presidential
nomination of 1920. Two years later he was nominated by his party for U.S. Senate, and in the contest of 1922 defeated Joseph S.

Frelinghuysen by the unprecedented plurality of 89,000 votes. In the senate he denounced various prohibition measures and favored the World Court, McFadden Bank Bill, World War loans and the reduction of the income tax. He failed to be reelected in 1928. He was married to Jule Blance Smith in 1888, and had two children. He died in Jersey City.

SILZER, GEORGE S.— (1870-1940), forty-fifth governor of New Jersey (1923-26), was born in New brunswick, New Jersey, to Theodore and Christina zimmerman Silzer. Silzer attended public high schools of his town and later prepared himself for a legal career. Admitted to the New Jersey bar in 1892, he immediately opened an office in New Brunswick for the practice of law. His political life began almost immediately, for he was made a member of the board of aldermen of New Brunswick in 1892, serving for six years. In addition to his regular practice, he was chairman of the Middlesex County Democratic Committee for ten years and was elected to the New Jersey senate in 1906 and 1909. In 1912 he was nominated prosecutor of the pleas of Middlesex County by Governor Woodrow Wilson, and filled that position with success until 1914, when he resigned to accept Governor Fielder's appointment of him as a circuit judge. Silzer was so serving in 1922 when he became the Democratic candidate for governor of New Jersey. He was elected by a large plurality and six days after his inauguration he went in person before a hostile legislature and removed the state highway commission just after $40 million had been appropriated for road improvement. His brief announcement, "I have this day removed the present state highway commission," caused a sensation in the Republican state legislature which, with its three Democratic members, was antagonistic to him. He appointed a new bipartisan commission but the senate tried to force him to place two appointees of their own in place of two members, who were Republicans, and a deadlock ensued. He held firm, however, and after a delay of several weeks the appointments were confirmed. The new commission devoted itself to state highway improvement. During a serious trolley strike in Newark in 1923, the dispute was over wages and, in the resulting deadlock, the public service railway company refused to run its cars. For nearly a month the city was practically without transportation. The governor announced that the streets of the state belong to the public and not to the public service company and that the use of the streets was given the company in return for adequate transportation facilities to the public. He requested the attorney general to bring action immediately to recover the streets to the state and remove the railway company. A suit was quickly filed and within two weeks the strike was over and the streetcars were in operation. During his administration he was opposed to so much proposed legislation that he won the nickname of "veto governor." In his annual message in 1925 he urged more drastic penalties to lessen crime and pleaded for a federal ban on firearms. In an address before the New York bar Association during the coal strike of 1925-26, he urged the "compact clause and the Constitution" as affording a means to counteract the modern tendency toward centralized administration in Washington. among the bills passed during his administration was one eliminating night work for women in the state's factories. He advocated enforcement of the 18th Amendment, saying, "No matter what the individual views may be on this question, there can be no two views on the subject of law observation and law enforcement." One of the outstanding achievements of his administration was the completion of the plans and virtual completion of the bridge to link New Jersey with Philadelphia. Funds for this bridge were raised by a bond issue which also made possible the construction of two vehicular tunnels between New York and New Jersey. After leaving the office of governor in 1926, Silzer returned to his law practice in Newark. He also became active in banking circles, and soon afterwards was appointed chairman of the Port of New York Authority, an office he held during 1926-28, supervising the construction of the Washington Bridge. In 1932, Silzer headed an independent bondholder's committee which successfully sought removal of the City Bank and Farmer's Trust Company, as trustee of $100 million in bonds of the International Match Company. As a lawyer he was identified with a number of well-publicized cases. With others he defended Arthur "Dutch Schultz" Fleganheimer in an income tax trial, and later was attorney for Ellis H. Parker, Sr., a detective charged with conspiracy to kidnap Paul Wendel, a Trenton attorney, and force him to make a false confession of the kidnapping of Charles Lindbergh's baby. The LL.D. degree was conferred on him by Rutgers University in 1923. Silzer was married at Metuchen, New Jersey in 1898 to Henrietta Waite, and had one son. His death occurred at Newark.

MOORE, ARTHUR HARRY— (1879-1952), forty-sixth, forty-eighth and fiftieth governor of New Jersey (1926-29, 1932-35 and 1938-41), was born at Jersey City. His parents were Robert and Martha McComb Moore. His family was poor and he had to work odd jobs while attending public school. He also had private tutoring which he paid for from his savings during the off school season and later he attended Cooper Union, New York, and the New Jersey Law School at Newark. He was graduated in 1924, having been admitted to the New Jersey bar two years earlier. He showed an early interest in public affairs for he was a natural born leader and like his father began his political career as a Democrat. While he did not begin his legal career in Jersey City until 1920 he had long been in public service which began when he was appointed secretary to Mayor Wittpen in 1908. Three years later he was chosen city tax collector for a term of two years. While in office in Jersey City he became convinced of the necessity and prudence of a commission form of city government and urged the passage of the Walsh Act for this purpose. After it became law he was one of ninety-two candidates for nomination for commissioner and when the vote was counted Moore was one of those at the top of the list. In the general election he was one of the five first successful candidates and was assigned to the department of public parks and property. He held that office until 1924 when he became director of revenue and finance. Meanwhile his popularity was growing. As a candidate for reelection in 1917 he led the ticket; in the election of 1921 his majority was increased and in 1923 he polled over 70,000 votes out of a total of 80,000. As commissioner of Jersey City he became interested in the welfare of children, and he undertook to organize civic clubs and extend the park and recreation systems of the city. He founded athletic fields for both winter and summer sports, improved the waterfront and helped end the pollution of beach waters that endangered the health of summer bathers. He mapped out a plan of city development which provided for new residential and commercial sections to relieve the congestion. The development of streets and highways was a part of his plan of city improvement and he was the originator of the enclosed highway connection with the Hudson River vehicular tunnel. Moore was elected governor of New Jersey in 1925, as a Democrat on a platform calling for the repeal of the 18th Amendment and modifying the Volstead Act, and was inaugurated in early 1926. Governor Moore set up a commission to revise the state's "Blue Laws" and worked to help strikers in labor disputes. He was not able to succeed himself under the 1844 Constitution, so he waited for one term until he could be reelected in 1931. His second term was concerned with the problems of the Depression, as many citizens were out of work or near-starving. Also, new regulations on narcotics and liquor were passed. In 1935 he resigned the governorship to begin his term as a U.S. Senator. He served in Washington under the "New Deal" administration until 1938, when he was once again elected Governor of New Jersey. This third term was concerned with legalized horse race betting, price fixing of gasoline and liquor sales and other price controls. Moore returned to his law practice after 1941, and died in Jersey City.

LARSON, MORGAN F.— (1882-1961), forty-seventh governor of New Jersey (1929-32), was born in Perth Amboy, New Jersey. His parents were Peter and Regina Knudson Larson, Danish immigrants. He received a public school education at his home town, and then studied engineering at Cooper Union (B.S. 1907 and C.E. 1910). While attending college at night, he supported himself by working with a surveying corps in Perth Amboy and during the period he was studying for his second degree he served as county engineer for Middlesex County in 1907-10. He then organized the engineering firm of Larson & Fox, Perth Amboy, and he continued as a partner in this enterprise until 1953. He was also interested in banking and was a director of the Perth Amboy Trust Company and of other financial institutions. Larson was in charge of a number of engineering projects for city and county governments, which gave him an interest in the workings of politics. He was a Republican. In 1917-23 he was city engineer at Perth Amboy and in 1923-27 was Middlesex County's chief engineer. In 1921, Larson was elected to the state senate, serving for three terms all together. He was majority leader in the 1925 session, and president of the senate in 1926. He left the senate in 1928 when he was elected governor of New Jersey, a seat he held for one three year term before former Governor Arthur Moore took over again. When he left he resumed his engineering work in Perth Amboy as a consultant. He was named the first state commissioner of conservation in 1945, and held the post until 1948. He was then a consulting engineer at the Division of Water Policy and Supply of New Jersey, position he held until he died. For a number of years he was also a consultant to the Port Authority of New York. Larson was a specialist in water conservation and management in New Jersey. Private water companies as well as city governments called upon his services when they needed help. Larson was also interested in state highway development, as evidenced in his state senate bills. After he became governor he continued these efforts, and in 1930 was able to submit a referendum to the voters for a $100 million bond issue for the construction of public roads, which was passed that year.

Throughout his term, Larson tried to stem the growth of overlapping commissions in the legislature. This caused a rift between him and the lawmakers, but he was able to get a ruling passed that required lighterage fees between New York and New Jersey to be equalized. New York City was also forced to stop disposing garbage off the New Jersey coast, by order of the Supreme Court after Governor Larson's complaint. He also established friendlier relations between New Jersey and Delaware so that a 150 years old boundary dispute was resolved. A state Tax Department and a State Purchasing Department were also created during his term. After leaving the governorship, Larson continued his consulting business, working with charitable organizations in Perth Amboy until his death there. He received an honorary LL.D. degree from Rutgers University in 1929.

PRALL, HORACE GRIGGS— (1881-1951), acting governor of New Jersey (1935), was born to Abraham J. and Mary Hill Prall at their farm near Ringoes, New Jersey. He studied at the State Model School at Trenton and then was accepted to Harvard University, from which he received a B.A. in 1906. Two years later, New York University Law School graduated him with an LL.B. degree. He first practiced in New York, but was admitted to the New Jersey Bar in 1915. He opened an office in Lambertville in 1916. He was elected to the state assembly in 1926 and 1927, and then held a seat in the state senate until 1936. As president of the senate, he was appointed to assume the governorship when A. Harry Moore resigned. He held the seat for only one week, however, until Governor-elect Hoffman could be inaugurated. After his senate term was up, Prall was a judge of the New Jersey court of common pleas in 1937-42. He then returned to his practice in Lambertville and was active in the Delaware Valley Protective Association. He died in Trenton.

HOFFMAN, HAROLD G.— (1896-1954), forty-ninth governor of New Jersey (1935-38), was born in South Amboy, New Jersey, the son of Frank and Ada Crawford Thom Hoffman. He attended the public schools in town, graduating from high school in 1913. He enlisted as a private in the New Jersey infantry in 1917 as the war in Europe intensified. He was a captain by the time of his discharge in 1919, and returned to South Amboy. There, he was elected secretary-treasurer of the city in 1920, serving five years. Meanwhile, he was a New Jersey assemblyman in 1923 and 1924.

He was elected mayor of South Amboy in 1925-27. He was also an active Republican, being elected a delegate to the 934, 1935, 1936 and 1937 state conventions and to the 1936 national convention. He served two terms in the U.S. House of Representatives (1927-31), and then was made commissioner of motor vehicles for New Jersey in 1931. He ran for governor of the state in 1934 successfully, and was inaugurated in January 1935. The legislature, influenced by New Deal politics, was not receptive to the conservative Hoffman's plans for funding programs for the unemployed and needy. A new two percent sales tax was first approved and then repealed within few months. Many new commissions were organized during this term, however, and new trade laws were established. Hoffman left office to become director of the New Jersey Unemployment Compensation commission, where he served until 1942 when he left to join the Army. He began service in World War II as a major, and left in 1946 with the rank of colonel. At that time, he returned to his former directorship of the Compensation Commission. He died several years later at New York City. Hoffman wrote *Getting Away With Murder, Mile a Minute Men* and *The Crime, The Case, The Challenge* .

EDISON, CHARLES— (1890-1969), fifty-first governor of New Jersey (1941-44), was born in West Orange, New Jersey, the son of the inventor Thomas Alva Edison and Mina Miller Edison. He received his preparatory education at the Dearborn-Morgan school and Cartaret academy in Orange, New Jersey, and the Hotchkiss School in Lakeville, Connecticut. He attended the massachusetts Institute of Technology during 1909-13. He then spent a year with the Edison Illuminating Company in Boston. Returning to Orange in 1915 he performed various duties with the Edison industries, developing an unusual gift for organization and management, but unlike his famous father, no talent for mechanical invention. Shortly thereafter he was made acting manager of certain divisions of the Edison plant at West orange temporarily without a manager, including the Edison Phonograph Works and the Edison Storage Battery Company. In 1916 he became chairman of most of the directing boards of the Edison Industries, in which capacity he supervised the manufacture of war materials at the Edison plant during the first World War. During this period he also served as assistant to his father, who was chairman of the naval consulting board, and as chairman of the West Orange Liberty Loan organization. In 1926 Edison became president and director of Thomas A. Edison, Inc., and of its subsidiaries. In addition to his Edison interests he was also president or director of several manufacturing companies. Edison was first drawn to politics by the Depression in 1933. In that year he was appointed to the New Jersey state recovery board and became a member of the regional labor board organized under the national industrial recovery act. Later he was compliance director for the national recovery administration and state director of the New Jersey division of the national emergency council, a group charged with the responsibility of coordinating the activities of various governmental agencies. In the summer of 1934 he spent much of his time in Washington, assisting in drafting the federal housing administration for the states of New Jersey, Pennsylvania, Delaware and Maryland. In April 1935 President Roosevelt appointed him a member of the national recovery board. In November 1936 the President made him assistant secretary of the Navy to succeed Henry Roosevelt, which office he assumed January 18, 1937. As assistant secretary of the navy he was not only in charge of the shore establishments, including the bureaus of yards and docks, engineering, construction and repair and supplies and accounts, but also had much to do with the bureaus of aeronautics and ordnance. Owing, however, to the illness of the secretary of the Navy, Charles Swanson, he was in reality acting secretary. When Swanson died in 1939, President Roosevelt appointed Edison to fill the vacancy. In 1940, when he received the Democratic nomination for governor of New Jersey, he soon repudiated Mayor Frank Hague's hold on Jersey City, denouncing his "boss" politics. Edison continued his military interests once elected by strengthening New Jersey's defenses. The legislature gave him the right to investigate state departments, and he created a Mediation Board for the state. After leaving office, he was chairman of the board of trustees of Town Hall, Inc. (1944-47), and continued his Edison Company interests. He died in New York City.

DRISCOLL, ALFRED E.— (1902-1975), fifty-third governor of New Jersey (1947-54), was born in Pittsburgh, Pennsylvania to Alfred Robie and Mattie Eastlack Driscoll. He graduated from high school in Haddonfield, New Jersey, and received a B.A. degree from Williams College in Massachusetts in 1925. Three years later he received an LL.B. from Harvard. The next year he began his practice in New Jersey, and became active in Haddonfield politics. In 1938., he was elected to the state senate where he was concerned with housing regulations and laws bearing on juvenile delinquency, provisions for additional funds for handicapped children, and social legislation for black. He was made majority leader of the state senate in 1940. His term ended in 1941, at which time he was appointed commissioner of the State Alcoholic Beverage Control Agency. He held that post until 1947, when he was inaugurated governor after a very successful election. Governor Driscoll was faced with a historic period in the state, as the 1844 Constitution was about to be revised. The old cumbersome document was honed down to a concise 10,000 words, containing the Bill of Rights, provisions for collective bargaining among workers and industrial companies, and for more power in the governor's office. Also, the English-based, overlapping court system was updated, and 100 state departments were reorganized into twenty larger ones. Governor Driscoll also supported a new road act that alloted $5 million each year to local governments for highway improvement and development. In 1948, he also created a turnpike Authority to oversee the toll roads. To pay for these new programs, the governor advocated a small sales tax, and fees for public services. Driscoll was reelected for a second term under the new Constitution, but he was not able to try for a third term. He left office in 1954 and became involved with the Warner-Lambert Company as president until 1967. He was also vice chairman of the President's Commission on Intergovernmental Relations in 1954-55 and was president of the National Municipal League in 1963-67. From 1969 until his death, he was chairman of the New Jersey Turnpike Authority, which he created, as well as the state Tax Policy Commission.

MEYNER, ROBERT B.— (1908-), fifty-fourth governor of New Jersey (1954-62), was born in Easton, Pennsylvania, the son of Gustave Herman and Mary Sophia Baumle Meyner, German immigrants. He attended public schools and then Lafayette College, from which he received an A.B. degree in 1930. The Columbia School of Law gave him an LL.B. degree three years later. He began practice in 1934, serving as a clerk until he could open his own office in Phillipsburg, New Jersey in 1936. The U.S. Supreme Court admitted him to practice in 1940. He began his political career in Warren County as a counsel in 1942, and was unsuccessful in his other attempts for office until 1947, when he was elected to the New Jersey senate. In 1950, he was senate Democratic minority leader, calling for more investigation of organized crime in the state, an issue that would become more important in the 1953 campaign. He was chair of the 1951 Democratic state convention, and two years later was elected governor for a four year term. At the end of this term, he was reelected by a larger margin than the first time. Governor Meyner's administration concentrated on fighting organized crime and official corruption. Also, the budget for state education tripled and the highway programs were substantially enlarged. State employees received pay increases and a better pension system under Governor Meyner's administration. Also, $60 million worth of additional land was bought for parks and recreation under the Green Acres Bond Act. Meyner resumed a law practice in Newark with two other lawyers after his terms. He has also been director of the Prudential Insurance Company and the Phillipsburg National Bank and Trust Company as well as the First National State Bank of Newark.

HUGHES, RICHARD J— (1909-), fifty-fifth governor of New Jersey (1962-70), was born in Florence, New Jersey to Richard P. and Veronica Gallagher Hughes, who were active in the Democratic party. He attended parochial school in Trenton and then took prelaw courses at St. Charles College in Maryland and at St. Joseph's College in Philadelphia. New Jersey Law School gave him an LL.B. degree in 1931, and the next year he began a law practice in Trenton. He soon began working for the Democratic party of Mercer County and was elected president of the young Democrats for new Jersey in 1937. The next year he lost an attempt for a seat in the House of Representatives, but gained attention from important political leaders. In 1939 he was named assistant U.S. attorney for the state, and held the post through the World War II years. In 1945, he resigned to form a law partnership with U.S. Attorney Thorn Lord. The two sought to revitalize the Democratic party in New Jersey and campaigned vigorously for all fellow members who ran for office. In 1949, Hughes was named a judge on the Mercer County court. Republican Governor Driscoll was so impressed with Hughes' record that he named him a judge on the New Jersey Superior Court, and later to the state supreme court's committee on juvenile and domestic relations courts. From 1952 until 1960 he was a member of the advisory council of judges of the National Probation and Parole Association. He worked in Union County, with an office in Elizabeth, but moved to Trenton in 1957 when he was appointed to the New Jersey Superior Appellate Court. However, he resigned the same year for personal and financial reasons, and resumed his private law practice. He ran for governor in 1961 and won by a slight margin after a tight race. In office, he introduced legislation to build local junior colleges, increase teacher's salaries, prohibit discirimination in housing and establish conflict of interest guidelines for state officials. He also cleared the way for development of the Hackensack Meadowlands, which subsequently became the site for a large sports complex. Hughes also approved a three percent sales tax to pay for many new programs and to keep up with inflation. Hughes was reelected in 1965 for another term. When he left office in 1970, he returned to Newark to practice law. In 1973 he was named Chief Justice of the New Jersey Supreme Court. Hughes and his wife Miriam McGrory Hughes have ten children.

CAHILL, WILLIAM T.— (1912-), fifty-sixth governor of New Jersey (1970-74), was born in Philadelphia, Pennsylvania, the son of William P. and Rose Golden Cahill, Irish immigrants. He attended parochial schools and after high school graduation in 1929 began studies at St. Joseph's College in Philadelphia, where he received a B.A. degree in 1933. In 1937, he completed his law studies at Rutgers University. He then worked as a special agent for the F.B.I., traveling to Washington, D.C., Little Rock, Arkansas and St. Louis, Missouri as part of his job. In 1939, he was admitted to the New Jersey bar, and began practice in Camden. He was elected city prosecutor in 1944-46, and in 1948-51 was assistant prosecutor of Camden County. As a special deputy attorney general of New Jersey, he helped investigate organized crime in 1951. That year, he was also elected to the state assembly. Two years later, he returned to his private law practice, setting up a partnership in Camden in 1956. In 1958, he was elected to the U.S. Congress, representing an urbanized, largely Democratic district, although he was a Republican. He served from 1959 to 1970, when he was inaugurated governor of New Jersey. At the beginning of the 1970s, Cahill was faced with governing a state that was the most densely populated in the nation, with a growing business climate, but with very low taxes, posing huge problems in the state budget. His administration increased the sales tax from three to five percent, and the State tax Commission was reorganized. He also changed the status of county prosecutors to a full time position appointed by the governor, which freed the office from the influence of organized criminals. A state Housing Authority was also created during his term. Cahill switched parties in the 1973 election, but did not receive the Democratic nomination for reelection. Instead, he resumed a law practice in Camden.

BYRNE, BRENDAN T.— (1924-), fifty-seventh governor of New Jersey (1974-82), was born in West Orange, New Jersey to Francis A., an Essex County official, and Genevieve Brennan Byrne. His family was active in Democratic politics, and young Brendan followed suit. After serving in the Air Force during World War II, he entered Princeton University, from which he obtained a B.A. in 1949. In 1951, he received an LL.B. degree from Harvard and began a practice in Newark. He was assistant counsel to Governor Robert Meyner in 1955-56, and then executive secretary to the governor in 1956-58. The governor then named him prosecutor of Essex County, in which position he investigated corrupt construction contractors and an infamous organized crime leader Anthony "Tony Boy" Boiardo. In 1968, he was appointed president of the New Jersey Public Utilities Commission. Two years later, Governor Cahill appointed him to be a judge on the state Superior Court, where he declared the state's capital punishment laws unconstitutional. In early 1973, he announced to Governor Cahill that he would contest him in the next election. There were some questions about corruption within Cahill's administration, and the financing of his 1969 campaign, so Byrne appeared a "clean" politician, free of the dark influence of political bosses and organized criminals. Byrne won by a 721,000 majority. His first few months in office were relatively easy, but in 1973, the state supreme court declared that funding of public schools by property tax revenues was unconstitutional. Another funding source had to be found, but the legislature and the voters were opposed to a state income tax. However, when the public schools were closed for lack of funds in 1976, the legislature finally approved the first income tax. Governor Byrne also had to order gasoline rationing during the 1974 shortage, as well as the nation's first auto emission standards testing. He supported public financing of gubernatorial campaigns, and approved legalized gambling in the casinos of Atlantic City, which did much to boost the state's economy. He was reelected in 1977, but could not succeed himself for a third term under the 1947 constitution.

KEAN, THOMAS— (1935-), fifty-eighth governor of New Jersey (1982-), was born in Livingston, New Jersey. His father was a wealthy Congressman who represented the state for twenty years. Young Thomas attended St. Mark's School in Massachusetts before entering Princeton University. He graduated with a degree in history in 1957 and immediately entered the Army National Guard for one year. he helped his father in an unsuccessful race for U.S. Senator in 1958, gaining his first experience in public speaking and politics. However, he wasn't interested in his own political career at this point. Instead, he moved to New York City where he worked for and investment company and for a Ph.D. in history and education from Columbia University. In the early 1960s, he abandoned his studies to teach school at St. Mark's academy and to help former Pennsylvania governor William Scranton in his Presidential campaign. By 1967, Kean was promoting his own campaign for a state legislative seat, which he won. For ten years he sat in the assembly, acting as its speaker for one year. Kean tried to win a seat in Congress in 1974 and the position of Governor of New Jersey in 1977, but was unsuccessful until 1981, when he defeated the popular James Florio. The election was close, but Kean found support from New Jerseyans who believed Republican fiscal policies could help the state's ailing economy. Kean has been called a very frugal man, and he admits, "I'm cheap." Kean and his wife, the former Deborah Bye, have three children.

Biographies
of
Famous New Jerseyans

BURR, AARON— (1756-1836), Revolutionary War soldier and Vice President of the United States, was born in Newark, New Jersey to the clergyman Aaron and Ester Edwards Burr. The parents died while he was a toddler, and he and his sister went to live with an uncle in Elizabethtown, where he was educated by private tutors and religious men. When he was only thirteen, he began studies at Princeton college and graduated in 1772. At first, he aspired to become a clergyman, but after some study, denounced the gospel and began to study law in 1774. Soon afterwards, however, he joined the Revolutionary Movement, first under General Benedict Arnold, and then as a member of General Washington's staff. In 1778 he was made a lieutenant-colonel, and led a regiment from West Orange, New York, but war ravaged his health and morale, and he was forced to resign in 1779. He returned to his law studies in 1780 at Raritan, New Jersey under William Paterson (q.v.), and by 1782 was licensed as an attorney. That same year he married Theodosia Bartow Prevost, the widow of an English officer. He moved to New York the following year to practice in the city, where he accumulated a small fortune from his work. Although he was often opposed by Alexander Hamilton (q.v.) and his associates, Burr entered politics and was eventually elected to the New York assembly (1797-99) and as the state's attorney general (1788). He was a U.S. Senator in 1791-97 and in 1800 was elected Vice President, having received the second highest number of votes after Jefferson, who became President. However, Burr was still seething with hostility against Alexander Hamilton, who was trying to undo Burr's political power. Burr had tried for the New York governorship in 1804, but Hamilton had worked diligently to undermine Burr's reputation, and he lost the election despite early signs of success. This was more than Burr could bear. He challenged Hamilton to a duel, and on July 11, 1804, fatally shot Hamilton. Burr was subsequently indicted for murder, and he fled to his daughter's home in South Carolina to escape the heat. Although the clamor for his conviction eventually died down, and he was able to finish his term as Vice President, Burr was a social outcast while in Washington. Afterwards he engaged in a number of reckless schemes to regain his power. He organized a group intent on taking over a vast tract of land in Mexico and Texas and claiming a new country with Burr as its leader. He also tried to construct a canal around the falls of the Ohio River. He was later accused of talking about seizing the U.S. President and cabinet and establishing himself as a dictator in Washington. While traveling through Ohio, he gained the financial support of the wealthy plantation owner Harman Blennerhasset, and plotted the separation of the Western States and territory from the Union. He was three times tried by federal juries for his schemes, but it wasn't until 1807 that the Virginia U.S. Circuit Court held him for a misdemeanor in organizing an illegal expedition in Spanish territory, but he could not be convicted of an "overt" act of treason. In 1808, Burr went to England, and then on to other European countries in search of support in a takeover of Mexico. He received no such support, and returned to the U.S. in 1812. Until his death, he resided in New York and kept a fairly lucrative law practice. He remarried in 1833, but they divorced before his death at Staten Island. He is buried in Princeton, New Jersey.

CRANE, STEPHEN—(1871-1900), novelist and poet, was born in Newark, New Jersey, the son of Dr. Jonathan and Mary Peck Crane, of a large family. He studied at the Pennington Seminary in New Jersey and at the Hudson River Institute in Claverack, New York. He also attended courses at Lafayette College and Syracuse University, but did not graduate. He moved to New York City to work as a writer for the *Tribune*, but was fired when his account of a parade at Asbury Park, New Jersey was deemed too "satirical." He then worked at the Newark *Morning News*, but spent much of his time with his own writing. His *Maggie, A Girl of the Streets*, which gained the attention of William Dean Howells, among other important literary men of the day. He then published *The Black Riders, and Other Lines*, a book of poems inspired by Emily Dickinson in 1895. He also published his famous *Red Badge of Courage*, an account of the Civil War, the next year. This short story had been written in the summer of 1895, and was a favorite of Howells' who claimed Crane's genius "sprang to life fully armed." The author traveled to Nebraska, Texas and Mexico in the next few years, which inspired his *The Blue Hotel* and *The Bride Comes to Yellow Sky*. In 1896, a boat that was to carry him to Cuba sank offshore of Florida and he suffered fifty hours on the open sea before help came. Crane went to Greece during the Turkish War as a reporter, but returned to the U.S. when culture shock and dysentery became too much of a handicap. Afterwards, he married Cora Taylor and moved to London, where he met Joseph Conrad. He worked as a reporter in Cuba for a few months, but returned to England and lived in a medieval house in Sussex until his death of a hemorrhage while on a vacation at Badenweiter, Germany. Much of his work was collected in the 1921 volume, *Men, Women and Boats.*

EINSTEIN, ALBERT— (1879-1955), physicist, was born in Ulm, Germany, to Hermann and Pauline Koch Einstein. The family lived in Munich for awhile, where his father began a small electrical supply factory. Although his early education was troubled, young Albert amazed his later teachers by his mastery of calculus, analytical geometry and physics when he was only fourteen. He moved with his family to Milan, Italy in 1894, and the next year he began studies at the Polytechnic academy of Zurich, Switzerland. He graduated in 1900 from this school, but was not honored because he had not been very attentive in his lectures; he preferred his own studies in physics and higher mathematics to any of the other subjects taught. He began a job at the Patent Office at Bern, Switzerland, which allowed him time enough to develop five papers on thermodynamics, electrodynamics and the Brownian Movement. He also married Mileva Maric, a Hungarian woman he had met at the Zurich Technical Academy. For his 1906 paper, "A New Determination of Molecular Dimensions," he gained a Ph.D. degree from the University of Zurich, and was appointed a lecturer at the University of Berne. His first lecture before fellow scientists was in 1908, when he delivered a speech on relativity and the constitution of light in Salzburg, Austria. In 1909, the University of Zurich made him a professor, and two years later he was a professor at the German University at Prague. In 1912, he was made professor of physics at his alma mater in Zurich, while serving as a non-resident professor at the University of Leyden. The Royal Prussian Academy of Sciences in Berlin awarded him an honorary professorship in 1914, which gave him the funds to pursue his interests full time. He also became director of the Kaiser Wilhelm Institute for Theoretical Physics in Berlin, all of which enabled him to develop his famous general theory of relativity by 1915, when he was only 35. Einstein had worked on this theory since 1907, when he proposed the equation $E = MC2$. It helped scientists to understand the motions of planets, providing a new explanation of gravitation in terms of the geometric properties of space and time. This theory was successfully tested in 1919, when British scientists examined the light beams passing near the sun during a solar eclipse. Einstein was then propelled into the public limelight and he used his position to promote the Jewish cause and attempts to regain the homeland in Israel. He won the Barnard Gold Medal in 1920 from the National Academy of Sciences, and the Nobel Prize for Physics the next year, among many other awards and honors. Unfortunately, his personal life at the time was in a turmoil; he separated from his first wife in 1914, and remarried a distant cousin, Elsa Einstein, in 1919. During the 1920s, Einstein worked on a "unified field theory" to connect the properties of gravity with electromagnetism. although he laid the groundwork for the quantum theory, he finally rejected it because he thought it depended too much on chance. "God does not play dice," he later explained. The Nazis took over Germany in 1933, while Einstein and his wife were in the U.S. He immediately asked for asylum in America and declared he would not return to his native country. Instead, he was named a professor for the Institute for Advanced Study at Princeton, New Jersey. He failed to develop a unified theory, but continued lecturing, and writing such works as *The World As I See It* (1934); *The Evolution of Physics* (with Leopold Infeld, 1938); and *Out of My Later Years* (1950). In 1938, Einstein warned President Roosevelt of the Nazis' possible development of nuclear bombs, and their devastating effect. However, Einstein always promoted peace; he wrote *Why War?* in 1933 with Sigmund Freud. After World War II, Einstein remained in New Jersey, promoting an international congress as well as peace, before his death at Princeton.

FENWICK, MILLICENT HAMMOND— (1910-), U.S. Congresswoman from New Jersey (1975-), was born in New York City to Ogden H., a financier, and Mary P. Stevens Hammond. Her mother's side of the family was descended from the early railroad builder, John Stevens, and founded the Stevens Institute of Technology in Hoboken. Young Millicent began her education at the private Foxcroft School in Virginia and then lived for a time with her father, who had been named Ambassador to Spain. She then took courses at Columbia University (1933) and the New School for Social Research (1942). She worked as a model for *Harper's Bazaar*, and during the Depression, as an associate editor for Conde Nast Publications. In 1938 she began writing for *Vogue* , and eventually wrote *Vogue's Book of Etiquette* . She left this work in 1952, when family inheritance and investment profits made her independently wealthy. Afterwards, she pursued public affairs more earnestly; she had been on the Bernardsville Board of Education and now she began working for Republican candidates at election time. In 1958-64 she was on the Bernardsville Borough Council, where she gained valuable political experience. Fenwick was chosen vice president of the New Jersey advisory committee to the U.S. Commission on Civil Rights in 1958 as well. In 1969 she ran as a Republican for the New Jersey Assembly, but her two terms in office did not show that she was a conservative by her actions. Instead, she fought for civil rights, consumer needs, prison reform and even an equal rights amendment for women — several years before it became a national issue. Governor Cahill named her director of the state Department of Consumer Affairs in 1972. Two years later, at the age of 64, Ms. Fenwick won a seat in the U.S. Congress. Her success was dubbed a "geriatric triumph" in one newspaper, but she proved capable of handling the busy life of a Congresswoman. She represents the Fifth District of Somerset and Essex Counties, an area of high income suburbs that includes Bernardsville, Fenwick's home. She became a member of the committees on banking, small business and housing. She traveled to Indochina in February 1975 with seven others to study the conditions there and the need for aid. She was on the House ethics committee during her second term; in 1979 she left this and the banking committee to join the foreign affairs and District of Columbia committees, and in 1981 she began working on the education and labor committee. Fenwick remains popular in her district; she gained 78 percent of the vote in 1980. However, an attempt at a U.S. Senate seat in 1982 proved abortive. New Jersey voters elected the Democratic candidate in the face of President Reagan's economic policies. Millicent Fenwick works long hours at her office and at home, but she is able to relax in front of reporters, even lighting up her favorite pipe when she feels like it. She was married, briefly, to Hugh Fenwick (1934-38), and has two children and eleven grandchildren.

FRENEAU, PHILIP M.— (1752-1832), a poet and journalist, was born in New York City. He studied at the College of New Jersey (Princeton), graduated in 1771, and spent the next years perfecting his poetry. He also taught school to support himself, and published General Gage's *Soliloquy* in 1775, among other Revolutionary treatises. However, when independence was declared from England, Freneau was in the West Indies, as an assistant to a Santa Cruz island planter. Before his return to the U.S. in 1778, he had written several poetic tributes to the beauty of the Caribbean island. He joined the New Jersey army in 1778, and began submitting his works to the new *United States Magazine*. In 1780 he visited the West Indies again, and was captured by a British cruiser and held as a prisoner in New York harbor for nearly a year. His experiences there led to his poem, *The British Prison Ship* (1781). *The Freeman's Journal* in Philadelphia began publishing his patriotic poems, but land could not hold him for long and he was a ship captain again in 1784-89. In 1790 he was made editor of the New York *Daily Advertiser*, and soon afterwards was appointed as translator for President Jefferson's State Department. Freneau received Jefferson's support in publishing the *National Gazette* at this time, which criticized Alexander Hamilton. The paper went bankrupt in 1793 and Freneau moved to Mount Pleasant, New Jersey to found the *Jersey Chronicle*. Freneau's later newspaper involvements were with the New York *Time-Piece* (1797-1800), a literary journal. He quit writing when he was only forty-five, after publishing "Tono Checki: The Creek Indian in Pennsylvania." His collected poems were published in 1809 in *Poems Written and Published During the American Revolutionary War* and in 1815 in *A Collection of Poems, on American Affairs*. Freneau never wrote for the aristocrat in early America; his poems were for the common man in a new democracy. He was never well-to-do, and disdained special privileges for any man above another. Jefferson credited him with saving the Constitution, "which was galloping fast into Monarchy," with his poems and essays. Freneau died a very old man in Monmouth County, New Jersey, in a hiking accident.

GRIMKE, ANGELINE E.— (1805-1879), abolitionist who met with other reformers in New Jersey, was born in Charleston, South Carolina, the daughter of Judge John F. Grimke and his wife, who owned a number of slaves. She was educated at home. Following her older sister Sarah's disgust with the slave-owning society, she joined the Quakers in Charleston, but failed to get any of her other family members to stop keeping slaves. When their parents died in 1826, Sarah and Angelina freed all the slaves. Angelina then joined her sister in "voluntary exile" from the South, becoming a member of the Philadelphia Society of Friends in 1831. She wrote an abolitionist article for the

Liberator journal in 1835, which made her prominent in anti-slavery circles. Her "Appeal to Christian Women of the South" was published in London in 1836 and widely distributed by American Quakers. The American Anti-Slavery Society in New York invited her to lecture to men and women in private houses. The Grimkes also actively pursued equal rights for women with their articles "Letters to Catherine Beecher," and "Letters on the Equality of .the Sexes and the Condition of Women," both published in 1838. That same year, Angelina married abolitionist Theodore Weld, a Presbyterian, which caused her ouster from the Society of friends. The Welds and Sarah Grimke then moved to New Jersey, in Raritan Bay Union at Belleville. There they founded a communal group with a school where anti-slavery proponents could develop their ideas. Angelina had three children which she reared there. After 1865 , she moved to Hyde Park, Massachusetts to teach in the Lewis Progressive School. She died there after many years of advocating women's rights and abolition.

HAMILTON, ALEXANDER— (1757-1804), early American statesman and first U.S. Secretary of the Treasury, studied grammar at Elizabethtown, New Jersey, although he was born on an island in the West Indies. Originally intending to become a physician, he studied at King's College (now Columbia University), New York (1773-74) until the Revolution interrupted his studious interest. In 1774, he attended a public meeting near school and although he was only seventeen he addressed the crowd as to the importance of the colonies' cause. In that year he also published a pamphlet against the "calumnies of the enemies" and began writing for Holt's New York *Journal* against British measures. He was soon looked upon as an intellectual prodigy and was dubbed the "Vindicator of Congress." Soon afterwards, he studied military tactics and received a commission in 1776 to command an artillery company authorized by the colonial convention. His success in drilling the men led to an introduction to General Washington, who asked him to become a member of his staff. In 1777, Hamilton was made aide-de-camp and private secretary to Washington with the rank of Lt. Colonel. Although he fought physically throughout New England with the general, his true weapon was his pen, and he used it in correspondences with Congress as well as in his military advice to the most prominent patriots of the time.

In 1780 Hamilton exhibited the first signs of his exceptional financial ability when he brought forth a plan for a U.S. bank, with a main purpose of supplying the army with provisions and ammunition. In a letter to Robert Morris, he also pushed for a constitutional convention, and a representative government. Washington appreciated his foresight and granted him a commandership of an infantry regiment in Lafayette's corps. At the Seige of Yorktown, he helped bring down an important British regiment.

After the war, he rented a house in Albany, New York and studied law with the intention of retiring to private life. Before admission to the bar, he wrote a *Manual on the Practice of the Law* . However, he was soon to return to the politics of the new nation and sat in the Continental Congress of 1782. While there he devoted his time to energizing the new government, especially by establishing a permanent national revenue. He looked for a centralization of the government, writing to Washington, "I have an indifferent opinion of the honesty of this country and ill foreboding of its future system." Although he retired from Congress, he soon reentered public life when in 1786 the convention he had called for all along was held in Annapolis, Maryland. He began writing the greater portion of *The Federalist* , and when Washington was selected president under the new constitution in 1789, he was chosen secretary of the treasury. His quick work and judgement led to the rapid creation of a public credit system by uniting the federal government's properties interests; also gave the country a currency system, banking facilities and important new industries.

However, Hamilton was not modest about his abilities and importance to the government, and this caused conflict with Thomas Jefferson, among others. Hamilton said of Secretary of State Jefferson in 1792 that he was a man of "profound ambition and violent passions," and Jefferson condemned Hamilton's Treasury Department as a "corrupt squadron." At the 1796 election, Hamilton supported John Adams, but when Jefferson was elected four years later, Hamilton left government concerns to retire in New York. Hamilton also opposed Aaron Burr's attempt for the governorship of New York, causing Burr to challenge him to a duel in revenge for his unsuccessful campaign. In the early morning of July 11, 1804, Hamilton fell at the first shot near the banks of the Hudson and died the next day.

HAGUE, FRANK— (1876-1956), Democratic party leader in New Jersey and mayor of the town he was born in, Jersey City (1917-47). He left formal schooling at a young age to become involved in local politics while working as a city hall janitor. He was elected mayor of Jersey City in 1917, and as his influence spread he became one of the most powerful political bosses in U.S. history, with an invincible organization in the city that lasted thirty years. In fact, in 1937 he was able to claim, "I am the law in Jersey City."

His power was not confined only to that area, however. From 1924 on he held the vice chairmanship in the Democratic National Committee and was extremely influential in presidential nominations. He supported Alfred E. Smith in 1932, but quickly joined in Roosevelt's support when he got to the convention, because he knew the candidate's importance to the party. In 1940, he vigorously supported Charles Edison for New Jersey's governor, but after the election Edison refused to conform to Hague's machinery. A bitter feud developed between the two, resulting in Hague's blocking of Edison's attempt to ratify a new state constitution.

Much of Hague's opposition stemmed from his hard line ambitious politics. Jersey City's police force was often used to break up strikes in the city; Hague tolerated no rivals from the state labor groups. In 1931, for example, when the Pulaski Skyway was under construction, Hague sanctioned the hiring of non-union workers despite protests from labor organizers. When Theodore "Teddy" Brandle of the New Jersey Building Trades Council fought back, Hague called him a "labor racketeer" and soon Brandle was powerless and bankrupt.

Hague left the mayoral throne in 1947 and his nephew, Frank Hague Eggers took over. Two years later, however, Eggers lost the city election and the Hague era ended. Hague died in New York City seven years later.

KILMER, A. JOYCE— (1886-1918), poet, was born in New Brunswick, New Jersey to Frederick B. and Annie Kilburne Kilmer. He studied at Rutgers College in 1904-06 and Columbia University, from which he received an A.B. degree in 1908. In the next year, he taught Latin at Morristown (New Jersey) High School, and was hired to help edit the *Standard Dictionary* in 1909. He had married Aline Murray in 1908 and they began their family of four children. In New York, he worked on magazine articles when not editing the dictionary, and in 1912 was made literary editor for the *Churchman* , a publication of the Episcopal church. The next year he began work with the *New York Times Magazine* and *Review of Books* . At the same time, he worked on the poetry section of the *Literary Digest* and *Current Literature*, and was asked to write criticism and prefaces for several new books of the time. He published *Summer of Love* in 1911, *Trees and Other Poems* in 1914, and *Main Street and Other Poems* in 1917 before joining the U.S. Army as a private. The war brought him to France, where he was eventually promoted to sergeant. He died while investigating enemy territory in the Ourcq region of France in July 1918. Kilmer's poetry was inspired by his adopted religion of Catholicism, his love for his wife, and his emotions about war, as in "The White Ships and the Red," and "Prayer of a Soldier in France."

KIRSTEN, DOROTHY— (1917-), opera singer, was born in Montclair, New Jersey to an extremely musical family. Her grandfather was James Beggs, conductor of the Buffalo Bill Band, and her mother and siblings were all involved in music. She took music, dramatics and voice lessons in high school, and then took a job as a "trouble shooter" for the New Jersey Bell Telephone Company in Newark to finance her singing lessons. She was able to sing in radio commercials from time to time and in 1938 began her own daily show. Singer Grace Moore heard her voice later that year, and provided Kirsten with the opportunity to study singing in Rome, Italy. This training helped her to gain volume and range in her voice enough to begin in the opera. She made her concert debut at the 1940 New York World's Fair, and her opera debut a few months later with the Chicago Civic Opera Company as Musette in *La Boheme*. She continued singing with this company until 1942 when she returned to New York to join Fortune Gallo's San Carlo Opera Company. She also sang on the Telephone Hour and the Prudential Family Hour on the radio. In later 1942, she played Vilia in Lehar's *The Merry Widow* at Milburn, New Jersey. In all, she sang in thirty-eight states during the 1942-43 season, having a many as fifteen engagements per month. In 1945, she was hired by the Metropolitan Opera Company, but continued to appear with other companies in Chicago, San Francisco, Mexico and New Orleans. She made her Lewisohn Stadium debut in 1947 for the Metropolitan, performed as Mimi in *La Boheme* (1945), Juliette in *Romeo and Juliette* (1945), and the queen in *L'Amore dei tie re* (1948). She has also sung the roles of Violetta, Cho Cho San, Manon Lescout, Nedda, Fioria, Tosca, Cressida, among many others. She appeared in the movies, *The Great Caruso* and *Mr. Music*. Since her retirement, she has resided in New York City.

LINDBERGH, CHARLES A.— (1902-1974), aviator, was born in Detroit, Michigan, the son of Charles and Evangeline Land Lindbergh. He attended high school in Little Falls, Minnesota, and began mechanical engineering courses at the University of Wisconsin, but was more interested in aviation so he quit school to learn to fly at Lincoln, Nebraska. An expert mechanic and an apt student, Lindbergh was soon performing acrobatic feats with the early airplanes In 1923, he purchased an army surplus plane and practiced with it until he gained a job the next year as a "barnstormer". He trained at U.S. Army flying fields in Texas, and in 1925 was made a first lieutenant in the air corps reserve. In 1926-27 he carried mail between St. Louis and Chicago for the Robertson Aircraft Company. Soon, he began making plans to try to cross the Atlantic on his new monoplane, the *Spirit of St. Louis*. He gained the support of several bankers and businessmen, and after flying from San Diego, California to New York's Roosevelt Field, he set off across the Atlantic on the morning of May 20, 1927. Although he encountered bad weather along the way, he was able to land safely in Paris the next night (Paris time), after thirty-three hours in flight. Lindbergh won worldwide acclaim, and was an instant hero. Later in the year, he made the first non-stop flight between Washington, D.C. and Mexico City, which propelled him even further into the limelight. In Mexico, he met Anne Morrow, daughter of an American diplomat, whom he married two years later. He continued making "good will" tours of many countries in the next few years, collecting hundreds of medals and honors along the way. He became a consultant to Transcontinental Air Transport Company and Pan American Airways in 1929. At that time, he and his wife settled in a large estate near Hopewell, New Jersey, but the two continued flying to exotic places. He set another record in 1930 by flying from California to New York in only fourteen and three quarters hours. Mrs. Lindbergh has described their flying tour of Asia in 1931 in *North to the Orient* (1935). However, the couple's happiness was bashed in 1932 when their first child, Charles III, was kidnapped from their home. Although they paid the $50,000 ransom for his safe return, the Lindberghs were horrified to discover he had been murdered. A German-born carpenter named Bruno Hauptmann was arrested and convicted after many months of sensationalism in his New Jersey trial. The reporters didn't stop hounding the Lindberghs after the case was closed, and they moved to England in 1934 for privacy. In 1936, Lindbergh went to Nazi Germany and reported on their increasing air power, which he found much superior to other European forces. The Nazis bestowed a service cross of the German Eagle on him in 1938, which produced a strong protest from leaders in England and the U.S. He was a colonel in the Army Air Corps upon his return to the U.S. in 1939, but he argued against American involvement in the World War. However, he did serve as a consultant to the Army Air Corps, United Aircraft and the Ford Motor Company during the war. Afterwards, he moved to Connecticut and began writing *Of Flight and Life*, which was published in 1948. In 1953 he published his autobiography, *The Spirit of St. Louis,* which receivd a Pulitzer Prize. In 1954, he was made a general by President Eisenhower and he advised the Department of Defense on the air force during war times. In his later years, Lindbergh was a champion of environmental protection. He remained somewhat of a recluse throughout life, which caused all sorts of the speculation in the more sensational media. Perhaps because of all the sorrow newspaper and radio brought to him, Lindbergh often disdained the "common people," and the mass mentality that surrounded his fame. He died of cancer in Maui, Hawaii, and is buried there.

MCPHEE, JOHN— (1931-), author, was born in Princeton, New Jersey, the son of Harry R., a physician, and Mary Zigler McPhee. He studied at the University in his home town, and after receiving his B.A., traveled to England to pursue graduate studies at Magdelene College, Cambridge in 1953 to 1954. He used his literary talents as a playwright for the Robert Montgomery Presents television show in 1955-57, and the next year began working as an associate editor for *Time*. His wife, the former Pryde Brown and he began a family of four children as he pursued his writing career. In 1963, he was hired as a staff writer for the *New Yorker*, which allowed him the time to work on his first book, *A Sense of Where You Are,* published in 1965. He wrote a biography of Frank Boyden of the Deerfield Academy in 1966 in *The Headmaster*, and a whimsical scientific account of *Oranges* in 1967. He described New Jersey's wild country in *The Pine Barrens* (1968), and other biographical books in the next few years. He remarried in 1972 to the horticulturist Yolanda Whitman, gaining four stepchildren in the process. He continued to write at least one book per year in addition to his *New Yorker* articles and pieces for *Holiday, National Geographic, Playboy* and

Atlantic. He chooses unlikely topics such as an experimental airplane in *The Deltoid Pumpkin Seed* (1973), and disposal of nuclear waste in *The Curve of Binding Energy* (1974). His articles were collected in *Pieces of the Frame* in 1975, and *The John McPhee Reader* (1977) before he wrote his well-read account of a maturing Alaska in *Coming Into the Country* (1977). For this work, he received an award in literature from the American Academy of Arts and Letters (1977) and an honorary Ph.D. degree from Bates College in 1978. He continues to write for the *New Yorker* and other magazines and to live in Princeton, New Jersey, where he often lectures on journalism.

MAILER, NORMAN— (1923-), author, was born in Long Branch, New Jersey, the son of Isaac B. an accountant, and Fanny Schneider Mailer. The family moved to Brooklyn in 1927, where he attended Boys High School and kept himself busy building model airplanes and writing "An Invasion of Mars," which filled two school notebooks. He entered Harvard University as an engineering student when he was only sixteen, but he began to write more seriously, and this took up much of his time. His short story, "The Greatest Thing in the World," won the 1941 college contest at *Story* magazine. In the summer of 1942, he worked at a state mental hospital, which inspired him to write "A Transit to Narcissus," although it was never published. He gained his engineering degree from Harvard in 1943, but was soon drafted into the Army. He served in the Phillippines and Japan until 1946, when he returned to New York City and began writing his first novel, *The Naked and the Dead* (1948). This book sold nearly 200,000 copies in its first year, and made Mailer an overnight success. he followed this with *Barbary Shore* in 1951, which wasn't so well received because of its twisted dealings with Communism, and the authoritarian American government of the post-war years. His political concerns bought him into writing non-fiction articles as well, for the *Village Voice, Dissent, Esquire* and *Life*. He had helped found the *Village Voice* newspaper in Greenwich Village, New York, in 1951, and began to espouse his philosophy of "Hip" or "American Existentialism" within its pages. His third novel, *The Deer Park* (1955), shocked readers with its unusual sexuality. At this time, a friend has said, Mailer "was living up to the code that the worst violation of life was to play it safe." Apparently, his second wife, Adele, fell victim to this code in 1960, when Mailer wounded her with a pen knife. However, Adele refused to press charges. Mailer quieted his life a bit after this, writing articles for *Esquire* on John F Kennedy as well as poetry, which was collected in *Deaths fo. Ladies, and Other Disasters* (1962). He wrote a horror-filled novel, *An American Dream* in 1965. and then a politically pointed work of fiction, *Why Are We in Vietnam?* in 1967. The next year he wrote *The Armies of the Night*, a "history as a novel, the novel as history" of the great anti-war protests of the time. His next works were semi-fictionalized as well as non-fictional. His *Marilyn*, a photo-biography of Marilyn Monroe was a bestseller in 1973, and he continued writing in the 1970s. In 1980 he published *The Executioner's Song*, which he called "A True Life Novel" about convicted killer Gary Gilmore and his execution. Mailer was more recently connected with another prisoner, whom he found to have writing talent. The convict was released from prison after Mailer and other writers vouched for his rehabilitarion, but soon afterwards the man killed a disagreeable waiter in a restaurant, and was sent back. Mailer has been married six times and has six children. He published *Ancient Evenings* in 1983.

ORATAMIN— (?-1667), also spelled *Oratam, Oratan, Oraton, o Oritany*, was a seventeenth century Hackensack chief in present new Jersey who exercised prominent roles in treaty relations between the Dutch and neighboring Indian tribes, especially the Esopus. A period of border warfare between the Dutch and ten o eleven area tribes was caused by the slaughter of 80-120 Indian. at Pavonia and Corlaer's Hook (February 25, 1643). Oratami represented the Hackensack, Tappan, Manhattan, Kitchawan and Sitsink in a treaty of forgive and forget signed April 22, 1643 Although new hostilities led by younger warriors erupted im mediately, a new treaty drawn at Fort Amsterdam. New Netherlands (August 30, 1645) through Oratamin's efforts led to general peace among all the Indians. Through 1660 Oratami participated in and often initiated discussions that establishe the principle of negotiation to settle all inter-tribal and triba settler disputes, and brought about peace treaties between th Dutch and Wappinger (May 18, 1660) and finally Esopus (Jul 15,1660), who had been the constant enemy of the settlers and disgrace to the surrounding Indian nations. The Wappinger aide the Esopus in hostility against the Dutch. wishing to contain th war, Oratamin served as an intermediary and "intelligence o ficer" for Peter Stuyvesant, governor of New Netherlands. Oratamin, with the Nyack chief Matteno, was called upon to establish negotiations between the two sides. By November 1663, after the Wappinger and Esopus were informed that the British would not assist them, an armistice was called. With the return of Dutch captives held by the Indians, three Esopus chiefs presented themselves at Fort Amsterdam and formalized a peace treaty (May 16, 1664) ratified by most of the surrounding Indian nations and for which Oratamin and Mateno offered themselves as security.

PIKE, ZEBULON— (1779-1813), soldier and explorer, was born in Lamberton, New Jersey, the son of Major Zebulon and Isabella Brown Pike. He attended country schools before entering his father's regiment as a cadet. By the age of 20, young Zebulon was made a first lieutenant serving along the western U.S. frontier. He was assigned to explore the source of the Mississippi in 1805 at the head of a company of twenty men, but only got as far as Lake La Sue (now Leech Lake), Minnesota, and believed that to be the big river's source. He returned to St. Louis in 1806 with the false information, but his proven ability as a pioneer gave him another appointment to explore the Louisiana Purchase up the Missouri River and on to the source of the Red (Canadian) River. He reached Pawnee County in September 1806 and in November caught his first glimpse of the Rocky Mountains. He explored the head of the Arkansas, the South Platte and then back to the area now known as Royal Gorge. On one hiking trip into the mountains, he saw the 14,000 foot peak that now bears his name, but which he called "Grand Peak." It wasn't until the 1830s that it became known as Pike's Peak. After this exploration, he followed the Rio Grande del Norte until he met some Spanish guards who claimed he was on their territory. The New Mexico governor connected Pike with Aaron Burr's conspiracy to take over Mexico, but let him go back to the United States Territory in mid 1807. Soon afterwards, he was promoted to captain and then lieutenant-colonel in 1809. Although he was still connected with the Burr scheme, Secretary of War Henry Dearborn dismissed all of these charges. He was commissioned colonel in 1812, and when the War broke out against Britain, Pike was made brigadier general, and was assigned to lead men at Toronto. His regiment won the battle, but he died when a British gunpowder magazine exploded. Pike had published *An Account of Expedi-*

tions to the Sources of the Mississippi and Through the Western Parts of Louisiana in 1810. Monuments to the explorer stand at Cortland, Kansas and Colorado Springs, Colorado.

PITCHER, MOLLY (MARY LUDWIG MCCAULEY)— (1744-1832), Revolutionary War heroine, was born near Trenton, New Jersey, the daughter of German immigrant John George Ludwig Hass, who dropped his surname when he arrived in America. She became a servant to Dr. William Irvine of Carlisle, Pennsylvania in 1769 and soon afterward married John C. Hays. He enlisted as a Revolutionary soldier in 1775 and in 1777 joined the seventh Pennsylvania Regiment. Mrs. Hays joined her husband at camp, washing the officers' clothing and tending the wounded. At the Battle of Monmouth, New Jersey, which was conducted in 96° heat, she carried water from a nearby spring to the soldiers, which gained for her the now-famous nickname of "Molly Pitcher." Molly's husband was wounded during a British charge in this battle, and when his company wanted to remove their cannon because of it, Molly seized the musket and vowed she would revenge her husband's injury. Her hard work helped the American side to win, and the next day General Washington commissioned her sergeant. She may have served in the army for eight years afterward, and then lived with her husband at Carlisle as a cook and laundress for the soldiers. She also worked as a nanny and owned a small store for a time. Hays died in 1789, and a few years later she married Sgt. George McCauley, but he didn't work and often beat her. The Pennsylvania Assembly recognized her services during the Revolution by presenting her with an award of forty dollars in 1822, along with a guaranteed annuity of the same amount, which helped her through old age. She died in Carlisle, and her grave was marked with monuments in 1876 and 1916. She is also depicted in a marker at the site of the Battle of Monmouth.

ROBESON, PAUL— (1898-1976), singer and actor, was born in Princeton, New Jersey, the son of Anna L. (Bustill) and William D. Robeson, a former slave who eventually became a Lutheran minister. Young Paul did well in his early education and then was able to attend Rutgers College on a scholarship. He graduated with honors for both his studies and his athletic achievements in 1919, and then worked on his LL.B. degree from Columbia

University (1923). He worked for a law firm in New York, but soon abandoned this career for one in acting. he had impressed playwright Eugene O'Neill so much when he had played in an amateur Y.M.C.A. production that in 1923 he offered him a role in *Taboo* and later *Emperor Jones*, which showed both in New York and London. It was in this last play that Robeson began using his voice, and, encouraged by friends, he studied singing. He continued acting, in *All God's Chillun Got Wings* in 1924, and then in *Show Boat* and *Othello*. His concerts of Negro Spirituals were the most well-received, however, and took him all over the U.S. and Western Europe as well as the Soviet Union. Returning to America in the Great Depression, he continued to sing in concert and in musicals, but he preferred Europe, especially Russia where he had seen no racial prejudice. He returned to Broadway in 1940 in *John Henry*, and then sang for radio and made over 300 recordings. In the next few years, he appeared in such films as *Emperor Jones, King Solomon's Mines, Dark Sands, Jericho* and *Song of Freedom*. During World War II, he campaigned for the sale of War Bonds. But Robeson was not unreservedly patriotic; he had quit the law profession because of discrimination more than to pursue his acting abilities. He sent his son to the Soviet Union for school in hopes of escaping this sense of injustice, and often showed more kinship with Europe than America. Robeson was not content to be a token black person in show business. He used his fame and influence to help any cause he saw to be good for black people. As he grew older, he refused stereotypcial roles that were offered to him, and began experimenting with African rhythms in his concerts and recordings. he believed in the "oneness of humankind," and could not tolerate bigots. This advocacy, often bordering on radicalism, put his career at a standstill after 1950. For over a decade he toured Europe, but returned to his home in New York City in 1963.

ROTH, PHILIP— (1933-), author, was born in Newark, New Jersey, the son of Herman and Bess Finkel Roth. His Jewish family life was the setting for many of his later novels and short stories. He attended Rutgers University in New Jersey in 1950-51 and then received his A.B. degree from Bucknell University in 1954. Afterwards, he studied and taught English literature at the University of Chicago, from which he received an M.A. degree in 1956. He was a visiting lecturer at the University of Iowa in 1960-62, and taught at Princeton and the University of Pennsylvania after his writing career was established. His first stories appeared in small literary journals during the 1950s, a period that has been called a "Jewish Renaissance" in literature. His first novel, *Goodbye, Columbus*, was published in 1959, and won the National Book Award for fiction. It was made into a movie ten years later. his works were sometimes called "dark" and "brooding", but his 1969 novel *Portnoy's Complaint* was an attempt to rewrite the gloominess of Kafka into a slapstick, Marx Brothers manner. The book sold half a million copies in its first hardcover year, and millions more in paperback in subsequent years. It was called a "technical masterpiece," which brought "the genre of the so-called Jewish novel to an end on a new point of departure." A Jewish writer writing about Jewish life, Roth was not always flattering, which raised a storm of protest from people who claimed he was anti-Semitic. Roth carried a Kafkaesque story to a ridiculous extreme again in 1972, with his novel, *The Breast*, in which a man wakes up to find he has metamorphosed into a large female breast. Roth's sexual imagery has been linked to comedian Lenny Bruce's influence. Many reviewers criticized women's non-role in Roth's books, especially in *Portnoy's Complaint*. His later novels are *The Professor of Desire* (1977) and *The Ghost Writer* (1979), both published by Farrar, Straus.

SINATRA, FRANK— (1915-), singer and actor, was born in Hoboken, New Jersey to Anthony M. and Natalie Garaventi Sinatra, Italian immigrants. He played the ukelele as a boy, and was a member of the band at Hoboken Demarest High School, but it wasn't until he was twenty-one that he decided to become a professional singer. He worked as a copy boy at the *Jersey Observer* for awhile after high school, but then on a fluke he quit the job and began singing with local bands. In 1937 he won first prize with one band in the Major Bowes' Amateur Hour, a radio show, which allowed him to tour the country. He then sang at the Rustic Cabin, a New Jersey roadhouse, and in 1939 did a few local radio shows. He married Nancy Barbato that same year. Harry James, a trumpeter with Benny Goodman's big band at the time, heard Sinatra on one radio show and asked him to be the singer in his own new band. After only a few months with James, Sinatra joined Tommy Dorsey's band, however. The songs they produced became hit records and in 1942, Sinatra broke away to become his own star. He was billed as "The Voice," or "The Crooner" in large concerts and gained a loyal following. In 1943 he starred in

Higher and Higher , the first of many movies he sang and acted in. It also meant success and the Hollywood lifestyle, which eventually broke up his first marriage (1951) as well as marriages to Ava Gardner and other actresses. In the 1950s Sinatra had his own television show, first on CBS and then on ABC. As his earnings grew, he made more and more business investments some of which were questionable. He formed a "clan" of business associates, including Sammy Davis, Jr., which was often criticized in the press, and was vaguely connected with underworld activities. In the 1970s, Sinatra made a dramatic comeback in the popular music charts with his *Ol' Blue Eyes* album and concert tours. He performs in Las Vegas and large entertainment venues throughout the country, and resides in California, among other places.

SPRINGSTEEN, BRUCE— (1949-), singer and author of New Jersey's "unofficial rock theme," was born in Freehold in central New Jersey. His parents were Douglas and Adele Springsteen. He was not interested in his studies at a local parochial school, but was impressed with the singing of Elvis Presley and other rockabilly stars of the time. He bought his first guitar when he was thirteen and within a year he had learned enough to play with others in small bands. He attended a community college in New Jersey for awhile but dropped out to devote all of his time to playing and writing music. With such bands as Steel Mill and Dr. Zoom and the Sonic Boom, he performed in Greenwich Village cafes and high school dances. He moved to San Francisco for awhile, played at the Fillmore West with a band called Child, but returned to the East Coast after failing a record company audition. In 1972 he met producer Mike Appel, who became his manager and promoted him to an audition with Columbia Records. Columbia hired him after hearing Springsteen sing "It's Hard to be a Saint in the City." Talent development executive John Hammond said later that Springsteen sounded better than Bob Dylan had in his first audition. In 1973, *Greetings from Asbury Park* was released. The album was not commercially successful outside a small area of the Northeastern U.S., and neither was the second, *The Wild, The Innocent and the E Street Shuffle* . Springsteen and his E Street Band then went on a long concert tour, first as the opening act for major bands at large auditoriums and then at smaller clubs around the country, where he could get his hard times lyrics across to more receptive crowds. When *Rolling Stone* magazine editor Jon Landau saw him perform in Cambridge, Massachusetts, he exclaimed, "I saw rock and roll future and his name is Bruce Springsteen." This gave Springsteen a renewed faith in himself and began a long friendship between the songwriter and critic. Ironically, Landau co-produced Springsteen's next album, *Born to Run*, amid a barrage of legal complications with ex-manager Appel. *Born to Run* proved to be a phenomenal success, with several songs reaching the popular record charts. In 1980 the title song, "Born to Run," was voted New Jersey's unofficial rock theme by the state assembly, reaffirming the feeling people have to the lyrics of a native Jerseyan, even if the song is about *leaving* places like many New Jersey cities. After three years of legal squabbling with ex-manager Appel, Springsteen produced his next album, *Darkness on the Edge of Town* (1978), which was less rousing and more brooding than his previous works. His later albums were *The River* (1981), a two-record set, and *Nebraska* (1982). He draws huge crowds to his amphitheater concerts.

TEEDYUSCUNG— (c.1700-1763), was a Delaware Indian leader in colonial Pennsylvania and New Jersey during the period of land cessions and frontier wars which forced these Indians westward toward the Ohio country. He advocated a policy of resistance to white pressures and attained notoriety as a Delaware spokesman at numerous treaties and councils.

Teedyuscung was born about 1700 in New Jersey, near present-day Trenton, and lived with his kinfolk in the remnant Indian community there until about 1730, when the family moved across the Delaware River and settled along the Lehigh Valley. From this location the Indians were ousted in 1737 by the so-called Walking Purchase. The purchase allegedly covering these lands had actually been made years before but it was not until 1737 that, according to the provisions of a later agreement, two white men well-supplied walked off its extent in a day and a half. The Indians protest, charging that the intent had been to alienate far less land, and that the government of Pennsylvania was perpetrating a fraud. Resentment over the Walking Purchase was in large part responsible for Teedyuscung's and other Delaware Indians' demands at later treaties and eventually for the defection of Teedyuscung's band to the French side during the French and Indian War.

At first, however, Teedyuscung attempted to remain on the lands. But white settlers began to enter the Forks of the Delaware, and the Iroquois — who claimed authority of sorts over the Delaware — in 1742 ordered the Delaware of the Forks to vacate their lands and in 1749 the Iroquois purported to sell these and other lands to the Penns. Many of the Indians now left for new homes on the Susquehanna. But Teedyuscung remained, converting to the Moravian faith and going to live in the communal settlement of some 500 Christian Indians at Gnadenhutten, north of the Moravian headquarters at Bethlehem. He remained there until 1754, when along with most of the others, under Iroquois insistence, he removed to Wyoming, on the Susquehanna (where Wilkes-Barre now stands). His political career dates from that move.

Before 1754 and his death in 1763, Teedyuscung was active as a council speaker for the Delaware Indians. During the hostilities on New Jersey's and Pennsylvania's frontiers, he was a warrior and leader of the warrior's faction of the Delaware. The policy of this faction was to use the military crisis to extort concessions from the province of Pennsylvania, threatening (and occasionally carrying out) reprisal raids if redress were not offered for land grievances and if Pennsylvania did not cease to endorse (or even promote) the Iroquois claims to sovereignty over the Delaware. At a series of council meetings with whites from 1756 to 1760, he articulated the Delaware position in eloquent speeches. These speeches were set down in English translation and published in the minutes of Indian treaties printed by Benjamin Franklin. He came thus to be widely known as a persuasive spokesman for the Indian interest for the entire East Coast.

Teedyuscung was given political support by the Quakers of the province who wanted to embarrass their opponents, the Proprietary party, by publicizing the Delaware charges of misconduct in Indian affairs. This did not endear him to the government of Pennsylvania, or to Sir William Johnson, the Crown's superintendant of Indian Affairs, and they did much to discredit him. He died at Wyoming, Pennsylvania, however, in the course of resisting invasion of that place by Connecticut settlers; it is alleged that he was murdered.

Teedyuscung's diplomacy was unable to prevent the rapid erosion of the Indian position in the east. Whether or not his specific charges were valid may be questionable. However, he was a widely cited symbol of Indian resistance to white rapacity because of the publicity given to his cause by the Quakers and the printing of the Indian treaties. He and other Indian spokesmen like him were able to inspire among the whites who. working within their own political system, were able to insist on an Indian policy less destructive to the Indians than that desired by many frontiersmen and land speculators.

WESTON, EDWARD— (1850-1933), electrical engineer, was born in London, England. His parents sent him to the best schools and tutors in hopes of enabling him to become a doctor, but he turned his attention to physical science instead. He emigrated to the United States in 1870, beginning work at the American Nickel-Plating Company in New York City. There, he improved the company's plating methods. His leisure time was spent making electrical experiments and by 1872 his successes in these led to his quitting the Nickel-Plating Company to devote full time to electricity. In 1875, he established the first dynamo-electric machinery factory in the nation at Newark. The Weston Dynamo Company was organized in 1877, and in 1881 absorbed several rivals to become the Unites States Electric Lighting Company. He was electrician to the company until 1889, when Westinghouse bought it out, but Weston continued as a chief stockholder afterwards. He displayed his own electrical inventions at Philadelphia in 1884. Most of his dynamometers, ohm meters, volt-meters and incandescent lamps were developed at his Newark laboratory. The Weston Electrical Instrument Plant eventually made phonograph players, radio and aircraft instruments as well. Outstanding is Weston's "Photonic" photo-electric cell, developed in 1931. It was used at the Century of Progress Exposition in Chicago in 1933 to pick up rays from the star Arcturus which in turn powered the electric light that officially opened the exhibition.

WHITMAN, WALT— (1819-1892), poet and essayist, was born in West Hills, Long Island, New York, on a farm. His parents were Walter and Louisa Van Velson Whitman, and he had eight brothers and sisters. The family moved to Brooklyn in 1823, where Walter studied in the public schools, but his best memories were of summer trips to the seashore on Long Island. When he was only eleven, he quit school to become a lawyer's and then a doctor's assistant. In the meantime, Walter read voraciously, joining a lending library, and soon he was interested in printing and newspapers. He was a printer's apprentice at the Long Island *Patriot* and the *Star*, and then learned the compositor trade in New York. His family moved back to Long Island in 1833, and three years later the poet joined them. He began to write what he called "sentimental bits" for the *Patriot* as well as the New York *Mirror* . He also taught in rural schools and decided to start his own newspaper with his savings. In 1838-39, he published and edited the *Long Islander* at Huntington, but he soon wished to return to New York City. For a brief time, he was an active Democrat, speaking in 1841 at a Tammany Hall meeting. In the next few years he worked for several newspapers and magazines in the city. His contributions to the *Democratic Review* , a literary journal, made him known to the major writers of the day, such as Hawthorne, Longfellow, Poe, Thoreau and others. His first works were mostly stories and melodramatic poems. He traveled south to work on the New Orleans *Crescent* . However, he stayed (with his brother) only three months before setting out on a tour of St. Louis, Chicago and the Great Lakes. He returned to newspaper work in Brooklyn in 1848, while continuing his own writing on the side. He edited the Brooklyn *Times* in 1857-59, but by this time his *Leaves of Grass* had been published (1855), and he was attracting considerable attention in the literary world. Most critics hated it, especially those who couldn't understand the twelve untitled poems within it. Emerson, however, marveled at the "wonderful gift of *Leaves of Grass* ." He continued to work on poems, and eventually joined the company of other artists connected with New York journalism, in the "Bohemian Club." A second edition of *Leaves of Grass* was published in 1860, and soon literary critics in London recognized Whitman and praised him more than his compatriots had. As the Civil War began, however, he moved to Washington and from there to the battlefront, where he helped in army hospitals. During this time, he wrote constantly, but his *Drum Taps* and *Memoranda During the War* were published after 1865. Whitman contracted a paralyzing fever during his missions to the soldiers and while he was recovering, his mother died, which sent him into a second fit. He was physically handicapped for the rest of his life. Lincoln had appointed him a clerk in the Department of the Interior, but he was fired after the president's death because Secretary Harland didn't like having the author of a scandalous book in his department. The paralysis caused Qhitman to quit his next job in the Attorney General's office, and he moved to his brother's house in Camden, New Jersey. His works were then published under the titles *Specimen Days and Collected Poems* (1883); *November Boughs* (1885) and *Sands at Seventy* (1888). Meanwhile, *Leaves of Grass* was republished several times. He took short trips to Boston, to Canada (1880) and to Colorado (1879), but generally did not leave Camden. He died there after many years of illness. Although George Santanaya once called Whitman's work "barbarism," of the mind, Robert Louis Stevenson said later, "something straightforward, something simple and surprising distinguishes his poems. We fall upon Whitman...into the huge and thoughtful night."

WILLIAMS, WILLIAM CARLOS— (1883-1963), poet, author and physician, was born in Rutherford, New Jersey, where he attended local schools. His parents were William and Raquel Williams, who encouraged him to read the classics. However, young William was more interested in math and science, and began studying biology and then medicine at the University of Pennsylvania. There, he met Ezra Pound, who came to be his mentor and good friend. He joined with Pound and other poets in what is known as the Imagist movement, which delighted Williams because of the lack of concrete law and order, which he was growing tired of. He received his medical degree from the University in 1906 and moved to the "Hell's Kitchen" area of New York City. He did graduate work at the University of Leipzig, and then traveled through Italy and Spain before settling to him lifelong practice in Rutherford. As a doctor, he said he heard the "inarticulate poems" of his patients as he traveled with them into "those gulfs and grottos" of disease and of births and deaths. He even wrote some of his poems as they came to him in the doctor's office, on prescription blanks. His first works were published in *Poems* in 1909, and he grew more prolific as the years went on. Many of his poems were published only in avant-garde magazines. His most famous poem, *Paterson*, first published in 1946, became a five volume "epic", in which he describes modern America. Williams said in his preface to *Paterson*, "a man himself is a city, beginning, seeking, achieving and concluding his life in ways which the various aspects of a city night embody." Partly because of the recognition given him for his work, Williams was asked to become a Library of Congress consultant in 1949. He didn't take the job until 1952, but the publisher of the literary magazine *Lyric* accused Williams of Communist associations, citing his poem "Russia." The Library of Congress withdrew its appointment, which Williams was not able to contest successfully. During the 1950s, however, Williams gained a loyal following of young poets, including Allen Ginsburg. Williams suffered a series of strokes and heart attacks during these years, which caused him to quit his medical practice and to slow down.

This, according to his wife, helped him to think more clearly and do better work. His *Pictures From Breughel and Other Poems* won a Pulitzer Prize in 1962, and the next year he won a Ballingen Prize. He died after several months of illness, at Rutherford.

WOOLMAN, JOHN— (1720-1772), Quaker preacher and early abolitionist, was born in Ancocas, in the province of West Jersey (now Northampton, New Jersey), one of thirteen children of Samuel and Elizabeth Burr Woolman. He spent his youth on the farm, and attended the neighborhood Quaker school. here also read widely and was early acquainted with "the operation of divine love" as he called it. About 1742 he began his ministry by teaching poor children and speaking at meetings of the Society of Friends. he visited Friends in the back settlements of Virginia in 1746, beginning his life of continued travel. He also learned the tailor's trade at Mount Holly, and married Sarah Ellis of Chesterfield in 1749. Woolman's goal was to "raise an idea of general brotherhood," and he saw that "success in business did not satisfy craving; but that commonly with an increase of wealth, the desire for wealth increased." Besides his grammar school primer, Woolman published essays in pamphlet form. His first, "On the Keeping of Negroes" (1753 and 1762), warned of the sin of keeping slaves. In Virginia, he had soon "so many vices and corruptions increased by this trade (slavery), that it appeared to me a dark gloominess was hanging over the Land...the consequence will be grievous to Posterity." He continued to travel throughout the colonies, warning slaveowners of their evil trade, saying, "The burden will grow heavier and heavier till times change in a way disagreeable to us." In June 1763, he traveled as far west as Wyoming to preach to the Indians. His *A Plea for the Poor* was published the same year, and he continued to keep a journal (published posthumously in 1774) that held all of his thoughts on slavery and theology. In 1772, he traveled to England to visit the Quakers there, but died in York soon after his arrival, of smallpox. He remains one of the most important figures in Quaker and U.S. history. Although he saw little change in the slavery situation during his own life, he laid the groundwork for future abolitionists.

WRIGHT, PATIENCE L.— (1725-1786), sculptor and wax modeler, was born in Bordentown, New Jersey, the daughter of Quakers. Her earliest art work was of modeling miniature heads in relief in wax, which were popular with her neighbors and then in Pennsylvania around 1772. She was a widow with three children when she moved to England and exhibited her works, often cast in metal. She produced historical figures in busts and life-size proportions, which made her one of the most prominent sculptors of the time, and very wealthy. Her life-size figure of Lord Chatham was placed in a glass case in Westminster Abbey in London. She remained loyal to America when the Revolution began, carrying on a correspondence with Benjamin Franklin, in which she told him of British military plans. She was also a friend of Benjamin West. Her eldest daughter became a painter under West's direction. She painted a portrait of the Prince of Wales in 1783, and later of George and Martha Washington. Mrs. Wright enjoyed favor in London and she lived there until her death.

Elizabeth

Population: 106,201   Area Code 201   Elev. 36'

Newark is southernmost in a chain of old cities--now heavily industrialized-- that form continuous links along the northeast Jersey shore in the metropolitan area. The city's northeastern boundary is a purely theoretical line marking the place where Newark begins. The centers of the two cities are only five miles apart, and the business and residential continuity between them is unbroken. The Newark airport juts into Elizabeth's northern boundary as well.

Elizabeth has seen its native American population augmented by an influx of workers from this country and Europe, and has watched old landmarks succumb to the demand for factories, apartment houses, and service stations. With a waterfront on Newark Bay and Staten Island Sound, the city was the natural terminus of the earliest highways and the first railroads. Although it is no longer an important terminal, Elizabeth has grown in stature as an industrial and residential area.

The better residential section has a handsome assortment of shade trees and gardens. Blue iris brightens many front yards in May; the somber leaves of the copper beech stand out against a cheerful background of blossoming horse chestnuts and catapas, and the omnipresent maple. The colors of the town, with the exception of the greenery, are those of a manufacturing place; faded and stained reds, grays, yellows, and browns. The white clapboard dwellings that might be expected from Elizabeth's early American heritage are rarely found.

179

Houses range from the yellow brick flats and nondescript frame structures of the poorer sections to the commuters' and businessmen's modern homes in the early American bungalow, or English cottage style. Characteristic of the older residential district are the semi-mansions of the late nineteenth and early twentieth centuries: bulky structures, often with commodious corner towers and bay windows, built in combinations of brick and stone, shingle and clapboard, stucco and half-timber; decorated with a fantastic variety of porch columns and moldings.

Business buildings include a full quota of the heavy-corniced brick structures of 100 years ago. Others, of more recent construction, are simply designed. One large office building is a 13-story structure modernly individualistic in design, its exterior richly decorated with aluminum panels and terra cotta ornaments. Red brick factories and a few modern industrial buildings fringe the city.

The northern end of the business district has a reminder of the days when Elizabeth was an important railroad terminal. This is "the Arch," where Broad Street dips to pass under a broad stone arch of the Jersey Central. Trolley cars no longer thump along Broad Street under the Arch. Above is an almost unending roar of freight and passenger trains on the two railroads. The decline of water transportation was followed by relocation of the city's industrial life; factories were clustered mainly along the railroads more than a mile inland. Now they line the highways.

Elizabethans, because of the city's location on the metropolitan fringe, are a mingling of the urban with the suburban. Their culture is influenced by contact with New York's theaters, concert halls, and social movements. The city is well stocked with churches, some of them outstanding native specimens, others of European inspiration.

The labor movement is more advanced in Elizabeth than in the outlying communities. For nearly 90 years the *Labor Advocate* , one of the state's very few labor newspapers, has been published monthly in Elizabeth.

The history of Elizabeth, oldest English settlement of the state, began in 1664, when the English ended Dutch control of New Netherland. In that year three Long Islanders, *John Baily, Daniel Denton,* and *Luke Watson* , received written license from the new English Deputy Governor of New York, *Richard Nicolls* , and bought from the Indians for the customary quantity of coats, gunpowder, and kettles a large tract extending from Raritan River to Newark Bay.

Farming operations were scarcely a year old when *Philip Carteret* arrived as the first English Governor of New Jersey. For his capital he picked a spot in the territory of the Long Island emigrants and named it Elizabethtown in honor of the wife of his cousin, *Sir George Carteret*. *Sir George* and *Lord John Berkeley* were at that time the sole Proprietors of all New Jersey.

In Elizabethtown *Carteret* compromised with the 80 Associates on division of the land. Houses were built by joint effort; so was a church, put up on the Broad Street site now occupied by the graveyard of the first Presbyterian Church.

In 1668 *Governor Carteret* summoned the first general assembly to his new capital. Two years later the Province was in turmoil over a dispute that has not yet been settled. The original settlers had obtained license to buy Indian lands from *Colonel Nicolls*, and they refused to pay annual quitrents to *Carteret*. *Carteret*, unable to maintain authority, went to England and returned with a compromise that kept peace for a time. Eventually control of all lands passed to an organization known as the Proprietors of East New Jersey. When the Proprietors attempted to revive the collection of quitrents, the inhabitants promptly retorted that they had bought their property from the Indians and owed not a cent to the Proprietors or anyone else. In 1745 the controversy landed in Chancery Court; land riots followed, and the suit, interrupted by the French and Indians Wars and the Revolution, was never settled.

The Proprietors, with a flair for mismanagement, transferred the capital to Perth Amboy in 1686, thinking that this village was destined for greater things than Elizabethtown. But Elizabethtown withstood the shock and in 1740 obtained from *George II* a charter as the "Free Borough and town of Elizabeth," which called for a borough hall and a courthouse. These were built on the site of the present Union County Courthouse. A second charter was granted by the state legislature in 1789, and a city charter was issued in 1855 and amended in 1863.

Elizabeth's industry developed along characteristic Colonial lines. By 1670 a merchant had established his shop; and six years later a brewer, *William Looker*, began catering to the powerful thirst aroused by day-long work in the fields and woods. Mills were established for the production of lumber and meal. Good grazing promoted the raising of sheep, swine, and cattle, which were shipped to New York. The tanning industry received an early start and by 1687 Elizabethtown was shipping leather to all of the Colonies. Ships of 30 and 40 tons sailed up the Elizabeth River as far as Broad Street. Soon Elizabeth was building its own vessels for pursuing whales, abundant off the Jersey coast.

The Revolution halted Elizabeth's development. The city was an important point in Washington's New Jersey maneuvers; it was, in fact, the Achilles heel in his defenses against the British in New York and Staten Island across the Kill from Elizabeth. Time and again the British from Staten Island made quick thrusts into the city, burning and pillaging. The year 1780 was a particularly bad one for the village, marked by major encounters at nearby Connecticut Farms (now Union) and Springfield, and a series of minor skirmishes through the countryside.

Impetus to industrialization came from New York in 1835 when a group of New York businessmen, aware of what the new railroads would mean to Elizabeth, bought a tract of land fronting for a half-mile on Staten Island Sound. They laid it out in long rectangular plots and named it "The New Manufacturing Town of Elizabeth Port."

During these years the water front was busy with fishermen and oystermen. It was called "downtown" as opposed to the "uptown" district around Broad Street, and there was violent antagonism between the two sections. The downtown men were known as "salt water boys." At irregular intervals they declared a "salt water day" that was celebrated by throwing every available uptowner off the dock.

Formation of volunteer fire companies in 1837 made for further breaches of the peace. There was sharp competition between the fire companies, not because of anxiety over the burning building, but to obtain a hydrant for the water fight that followed every fire. Downtown Red Jacket Engine Co. No. 4 had the jump in early morning blazes on its rivals in the uptown Hibernia Engine No. 5, for the Red Jackets were up at 2 a.m. getting ready to sail for Newark Bay oyster beds. Early evening fires provided the best competition; the Hibernians armed a man with a poker to prevent the Red Jackets from cutting their hose.

As a change from fighting with the uptowners, the oystermen used oars, oyster rakes, and boathooks in repelling Staten Island oystermen who ventured into Jersey waters. Every morning the fleets started up the bay, returning at 5 p.m. At daybreak oyster dealers from Prince Bay, Staten Island, would arrive with a large basket at the masthead, a signal that oysters were being bought, whereupon the men would flock out to sell.

There was one downtowner who was welcome all over the city—the clam vendor who drove his little horse cart slowly through the streets, singing hoarsely:

Fine clams, fine clams,
Fine clams, I say,
They are good to stew,
And good to fry;
And are good to make
A good clam pie.

In 1873 the first important industry, the Singer Sewing Machine Company, came to Elizabeth and "The New Manufacturing Town of Elizabeth Port" began to develop. Railroad extensions to the Pennsylvania coal fields resulted in the building of docks at the Elizabeth and Somerville Railroad Terminal, foot of Broadway, where freight and passengers were transferred to boats for New York. The "Pig Iron Dock" was the center for pig iron brought in barges from northern New Jersey and New York and shipped by train to iron mills elsewhere in the country. The railroads stimulated the immigration of large numbers of Germans and Irish to the city. World War production brought thousands of Slavs and Italians to man Elizabeth factories.

Elizabeth now has hundreds of manufacturing plants. Products include Simmons beds, sewing machines, Kelly presses, refined petroleum, soap, chemicals, paper supplies, clothing, furniture, iron and steel machinery and other commodities.

During World War II, these products helped supply the Allied Forces, and many products were shipped from Elizabethport to Europe.

However, the boom died down after the war, and many young families moved outward to the newer, cleaner suburbs. The factories remained, though, choking out many old neighborhoods with their work. With the construction of the New Jersey turnpike in the 1950s, and other major toll roads and highways afterwards, Elizabeth became a major transportation center once again.

As Union County seat, Elizabeth is also looked upon as a leader in a vast metropolitan area. The *Daily Journal*, founded in 1785 in Elizabeth by *Shepard Kollock*, still provides news to this area. A large public library contains millions of volumes for the town's readers and researchers, and various historical sites are tucked away behind the vast manufacturing plants. The city is governed by a mayor-council system.

Some points of interest here are the Jonathan Belcher mansion, built before 1742, the Nathaniel Bonnell house, built before 1682, the Minute Man statue on First Avenue and High Street, and the First Presbyterian Church, constructed in the 1780s. Tours are available in the Singer Sewing Machine plant and the *Daily Journal* offices.

Jersey City

Population: 223,532   **Area Code 201**   **Elev. 11'**

The site of Jersey City was first important as a North Jersey gateway for the Dutch traders who settled Manhattan. That relationship was expanded when the settlers began bringing their farm products to New York. Probably the first permanent settlement was made shortly after 1629, when *Michael Pauw* bought a tract from the Indians. Under the colonization plan of the Dutch West India Company he was required to settle fifty persons on the land. *Cornelius Van Vorst* , sent by *Pauw* to establish a plantation named Pavonia, enjoyed civil and judicial power, and enough prosperity to entertain the directors general of New Netherland. The house that he built in 1633 is supposed to have stood near the present corner of Fourth and Henderson Streets. Later *Michael Paulez* (or Paulusen), the company's overseer of trade with the Indians, occupied a house at Paulus Hook.

Dissatisfied with the feudal patroon system, the company bought out *Pauw* in 1634 for about $10,000 and built two houses at Pavonia; another was erected at Communipau (Pauw's community). After 1638 the company's officers obtained grants from Director *General Kieft* .

Unscrupulous trade practices against the Indians, plus *Kieft's* demand for tribute and his subsequent massacre of innocent Raritans, resulted in bloody reprisals by both sides. When peace was declared in 1645 only the Van Vorst manor had escaped destruction. Ten years later the Indians raided the settlement again after another provocative act. *Governor Stuyvesant* refused to permit settlement until 1660, when he granted a petition on condition that the colonists live in a fortified community. The first court was established in 1661.

The village of Bergen was laid out as an 800-foot square surrounded by a log palisade. Two streets, now Academy Street and Bergen Avenue, intersected to form a public square, today known as Bergen Square. Within a year the settlement was large enough to require regular communication with New Amsterdam, and *William Jansen* began operating a rowboat ferry three times a week. For cattle and other cargo a flat-bottomed sloop was used. In 1662 the settlement hired a combination *voorleser* (sermon reader) and schoolmaster, being unable to afford an ordained minister.

The transition to English rule in 1664 took place smoothly, with thirty-three Dutch families later signing an oath of allegiance. At about that time a rough log church was built for the Dutch Reformed congregation; it was probably the first church erected in the Province. For many years the Dutch Reformed Church had an important role in the affairs of the growing community, which was chartered as a town in 1668 by *Governor Philip Carteret* .

During the next century the town was concerned with little besides farming. Establishment of improved ferry service in 1764 was followed several years later by the building of a race track at Paulus Hook. The opening of a new land route to Philadelphia made the Hook a vital link between New York and the south and west; formerly a monopoly had been enjoyed by Elizabethtown and Perth Amboy, which had better water connections with New York.

Close by the ferry was a tavern with stables, all under the same management. Schedules were carefully disarranged so that ferry passengers from New York arrived too late for the southbound stage in the morning, and had to stay overnight at the tavern.

An outpost of the British Army held a fort on Paulus Hook during the occupancy of New York. On the night of August 18, 1779, Major (Light Horse Harry) Lee led 300 men south from the American camp on upper Hudson River in a bold attack on the garrison. Crossing a moat at low tide, Lee's force stormed the fort at 3 o'clock in the morning and captured 159 men, about one-third of the defending force. The Americans lost only two killed and three wounded, and escaped northward before their retreat was cut off by other British detachments.

Speculative New Yorkers cast appraising eyes upon the site of Jersey City in 1804, immediately after *Col. John Stevens'* auction of lots in Hoboken. *John B. Coles* , a flour merchant, laid out city blocks in the Bergen area. *Anthony Dey* , a young New

York lawyer, acquired land and ferry for a perpetual annuity of 6,000 Spanish milled dollars.

Dey's company was incorporated as the Associates of The Jersey Company under a charter that made the organization, in effect, the civil governing body. The real estate boom however, was anything but resounding. Although a red brick tavern was built and a few small industries came, the political domination of the Associates hindered growth. Another obstacle was New York's claim to riparian rights up to the low-water line on the Jersey shore, which hindered the building of piers and wharves. The boundary dispute was unsettled for many years.

Steam ferry service began in 1812 with the *Jersey*, built by *Robert Fulton*. A passenger reported that the crossing was made in fourteen minutes as thousands watched from both shores, all "gratified at finding so large and so safe a machine going so well."

During this period, when the population consisted mainly of boatmen and transients and the town had neither jail nor policemen, the Hook became known for dog fights, bull baits, and drunken brawls. Efforts to obtain an autonomous government were balked by the Associates, who had great influence with the legislature. Finally the citizens succeeded in incorporating the City of Jersey in 1820, but the Associates retained special powers until 1838.

The year 1834 was a turning point in the city's growth. A treaty setting the line between New York and New Jersey in the middle of the Hudson River, while New York got Staten Island, gave the city access to its own water line. Terminals of the New Jersey Railroad (later the Pennsylvania) and the Paterson and Hudson Railroad (later the Erie) were established in Jersey City. Horse-car service to Newark, begun in September 1834, was replaced by steam in 1838. Meanwhile the Morris Canal, with its western terminal on Delaware River, had been extended from Newark to Jersey City in 1836.

Several important industries had already been established. As early as 1760 the Lorillard Tobacco Company had started a snuff factory. In 1884 the firm opened a night school for the 250 children then employed. Dummer's Jersey City Glass Company, later famous for its flint glass, began operations in 1824. The fireworks factory built by *Isaac Edge Jr.* became a training school for American pyrotechnists. Some of the foremost American potters learned their trade at the plant of the American Pottery Company, which was one of the first factories to compete successfully with leading English producers.

Other industries included Colgate soaps, Dixon pencils, steel, paper, beer and whisky. By 1860 the population was 29,000, an increase of almost 150 percent in nine years. Jersey City opened its first stockyards in 1866, and it was also for a time the western terminal of the Cunard Line, beginning in 1847.

The city was an important station on the Underground Railroad. Slaves were sent North hidden in the dead air space between cabins on Erie Canal boats. During the Civil War thousands of troops passed through the railroad stations and the city contributed full quotas of men.

Railroad and political battles colored the latter part of the nineteenth century. The monopolistic hold of the United Railroads (later the Pennsylvania) on the Jersey City water front was broken when the Jersey Central dumped New York refuse on tidal flats and built a terminal. Another terminal was established when the Erie Railroad blasted a tunnel through Bergen Hill.

The political struggles supplied such incidents as the Hudson County "Horseshoe," which gerrymandered nearly the whole Democratic vote into one assembly district, and an election in which ballots were printed on tissue paper so that more could be stuffed into each ballot box. Consolidations with neighboring communities were preceded by street and sewer contracts whose addition to the merged public debt caused an intolerable tax burden. The election of *Mark Fagan* , a New Idea Republican, as mayor in 1901 temporarily halted political scandals.

Construction of a railroad tunnel to Manhattan had been attempted as early as 1874. But it was not until *William G. McAdoo* , later Secretary of the Treasury, became interested in the project that it was completed (1909-10). The Hudson Tubes brought an increase in the number of factories and in the working population.

The Black Tom explosion on the Communipaw water front during the night of July 30, 1916, has been called the only successful German war plot in the country, although international litigation to fix responsibility and damages has not been concluded. Ammunition-laden railroad cars blew up with such violence that residents of Connecticut and Maryland felt the shock. The damage was estimated at $20,000,000, of which the greater part was in Jersey City. Loss in broken windows in the metropolitan area amounted to more than $1,000,000. Only seven lives were lost, although 75 mm. shells struck Ellis Island and other nearby places. After the United States entered the war, the city's factories were busy supplying materials to the government.

St. Peter's College, chartered in 1872, closed during the war when more than half of its faculty and students enlisted. The college, conducted by the Society of Jesus, reopened in 1930 and now has more than 400 students.

World War II brought a temporary prosperity to heavily industrialized Jersey City. Thousands of new residents flocked to the city to find jobs in manufacturing plants. The city government, ruled by Mayor and political boss *Frank Hague* until 1947, was later controlled by *John V. Kenny*, political leader of Hudson County. *Kenny* remained in power for two decades, perpetuating the corruption that marked *Hague's* regime. But Jersey City continued its support for the Special Service Bureau, an institution for the treatment of juvenile delinquency that had attracted nationwide attention. The Bureau coordinated the work of police and the Board of Education, in the process keeping many young offenders from acquiring jail records.

Starting about 1950, when it had 299,017 residents, the city lost population steadily. Inner-city "blight" also forced many businesses to move their offices and other facilities. *Kenny* and a number of his associates were convicted of extortion and similar crimes in 1967. The city began to plan more intensively for the future.

The Journal Square Transportation Center opened in 1974, a major step toward rehabilitation of the central city. The Center housed a bus terminal, a rapid transit railroad station, and a shopping area. To reverse its continuing population decline, Jersey City also drew up plans for a new shipping, housing, and industrial complex, to be located next to a state park. In 1976 the Liberty State Park on the waterfront, a $14 million project that was described as New Jersey's largest state park, was opened as part of the city's bicentennial celebration. The park covered 800 acres.

By the early 1980s Jersey City had some 500 factories producing such diverse goods as clothing, electrical equipment, and chemicals. Some 20 million vehicles were using the Holland Tunnel, connecting Jersey City and New York City, each year. The city had a population exceeding 222,000, remaining the second largest city in New Jersey.

Newark

Population: 330,104   **Area Code 201**   **Elev. 146'**

Newark is the principal city in northeast New Jersey, occupying the western bank of the Passaic River where it joins Newark Bay. Westward, the wooded skyline of the Watchung Mountains overlooks the city and its suburbs. Eastward the city faces the gaunt flatlands of the Hackensack, with Jersey City and New York often visible from its taller buildings.

Newark was settled in 1666 by *Capt. Robert Treat* and 30 families from New Haven and the vicinity. The village on the Passaic was the result of five years' search for a site where these former Connecticut citizens could obtain self-government and religious freedom.

In his haste to develop the territory, *Governor Philip Carteret* had promised to eliminate the Indian title to the settlement. His neglect in this detail brought the colonists face to face with angry Hackensack Indians almost as soon as they had disembarked. Complete peace was established in 1667 when the settlers purchased a tract extending from the Passaic River westward to the Watchung Mountains.

The source of the name Newark remains buried with the original settlers. It has recently been disproved that the inspiration came from Newark-on-Trent, the supposed English home of the *Reverend Abraham Pierson*, pastor of the first church. Scholars have therefore returned to the older interpretation that the name was originally the Biblical New Ark or New Work, meaning a new project.

Whatever the origin of its name, Newark was unmistakeably founded as a theocracy with the Puritan Congregational Church securely in control of village affairs. The church quickly erected a barrier around the religious freedom won by emigrating from New Haven. Church membership was a prerequisite to owning land, holding public office and voting. The church maintained such strict supervision over personal and public life that early Newark was more Puritan than much of New England itself.

The severity of ecclesiastical rule discouraged new settlers. Like many other religious communities, Newark grew slowly within a narrow arc prescribed by its Puritan leaders. They established a school in 1676, laid out military training grounds and encouraged gristmills, tanneries and small shops which made the little community self-sustaining.

The Puritan hegemony was first openly challenged in 1687. The *Rev. Abraham Pierson Jr.*, who succeeded his father as the town pastor, clashed with the conservatives. Five years later they coldly permitted him to retire and return to Connecticut, where he became the first president of Yale College.

It took another generation, however, in which more liberal Englishmen settled in Newark, to break the religious monopoly of Old First Church. About 1733 *Col. Josiah Ogden*, a pillar of this organization, which had become Presbyterian in 1719, gathered in his wheat on the Sabbath rather than let it be ruined by the rain. He stoutly defended himself before the outraged membership and finally withdrew from the church. *Ogden* then joined with the local Church of England missionaries and founded Trinity Church.

Despite this rupture, Newark moved through the eighteenth century as a Puritan town, with a Puritan interest in education and commerce and a Puritan horror of secular art and pleasure. In 1748 the College of New Jersey, afterward Princeton University, moved from Elizabethtown to Newark with the *Rev. Aaron Burr Sr.*, pastor of Old First Church, as president. The college remained until 1756, when it was transferred to Princeton. In the same period forges and foundries began to work the products of nearby iron mines. Before the time of the Revolution, Newark was of sufficient commercial importance to warrant the building of roads connecting with ferries to New York.

The war itself divided Newark into Tories who gave ample aid to *Lord Cornwallis* and other British commanders who encamped here, and Revolutionaries whose cooperation won the praise of Colonial generals. *Washington* used Newark as a supply base on his retreat across the state in 1776. In addition to a number of raids and skirmishes in the center of the village, two battles and a skirmish were fought at Springfield, part of which was then Newark.

The value of trade and manufacture was one of the lessons learned by the city from the Revolution. Factories increased. In about 1790 *Moses Combs* founded the shoe industry and a few years later one third of Newark's working population was engaged in some form of the leather trade. The impetus came from an abundant stand of hemlock trees on the nearby Orange Mountains, which provided bark for tanning.

Hand-in-hand with prosperity went an escape from religious scrutiny, and the town supported three of the finest taverns in the country. Possibly attracted by a carefree society group, the exiled Frenchman, Talleyrand, visited Newark in 1794 and stayed at what was later the David Ailing House on the corner of Broad and Fair Streets. The length of his stay is uncertain but it is likely that while in Newark he devoted much time to study and writing. In the next decade *Tom Moore* , the Irish poet, was entertained by the *Ogden* family, and *Washington Irving* was inspired to write the *Salmagundi* papers by many gay evenings at old Cockloft Hall, the Kemble Mansion, which stood on the corner of Mt. Pleasant Avenue and Gouverneur Street.

Finance, commerce and industry quickened the conversion of Newark from a sprawling agricultural village into an important business center. The first bank, the Newark Banking and Insurance Company, was organized in 1804, and six years later the Newark Fire Insurance Company wrote the first of millions of Newark policies. One of the Newark companies established in this period has preserved from its earliest days a yarn to the effect that when an Elizabeth woman, who was insured for $500, fell critically ill, the officers became alarmed lest the company expire with her. Accordingly, the president had the best local doctor attend her and sat at her bedside himself until she recovered.

After the War of 1812, new industries pushed Newark into the position of New Jersey's leading city, which it has held ever since. In two decades the manufacture of jewelry, begun by *Epaphras Hinsdale* in 1801, had become a leading occupation; *Seth Boyden's* work in patent leather gave tremendous impetus to the leather trade; and by 1831 hat making and brewing occupied large numbers of workmen.

Transportation developments began to link the growing city with the rest of the eastern seaboard. One of the state's earliest railroads--the New Jersey Railroad and Transportation Company--began operation in 1834 from Newark to Jersey City, while the Morris Canal, completed to Phillipsburg three years earlier, provided an outlet for Newark's products in Pennsylvania and the west.

In 1836 Newark was incorporated as a city with *William Halsey* as its first mayor. The population of nearly 20,000 was no longer exclusively of Puritan gentry; the growth of industry had resulted in the formation of 16 trade societies, chiefly among plasterers, bricklayers, and corset makers. By 1836 they were bidding for political power as labor organizations.

For two decades following the panic of 1837 economic progress was slow, but this period witnessed an increased interest in social reform and entertainment. Criminals were better treated and the mentally ill were regarded less as offenders against decent society. In 1848 a theater inaugurated a long history of romantic and tragic drama in Newark. By 1855 Germans had settled Newark in large numbers, and their Saengerfests made the city one of the national centers of German music.

The outbreak of the Civil War seriously threatened a large intersectional trade which Newark had established with the South. As an offset, however, to the manufacturers' fears, the war boomed industry; hat and shoe factories operated at full capacity to fill army orders and a general prosperity was enjoyed. A visit from *Abraham Lincoln* en route to his first *Washington* inaugural helped to solidify community sentiment. Newark sent 10,000 to the Union armies.

Modern Newark dates from the close of the Civil War. An industrial exposition in 1872 showed that the city was becoming more and more diversified in its manufacturing interests, although brewing, jewelry, and leather still maintained the lead. But while these industries were at their peak, the scientific age was beginning to transform completely the city's industrial character. In 1869 *John Wesley Hyatt* invented celluloid and laid the basis for the important plastic industry. Eighteen years later he turned celluloid into film for photographic negatives. *Thomas A. Edison's* invention of the electric light bulb in nearby Menlo Park was responsible for the rise of a new industry in Newark. Later *Edward Weston* carried on the *Edison* tradition with many important electrical inventions.

The post-Civil War period was marked also by the city's finest literary flowering. *Stephen Crane* (1871-1900), the novelist, was its greatest literary figure. His contemporary, *Mary Mapes Dodge* (1838-1905), created the children's classic, *Hans Brinker or the Silver Skates*, and *Edmund Clarence Stedman* (1833-1908), banker-poet-editor, conducted literary salons in and around Newark for a decade. *Richard Watson Gilder* (1844-1909), editor of the *Century*, worked for a time after the Civil War on the old Newark *Advertiser* and with *Newton Crane* founded the Newark *Morning Register*. *Noah Brooks* (1830-1903), well known at the end of the last century as a journalist and author of books for boys, was editor of the Newark *Daily Advertiser* in 1884.

By the turn of the century the newer, electrified industries were crowding out the old steam crafts and preparing Newark for its future leadership in heavy, mass industrial enterprise. Municipal government under *Mayor Joseph Haynes* aided the upswing with improved water facilities, new buildings and sincere efforts to harmonize the interests of industry and the city. Similarly, the once independent unions contributed toward stabilization by consolidation into the American Federation of Labor.

The completion of the Hudson and Manhattan Railroad in 1911 between Newark, Jersey City, and New York under the direction of *William Gibbs McAdoo* greatly accelerated the intermingling of the population and speeded the development of the city. The new rapid transit attracted thousands from Manhattan to Newark and its suburbs, and in turn made "going to New York" for business or pleasure a Newark habit. Today, uncounted thousands commute daily to Manhattan offices and shops on the jerky red trains of the Hudson & Manhattan Railroads--known to everyone as "the tubes." The same trains bring a substantial number of New Yorkers to jobs in Newark. Additional thousands of men and women who work in the banking, insurance and industrial offices of Newark have homes and interests in outlying suburbs. Like the New Yorkers they are only daytime Newark residents.

Far-reaching demographic changes took place in Newark starting about 1940. Attracted by jobs in defense, tens of thousands of southern Blacks crowded into the city's poorer districts. At the same time, thousands of middleclass families were moving to the suburbs. By 1960, the city's population had declined to about 405,000. Racial tensions were mounting, partly because Black citizens had little political power. Also, the city had inadequate resources for coping with social problems. including unemployment and poverty.

The commission form of government that had been established in Newark in 1917 was terminated in 1954. On July 1 of that year the city adopted a charter form of government including a mayor and a city council. The mayor exercised executive power while the council served as the legislative authority. Administrative power was vested in an appointed business administrator.

Encouraged by the governmental changes, a number of Newark-based businesses decided to remain in the city rather than move. The Mutual Benefit Life Insurance Company announced in late 1954 that it would build a 20 story headquarters in the city's center. Construction began about the same time on a 24 story home office for the Prudential Insurance Company. Complementing such expressions of confidence, the city included in its slum clearance program plans for additions and expanded facilities for Rutgers University, the state university; Newark College of Engineering, and a brand-new medical center. Such construction and rehabilitation projects, some on former slum land, accounted for about $1 billion in investment funds in the next two decades.

Riots that broke out in Newark in July of 1967 went quickly out of control. Twenty-six persons died. Rioters caused an estimated $10 to $15 million in property damage. Investigations were undertaken after the riots in an effort to confirm or refute charges of corruption among city officials. The investigations led to the trials and convictions of *Mayor Hugh Addenizio* and other local politicians for illegally accepting refunds on city contracts. In 1968, the assassination of *Rev. Dr. Martin Luther King* in Tennessee touched off new riots, looting, and burning. The city's voters in 1970 elected *Kenneth A. Gibson* mayor. *Gibson* was Newark's first Black mayor.

The efforts to improve Newark's housing situation that had gotten under way in the 1950s continued into the 1970s against a background of other projects that were scheduled or already completed. A $200,000,000 program effected modernization and expansion of Newark Airport starting in the late 1960s. At the same time the city undertook, with Port Elizabeth, channel and operational development of the Port of Newark. The changes enabled the port to adapt to new demands imposed by containerization and automation. The establishment of Essex County College in 1968 helped bring educational opportunity to thousands. By the 1980s, the city was working to cope with its urban challenges. Its population stood at slightly more than 330,000.

Paterson

Population: 137,970   Area Code 201   Elev. 100'

Paterson is capital of Passaic County, located in north New Jersey. Dutch settlers were early attracted to the great cataract on the Passaic which had been described to them by the Indians. In 1679 they obtained the first tract of land within the present bounds of Paterson. Many of the Dutch pioneers bore names still common in the city. For more than a century the Falls were merely an attraction for visitors, and the settlement remained small.

Then in 1791 *Alexander Hamilton*, Secretary of the Treasury, helped form the Society for Establishing Useful Manufactures (S.U.M.). The New Jersey Legislature voted the company perpetual exemption from county and township taxes and gave it the right to hold property, improve rivers, build canals, and raise $100,000 by lottery. The company selected, from a number of sites offered, the Great Falls of the Passaic River, which at that time had "no more than ten houses." *Hamilton* had favored this place, which he had seen during the Revolution, but he "did not make public this idea of his at the time, for fear that some of the men who did not live near the Passaic Falls might not contribute." Money was set aside by the S.U.M. for factories, and *Major Pierre L'Enfant*, designer of Washington D.C., was hired to build a system of raceways.

Paterson grew out of the Society's 700 acres above and below the Passaic Falls and was named for *William Paterson*, then Governor of New Jersey. It was a company town, and its workers began to exhibit signs of dissatisfaction. S.U.M. records tells of "disorderly" calico printers as early as 1794. This resulted in the closing of the mill--the first lock-out in American history and the forerunner of a long string of industrial struggles.

197

The town continued to grow as an industrial center. When one industry failed, others replaced it. About 1825 Paterson became known as the "Cotton Town of the United States." Oxen are reputed to have provided power for the first cotton spinning here in a mill known as the Bull House.

In 1828 Paterson gave America its first factory strike when cotton workers quit their looms to protest a change in the lunch hour. The owners had asserted that the health and comfort of child workers would be improved by a 1 o'clock dinner instead of a meal at 12, making a more equal division of the day. The employees countered with a surprise demand for reduction of working hours from 13 1/2 to 12. Carpenters, masons and mechanics of Paterson also walked out, the first recorded instance of a sympathy strike in the United States. Although the strike was lost, it made a strong impression on the community, and the owners afterward restored the 12 o'clock lunch hour.

In 1831 the Morris Canal, penetrating the coal fields of Pennsylvania, was opened. The railroad came to town a year later when the tracks of the Paterson and Hudson River Railroad were laid. Both the canal and the railroad gave impetus to the town's development. In 1836 *Samuel Colt* established his mill, and the original Colt repeating revolvers were manufactured. In 1837 *John Clark's* modest machine shop produced one of the earliest American locomotives, the *Sandusky* , which was fashioned after an imported English model. Within 44 years 5,871 engines were made in Paterson and shipped to all parts of North and South America.

Silk manufacturing was permanently introduced to Paterson in 1840 when a plant under the supervision of *John Ryle* was established in the Old Gun Mill. By 1850 the new industry surpassed cotton and Paterson became known as the "Silk City." One year later the town was incorporated, and by 1860 its population reached approximately 19,600. Attracted by the rising silk industry, immigrants from Ireland, Germany, Italy, and Russia poured into Paterson, so that by 1870 the city had enough skilled workers to handle two-thirds of the raw silk imported into the United States.

Many of the foreign workers had been forced to flee Europe for championing various liberal causes. When, in 1886, conditions in local silk mills became unbearable, they led in calling a three-hour strike. The next important strike was a three-week walk-out in 1902, led by *McQueen* and *Grossman* , two Philosophic Anarchists.

That year brought a series of major disasters to the city. A fire started on February 8 and destroyed almost 500 buildings, including the City Hall and the entire business section. It was halted a mile from its starting point with the help of Jersey City and Hackensack firemen, who fought the blaze from roofs. Ruins of the fire had barely cooled when on March 2 the swollen Pasaic River engulfed the lower portions of the city and swept away bridges, homes and buildings, causing damage of more than $1,000,000. Several months later a tornado struck the city, uprooting trees and houses and crippling vital services.

The silk industry reached its peak in 1910 when 25,000 workers in 350 large plants wove close to 30 percent of the silk manufactured in this country. Three years later all mills came to a standstill when workers, under the leadership of the Industrial Workers of the World, struck for the maintenance of the two-loom system (two looms for each worker to tend) against the owners' plans for an increased number.

The workers walked out on February 15; the employers raised the American flag on their empty mills and declared a lock-out. *Carlo Tresca*, *Elizabeth Gurley Flynn*, *"Big Bill" Haywood*, and *John Reed*, the young Harvard poet, came to lead the picket lines. When one picketer was killed, *Haywood* led 15,000 workers in the funeral procession. School children struck in sympathy with their parents, and gigantic mass meetings were largely sympathetic. *Reed* who was jailed during the walk-out, staged the famous "Paterson Pageant" in Manhattan's Madison Square Garden for the benefit of the strikers. It was the greatest strike in Paterson history, but the workers went back to their looms in July, defeated.

In 1924, 20,000 workers waged an unsuccessful fight against the four-loom system. Manufacturers, blaming labor troubles, began hunting for sites with lower taxes, cheaper power, and more docile workers. By 1925 the exodus had begun. There were 700 plants then, but the factories were much smaller than formerly.

Today, Paterson's widely diversified industries do not allow for the silk and dyers' monopolies of past years. This is also a retail center; with over 2,000 retail outlets and over 700 wholesale houses in town. During World War II, Paterson's mills and aircraft and metal factories produced at record levels, making this one of the nation's "Arsenals of Democracy."

Although many people moved out to the suburbs in the 1950s and '60s, the metropolitan area around Paterson grew substantially as workers continued to commute into the city each day.

Paterson is the site of many educational facilities, including a branch of the state university, Rutgers. Seton Hall University also has a campus here, as does Paterson State College, formerly a normal school for teachers. The large Danforth Memorial Library is also in town. The Paterson Museum exhibits New Jersey minerals and Indian relics.

Relics of Paterson's past are hidden throughout the city. At the museum is *John Holland's* first submarine, which was sunk in the Passaic River in 1878 and salvaged by the city in 1927. At Westside Park is his first practical submarine, *The Fenian Ram* , built in 1881. City Hall was built in 1894 from designs of *John Carrere* . The Old Gun Mill on the riverbanks was originally built as a revolver factory by *Samuel Colt* in 1836. It is still in use, as a textile mill.

Residents of the city enjoy ball games and concerts at the Hincliffe City Stadium in town. On warm summer days and clear nights they go up to Garret Mountain Reservation, a 570 acre park on that 500 foot high hill. Woodland trails, picnic facilities, and an observatory over the sweeping Passaic Valley are maintained by the county park district. Garret Mountain is said to have been named in the nineteenth century for a secret society that met in the garrets of its members here. A castle-style mansion, built by *Catholina Lambert* in 1891, is also in the reservation, and now houses a historical museum. A Festival of Nations is held in town each June.

A mayor is elected every two years in Paterson, under a system enacted in 1907.

Trenton

Capital of New Jersey

Population: 92,124   Area Code 609   Elev. 50'

Located in west New Jersey, Trenton is primarily a manufacturing center. Residents are proud of its history, and there are plaques, monuments, and historic houses throughout the city. Nevertheless, Trenton chooses to identify itself by a sign almost as wide as Delaware River, fastened to the steel arches of the main highway bridge: "Trenton Makes--The World Takes."

The city lies on a low plateau at the head of naviagation on Delaware River. Thanks to the rocky channel and rapids (known from earliest settlements as the Falls) that have made commercial development impractical along most of the shore, the river front is bordered by the trees and grass of an extensive park, making a green backyard for the state buildings and for the western residential section.

Assumpink Creek, site of a Revolutionary battle, bisects the city, closely paralleled by the depressed main line tracks of the Pennsylvania Railroad. Once this tributary of the Delaware was clear-flowing and tree-lined; it is now hemmed by retaining walls, spanned by many bridges, and burdened with the refuse of factories.

It is possible that Trenton's history dates back to the Stone Age man. *Dr. Charles C. Abbott* made an exhaustive study of gravel deposits on his Trenton farm and reported in 1872 that crude implements he had discovered were of the glacial period. The weight of archeological opinion seems, however, to be against this theory. In 1650 about 200 Sanhicans, a clan of the Unami subdivision of the Lenape, occupied part of this area. This agricultural group was noted for its skill in making lanceheads and arrowheads of quartz and jasper.

The first white settler was *Mahlon Stacy*, an English Quaker, who took up a grant of land in 1679 at "ye falles of ye De La Warr" and built a log mill and a clapboard house. The little hamlet that developed around this nucleus was called The Falls.

Recognizing the commercial possibilities of the site, *William Trent*, a Philadelphia merchant, in 1714 bought of *Mahlon Stacy Jr.* the remainder of his father's holdings of 800 acres on Assumpink Creek (Ind., *stone in the water*). Trent replaced the log mill with one of stone and *c.* 1719 built himself a fine house later called Bloomsbury Court; now the oldest in the city. In the same year court sessions of Hunterdon County were held in the village. *Trent's* energy and financial backing launched the settlement, which he called Trent's Town, into a period of steady growth. Its position at the head of sloop navigation made the town a shipping point for grain and other products of the area, and a depot for merchandise between New York and Philadelphia. Overland travelers found the village a convenient stopping place on King's Highway, while a ferry, chartered in 1727, afforded communication with Pennsylvania.

In 1745 the town received a royal charter of incorporation as a borough and town, although the charter was voluntarily surrendered five years later when it failed to bring any material benefits.

The townspeople hurried to the waterfront in 1746 and cheered the first raft of timber from the upper Delaware as it passed through the rapids on its way to Philadelphia. Many others followed during the next century; some carried from 500 to 600 bushels of wheat.

The first chief burgess, *Dr. Thomas Cadwalader*, ranked high in his profession. One of the first advocates of innoculation as a disease preventive, he is said to have introduced the practice in Trenton to combat smallpox. In 1750 *Dr. Cadwalader* gave 500 pounds to found the Trenton Library Company, the first "public" library in New Jersey. It was almost wholly destroyed by British soldiers in December 1776 but revived in 1797 and lasted until 1855.

John Adams reported in 1774 that Trenton, as it soon became known, was "a pretty village. It appears to be the largest town we have seen in the Jerseys." Trenton resembled the shire towns of England, its hip or gable roofed dwellings facing the street, with gardens on both sides. The wharves were busy, and there were four churches, a courthouse, and a jail. In 1776 Trenton was a village of about 100 houses, mainly clustered along King and Queen Streets (now Warren and Broad Streets).

On the morning of December 26, 1776, Trenton was the scene of one of the most decisive battles of the Revolution. *Washington*, his prestige seriously reduced after his army had been harried across the state and into Pennsylvania by closely pursuing British, turned with about 2,500 troops upon his foe by executing the famous crossing of the ice-choked Delaware.

Washington had planned his surprise attack on the Hessians in Trenton for 5 a.m., expecting to find them asleep after a boisterous Christmas celebration. The difficult crossing of the river and the icy roads on the nine-mile march delayed until 8 o'clock the arrival of his two divisions, one marching by the lower road and one by the upper road, but apparently few of the Hessians were awake even then.

The prisoners numbered 23 officers and 886 men. *Colonel Rall* ; the Hessians' commander, was mortally wounded; *Washington* estimated the enemy's dead at "not above twenty or thirty," while the Americans' casualties were "only two officers and one or two privates wounded." One of the wounded officers was *Lieut. James Monroe* , later President, who helped to capture a Hessian battery. About one-third of the Hessian force escaped down the river road toward Bordentown.

After resting a few hours in Trenton, the American troops returned to the Pennsylvania shore. Two men died from the cold. Revolutionists throughout the Colonies were heartened by the unexpected success at Trenton and the British command was correspondingly alarmed. *General Howe* dispatched *Cornwallis* with 4,000 to 5,000 troops to intercept *Washington* should he attempt to recross New Jersey. The American Army, meanwhile, had recrossed to Trenton on the then frozen river.

Cornwallis arrived shortly before sunset on January 2 and found the Continental troops drawn up on higher ground on the farther side of Assunpink Creek. The engagement that followed, often confused with the Battle of Princeton on the next day, is known locally as the second Battle of Trenton, or Battle of the Assunpink.

Three times the British charged up to the bridge and even onto it, but each time the assault was broken by a hail of Continental lead. An eyewitness wrote that when the first attack crumbled, "...our army raised a shout, and such a shout I have never since heard; by what signal or word of command, I know not. The line was more than a mile in length, and from the nature of the ground the extremes were not in sight of each other, yet they shouted as one man..."

A contemporary observer estimated that 150 enemy troops were killed. *Washington* knew, however, that a more determined asault would be made in the morning, which might overwhelm his poorly equipped army. Since a thaw had broken the ice sheet across the Delaware, an escape to the Pennsylvania shore was impossible. That night *Washington* and his officers conferred in the Douglass house to find a way out of the trap. It was *General St. Clair*, according to some historians, who suggested the retreat to Princeton by a little-used back road.

By good fortune the temperature dropped sufficiently to freeze this ordinarily bad road so that artillery wheels could be supported. The army marched off to whispered orders. To deaden the rumble of artillery wheels, rags were wrapped around the rims. "Rags were plentiful, but they were all on the backs of the soldiers," one historian commented. A skeleton force was left behind to keep the camp fires burning in sight of the British, who were singing around well-filled kettles only a short distance away. It is said that *Washington* even ordered dummy cannon mounted to aid the deception, a device used as recently as 1937 by Chinese defenders of Shanghai.

In the morning *Cornwallis* got hurried news of the Revolutionaries' success in overcoming the British garrison at Princeton. Fearing for the safety of a treasure chest of 70,000 pounds and a large supply of military stores at New Brunswick, the British commander started his army in quick pursuit. But the American troops had turned off to find shelter in the Watchung Hills.

Trenton was chosen as the state capital in 1790 and two years later, still nothing more than a village, was incorporated as a city. The residents' earlier hopes of bringing the national capital to the bank of the Delaware, defeated by the opposition of southern states, were temporarily fulfilled when recurring epidemics of yellow fever caused the removal of national offices from Philadelphia. In 1794 and 1798 Trenton had several federal offices, and in 1799 practically all of the departments were represented; even President Adams and his wife were temporary residents.

A covered bridge 1,100 feet long was built across Delaware River in 1806, described by the historians, *Barber and Howe*, as "one of the finest specimens of bridge architecture, of wood, in the world." Perpendicular iron rods, hung from arches, provided such sturdy support for the floor that the structure was used later by railroad trains.

Development of water power by the Delaware Falls Company, construction of the Delaware and Raritan Canal, and building of the Camden and Amboy Railroad resulted in industrial activity that made Trenton a city in fact as well as in name. *John A. Roebling* moved his wire mill from Pennsylvania in 1848 and continued the manufacture of steel cable. The erection of Brooklyn Bridge a generation later publicized *Roebling* and Trenton throughout the world.

Pottery making, a Colonial industry, began to thrive after 1850. Craftsmen were imported from England and Ireland to teach local apprentices the art of producing wares that, by 1880, made Trenton known as the Staffordshire of America. The Ott and Brewer Company made in 1882 the first piece of American Beleek. *Walter Lenox*, one of the young apprentices, later laid the foundations for Lenox China. From Trenton potteries came, in 1873, the first porcelain sanitary ware in the United States. Trenton workers had formed trade unions as early as 1835, and in that year conducted a largely successful strike for a 10-hour day.

Growth of industry had by 1860 eliminated much of the city's quiet charm. Factories and houses for workers claimed terrain once dominated by Colonial dwellings. Down the center of North Broad Street (then Greene Street) ran the Street Market, two buildings stretching from State Street out to Academy Street.

In this period Trenton's most prolific writer--now largely forgotten--began his career. He was *Edward S. Ellis*, a school teacher who was one of the originators of the dime novel. At the age of 20 he wrote *Seth Jones*, or *The Captive of the Frontier*, which was published in 1860 by Beadle Brothers, New York, and sold 600,000 copies. *Ellis* produced about one hundred novels afterward.

In the early 1880's, the potters of Trenton were victimized by the blacklist. By agreement among the manufacturers, no worker could change employers without a written release from his last employer. The *Sunday Advertiser*, in an article headed "Local Fugitive Slave Law," reported in May 1883 the suit of *Mary E. Slattery* against the American Crockery Company for damages because of the girl's inability to get work elsewhere in Trenton. A judgment for $72 was finally given in 1884.

The city's greatest expansion occurred between 1880 and 1920, when the population increased by 90,379 as foreign labor poured in to man factories and mills. During this period the adjacent boroughs of Chambersburg and Wilbur, Millham Township, and parts of Ewing Township were annexed.

The population decline that had begun in Trenton in the 1920s continued in the 1940s and 1950s. The pattern of demographic change that saw Black and Spanish-American workers moving into poorer districts had a complementary effect: many middle-class workers and professional people moved out into the suburbs and into the countryside. Government, however, remained the major industry in the city; personnel employed by the state, city, and other levels of government continued to make up as much as one-third of Trenton's population. About 30 percent of the city's workers were employed by government in the late 1970s.

The government itself underwent changes. The municipal manager form of government, only four years old in 1939, gave way to a commission form. In November, 1961 the city's voters approved for implementation as soon as possible. The city continued to own the Newark port facilities while owning and operating the waterworks and the sewage treatment plant.

A long-term modernization program began in the 1950s. By the mid-1970s, the city had closed two blocks of its main street to traffic and created a mall called Trenton Commons. Construction of a downtown complex named Capital Place also went into the planning stage. Attracted by new construction and improving civic conditions, middle-class residents were moving back into the city. On the city's 300th anniversary in 1979, some authorities were calling the rehabilitation effort "Trenton's Reeducate/Invigorate Program (TR/IP)." In the early 1980s Trenton had a population of more than 90,600, the fifth largest city population in the state of New Jersey.

A DICTIONARY
OF
PLACES

It is our intention in this section to list every place in the state. These places include political and administrative units, civil divisions, physical and cultural features. Since this is a totally new editorial creation without prior model to follow and with the necessity to meet a deadline, it must be expected that there will be minor omissions. By the time this first edition is circulated, our editors will have already started updatings for the next edition. All populations are taken from either the preliminary or final counts of the 1980 Census. We believe this dictionary of places provides the basis for what will be a continuously evolving guide.

•**ABSECON**, City; Atlantic County; Pop. 6,787; Area Code 609; Zip Code 08021; Elev. 24'; 5 miles NW of Atlantic City in SE New Jersey on the Atlantic Ocean; is named from Absegami (an Indian tribe) meaning place of the swans. Many of the residents earn their living in Atlantic City, catering to the needs of its year round influx of visitors.

Many travelers on their way to Atlantic City stop here long enough to sample wines at Gross' Highland Winery. *Johann Gross* brought vines here in 1934, and today over 20 varieties of wine are produced, bottled and sold here.

•**ABSECON BEACH**, Beach, Atlantic County, within SE limits of Atlantic City on Atlantic Ocean S of the Boardwalk. Sunbathing facilities available.

•**ALLAMUCHY**, Township; Warren County; Pop. 2,541; Area Code 201; Zip Code 07820; NW New Jersey; named from the Indian meaning "place within the hills."

•**ALLENDALE**, Borough; Bergen County; Pop. 5,900; Area Code 201; Zip Code 07401; Elev. 375'; 10 miles N of Paterson in NE New Jersey; named after *Col. Wm. C. Allen*, who was a surveyor for the Erie Railroad.

•**ALLENHURST**, Borough; Monmouth County; Pop. 875; Area Code 201; Zip Code 07711; Elev. 24'; E Central New Jersey; on the Atlantic; named for an early resident, *Abner Allen*.

•**ALLENTOWN**, Borough; Monmouth County; Pop. 1,967; Area Code 201; Zip Code 08501; Elev. 82'; E Central New Jersey on the coast; named for *Nathan Allen*, who was the son-in-law of *Robert Burnet* an early settler of this area.

•**ALLOWAY**, Township; Salem County; Pop. 2,669; Area Code 609; Zip Code 08001; SW New Jersey; named for an Indian chief *Aloes Alloway*.

•**ALPHA**, Borough; Warren County; Pop. 2,653; Area Code 201; Zip Code 08865; Elev. 273'; 5 miles SE of Phillipsburg in NW New Jersey; named after the Alpha Cement Works Company.

•**ALPINE**, Borough; Bergen County; Pop. 1,557; Area Code 201; Zip Code 07620; Elev. 410'; NE New Jersey; named after the Alps Mountains in Europe; is hidden among the rocks and trees of the Palisades. Hundreds of Sunday afternoon hikers from New York City come here to follow footpaths along the top of the Palisades or trails along the river bank.

•**ANDOVER**, Borough; Sussex County; Pop. 865; Area Code 201; Zip Code 07821; Elev. 634'; is the site of Andover Mine were parts of a tract of 11,000 acres obtained from *William Penn's* heirs by furnace builders. In October 1932, *Arthur Barry*, the cultured criminal was captured on a nearby farm where he had lived 15 months.

•**ARTHUR KILL**, River; NE New Jersey; Flows S approx. 10 mi. from Newark Bay to Raritan Bay between industrialized New Jersey cities of Elizabeth and Linden and Staten Island, New York.

•**ASBURY PARK**, City; Monmouth County; Pop. 16,675; Area Code 201; Zip Code 07712; Elev. 21'; 25 miles SE of Perth Amboy in NE Central New Jersey, on the Atlantic Coast; named after the first Methodist bishop in America who was *Francis Asbury*; is one of the best-known resorts in northern New Jersey. In 1870, when this region was a wilderness, *James A. Bradley*, a New York businessman, visited the adjoining Ocean Grove camp meeting. He saw possibilities of developing a large summer resort and bought 500 wooded acres, which he developed primarily as a summering place for temperance advocates so that no bad influences might encroach on the adjoining camp meeting.

•**ATLANTIC CITY**, City; Atlantic County; Pop. 40,199; Area Code 609; Elev. 8'; 60 miles SE of Philadelphia in SE New Jersey on the Atlantic Ocean, from where it derives its name.

Atlantic City has developed as a super-resort of New Jersey. Each season brings its characteristic crowd: honeymooners, teachers, elderly retired couples, vacationing white collar workers, businessmen and their families. Uncoaxed, they come and get it. Of the whole American population, only trailer-travelers who wish to bring their trailers into the city limits are prohibited by city ordinance. The hotels and rooming houses have no desire to see "The World's Health and Pleasure Resort" re-established on a freewheeling basis.

Except for the fact that the city fronts the Atlantic Ocean, Atlantic City's geography is unimportant to the visiting host. Yet it plays a vital part in their pleasure. The Philadelphians and Camdenites who come mostly for a day or a week-end's bathing seldom learn that the peculiar coast curve shields the section from devastating northeastern storms. Nor do the New Yorkers, who are more likely to spend a week or a fortnight, often realize that the Gulf Stream comes near enough Atlantic City to temper its winter climate. Finally, few of the visitors from all over the land notice that their mecca is actually an island: for the immense marshes crisscrossed by highways and railways, over which every visitor gets his first skyline glimpse of Atlantic City, hide deep channels that completely cut off this densely populated strip of beach from the mainland.

These natural considerations are subordinated to one of the most fascinating man-made shows playing to capacity audiences anywhere in the world. Here *Madame Polaska* reads your life like an open book; here *Ruth Snyder* and *Judd Gray* sit for eternity in horror-stricken suspense on an electric chair that fails to function; here an assortment of the World's Foremost Astrologers reveal the future at so much a glimpse; here hundreds sit and play Bingo; here the bright lights of Broadway burn through a sea haze; here Somebodies tumble over other Somebodies and over Nobodies as well.

Atlantic City is an amusement factory, operated on the straight-line, mass production pattern. The belt is the boardwalk along which each specialist adds his bit to assemble the finished product, the departing visitor, sated, tanned, and bedecked with souvenirs.

The boardwalk is unique. Sixty feet wide for much of its length, it is of steel and concrete construction overlaid with pine planking in herringbone pattern. Miles of planks are used each year to keep it in repair. Along its four-mile length the city side is lined with huge hotels, broken by blocks of new casinos, shops, restaurants, exhibit rooms, booths, auction houses, and occasional bank and even a private park. Architecturally the motifs are mixed, but functionally they unite in presenting a glittering, luxurious front.

The shops are a melange. Like the super-salesmen who operate them, they sell anything--Ming vases from China, maple furniture from Grand Rapids, laces from the Levant, jewelry from Newark, shawls from Persia, and ladies' ready-to-wear from New York. Confectionery shops, where one of Atlantic City's famous products, salt water taffy, is made and sold, radiate a sickly sweet fragrance among motion picture houses, circus side shows, frozen custard emporiums, shooting galleries, restaurants and hot dog and hamburger stands. Commercially, the boardwalk achieves its greatest dignity in the permanent display shops of leading national advertisers and the smart shops studding the first floors of the large hotels and casinos.

The visitor may tire physically of the boardwalk, but he seldom leaves it. More than a dozen business firms and the city provide pavilions and benches where visitors may watch the passing show or gaze into the vastness of the ocean.

The history of Atlantic City is a story of a city that knew what it wanted to be from its very infancy. Before 1852, when construction of the Camden and Atlantic Railroad began, Atlantic City was an island waste 5 miles off the mainland and separated from it by a series of bays, sounds, and salt meadows. It was known as Absecon (Ind., *place of swans*) Island or Absecon Beach where, historians say, "The frequency of shipwrecks and the undisturbed isolation of the island must have made it an attractive spot for refugees from war or justice." One historian repeats a story "that in the cupola of the first church...was stationed a look-out during the hour of service to acquaint the congregation of a vessel drifting in, in order that the Barnegat and Brigantine Beach people should not forestall them in reaching the scene of disaster and appropriating the best of what the waves would wash in."

Once the climate and beach of the Island were appraised, it was not long before a railroad from Camden was under construction. The railroad company assigned one of its engineers, *Richard B. Osborne* , to lay out the city. To the streets running across from the beach to the marshes he gave the names of the states; for those paralleling the beach he borrowed the names of seven seas: Atlantic, Pacific, Arctic, Baltic, Adriatic, Mediterranean, Caspian. Let Mr. Osborne give his own reasons: "Its proud name is the the nation; it has made her prominent, and will, every year of her existence, prove more and more appropriate as she reaches her manifest destiny--the first, most popular, most health-giving and most inviting watering-place..."

The year 1854 was a crowded one. The city was incorporated March 3. At the first election 18 of the 21 voters pushed their ballots through the slot of a cigar box, fastened with tape. In the same year the first train arrived from Camden, bringing 600 passengers. Many dined at a still uncompleted hotel. Other hotels were soon being built.

Meanwhile the Camden and Atlantic Land Company had bought land at $17.50 an acre and, as a contemporary newspaper reported, planned "to sell it some day for as high as $500 per lot." By 1877 the pressure of traffic was so great that a second railroad to Camden, 54 miles away, was built in the fast time of 98 days. This was known as the Narrow Gauge Railroad because of its 3 1/2-foot gauge, 14 inches less than standard. The West Jersey Railroad, known as the Electric, opened in 1906.

The boardwalk was the joint conception in 1870 of a local hotel man, *Jacob Keim* , and a conductor on the Camden and Atlantic, *Alexander Boardman* . They agreed that the beach was the principal attraction of Atlantic City and noticed that this attraction was nullified by cool or cloudy weather. They had their fellow citizens sign a petition to council, and on June 26, 1870, the first boardwalk was completed. It was set directly upon the sands, and was only 8 feet wide. The present structure, the fifth, dates from 1896.

The next milestone in the history of the resort was the invention of the rolling chair in 1884. *M.D. Shill* , a Philadelphia manufacturer of invalid chairs, gocarts and perambulators, came to Atlantic City and opened a store to rent out baby carriages to summer families. He also rented out invalid chairs for convalescents and handicapped persons. Within a few years these invalid chairs evolved into the double chair with a pusher. Triple chairs followed, completing the fleet of comfortable sightseeing chairs of today.

In 1895 the picture postcard was naturalized in Atlantic City. In that year the wife of *Carl M. Voelker* , a local resident, visited Germany and returned with the idea. *Mr. Voelker* turned them out in his printing shop as an advertising medium for the beach front hotels, and the fad spread across the country.

During these late years of the nineteenth century the making of salt water taffy became a thriving industry. The name was derived from association rather than ingredients. The product is really a form of pulled taffy and is sold now by three large firms operating chains of stores along the boardwalk.

Atlantic City's showmanship achieved real individuality with the creation of the amusement pier, the first of which was built in 1882. The economic principle was the same as that of the skyscraper, except that it operated horizontally, the aim being to occupy little space on the boardwalk, yet to pack as much amusement behind the entrances as was physically possible. After the first of these ingenious structures dipped its spindly legs into the Atlantic's surf, others followed quickly. Their construction was facilitated, it is said, through the accidental discovery of a black laborer, who, while working in Delaware Bay, noticed the effect of water running swiftly from a hose upon the sand. His discovery of jetting was used in sinking foundation piles for the piers.

With the establishment of the amusement pier, Atlantic City's mold was almost unalterably shaped. Since the turn of the century the resort has largely devoted itself to improving and modernizing the basic amusement equipment and refining its technique of entertainment.

Power politics marked Atlantic City's glittering history even after *Enock L. 'Nucky' Johnson*, Republican Party leader in the city and treasurer of Atlantic County, was convicted of income tax evasion in 1941. *Johnson's* successor was *Frank "Hap" Farley*, who dominated the city's political scene for the next three decades. The city fathers began a slum clearance program in the mid-1940s. Despite such programs, the city continued the decline begun during the Great Depression. Civic leaders sought to revive the tourist trade and to bring more industry into the city.

In 1936 the city government had announced plans to turn Atlantic City into a "super resort." The rebuilding program was to continue for 25 years. The plan was still in effect, at least nominally, in 1954 when the city, as part of its centennial celebration, commemorated the first attempt--in 1910-- to fly across the Atlantic Ocean in the dirigible "America." In 1964 the Democratic Party held its national convention in Atlantic City. While nominating *Lyndon B. Johnson* as the Democratic presidential candidate, the convention helped to focus attention on the city's rehabilitation programs.

A new effort began in the early 1970s. Atlantic City had New Jersey's highest poverty rate and one of the United States' highest crime rates. In 1976, a state referendum on the question of casino gambling was approved. On May 27, 1978 Resorts International Casino opened for business in Atlantic City; a second casino opened the following year in the midst of a new wave of prosperity. Plans for some 40 other casinos were under discussion. But numerous complaints revealed that the city's elderly and minority-group citizens were not sharing in the economic renaissance. The city had a population of about 38,000 in 1981.

Atlantic City today is quickly become the "second Las Vegas" in America. It boasts of large casino-hotels, expensive restaurants and dazzling floor shows in its downtown area. The nation's longest boardwalk is along the beach here, and the street names of this boom town were the inspiration for the "monopoly" board game. A "Miss America" is chosen here each year in a televised pageant.

•**ATLANTIC COUNTY**, Southeast Coast; Area 575 sq. miles; Pop. 194,119; Seat-Mays Landing; Established Feb. 7, 1837; Named after the Atlantic Ocean.

•**ATLANTIC HIGHLANDS**, Borough; Monmouth County; Pop. 4,895; Area Code 201; Zip Code 07716; 15 miles SE of Perth Amboy at the end of Hwy. 36 on the S beach of Sandy Hook peninsula in E Central New Jersey; named after the Ocean.

•**AUDUBON**, Borough; Camden County; Pop. 9,546; ; Area Code 609; Zip Code 08105; Elev. 58'; 5 miles SE of Camden in SW New Jersey is a suburb of Camden; named after *John James Audubon* , the naturalist and founder of the Audubon Society.

•**AVALON**, Borough; Cape May County; Pop. 2,192; Area Code 609; Elev. 6'; S New Jersey; named after the island of Welsh mythology.

•**AVON BY THE SEA**, Borough; Monmouth County; Pop. 2,286; Area Code 201; Zip Code 07717; Elev. 22'; E Central New Jersey of the Atlantic Coast; named after Avon, England.

•**BARNEGAT**, Township; Ocean County; Pop. 8.568; Area Code 201; Zip Code 08005; Elev. 35'; located on the eastern coast of New Jersey.

The town's name was originally, but never officially Barendegat (Dutch, breaker's inlet). Often the place is confused with the smaller Barnegat City across the bay, where the famous Barnegat Light stands.

For generations Barnegat's life has been linked to salt water. The Revolution brought a busy shipbuilding industry and a salt works to the place. The settlement had earlier produced pirates who in whaleboats preyed on grounded vessels lured from their course by false beacons.

•**BARNEGAT BAY**, E New Jersey; Extends approx. 20 mi. along coast, protected from Atlantic Ocean by Long Beach barrier island. Fishing and boating are popular along the bay, which is part of the Intracoastal Waterway. At S end is the Barnegat National Wildlife Refuge.

•**BARNEGAT LIGHT**, Borough; Ocean County; Pop. 616; Area Code 201; Zip Code 08006; Elev. 10'; E coast on Atlantic Ocean at the N tip of Long Beach Island in Eastern New Jersey. Island Beach State Park is N of town, with an old lighthouse and miles of bathing beaches along the long barrier island.

•**BARRINGTON**, Borough; Camden County; Pop. 7,426; Area Code 609; Zip Code 08007; Elev. 81'; 5 miles SE of Camden in SW New Jersey.

•**BAYHEAD**, Borough; Ocean County; Pop. 1,336; Area Code 201; Zip Code 08742; Elev. 5'; E Coastal; derives its name from the location at the head of Barnegat Bay; the northermost and largest of a series of small summer resorts. This is the starting point for the popular sailing and motorboat races that take place on the bay.

•**BAYONNE**, City; Hudson County; Pop. 65,047; Area Code 201; Zip Code 07002; Elev. 27'; 5 miles SW of Jersey City in NE New Jersey; named after Bayonne, France.

Nothing remains in the city to recall its setlement. In March 1646, thirty-seven years after *Henry Hudson* stopped at the site of Bayonne before his sail up Hudson River, *Jacob Jacobsen Roy*, a gunner at New Amsterdam, received patent to a tract of land, called after him Konstapel's Hoeck (Dutch, *gunner's point*). Other grants were not issued until December 1654; a year later shelters were built as centers for Indian trading. Shortly after, the Indians, enraged at the Dutch trading tactics, drove out the settlers. Resettlement was made several years after the Dutch made a treaty with the tribesmen in 1658.

The peninsula was called Constable Hook when the British gained control of it in 1664, and later it became Bergen Neck. Trading shacks and forests gave way to homes and large estates. During the next century, the area became a pleasure center for the socialites of the New World.

Separated as it was from New Jersey's mainland and New York, Bayonne was the scene of only a few unimportant skirmishes during the Revolution. With the War of 1812 came the first industrial plant, the Hazard Powder House, which produced some powder for the Navy and for the forts in New York Bay.

To speed the movement of troops and munitions during the Civil War, the first railroad trestle was built across Newark Bay from Elizabethport, which until 1864 was the railhead.

In 1869 the township, which comprised Constable Hook, Bergen Point, Centerville, and Saltersville, was incorporated as the City of Bayonne with a population of 4,000.

The establishment of the Prentice refinery in 1875 marked the beginning of the city's change. The concern employed 20 men and produced 600 barrels of kerosene daily. The rural atmosphere gave way to increasing industrial clatter as in rapid succession the Standard Oil Company, the Tide Water Oil Company and other refineries, attracted by the natural advantages of the location, moved in. Four docks were constructed to take care of increasing tonnage; railroad tracks were laid; and pipe lines were built to bring crude oil directly from Oklahoma and from Illinois. Kerosene was the chief product of the cracking stills, with greases and lubricating oils as byproducts. Pollution from gasoline products, at first generally dumped into the bay, spoiled swimming and fishing.

Several times the Bayonne water front blazed with spectacular oil fires, one of which (1900) lasted for three days. The last big fire was in 1930, when 18 tanks and dockage facilities of the Gulf Refining Company were destroyed by fire and a series of explosions with a $3,000,000 loss. Blazing barges drifted into New York Harbor, pursued by fireboats and tugs.

Twice the Standard Oil plant was the scene of strikes that left a heavy toil of dead and wounded among the employees. In 1915 one hundred still cleaners, striking for overtime pay, were joined by 5,000 other workers. At an expense of $250,000, the company called in a strikebreaking organization led by *Pearl Bergoff*. Five men were killed by police or imported strike guards. Sheriff *Eugene F. Kinkead* arrested the strike leader, *J.J. Baly*, and, when the strike was almost ended, he jailed 99 special company guards. The company finally yielded a small increase, but wages still remained below the prevailing level.

A year later the workers struck for a 30 percent wage increase for men earning less than $3 a day and a 20 percent rise for all others. The result was another series of battles that left eight workers dead and twenty-five seriously hurt. Strikers complained that their leaders were hampered in entering the city and that some of their local sympathizers were forced to leave their homes. The strike ended with nothing gained. Afterward Standard Oil became one of the pioneers in establishing a company union, or employees' representation system.

One of the strangest strikes in the history of the city began in the fall of 1937 when eight members of the American Newspaper Guild walked out of the Bayonne *Times* office after the publisher failed to put a wage and hour agreement into effect. Most of the leading Bayonne merchants and thousands of citizens gave their support to the small band of strikers, who finally won a sweeping victory despite a Chancery Court injunction that practically prohibited any strike activities.

•**BEACH HAVEN**, Borough; Ocean County; Pop. 1,714; Area Code 201; Zip Code 08008; Elev. 10'; E New Jersey.

•**BEACHWOOD**, Borough; Ocean County; Pop. 7,687; Area Code 201; Zip Code 08722; Elev. 25'; located in Eastern New Jersey; is a summer colony. A 150 years ago it was the terminal of a mule-powered wooden railway that ran from charcoal-burning pits at Lakehurst to Toms River; stockholders and mules went back to the plow when the coal mines killed the charcoal trade. A few traces of the old railway remain. Named for its location.

•**BEDMINSTER**, Township; Somerset County; Pop. 2,469; Area Code 201; Zip Code 07921; named for Bedminster, England.

•**BELLEVILLE**, Town; Essex County; Pop. 35367; Area Code 201; Zip Code 07109; Elev. 69'; located in NE New Jersey; is an old Dutch settlement on the steep bank of Passaic River. At first only the "Second River Section" of Newark, the town became a separate community in 1839. Second River was the scene of a rear guard action in 1777. The first low pressure steam engine made in America was manufactured at a plant in Belleville for *John Stevens* in 1798. The engine was installed in a boat that ran under steam power down the Passaic to New York. This was nine years before Fulton operated the Clermont, but eight years after *John Fitch* ran a steamboat on the Delaware. The name is French, meaning "beautiful city."

•**BELIMAWR**, Borough; Camden County; Pop. 13,752; Area Code 609; Zip Code 08031; Elev. 44'; located in SW New Jersey, 5 miles South of Camden; originally known as Heddings for a church built here in 1865, the community changed its name when a post office was established. Named for *Ernest C. Bell*, horse breeder.

•**BELMAR**, Borough; Monmouth County; Pop. 6,771; Area Code 201; Zip Code 07719; Elev. 19'; located in E New Jersey; is named for the Italian word meaning "beautiful sea."

•**BELVIDERE**, Town; Warren County; Pop. 2,475; Area Code 201; Zip Code 07823; Elev. 28'; name is Italian word meaning "beautiful to see."

•**BERGEN COUNTY**, Northeast New Jersey borders New York State; Area 233 sq. miles; Pop. 845,385; Seat- Mays Landing; Established March 1, 1683; named for Bergen-op-zoom, Holland.

The county lies just a George Washington Bridge-length from Manhattan and is criss-crossed by Interstate 80, the New Jersey Turnpike and the Garden State Parkway. The football Giants and the soccer champion Cosmos (and soon the basketball Nets) play here to audiences in the Meadowlands Sports Complex. A growing number of *Fortune* 500 corporate headquarters, haute cuisine restaurants, higher education facilities, ski slopes and swimming pools, sparkling luxury apartment buildings and thousands of well manicured lawns are all part of the Bergen scenery.

Bergen County was first recorded by *Robert Juet*, a ship's officer on *Henry Hudson's Half Moon* in 1609 as it sailed between the County and what the Indians called Man-a-hat-ta. Juet's *Journal* recorded the area as one of "good furres," "skins of divers sorts," "white green cliffs," and "copper or silver myne" hills. It was "a pleasant Land with grasse and flowers and goodly trees." It still is.

Chief Oratam, the great Sachem of the Achensachy (Hackensack) Indians, a tribe of the Lenni Lenape which occupied what is now Bergen, welcomed the early white settlers from Holland. The first settlements were river towns of Fort Lee on the Hudson and Hackensack and New Milford on the Hackensack. The English took control from the Dutch in 1664. Bergen was designated a "County" or judicial district in 1675 and in 1683 its borders were set by an Act of the Assembly. Bergen and New York State finally set its border firmly in 1769. Hackensack became the county seat in 1710 and remains so to this day. Bergen played an important role in the Revolutionary War and Washington camped out here often. The British, to our dismay, managed to burn the Hackensack courthouse in 1780. Historical sites and buildings abound, particularly at the New Milford-North Hackensack complex which boasts a number of colonial homes; at the Fort Lee terminus of the George Washington Bridge; Paramus (where a red mill built in 1745 made blankets and uniforms for the Continental Army); and many other locales.

The first official census taken in 1790 reveals Bergen had a population of 12,601. Today it is near the million mark. The biggest stimuli to growth were construction of the railroads after the Civil War and the opening in 1931 of the graceful span over the Hudson, the George Washington Bridge, linking the county with the great megalopolis. The county's population in 1930 was 365,000.

•**BERGENFIELD**, Borough; Bergen County; Pop. 25,568; Area Code 201; Zip Code 07621; Elev. 92'; located in NE New Jersey.

•**BERKELEY HEIGHTS**, Township; Union County; Pop. 12,549; Area Code 201; Zip Code 07922; located in NE New Jersey; named after *Lord John Berkeley* , Proprietor.

•**BERLIN**, Borough; Camden County; Pop. 5,786; Area Code 609; Zip Code 08009; Elev. 155'; 15 miles SE of Camden in SW New Jersey; owes its existence to the fact that it was just about here that passengers on the stagecoach from the coast to the Delaware River ferry began to be hungry. The stage, due at 3 p.m. was usually late. Hence the old name, Long-a-Coming, given to the town by impatient passengers. The change to Berlin came when a post office was established in 1867. Named for Berlin, Germany.

•**BERNARDSVILLE**, Borough; Somerset County; Pop. 6,715; Area Code 201; Zip Code 07924; Elev. 400'; located in N New Jersey; named after *Francis Bernard* , Governor 1758-60.

•**BEVERLY,**, City; Burlington County; Pop. 2,919; Area Code 609; Zip Code 08010; Elev. 28'; located in S New Jersey; named for Beverly, England.

•**BLACKWOOD TERRACE**, Township (also included in Deptford Township); Gloucester County; Pop. 900; Area Code 609; Zip Code 08096; located in SW New Jersey.

•**BLAIRSTOWN**, Township; Warren County; Pop. 4,360; Area Code 201; Zip Code 07825; Elev. 350'; located in NW New Jersey;

covers the northern slope of Paulins Kill Valley and extends to the highway; is a preparatory school for boys, founded in 1848 by *John I. Blair*, the Lackawanna R.R. millionaire, in which the township is named. More than a century ago the town was known as Gravel Hill. It was aided in its growth as an educational center and as a shipping point for farm produce by *John Blair*.

•**BLOOMFIELD**, Town; Essex County; Pop. 47,792; Area Code 201; Zip Code 07003 ; Elev. 131'; located in NE New Jersey; an old settlement that has developed as a modern residential and industrial extension of Newark. Originally known as Wardsesson (Ind. crooked place), it got its present name when a town meeting decided in 1796 to honor *Joseph Bloomfield*, Revolutionary general and later Governor (1810-1812).

Montclair, Belleville, Glen Ridge, and Nutley have all been formed from the 20 square miles that was once Bloomfield. The city's factories, producing a wide variety of goods, have been built along its two railroad lines.

BLOOMFIELD COLLEGE AND SEMINARY, facing the green at Broad, Franklin and Liberty Sts., is a Presbyterian institution founded in 1810.

Bloomfield was the birthplace of *Randolph Bourne*, prominent pacifist, author of Education and Living, and philosopher of the American youth movement during the pre-World War I literary renascence. Bourne died at the age of 32 in 1918, leaving an unfulfilled future but a decisive influence on his contemporaries.

•**BLOOMINGDALE**, Borough; Passaic County; Pop. 7,867; Area Code 201; Zip Code 07403; Elev. 257'; located in N New Jersey; name is descriptive of location.

•**BLOOMSBURY**, Borough; Hunterdon County; Pop. 864; Area Code 201; Zip Code 08804; Elev. 279'; located in NW New Jersey.

•**BOGOTA**, Borough; Bergen County; Pop. 8344; Area Code 201; Zip Code 07603; Elev. 100'; located in NE New Jersey; named for Bogert family, early settlers.

•**BOONTOWN**, Town; Morris County; Pop. 8,620; Area Code 201; Zip Code 07005; Elev. 431'; located N of New Jersey; is built high into the ledge that overlooks precipitous Rockaway Gorge. Named after Governor Thomas Boone, 1760-61. Settled in 1762. Incorporated in 1867. An early iron works was established here and for about 50 years in the middle of the nineteenth century, when iron rails were demolishing the West's frontiers, the town was one of the largest iron centers in the country.

•**BORDENTOWN**, City; Burlington County; Pop. 4,441; Area Code 609; Zip Code 08505; Elev. 72'; located in S New Jersey; settled in 1682 by *Thomas Farnsworth*, an English Quaker, the village was first known as Farnsworth's Landing. It became a busy shipping center, thanks to its location at the confluence of Delaware River and Crosswicks Creek. By 1734 the Landing had a stage line and packet service, making connections at Philadelphia and at Perth Amboy for the New York boat. This enterprise was established by *Joseph Borden*, for whom the town was soon named.

The pleasant site attracted the fashionables of Philadelphia as summer visitors. Among the Morrises, the Shippens, the Chews, the Norrises, and the Hopkinsons a gracious social life developed.

Patience Lovell (1752-1785), born in Bordentown of Quaker parentage, began as a child to model in bread crumbs and clay. As a young woman she went abroad to study art, but it was not until she was 47 and a widow with four children that her work received recognition. She won international attention for her figures in wax, notably one of Sir William Pitt which was placed in Westminster Abbey.

Bordentown was severely punished by the British for the famous "mechanical keg plot" of the Revolution. In January 1778 the British fleet was anchored in the Delaware at Philadelphia. One night the patriots upstream launched a flotilla of kegs filled with gunpowder, depending upon the river current to carry them to the fleet, which--unknown to the Colonials--had just been removed from its exposed position. Only one of the primitive mines exploded, but it killed four men and created a panic among the British. Thereafter every piece of flotsam was viewed with suspicion and orders were given to fire without warning upon any unidentified log, keg or barrel.

The mechanical kegs had been built in the cooperage of *Col. Joseph Borden*. It was his son-in-law, the talented *Francis Hopkinson*, who promptly wrote one of the best jingles of the Revolution, *The Battle of the Kegs*, 22 verses that were published throughout the Colonies and caused some British officers to wear countenances no less scarlet than their uniforms.

Angered no less by Hopkinson's verses than by the plot to blow up the fleet, the British sent five armed vessels and 24 flat-bottomed boats with about 800 soldiers to Bordentown in May 1778. At their approach, the townspeople destroyed more than 20 American vessels that had been lying at the White Hill. Disappointed, the British turned on the town and razed the home and store of *Colonel Borden* . *As the colonel's wife sat in the middle of the street and watched the destruction, a British officer expressed his sympathy. The proud old lady retorted: "...This is the happiest day of my life. I know you have given up all hope of reconquering my country, or you would not thus wantonly devastate it." Before they left the British also burned two Continental galleys that had been moored up Crosswicks Creek.*

Thomas Paine , the firebrand of the Revolution, made his home in Bordentown with *Col. Joseph Kirkbride* in 1783 before buying his own house. Here he received a cordial invitation from Washington to visit him at Rocky Hill. *Paine* had been virtually ignored, and Washington hoped thus to remind Congress of the value of his Revolutionary services.

After *Paine* had been rewarded by appointments to several responsible positions he was often visited at Bordentown by *Benjamin Franklin* , *Gouverneur Morris* , and other distinguished men. The gunsmith and dreamer, *John Fitch* , came with plans and a proposal of partnership in the building of a steamboat. Although *Paine* offered mechanical suggestions he was not further interested.

When *Paine* returned to Europe and became embroiled in the affairs of the French Revolution he still held an affectionate memory of Bordentown. In one letter he wrote "...my heart and myself are three thousand miles apart; and I had rather see my horse, Button, eating the grass of Bordentown, than see all the show and pomp of Europe."

Following his escape from the guillotine and the publication of the *Age of Reason* , *Paine* again sought the comfort of the pleasant river town and, more particularly, of his friend, *Colonel Kirkbride* . His liberal religious views had outraged most of his former admirers, and there were few who cared or dared to greet him. But *Colonel Kirkbride* welcomed his old friend--only to flee ‑ with him from a mob of jeering pursuers who forced their way into the quiet garden and literally ran *Paine* out of town.

In the summer of 1790 the townspeople gathered on the bluff to cheer the first commercially operated steamboat in America. *John Fitch* , the ridiculed inventor, had at last succeeded in building a steam packet for a service along the Delaware, and Bordentown was a scheduled stop. Two years earlier *Fitch* had made an experimental trip from Philadelphia to Bordentown.

In 1816 *Joseph Bonaparte*, exiled King of Spain and brother of *Napoleon*, bought about 1,500 acres, which he developed into an elaborate estate on the outskirts of the town. No alien was then permitted to own property in the United States, and transference of title was delayed a year pending passage of a special act by the legislature. The little kingdom on the edge of the Delaware River earned for New Jersey the sobriquet of "New Spain."

Bordentown was the scene of a peacetime mechanical feat no less remarkable than the launching of the powder kegs. In 1831 there arrived from England a strange assortment of iron plates, pipes, bolts, nuts, rods, and other parts. These were the makings of the first locomotive to run on the new Camden and Amboy Railroad. To *Isaac Dripps*, a young mechanic of Bordentown who had never seen a locomotive, fell the task of assembling these parts without the aid of a shop drawing--the only item omitted by the British manufacturers. After 2 weeks of dogged effort, *Dripps* had the *John Bull* ready for service, and on November 12, 1831, tested in a run with two coaches filled with distinguished passengers.

Shops employing hundreds of skilled mechanics were established in Bordentown for the construction and repair of locomotives and coaches. Meanwhile the Delaware and Raritan Canal was completed in 1834 from New Brunswick to Bordentown. For the succeeding 30 years the canal as a freight carrier made the town an important water transport center.

Bordentown was incorporated as a borough in 1825, and rechartered as a city in 1867. Population expanded to 6,000 with an influx of Irish and German immigrants, employed on the railroad and canal. As the town changed its character many of the aristocrats left their fine mansions.

In 1871 the Pennsylvania Railroad dealt a double blow to Bordentown. After it had leased both the railroad and the canal, it removed the railroad shops to its own locations in Altoona, Pa., and Newark, and stifled canal commerce by refusing to allow coal to be water-hauled in competition with the railroad. Bordentown has never recovered the commercial importance lost in those years after the Civil War.

•**BOUND BROOK**, Borough; Somerset County; Pop. 9,710; Area Code 201; Zip Code 08805; Elev. 48'; located in North Central New

Jersey; the site of a British Raid is marked by a boulder at Main and East Sts. Near it stood a blockhouse garrisoned by 500 of Washington's troops. On April 13, 1777, a British force of 4,000 under *Cornwallis* surprised the sleeping Continentals. Named for boundary in Indian deed.

•**BRADLEY BEACH**, Borough; Monmouth County; Pop. 4,772; Area Code 201; Zip Code 07720; Elev. 26'; named after *James A. Bradley*, founder.

•**BRANCHVILLE**, Borough; Sussex County; Pop. 870; Area Code 201; Zip Code 07826; Elev. 529'; located in N New Jersey; named Branchville as it's the main branch of Paulins Kill.
•**BRICK**, Township; Ocean County; Pop. 53,629; Area Code 201; Zip Code 08723; located in E New Jersey; named after *Joseph W. Brick*, resident.

•**BRIDGETON**, City; Seat of Cumberland County; Pop. 18,795; Area Code 609; Zip Code 08302; Elev. 40'; located in SW New Jersey; Quakers founded Bridgeton in 1686, though a few scattered settlers were here before them. A bridge built across Cohansey Creek about 1716 have the hamlet the name of Conhansy Bridge. Later it was changed to Bridge Town and then to Bridgeton.

•**BRIDGEWATER**, Township; Somerset County; Pop. 29,175; Area Code 201; Zip Code 08807; located in N New Jersey; named after Bridgewater, England.

•**BRIELLE**, Borough; Monmouth County; Pop. 4,086; Area Code 201; Zip Code 08730; Elev. 12'; located in E New Jersey; is at the mouth of Mansquan River where the stream joins the Atlantic Ocean. It has a large fishing fleet and boat yards. Named after commune in Holland.

•**BRIGANTINE**, City; Atlantic County; Pop. 8,318; Area Code 609; Zip Code 08203; Elev. 8'; located in SE New Jersey; named after Brigantine, a ship wrecked about 1710 in this area. North of town is long Brigantine Beach, popular with sunbathers from Atlantic City. A "natural area" was set aside here by the state.

•**BUDD LAKE**, Unincorporated; Morris County; Pop. 3,168; Area Code 201; Zip Code 07828; Elev. 940'; named for *John Budd* an early landowner. Budd Lake is a summer resort on the broad, shallow lake of the same name. Frame cottages line the low lake front, many of them adorned with the rustic namesigns that haunt most lake pleasure resorts: Dew Drop Inn, Wa-Kum-On Inn, Blue Heaven. High wooded hills guard the northwestern rim of the lake. Budd Lake has been popular as a training-ground for prizefighters.

•BUENA, Borough; Atlantic County; Pop. 3,642; Area Code 609; Zip Code 08310; Elev. 108'; located in SE New Jersey; named for battle of Buena Vista, Mexican War.

•BURLINGTON, City; Burlington County; Pop. 10,246; Area Code 609; Zip Code 08016; Elev. 12'; located in S New Jersey; the town owes its existence to the Quakers, whose influence has persisted to the present. Two companies of Friends, one from London and one from Yorkshire, began the settlement in 1677. *John Crips* , one of the settlers, wrote in that year: "...the country and air seems to be very agreeable to our bodies, and we have very good stomachs to our victuals...The Indians are very loving to us, except here and there one, when they have gotten strong liquors in their heads, which they now greatly love..." During the following year *Crips* wrote: "...I do not remember that ever I tasted better water in any part of England, than the springs of this place do yield; of which is made very good beer and ale; and here is also wine and cyder...As for the musketto fly, we are not troubled with them in this place..."

High Street was laid out with lots to the east for the Yorkshiremen and lots to the west for the men from London. The settlement, first called New Beverly, then Bridlington from the Yorkshire town, finally became Burlington. The land nurtured a steadily growing community and the new town soon took rank as one of the first permanent settlements in the western part of the Colony. The following year the ship *Shield* brought a second company of Quakers. A gristmill and a sawmill were built, and in 1681, after West New Jersey had become a separate province, the Colonial Assembly designated Burlington as the capital and port of entry. The Burlington yearly and quarterly meetings of Friends were established this year.

Burlington was one of the first settlements to provide for public education. In 1682 an act of the assembly gave Matinicunk Island in Delaware River to the town with the stipulation that the revenue be used for the education of youth. The money from farm tenants on the island is still spent for schools.

The first schoolhouse was a Quaker institution. Built in 1792 (now occupied by the Young Women's Christian Association), it was constructed partly with bricks from the meeting house erected in 1683. Members of the Church of England who came to Burlington were antagonistic to the Quaker classes that existed long before the school was built. In 1714 the Episcopal Society appointed as schoolmaster *Rowland Ellis*, who complained that his efforts were "beset with Heathenism, Paganism, Quakerism and God knows what." Ironically, a majority of the 20 pupils enrolled under *Ellis* at that time were Quakers.

The Episcopalians were no more friendly toward the very few Presbyterian newcomers. Of them, *John Talbot*, rector of St. Mary's said: "The Presbyterians here come a great way to lay hands one on another; but after all I think they had as good stay at home, for the good they do." Methodists and Baptists joined the settlement a good deal later. Burlington's fine old Colonial churches are its heritage from those first citizens.

The town was capital of the Province from 1681, alternating with Perth Amboy after the union of West and East Jersey in 1702. During this period Burlington was the residence of *Deputy Governors Samuel Jennings* and *Thomas Olive*, and *Governor Jonathan Belcher*.

A dozen years after its founding the town had a large pottery, salt house, and other industries. Shipbuilding became increasingly important. By 1744 Burlington ranked with New York, Philadelphia, and Boston as one of the busiest ports in the country.

In 1776 the little city, then numbering 1,000, was chosen as the meeting place of the Provincial Congress, which there adopted the state constitution. Secure in their prosperity, the citizens of Burlington did not take the Revolution too seriously. The invasion of the town by about 400 Hessians in December 1776, and the cannonading in the spring of 1778 by two British warships returning from an attack on American frigates farther up the Delaware, were accepted with equanimity. In fact British naval officers had to warn spectators from the Green Bank before the bombardment started.

Burlington's position on the main thoroughfare between New York and Philadelphia and the natural beauty of its site attracted many of the political and literary figures of the early days of the Republic. The town became a summer resort for the fashionables of Philadelphia.

An important contribution to agricultural methods was made by *Charles Newbold* of Burlington, who patented the cast-iron plow in 1797. Farmers first feared that it would poison the soil, but their prejudice was finally overcome.

About 1838 a silkworm industry was started with acres of mulberry trees, but the experiment failed. From the Civil War to the present Burlington's industries have developed substantially, but the once vital shipping trade has disappeared.

•BURLINGTON COUNTY, Central New Jersey; Area 819 sq. miles; Pop. 362,542; Seat- Mount Holly; Established May 17, 1694; Named for Burlington, England- a corruption from New Beverly/Bridlington.

•BUTLER, Borough; Morris County; Pop. 7,616; Area Code 201; Zip Code 07405; Elev. 315'; located in N New Jersey; is spread out over rolling wooded country. The community was founded in 1695; among its residents are descendants of Hessians who quit *King George's* service to remain in America after the Revolution had succeeded. Named after a early landowner.

•CALDWELL, Borough; Essex County; Pop. 7,624; Area Code 201; Zip Code 07006; Elev. 411'; located in NE New Jersey; named after a "fighting parson" during the Revolution, *Rev. James Caldwell* .

•CALIFON, Borough; Hunterdon County; Pop. 1,023; Area Code 201; Zip Code 07830; Elev. 411'; located in NW New Jersey; named for California.

•CAMDEN, City; Camden County; Pop. 84,910; Area Code 609; Zip Code 081+zone; Elev. 23'; located in SW New Jersey; is always aware of Philadelphia, and there is a custom--strictly confined to Camden--of referring to the "twin cities of the Delaware." Some years ago Philadelphians used to say vaguely, "Camden is over there in back of the Victor and Campbell's soup factories," and traveling Camdenites often said that they were from Philadelphia to forestall explanations. But an increasingly larger portion of the United States now knows that Camden is a city opposite Philadelphia.

The ties with Philadelphia are deeply rooted in the history of the two cities. Both were permanently colonized by the Quakers, fleeing from religious persecution in England. The first Camden settler was probably *William Cooper* , who built a home in 1681 on the point of land below Cooper River and named the tract Pyne Point. In the same year scattered families of Friends set up a meeting, still in existence, the third established in New Jersey.

After *Cooper* took over the ferry to Philadelphia the ssettlement became known as Cooper's Ferries. Virtually all the rest of the present site of Camden was taken by *John Kaighn*, for whom the old village of Kaighntown was named, and by *Archibald Mickle*, upon whose farm Camden proper developed later. But the settlement grew slowly and by the beginning of the eighteenth century there were fewer than a dozen clearings in the wooded points on the Delaware. Philadelphia was more attractive to the newcomers.

A real estate boom began in 1773 when *Jacob Cooper* Philadelphia merchant and descendant of *William Cooper*, laid out 40 acres as a townsite. He named the place Camden for the first Earl of Camden, the nobleman who had befriended the Colonies during their disputes with the mother country. Twenty-two communities in the United States have chosen the same name.

The Revolution checked development of the new village. During the British occupation of Philadelphia, Camden was held as an enemy outpost and a number of skirmishes occurred within the present city limits. Years after the end of the war Camden continued to be more a ferry terminal than a town.

About 1809 a small steamboat began operation as a ferry for passengers. Others followed, replacing the open boats that had double keels for use as runners when the river was frozen.

Originally part of Newton Township, Camden was incorporated as a city in 1828 and in 1844 was made the seat of Camden County. The city's real growth began in 1834 when it became the terminus of the Camden and Amboy Railroad, then the longest line in the country. All-iron rails, imported from England, were fastened to the ties with hook-headed spikes, the invention of *Robert Stevens*. The first locomotive, the *John Bull*, a duplicate of Stephenson's *Planet*, was also English-made.

For six years the line was the only through route between Philadelphia and New York. In 1840 the railroad company opened another line from Philadelphia via Trenton and New Brunswick direct to Jersey City, which reduced the importance of the Camden route but strengthened the transportation monopoly that gave New Jersey the name of the "State of Camden and Amboy."

On the night of March 15, 1856, the ferryboat *New Jersey* left its Philadelphia dock and caught fire in midstream. Ice floes made it impossible for the ferry to be beached, or for other craft to get to her aid. Sixty-one persons perished. This disaster, coupled with the financial panic of the following year, hindered the town's growth.

Following the Civil War, Camden was caught up in the tremendous industrial expansion that was the sequel to railroad building. Swiftly the water front was taken over by factories. When every site was filled, the shops and mills overran the town.

•**CAMDEN COUNTY**, Northwest New Jersey; Area 221 sq. miles; Pop. 471,650; Seat- Camden; Established March 13, 1844; Named for Earl of Camden.

•**CAPE MAY**, City; Cape May County; Pop. 4,853; Area Code 609; Zip Code 08204; Elev. 14'; located at the southernmost point of New Jersey on the Atlantic Ocean; dean of the Jersey shore resorts, for almost a century catered to the most prominent figures in American public affairs and society.

Cape May's recorded history as a summer resort goes back to 1801 when Postmaster *Ellis Hughes* advertised in a Philadelphia newspaper: "The subscriber has prepared himself for entertaining company who use sea bathing, and he is accommodated with extensive house room, with fish, oysters and crabs and good liquors."

To Cape May came Presidents Lincoln, Grant, Pierce, Buchanan, and Harrison. *Horace Greely, John Wanamaker*, countless Congressmen, and wealthy society leaders vacationed here.

The Cape, named for *Cornelius Jacobsen Mey* who sailed past in 1623 - 14 years after *Henry Hudson* - was purchased in 1631 by *Samuel Godyn* and *Samuel Blommaert*. Into the waters surrounding the Cape came whaling boats, British men-o'-war, and pirates-all attracted mainly by the fresh water supply of Lilly Pond, a 10-acre sheet of fresh water beautifully dotted with creamy white water lilies. *Captain Kidd* filled his water casks and supposedly cached part of his treasure near the pond. *Col. William Quary* unsuccessfully pursued *Kidd* to this region in 1699. During the War of 1812 British warships watered here until exasperated residents dug a ditch from the ocean to spoil the sweet water. The ditch was filled in after the war and the water gradually became fresh again.

Of all the resorts along the coastlines of America, one can lay claim to the title of the "Nation's Oldest Seashore Resort."

This is the City of Cape May, New Jersey's southernmost resort. Located between the waters of the Atlantic Ocean and

Delaware Bay, Cape May is at the southern end of the Garden State Parkway. It is only minutes away from the New Jersey terminal of the Cape May-Lewes Ferry.

Cape May has had historical recognition for well over 200 years. Its rich heritage has seen it prominent as a haven for pirates; as an important niche in the coastal sailing trade; as a fishing center and as an important link to the ships that have defended these shores over the years.

Throughout its span of history, Cape May has been indelibly marked with a rich Victorian culture and architecture, and much of this is preserved in the city's Victorian Village.

This exciting, growing venture into yesteryear is truly unique, with its old Victorian architecture in many of the public buildings and private homes.

Blended with new, modern motels, Cape May's old hotels, rooming houses and apartment houses offer the visitor a wide selection of accommodations. Activities are available for all seasons.

The Cape's namesake, *Cornelius Jacobsen Mey*, was a Dutch explorer who represented the Dutch West India Company. Mey explored the coast in 1621. Today, ocean-going vessels come daily to unload passengers and seafood catches, a good deal of which winds up on the table in area seafood houses or in nearby fish markets.

There is much to do and see in Cape May. A tour of the Victorian Village is a must. A promenade along the beach and a visit to one of the many restaurants helps visitors savor some of the food which has made Jersey Cape cooking well-known.

Other attractions include the Audubon Bird Sanctuary, the old trolley, famous Lake Lily, activities at Convention Hall and the U.S. Coast Guard Recruit Training Center.

One can pick up Cape May Diamonds, watch the sailboat races, visit the local shops to browse and buy and relax in the surf on the white, sandy beach.

Cape May, the "Nation's Oldest Seashore Resort," beckons and its more than 200 years of resort experience offers a vacation full of excitement, relaxation, history, and fun.

The League of Offices and art gallery are on the grounds of the Physick Estate at 1048 Washington St., Cape May.

Self-conducted tours of Dennisville, South Seaville, and Cape May Court House offer opportunities to explore the history of the mainland communities.

Early seaside classic construction can be found in the areas surrounding Ocean City's Tabernacle and Cape May's Victorian Mall. Many of the county's antique shops are actually housed in classic old structures which have been restored or kept up by their owners as part of the county's historical heritage.

Many of the old buildings are in use and can be visited by the public. The old Court House which was built in 1849 is still in active use. It graces the main street in the county seat in Cape May Court House. Other examples of historical architecture include the Cold Spring Presbyterian Church on Seashore Road (1823); Tuckahoe Grange on Route 50; the resident-built Woodbine Synogogue; Seaville's Friends Meeting House (1700) and Congress Hall on Beach Drive in Cape May.

•CAPE MAY COUNTY, Southern Coastal New Jersey; Area 267 sq. miles; Pop. 82,266; Seat- Cape May Court House; Named for *Cornelius Jacobsen Mey* , (Corrupted to May).

•CAPE MAY COURT HOUSE, County Seat; Cape May County; Area Code 609; Zip Code 08210; located in S New Jersey.

•CAPE MAY POINT, Borough; Cape May County; Pop. 255; Area Code 609; Zip Code 08212; Elev. 9'; located in S New Jersey.

•CARLSTADT, Borough; Bergen County; Pop. 6.166; Area Code 201; Zip Code 07072; Elev. 94'; located in NE New Jersey; is a bit of "Das Vaterland" planted in an American town on the rocky ridge between the Hackensack and Passaic valleys. The land was bought cooperatively from the original American owers by a group of German exiles, liberals and freethinkers who were seeking political liberty. The town, first called Tailor Town because many of the inhabitants worked for New York tailors, was later renamed Carlstadt (Carl's town) for *Dr. Carl Klein* , leader of the German group.

•CARNEY'S POINT, Township; Salem County; Pop. 2,680; Area Code 609; Zip Code 08069; located in SW New Jersey; 6 miles NE of Perth Amboy in Central New Jersey by Staten Island.

•CARTERET, Borough; Middlesex County; Pop. 20,598; Area Code 201; Zip Code 07008; Elev. 12'; located in Central New Jersey; named after the first English Governor, *Philip Carteret* .

•CEDAR GROVE, Township; Essex County; Pop. 12,600; Area Code 201; Zip Code 07009; located in NE New Jersey; descriptive name for stands of cedars.

•**CHATHAM**, Borough; Morris County; Pop. 8,537; Area Code 201; Zip Code 07928; Elev. 244'; 5 miles SE of Morristown in N New Jersey; located 10 miles West of Newark; was at one time known as Bonnel Town. Its antiquarians are fond of boasting that no British troops ever enterd the town Day's Tavern, a two-and-a-half-story frame building with wide front proch ws frequented a good deal by *Washington* and his officers. The current name comes from the Earl of Chatham who was friendly to the colonists.

•**CHERRY HILL**, Township; Camden County; Pop. 68,785; Area Code 609; Zip Code 080+ zone; E of Camden in W central New Jersey.

•**CHESTER**, Borough; Morris County; Pop. 1,433; Area Code 201; Zip Code 07930; Elev. 846'; located in North Central New Jersey on Hwy. 24 just E of Hwy. 206; was the first brick building erected in the town. It was built by *Zephaniah Drake* in 1812. Chester's first settlers, arriving in 1713, were attracted by the industrial possibilities offered by the waters of the Black River. They bult sawmills, gristmills and distilleries; later, woolen and threshing-machine factories were established, and until 1890 iron mines operated in the midst of this peach-orchard area. They are all gone. Named for Chestershire, England.

•**CINNAMINSON**, Township; Burlington County; Pop. 16,072; Area Code 609; Zip Code 08077; located in S central New Jersey; descriptive name derived rom Assan meaning "stone" and minna meaning "island."

•**CLARK**, Township; Union County; Pop. 16,699; Area Code 201; Zip Code 07066; located in NE New Jersey; named after a signer of the Declaration of Independence, *Abraham Clark* .

•**CLAYTON**, Borough; Gloucester County; Pop. 6,013; Area Code 609; Zip Code 08312; Elev. 130'; located in SW New Jersey.

•**CLEMENTON**, Borough; Camden County; Pop. 5,764; Area Code 609; Zip Code 08021; SE of Camden in SW New Jersey; named for *Samuel Clements* , industrialist.

•**CLIFFSIDE PARK**, Borough; Bergen County; Pop. 21,464; Area Code 201; Zip Code 07010; Elev. 57'; on the Hudson River, across from New York City, 10 miles NE of Jersey City; named for its location "Park by the cliffs."

•**CLIFTON**, City; Passaic County; Pop. 74,388; Area Code 201; Zip Code 070+zone; Elev. 70'; located in N New Jersey; named for location under Weasel Mountain.

•**CLINTON**, Town; Hunterdon County; Pop. 1,910; Area Code 201; Zip Code 08809; Elev. 195'; located in NW New Jersey; named for Governor of New York *De Witt Clinton* .

•**CLOSTER**, Borough; Bergen County; Pop. 8,164; Area Code 201; Zip Code 07624; Elev. 51; located in NE New Jersey; was the scene of a spontaneous strike in 1936 during the course of which a sympathizer was shot and eventually died. The killing provoked a vigorous controversy over civil liberties, accentuated when the police forbade a memorial mass meeting, which, however, was finally held after an injunction had been attained. The shop foreman was found guilty of the killing and was sentenced to serve from six to ten years in the State Penitentiary. The strikers were persuaded to return to work. Named after *Frederick Closter* , settler.

•**COHANSEY RIVER**, River, S New Jersey; Flows S and W approx. 30 mi. from source in Salem County to Atlantic Ocean at Cohansey Cove, Delaware Bay.

•**COLLINGSWOOD**, Borough; Camden County; Pop. 15,838; Area Code 609; Zip Code 08108; Elev. 20'; located in SW New Jersey, NE of Camden; named after Mother of *Edward Collings Knight* .

•**COLONIA**, Unincorporate village; Somerset County; Pop. 23,200; Area Code 201; NE New Jersey; In a suburban-residential area SW of Rahway.

•**COLTS NECK**, Township; Monmouth County; Pop. 7,888; Area Code 201; Zip Code 07722; Elev. 125; located in E New Jersey on Hwy. 537; was originally named Caul's Neck for an early settler. It became a famous breeding place for race horses, and a story persists that a colt of the renowned race horse, *Old Fashioned* , fell and broke its neck here.

•**CONVENT STATION**, included in Morristown; Morris County; Pop. est. 1,300; Area Code 201; Zip Code 07961; located in N New Jersey.

•**COOKSTOWN**, included in New Hanover and North Hanover townships; Burlington County; Pop. est. 300; Area Code 609; Zip Code 08511; located in S New Jersey.

•**CRANBURY**, Township; Middlesex County; Pop. 1,927; Area Code 201; Zip Code 08512; Elev. 110'; located in Central New Jersey; named for wild cranberries; is a center of a potato-growing district. Cranbury was settled in 1682 and here, 50 years later, *David Brainerd*, the young follower of *George Whitefield*, often preached to the Indians under one of the village elms.

•**CRANFORD**, Township; Union County; Pop. 24,573; Area Code 201; Zip Code 07016; Elev. 70'; located in NE New Jersey; named for the *Crane* family; is spread along the Rahway River Parkway. The name Nomhegan is a variation of Noluns Mohegans, as the New Jersey Indians were called in the treaty ending the Indian troubles in 1758. It is translated as Women Mohegans or she-wolves and was applied to them in scorn by the fighting Iroquois.

•**CRESSKILL**, Borough; Bergen County; Pop. 7,609; Area Code 201; Zip Code 07626; Elev. 43'; located in NE New Jersey; descriptive name, meaning steam full of cresses.

•**CUMBERLAND COUNTY**, Southwest New Jersey; Area 503 sq. miles; Pop. 132,866; Seat Bridgeton; Established Jan. 19, 1748; named for Duke of Cumberland.

•**DEAL**, Borough; Monmouth County; Pop. 1,952; Area Code 201; Zip Code 07723; Elev. 33'; located in E New Jersey; named for Deal, England.

•**DEERFIELD**, Township; Cumberland County; Pop. 2,523; Area Code 609; Zip Code 08313; Elev. 120'; located in SW New Jersey at the intersection of Hwy. 77 and 540; was settled in 1732 by colonists from nearby Greenwich and Fairfield. According to local tradition, the original cost of 1,000 acres here was 10 shillings an acre. Settlers protested at the exorbitant price, and the community consequently acquired the name of Deerfield. Named for Deerfield, Massachusetts.

•**DELANCO**, Township; Burlington County; Pop. 3,730; Area Code 609; Zip Code 08075; located in S central New Jersey; named for the location on the Delaware River and Rancocas Creek.

•**DELAWARE RIVER**, River; NE United States; Flows S appros. 295 miles from source in Catskill Mountains, NY, along New York-Pennsylvania and Pennsylvania-New Jersey boundaries to

Delaware Bay, Atlantic Ocean. Major New Jersey cities, such as
Camden and Trenton, grew up along its banks. Named for Lord
De La Warr, governor of Virginia, by an English explorer of the
region.

•**DELRAN**, Township; Burlington County; Pop. 14,811; Area
Code 609; Zip Code 08075; located in S New Jersey.

•**DEMAREST**, Borough; Bergen County; Pop. 4,963; Area Code
201; Zip Code 07627; Elev. 38'; located in NE New Jersey 15 miles
NE of Paterson; named by *Demarest* family, early settlers.

•**DENNIS**, Township; Cape May County; Pop. 3,989; Area Code
609; Zip Code 08214; located in S New Jersey.

•**DENVILLE**, Township; Morris County; Pop. 15,380; Area Code
201; Zip Code 07834; Elev. 540'; named for *Daniel Denton* , a landowner; at its southwestern tip is Indian Lake, a popular summer resort, and in summer the village's population jumps.

•**DEPTFORD**, Township; Gloucester County; Pop. 23,473; Area
Code 609; Zip Code 08096; located in SW New Jersey; named for
Deptford, England.

•**DOVER**, Town; Morris County; Pop. 14,681; Area Code 201; Zip
Code 07801; Elev. 585; located in N New Jersey; named for
Dover, New Hampshire; was sometimes called the "Pittsburgh
of New Jersey." Formerly an important port on the old Morris
Canal, Dover is the shipping center of an iron-ore area that at one
time made mining one of New Jersey's principal industries.

•**DUMONT**, Borough; Bergen County; Pop. 18,334; Area Code
201; Zip Code 07628; Elev. 104'; located in NE New Jersey; named for the first mayor.

•**DUNELLEN**, Borough; Middlesex County; Pop. 6,593; Area
Code 201; Zip Code 08812; Elev. 58'; located in Central New
Jersey 9 miles NE of New Brunswick; was conceived, planned
and established (1868) by the Central R.R. of New Jersey. An independent corporation, directed by Jersey Central officials, laid
out the streets and sold lots. The borough was incorporated in
1887. Though the derivation of the name is masked by countless
theories and smoking room jokes, the weight of authority rests
with the simple solution of *Mrs. Emily de Forest* , daughter of the

president of the railroad at the time. *Mrs. de Forest* says that her father took the first name of a friend, *Ellen Betts* , and prefixed the "dun" because he liked the sound of the combination. Named for Jersey Central R.R. Station.

•**EAST BRUNSWICK,** Township; Middlesex County; Pop. 37,711; Area Code 201; Zip Code 08816; located in Central New Jersey.

•**EAST HAVOVER,** Township; Morris County; Pop. 9,319; Area Code 201; Zip Code 07936; located in N New Jersey.

•**EAST ORANGE,** City; Essex County; Pop. 77,025; Area Code 201; Zip Code 070 + zone; Elev. 166'; located in NE New Jersey; is the largest of "The Oranges" and closest to the center of Newark, being less than two miles distant via Orange Street.

Newarkers first "went over" to what is now East Orange in 1678. The community remained a part of Orange until the Civil War when its Republicanism forced it to break from the parent city and assume the independent status of a town, and the name at East Orange. For the balance of the century it grew slowly; its population was only 30,600 when it was incorporated as a city in 1899.

•**EAST RUTHERFORD,** Borough; Bergen County; Pop. 7,849; Area Code 201; Zip Code 07073; Elev. 48'; located in NE New Jersey; North of Newark; is separated from Rutherford only by the tracks of the Erie R.R., is an industrial community. It was formerly called Boiling Springs Township because of a spring that bubbled from the earth.

Rising like a Phoenix from the former marshland garbage dumping area of the Meadowlands, a strip of land stretching from Newark Bay to the approach to the George Washington Bridge, is the $360-million Meadowlands Sports Complex in East Rutherford with the 76,000-seat Giants Stadium, home to the National Football League Giants and the North American professional soccer champions, The Cosmos and the 35,000-person Meadowlands Racetrack, the leading harness track in the nation and one of the finest thoroughbred tracks. Planned to open in 1979 is a 20,000-seat arena to house the New Jersey Nets professional basketball team and host hockey, tennis, boxing, indoor track and other sorts, music and expositions.

In its first year of operation (1977), the track passed the $500-million in handle, which no track had ever done in its initial year. So successful has it been that the dining capacity of the track has had to be increased from 1,000 to about 2,500. During 1977, some 6.7 million fans attended racing and Giants Stadium events. The first world championship event, Soccer Bowl '78, is to be played at Giants Stadium. In addition to the construction jobs, the new Sports Complex employs 800 full-time workers, 1,200 racetrack employees, 1,000 attendants at the Stadium. It has parking for 20,000 cars and 400 buses, a six-level enclosed grandstand at the track for 8,000 people and 12 barns housing 1,540 horses. The Complex also has a 130-acre preserve.

The State of New Jersey received about $10 million as a result of the 1977 operations and $12 million is expected from 1978 Sports Complex activities.

The Sports Complex has been the catalyst for what is now being called the second great phase of development in Bergen after the boom which came when the George Washington Bridge opened. The Meadowlands crosses 14 towns, mostly in Bergen, and has 12 lanes of the New Jersey Turnpike, five major and a dozen secondary roads., three railroads and is considered the most valuable piece of real estate in the world today. It is at the heart of a 19-million population and is being developed under the aegis of the Hackensack Meadowlands Development Commission created by the state legislature. The master plan calls for a population of 125,000 in six new residential areas, and allots 3,000 of its 20,000 acres to residential centers and shopping, cultural and health services, while 10,000 acres are set aside for industrial, commercial and transportation uses.

Corporate and industrial growth has been spurred in The Meadowlands, affecting the southern and central portions of the county. Mid-rise and highrise office complexes, the equal of any throughout the nation, have given a new vertical dimension to the county's community of offices. Modern facilities are available in a number of the communities at good rental rates.

Plans have been announced for a $100-million shopping center, one of the largest in the country, opposite the Sports Complex. It would have up to six major department stores and 125 shops in 1.25-million square feet on 125 acres.

•EATONTOWN, Borough; Monmouth County; Pop. 12,703; Area Code 201; Zip Code 07724; Elev. 46'; 5 miles NW of Asbury Park in E New Jersey; was named for *Thomas Eaton*, who came here from Rhode Island before 1685. He constructed a gristmill that ran until 1920 and was later razed. Something of a local Paul Bunyan was Indian Will, who refused to emigrate with his tribe when their land was sold. Angered by his individualism, the tribe dispatched on messenger after another to kill Indian Will in single combat; but Will always won.

•**EDGEWATER**, Borough; Bergen County; Pop. 4,628; Area Code 201; Zip Code 07020; Elev. 55'; located in NE New Jersey; named for location along the Hudson River.

•**EDISON**, Township; Middlesex County; Pop. 70,193; Area Code 201; Zip Code 088+zone; located in Central New Jersey; named after *Thomas Alva Edison* .

•**EGG HARBOR CITY**, City; Atlantic County; Pop. 4,618; Area Code 609; Zip Code 08215; Elev. 58'; located in S Central New Jersey on Hwy. 30; is a noted wine-making and grape-juice center surrounded by vineyards. There is a tantalizing odor when the wine presses are at work. *John F. Wild* in 1858 discovered that the soil and climate here were adapted to grape culture. The place had been founded eight years before by German immigrants who sought refuge from the Native American or Know-Nothing party; but its prosperity dates from Wild's experiments, which attracted many wine-grape growers from Germany. The industry experienced another boom after the Civil War with the influx of Italian growers. The vineyards, individually owned, are in most casts operated by the second and third generations of these families. American Renault wines, pressed from grapes of local growers and aged in old stone vaults, have become popular despite pressure from competing California districts.

Egg Harbor City was named in anticipation of a proposed canal to connect it with Gloucester Furnace and the Mullica River, 6 miles northeast. The canal was never dug, and the only maritime flavor of the community is its name. Named for its Gull's eggs. The Renault Winery, founded in 1864 by *Louis N. Renault* , now offers tours of its cellars and vineyards.

•**ELIZABETH**, See special article.

•**ELMER**, Borough; Salem County; Pop. 1,569; Area Code 609; Zip Code 08318; Elev. 118'; located in SW New Jersey; is named for *L.Q.C. Elmer* , New Jersey Supreme Court Justice.

•**ELMWOOD PARK**, Borough; Bergen County; Pop. 18,377; Area Code 201; Zip Code 07407; Elev. 50'; located in NE New Jersey; originally Eat Paterson; SE of Paterson in N New Jersey.

•**EMERSON**, Borough; Bergen County; Pop. 7,793; Area Code 201; Zip Code 07630; Elev. 46'; located in NE New Jersey; is named for author, *Ralph Waldo Emerson* .

•**ENGLEWOOD**, City; Bergen County; Pop. 23,701; Area Code 201; Zip Code 076 + zone; Elev. 44'; located in NE New Jersey.

•**ENGLEWOOD CLIFFS**, Borough; Bergen County; Pop. 5,698; Area Code 201; Zip Code 07632; Elev. 371'; located in NE New Jersey; is named for position atop Palisades.

•**ENGLISHTOWN**, Borough; Monmouth County; Pop. 976; Area Code 201; Zip Code 07726; Elev. 70'; located in E New Jersey; is where *Washington* made his headquarters, June 27, 1778, the night before the Battle of Monmouth. The building he used for a council with his officers was the Hulse House, in the center of the village. *Washington* slept in the house, then the home of *Dr. James English* , the night before the battle.

•**ESSEX COUNTY**, Northeast New Jersey; Area 128 sq. miles; Pop. 850,451; Seat Newark; Established March 1683; named for Essex County, England.

•**ESSEX FELLS**, Borough; Essex County; Pop. 2,363; Area Code 201; Zip Code 201; Elev. 387; located in NE New Jersey; named for *John Fells* .

•**ESTELL MANOR**, City; Atlantic County; Pop. 848; Area Code 609; Zip Code 08319; Elev. 78'; located in S central New Jersey; is one of the communities in the largest township of the state. The name is derived from the D'Estail family, French Huguenots who settled here in 1671. Long forgotten by industry, the village is remembered as the birthplace of the Jersey, or Leeds Devil. Here in 1887 a devil is reputed to have been born to a Mrs. Leeds, who in a testy moment expressed the wish that the devil might take here undesired child. The young devil spent his early years in the swampland, but on reaching man's estate struck out to seek his fortune among the residents of southern New Jersey. Named after *Estelle* family estate.

•**FAIR HAVEN**, Borough; Monmouth County; Pop. 5,679; Area Code 201; Zip Code 07701; Elev. 30'; located in E New Jersey; name is the remark of a ship's Captain.

•**FAIR LAWN**, Borough; Bergen County; Pop. 32,229; Area Code 201; Zip Code 07410; Elev. 100'; located in NE New Jersey; name of the *Ackerson* estate.

•**FAIRVIEW**, Borough; Bergen County; Pop. 10,519; Area Code 201; Zip Code 07022; Elev. 308'; located in NE New Jersey; named for the view of the Hackensack Valley. International Fireworks Co. Plant, one of the largest manufacturers of display fireworks. Here were made the elaborate fireworks for the inaugurals of Presidents Wilson, Hoover and Roosevelt. Routine business is the making of "True Lovers Knots" and "Fountains of Youth" for use at convention of fraternal orders and for civic celebrations.

•**FANWOOD**, Borough; Union County; Pop. 7,767; Area Code 201; Zip Code 07023; Elev. 184'; located in NE New Jersey; was named for *Miss Fannie Wood* , a writer, daughter of Jersey Central R.R. official. The Spence House was used during the Revolution by American soldiers. A strong room in the cellar with the name "George Washington" carved on a beam is believed to have served as a prison cell. The building has two wings covered with white clapboards, green slat shutters, and a shingle roof. A large red brick chimney has the date 1774 in white brick.

•**FAR HILLS**, Borough; Somerset County; Pop. 677; Area Code 201; Zip Code 07931; Elev. 220'; located in N New Jersey.

•**FARMINGDALE**, Borough; Monmouth County; Pop. 1,348; Area Code 201; Zip Code 07727; Elev. 79'; located in E New Jersey; named for center of farming area.

•**FLEMINGTON**, Borough; Hunterdon County; Pop. 4,132; Area Code 201; Zip Code 08822; Elev. 160'; located in NW New Jersey; was catapulted into the front pages of the world's newspapers in January, 1935, during the trial of *Bruno Richard Hauptmann* for the murder of *Charles A. Lindbergh Jr.* . Press stories at the time recounted the angry bewilderment of the local citizenry at the spate of strange people the trial brought into the community.

   John Philip Kase is generally credited as being the town's first settler, although the community takes its name from *Samuel Fleming* .

•**FLORENCE**, Township; Burlington County; Pop. 9,084; Area Code 609; Zip Code 08518; located in S New Jersey; named for Florence, Italy.

•**FLORHAM PARK**, Borough; Morris County; Pop. 9,359; Area Code 201; Zip Code 07932; Elev. 200'; located in N New Jersey.

•**FORT LEE**, Borough; Bergen County; Pop. 32,449; Area Code 201; Zip Code 07024; Elev. 313'; located in NE New Jersey; named after Revolutionary fort, for *Major General Charles Lee* .

During the Revolution this plateau at the crest of the Palisades was selected by *Washington* as the site of the fort. His plan was to prevent the British fleet from sailing up the Hudson River to West Point. From the rocky bluff, *Washington* watched the attack and surrender of his garrison at Fort Washington, directly across the river, in November 1776. A few days later he was forced to abandon Fort Lee.

Early in the twentieth century Fort Lee became one of the cradles of the motion picture industry. Before narrow, boxlike cameras, with reels on the top like the ears of *Mickey Mouse* , Cowboys and Indians exchanged fusillades and whoops as, respectively, they galloped madly to rescue the lovely maiden from a fate worse than death or to write another terrible chapter in frontier history.

•**FORT MONMOUTH**, part of Oceanport; Monmouth County; Area Code 201; Zip Code 07703; located in E New Jersey.

•**FRANKLIN**, Borough; Sussex County; Pop. 4,486; Area Code 201; Zip Code 07416; Elev. 621'; located in N New Jersey; named after *Benjamin Franklin* ; is the center of New Jersey's zinc-mining industry. Zinc dominates the land here; in the rocks, underground, and in row after row of gray shingled company houses. The highway itself is built over a maze of underground tunnels where 75 miles of electric railway connect mining operations.

The region contains one of the largest supplies of zincite, franklinite, and oxide of zinc in the world. Franklin was a mining town before the discovery of zinc. One hundred forty years ago it was a pig-iron center with two forges and a blast furnace.

•**FRANKLIN LAKES**, Borough; Bergen County; Pop. 8,769; Area Code 201; Zip Code 07417; Elev. 399'; located in NE New Jersey; named for *William Franklin* , the son of *Benjamin* and last Royal Governor of New Jersey.

•**FRANKLIN PARK**, Township; Somerset County; Pop. 31,116; Area Code 201; Zip Code 08823; Elev. 130; located in N New

Jersey; named for *Benjamin Franklin* ; was an early Dutch community. The Dutch Reformed Church was organized in 1710, and the *Rev. Theodore Frelinghuysen* , leader in the founding of Rutgers University, was pastor in 1720.

•**FRANKLINVILLE**, Township; Gloucester County; Pop. 12,396; Area Code 609; Zip Code 08322; located in SW New Jersey.

•**FREEHOLD**, Borough; Monmouth County; Pop. 10,020; Area Code 201; Zip Code 07728; located in E New Jersey; the first white settlement in the Freehold district was made about 1650. A permanent village was established here in 1715 by Scots from New Aberdeen (now Matawan), who had earlier left England because of persecution by *Charles II* . They chose the name of Monmouth Court House from Monmouthshire in England.

Coastal residents complained that politics was responsible for selection of a courthouse site in the inland wilderness, and the record shows that, at the very least, shrewd business sense was involved. In 1714, one year after passage of an assembly act designating Freehold Township as the site, *John Reid* bought an extensive tract of land. He sold part of his holdings to the county authorities for a courthouse site at the bargain price of 30 shillings, and immensely increased the value of the rest of his property.

Colonists gathered in the courthouse to protest the Boston Port Bill; later, in a more militant mood, they heard news of the battles of Lexington and Bunker Hill. In 1778 Freehold saw part of the Battle of Monmouth. On June 27, the day before the fighting, *Sir Henry Clinton* and his army, retreating from Philadelphia to New York, occupied the town. The British commander and his staff established themselves in the present Moreau House.

The first of two early attacks occurred near the present high school on the northeastern edge of the town. On the slight rise of ground now known as Monument Park, behind the present courthouse, *Col. Butler's* detachment of Revolutionaries fired a heavy volley in the second skirmish, dispersing a body of the Queen's Rangers, the celebrated Tory corps.

During the hot Sunday on which *Washington's* troops tried to shatter the British forces, soldiers of both sides thronged in and out of the village. *Lafayette* led a party of horsemen down Main Street past the courthouse; various buildings were converted into military hospitals; and local residents fired on the escaping British from the shelter of trees and fences. The New

Jersey *Gazette* later published a withering letter describing British outrages, and accusing *General Clinton* of conduct by no means to his credit.

The last important local episode of the Revolution was a public funeral in 1782 for *Capt. Joshua Huddy* , the Revolutionist who was summarily hanged by Tories as an act of vengeance.

By 1795 a post office was opened, under the shorter name of Monmouth. Six years later the name was changed to Freehold by postal authorities to avoid confusion with other Monmouths in the county. The first newspaper, the *Spirit of Washington* , appeared during the years 1814-15; and in 1834 the Monmouth *Democrat* , still in existence, was established. Several private schools were functioning at the middle of the century, one of which, the Freehold Institute, remains as the Freehold Military School, a preparatory institution.

A stage line with railroad connections at Hightstown enabled Freehold residents in 1836 to reach New York or Philadelphia in seven hours. Plank roads were built to Howell and Keyport, speeding the transportation of marl and farm produce for shipment by water. The Freehold and Jamesburg Agricultural Railroad began service in 1853, and the marl pits at Farmingdale were later tapped by the Squankum Railroad. Both are now part of the Pennsylvania Railroad. A line paralleling the old plank road to Keyport was finally opened as the Freehold and New York Railway in 1880, and was later taken over by the Jersey Central.

A disastrous fire destroyed the courthouse and a number of buildings in 1873. The heat was so intense that no trace of the courthouse bell, placed in 1809, was ever found.

•**FRENCHTOWN**, Borough; Hunterdon County; Pop. 1,573; Area Code 201; Zip Code 08825; Elev. 141'; located in NW New Jersey; is on the bank of the Delaware River. Named for fugitives from French Revolution.

•**GARFIELD**, Bergen County; Pop. 26,803; Area Code 201; Zip Code 07026; Elev. 80'; located in NE New Jersey; named after *President James A. Garfield* .

•**GARWOOD**, Borough; Union County; Pop. 4,752; Area Code 201; Zip Code 07027; Elev. 86'; located in NE New Jersey; is named for the *Unami* clan of Indians.

•**GIBBSBORO**, Borough; Camden County; Pop. 2,510; Area Code 609; Elev. 89'; located in SW New Jersey; dates back to 1775 when a German widow, *Catherine Stanger* , and her seven sons built a glass factory here. The cornerstone of the first plant is visible under the dining room of a building at 124 State St. Greensand and silica deposits boomed the glass industry, which reached its peak around 1840 when a bottle famous in the 1840 Presidential campaign was made here. Shaped like a log cabin, the flask was symbolic of candidate *William Henry Harrison's* supposed home. The bottles were filled by a Philadelphia distiller, *E.C. Booz* ; soon known as "Booz bottles," they widely popularized the word "booze" or "boose," which as early as 1812 had been a potent noun in the vocabulary of *Parson Weems* , American evangelist.

•**GLASSBORO**, Borough; Gloucester County; Pop. 14,574; Area Code 609; Zip Code 08028; Elev. 144'; located in SW New Jersey; named for it's early glass industry.

•**GLEN GARDNER**, Borough; Hunterdon County; Pop. 834; Area Code 201; Zip Code 08826; Elev. 415'; located in NW New Jersey; named after *Gardner* brothers, chair manufacturers.

•**GLEN RIDGE**, Borough; Essex County; Pop. 7,855; Area Code 201; Zip Code 07028; Elev. 187'; located in NE New Jersey; descriptive name for a ridge in glen formed by Toney's Brook.

•**GLEN ROCK**, Borough; Bergen County; Pop. 11,497; Area Code 201; Zip Code 07452; Elev. 114'; located in NE New Jersey; named by ridge in glen formed by Toney's Brook.

•**GLOUCESTER COUNTY**, Southwest New Jersey; Area 329 sq. miles; Pop. 199,917; Seat Woodbury; Established May 28, 1686; Named for Duke of Gloucester, Gloucester England.

•**GREAT BAY**, Bay, SE New Jersey; At mouth of Mullica River; Protected from Atlantic Ocean by several small islands and barrier island of Long Beach. At S shore is Brigantine National Wildlife Refuge.

•**GREAT EGG HARBOR AND RIVER**, Bay and River, SE New Jersey, both emptying into the Atlantic Ocean by way of Great Egg Harbor Inlet 10 mi. S of Atlantic City. Bay extends approx. 5 mi. along coast, protected from ocean by Peck Beach, a barrier island. River flows SE approx. 55 mi. from source in Camden County to the Bay, Atlantic County. Named for seagull's eggs.

•**GREAT SWAMP**, Morris County; located in N New Jersey; is about 7 miles long and 3 miles wide. Here, in the Ice Age, was a lake caused by the North American glacier's choking the old outlet of Passaic River. The river was diverted by the debris thrust ahead of the ice mass into its present hairpin course about 30 miles to the north, before finding a new outlet at Passaic Falls, Paterson, on its way to the sea. The remnant of the ancient lake, stagnant and decrepit under the weight of its 20,000 years, lingers in the Great Swamp in black pools oozing up between clumps of moss and stunted trees. At some spots near the edges drainage has produced hay crops, but there is no human habitation. The swamp's most important citizens are wary, beady-eyed muskrats who paid rent with their skins for centuries, first to the Indians and then to the white men.

•**GREENWICH**, Township; Cumberland County; Pop. 973; Area Code 609; Zip Code 08323; located in SW New Jersey; named after Greenwich, England.

•**GUTTENBERG**, Town; Hudson County; Pop. 7,340; Area Code 201; Zip Code 07093; Elev. 240'; located in NE New Jersey; name is a German word meaning, "good village."

•**HACKENSACK**, City; Bergen County; Pop. 36,039; Area Code 201; Zip Code 076+zone; Elev. 20'; located in NE New Jersey; the name Hackensack is supposed to be of Indian origin, but the exact derivation is vague. A favorite local pastime is the collection of different versions of the Indian spelling. These range from Achkinchesacky to Hockumdauchgue, and new contributions are constantly being made. It has also been suggested that the town was named after an old tavern called the Hock and Sack, which sold hock, a popular Rhine wine, and sack, an appetizing sherry. This theory is more colorful than probable.

Hackensack dates back to 1647 when the Dutch from Manhattan established a trading post on the lands of *Chief Oratam* . Governed by the Council of New Netherland, the region was later known as New Barbadoes after the island whence came the original grantees. By 1700 the village was stamped with a Dutch imprint despite the English conquest. Until 1921, when the town received a city charter, its official name was still New Barbadoes.

The Revolutionary period was a turbulent one in Hackensack, with Tory and patriot intrigue. Foraging parties of continentals and redcoats skirmished over the entire country. In 1780 Hessians and British plundered the village and set fire to the old courthouse on the Green.

After the war Hackensack continued to develop as a commercial and political center. In the early 1800's the Hackensack Turnpike was built, connecting the town with Hoboken, and making Hackensack the freight depot for northern New Jersey. The so-called "Windjammers of the Hackensack" plied the river and bay to New York City, further enhancing the community's shipping importance.

The conservatism of Hackensack's population was demonstrated when the Civil War broke out, popular sentiment favoring slavery to such an extent that an Abolitionist editor had his print shop raided, and the Union flag was publicly burned on the Green.

Construction of the New Jersey and New York Railroad station in 1869 accelerated Hackensack's growth as a residential community, the succeeding years being marked by large-scale real estate operations.

Incorporated as a separate governing unit in 1868, Hackensack, or New Barbadoes, had its affairs administered until 1933 by a group known as the Hackensack Improvement Commission, formed under an act of the state legislature in 1856. This body obtained mail delivery in 1858; introduced the gas street light in 1868; and the telephone exchange in 1882.

•**HACKENSACK RIVER**, River; Bergen County; located northeast New Jersey and southeast New York. Approximately 40 miles long. The river flows south from New York across the New Jersey state line and into Newark Bay.

•**HACKETTSTOWN**, Town; Warren County; Pop. 8,850; Area Code 201; Zip Code 07840; Elev. 560'; located in NW New Jersey; is situated in Musconetcong Valley between Schooleys and Scotts Mts. Originally called Helm's Mills or Musconetcong, it became known as Hackettstown about the middle of the eighteenth century after *Samuel Hackett* , largest landowner in the district.

•**HADDONFIELD**, Borough; Camden County; Pop. 12,345; Area Code 609; Zip Code 08033; Elev. 571'; located in SW New Jersey, 10 miles W of Camden; was founded by a Quaker girl of 20, *Elizabeth Haddon* . In 1710 *Elizabeth* was sent over from England by her father, who had no sons, to develop 400 acres of land. Within a year the young woman had started her colony, erected a home, and married *John Estaugh* , Quaker missionary, because she had the courage to propose to him. Longfellow tells the tory of the romance with the "Theologian's Tale" in Tales of a Wayside Inn.

Later the "great road or King's Highway" was laid through the Haddon estate on its route from Burlington to Salem. At the time of the Revolution it was the most important thoroughfare in this region.

•**HADDON HEIGHTS**, Borough; Camden County; Pop. 8,361; Area Code 609; Zip Code 08035; located in SW New Jersey; is named after *Elizabeth Haddon* , settler.

•**HAINESPORT**, Township; Burlington County; Pop. 3,236; Area Code 609; Zip Code 08036; located in S New Jersey; is named for *Barclay Haines* an early resident.

•**HALEDON-NORTH HALEDON**, Borough; Passaic County; Pop. 8,177; Area Code 201; Zip Code 075 + zone; Elev. 259; located in N New Jersey; is named after Haledon, England.

•**HAMBURG**, Borough; Sussex County; Pop. 1,832; Area Code 201; Zip Code 07419; Elev. 453'; located in N New Jersey; was the home of *Daniel Haines* , Governor of New Jersey in 1843 and the "first to advocate a free school system." Named after Hamburg, Germany.

•**HAMILTON**, Township; Mercer County; Pop. 82,801; Area Code 609; Zip Code 08690; Elev. 100'; was originally known as the Crossroads in Nottingham Township, and later was called Nottingham Square. The name was changed in 1842 to honor *Alexander Hamilton* .

•**HAMMONTON**, Town; Atlantic County; Pop. 12,298; Area Code 609; Zip Code 08037; Elev. 100'; located in SE New Jersey.

•**HAMPTON**, Borough; Hunterdon County; Pop. 1,614; Area Code 201; Zip Code 08827; Elev. 496'; located in NW New Jersey; is named for *Jonathan Hampton* , donor of church land.

•**HARRINGTON PARK**, Borough; Bergen County; Pop. 4,532; Area Code 201; Zip Code 07640; Elev. 50'; located in NE New Jersey; is named after *Harring* family, settlers.

•**HARRISON**, Town; Hudson County; Pop. 12,242; Area Code 201; Zip Code 07020; Elev. 30'; located in NE New Jersey; is named after *President William Henry Harrison* .

•**HARRISON**, Township; Gloucester County; Pop. 3,585; Area Code 609; Zip Code 08039; Elev. 10'; located in SW New Jersey; settled by Quakers at some time after 1673, was the site of a tavern popular in Civil War days. It was known as the Pig's Eye and for a time gave its name to the village and vicinity. Named after *President William Henry Harrison* .

•**HARVEY CEDARS**, Borough; Ocean County; Pop. 363; Area Code 201; Zip Code 08008; Elev. 5'; located in E New Jersey; the island's oldest settlement, drew whalers from Long Island and New England soon after the war of 1812.

•**HASBROUCK HEIGHTS**, Borough; Bergen County; Pop. 12,166; Area Code 201; Zip Code 07604; Elev. 130'; was founded by the *Kip* family in 1685, but the name was taken from another Dutch colonist.

•**HAWORTH**, Borough; Bergen County; Pop. 3,509; Area Code 201; Zip Code 07641; Elev. 64'; located in NE New Jersey; is named for Haworth, England.

•**HAWTHORNE**, Borough; Passaic County; Pop. 18,200; Area Code 201; Zip Code 075 + zone; Elev. 50'; located in N New Jersey; is named after *Nathaniel Hawthorne* , novelist.

•**HAZLET**, Township; Monmouth County; Pop. 23,013; Area Code 201; Zip Code 07730; located in E New Jersey.

•**HELMETTA**, Borough; Middlesex County; Pop. 955; Area Code 201; Zip Code 08828; Elev. 40'; located in Central New Jersey; is named after *Etta Helme* , daughter of snuff factory owner.

•**HEWITT**, included West Milford; Passaic County; Pop. 22,750; Area Code 201; Zip Code 07421; located in N New Jersey; is named for *Abram S. Hewitt* , ironmaster, mayor of New York.

•**HIGH BRIDGE**, Borough; Hunterdon County; Pop. 3,435; Area Code 201; Zip Code 08829; Elev. 332'; located in NW New Jersey.

•**HIGHLAND PARK**, Borough; Middlesex County; Pop. 13,396; Area Code 201; Zip Code 08904; Elev. 99'; located in Central New Jersey; a suburb of New Brunswick, is divided by Raritan River from that city. On the townsite was an Indian village in 1675, when the place was known as Raritan Falls, from a small cascade.

•**HIGHLANDS**, Borough; Monmouth County; Pop. 5,187; Area Code 201; Zip Code 07732; Elev. 104'; located in E New Jersey; formerly Parkertown, is a fishing village and summer resort close by the ocean.

•**HIGHTSTOWN**, Borough; Mercer County; Pop. 4,581; Area Code 609; Zip Code 08520; Elev. 84'; located in W New Jersey; founded in 1721, the town was named for *John Hight*, an early landowner and miller. In 1834 it became a station on the Camden and Amboy R.R., the first railroad built in New Jersey. The Peddie School is a private preparatory institution for boys, established in 1864.

•**HILLSDALE**, Borough; Bergen County; Pop. 10,495; Area Code 201; Zip Code 07642; Elev. 83'; located in NE New Jersey; is named for description meaning its "dale among the hills."

•**HILLSIDE**, Township; Union County; Pop. 21,440; Area Code 201; Zip Code 07205; located in NE New Jersey.

•**HOBOKEN**, City; Hudson County; Pop. 42,460; Area Code 201; Zip Code 07030; Elev. 5'; located in NE New Jersey; as early as 1640, the Lenni Lenape Indian territory of Hobocan Hacking *(land of the tobacco pipe)* was settled by the Dutch of New Amsterdam. Shortly after, the Indians, aroused by a ruthless Dutch massacre in 1643, drove the settlers out and burned all the buildings with the exception of a brewery. The first in America, it had been built in 1642 by *Alert T. van Putten*, one of the earliest settlers. *Peter Stuyvesant* bought the land back from the Indians and later his relatives sold it to *Samuel Bayard*.

Very little occurred to to differentiate Hoboken from other towns in New Jersey before the coming of *Col. John Stevens*, inventor and financier, who bought the whole area for $90,000 when the extensive land holdings of *William Bayard*, the Tory grandson of *Samuel*, were confiscated and ordered sold by the Bergen Court of Common Pleas. In 1804 *Stevens* mapped the territory into what he called the "New City of Hoboken" and auctioned the lots in New York.

Stevens put into service in 1811 the first regular steam ferry in the world, the *Juliana*. As early as 1808, however, he had operated the *Phoenix*, a steamship of his own design, as a ferry. He was forced to abandon the venture when *Robert Fulton*, who had secured sole rights to steam travel on the Hudson, objected. The *Phoenix*, sent south to Delaware River, was the first steamship to navigate at sea.

Colonel Stevens also devised the first iron floating fort, never completed although huge sums were spent on it; he drew plans for a vehicular tunnel on the bed of the Hudson, and for a bridge from Castle Point to Manhattan. In 1824, after arguing the feasibility of railroad transportation with doubting capitalists, *Stevens* built a locomotive and, on a circular track in Hoboken, conducted the first successful run in the United States.

Hoboken soon acquired world fame as a resort. Beer gardens, fireworks, mountebanks, and waxworks brought New York's citizens over in droves, and the beautiful country so close to the metropolis attracted society people and literary and artistic celebrities. *John Jacob Astor* built an extensive villa on the city's shores; *Washington Irving, William Cullen-Bryant, Martin Van Buren,* and other prominent people vacationed here. In Hoboken was founded the New York Yacht Club with *John Cox Stevens*, son of the colonel, as its first commodore. Organized baseball had its beginning in Hoboken. The first game was played in 1846 on the Elysian Fields by Hoboken's Knickerbocker Giants and New York.

The River Walk was soon packed hard and smooth by pleasure-seeking visitors, and Sybil's Cave became a lovers' rendezvous. The cave figured in one of Hoboken's early scandals when the body of *Mary Rogers*, a pretty young New York Tobacco shop clerk, was found floating in the river near the entrance. *Edgar Allan Poe* based his story, *The Mystery of Marie Roget*, on the newspaper accounts of the murder.

Hoboken's separation from North Bergen and its incorporation as a city in 1855 marked the beginning of a new development in its history. Industrialists were attracted by the ease of communication with New York and the advantages of the water front. An influx of labor, mainly Irish, came with the industries. Later the Hamburg-American Line made Hoboken its American terminus.

A $10,000,000 fire that resulted in 145 deaths broke out in the North German Lloyd line dock on the afternoon of June 30, 1900. Two blocks of the water front blazed, and several ships, including the *Main, Bremen,* and *Saale*, endangered shipping as they floated burning into the harbor. The fire probably started from a burning bale of cotton which, tossed overboard from a cargo ship, ignited a wooden pier.

When Hoboken was chosen as a major point of embarkation during the World War, strict military rule was imposed on the city. Anti-German feeling rose quickly and with disastrous effect on the German families who had made their homes here. The United States seized the larger portion of the steamship properties as a war measure and has held them ever since.

The labor required for the shipment of war supplies brought the population to abnormal high. After the War, the exodus of many workers caused the failure of a number of businesses established during the boom.

During 1928 and 1929 *Christopher Morley* and his associates brought back the sophisticated New York crowds that once pressed into the two old theaters by presenting the melodramas of another generation. *After Dark* and *The Black Crook* kept the Rialto and Lyric alive with eager sightseers; "Seidel over to Hoboken" became a national phrase. But the competition from Harlem was to strong in 1929. The novelty-seeking crowd drifted away, and the theaters were closed, to reopen as third-run moving picture houses.

•HO HO KUS, Borough; Bergen County; Pop. 4,129; Area Code 201; Zip Code 07423; Elev. 111'; located in NE New Jersey; the Zabriskie House was built in 1790 by *Caspar Zabriskie* ; it is a fine example of Georgian design in stone, two and one-half stories high. The place is now called Hohokus Inn.

The Hermitage was visited by *George Washington* in 1778. *Capt. Philip De Visne* , known as The Hermit, built his house of cut red sandstone in English Gothic style with steep pitched roof, dormer windows of diamond-shaped glass, and projecting wings. here *Aaron Burr* courted *Theodosia Provost* , a widow, who became his wife. *Lafayette* and *Mrs. Benedict Arnold* were also guests here.

In Colonial times Hohokus was known as Hoppertown, because of an early settler. The present name, from the Chihohokies Indians who had a chief town here, is still spelled Ho-Ho-Kus on the municipal building, but the post office, the U.S. Census Bureau, and the telephone company prefer the unhyphened form. Named for Mehohokus, meaning "Red Cedar."

•HOLMDEL, Township; Monmouth County; Pop. 8,447; Area Code 201; Zip Code 07733; Elev. 100'; located in E New Jersey; is one of the oldest settlements in Monmouth County. The name is derived from the *Holmes* family, leading landowners, and descendants of the *Rev. Obadiah Holmes* , who came from England in 1638 and became pastor of the Baptist Church at Newport, R.I. in 1676. This village was the original Freehold and bore that name probably 75 years before the present Freehold. The name was changed afterward to Baptistown.

•**HOLMDEL VILLAGE**, Township; Monmouth County; Pop. 8,447; Area Code 201; Zip Code 07733; located in E New Jersey; is named for the *Holmes* family.

•**HOPATCONG**, Borough; Sussex County; Pop. 15,531; Area Code 201; Zip Code 07843; Elev. 1,100'; located in N New Jersey; is named for Hokunk, "above," peek, "body of water," and, "hill" and Saconk, "outlet."

•**HOPATCONG, LAKE**, Lake, N New Jersey; In hilly stretches of Hamburg Mountains, approx. 35 mi. W of Paterson. Extends approx. 7 mi. from N tip at Woodport to S tip at the Hopatcong State Park.

•**HOPE**, Township; Warren County; Pop. 1,468; Area Code 201; Zip Code 07844; Elev. 470'; located in NW New Jersey; Moravian colonists from Bethlehem, Pa., settled here in 1774 after buying 1,000 acres from an earlier settler.

A peace-loving people, their conscientious refusal to fight in the Revolutionary War for a time labeled them as Tories; but they later won esteem by their devoted care of sick and wounded Revolutionists. A smallpox epidemic crippled the community in the early 1800's. Is named for description "Hope of Immortality" by Moravian missionaries.

•**HOPEWELL**, Borough; Mercer County; Pop. 2,001; Area Code 609; Zip Code 08525; located in W New Jersey; is named after "The Hopewell" which brought settlers.

•**HOWELL**, Township; Monmouth County; Pop. 25,065; Area Code 201; Zip Code 07731; located in E New Jersey; is named for *Richard Howell*, Governor 1792-1801.

•**HUDSON COUNTY**, Northeast New Jersey; Area 45 sq. miles; Pop. 556,972; Seat Jersey City; Established Feb. 1840; Named for *Henry Hudson*, English Navigator (1569-1611).

•**HUDSON RIVER**, River, NE United States; Flows approx. 300 mi. from source in Adirondacks Mountains, New York, S to Atlantic Ocean at New York Bay. Forms New York-New Jersey state boundary for approx. 25 mi. Major transportation route in early American history.

•**HUNTERDON COUNTY**, Western New Jersey; Area 435 sq. miles; Pop. 87,361; Seat Flemington; Established Mar. 13, 1714; Named for *Robert Hunter*, Governor, Royal Province of Virginia.

•**INDIAN MILLS**, Burlington County; Zip Code 08080; is the site of the first Indian reservation on the continent, established in 1758. On the site of an old one-room Schoolhouse, stood a church where the Indians worshiped; it burned in 1802. Behind it was the Indians' burying ground. Indian Mills today is a settlement of cranberry pickers and a few farmers. The land is perhaps even more barren than when it was set aside for the survivors of the South Jersey or Turkey brotherhood of Indians, at a time when the Colonial government was striving to end the costly Indian war on its borders.

      In August, 1758, an Indian delegation presented a formal request to the Colonial assembly for the allocation of this area. In three days the legislature complied, buying a 3,000-acre tract called Edge Pillock, or Edge-Pe-lick, on which were built several cabins and a log meeting house. Friends of the Indians renamed the place Brotherton. Here the last tribesmen lived but did not prosper; in 1801 they sold their land and left to join kinsmen in the Lake Oneida Reservation, New York. A small remnant moved later to Wisconsin and then to Oklahoma and to Ontario, where their descendants still live.

•**IONA LAKE**, Lake, Cumberland County; is 0.7 miles long, formed by damming the Maurice River. The lake once supplied power for early glassworks and gristmills. It once furnished excellent boating and fishing.

•**IRVINGTON**, Town; Essex County; Pop. 61,493; Area Code 201; Zip Code 07111; Elev. 185'; located in NE New Jersey; is named after *Washington Irving*, author.

•**ISELIN**, included in Woodbridge; Middlesex County; Pop. 18,400; Area Code 201; Zip Code 08830; Elev. 60'; was named for the *Iselin* family, prominent in New York financial and international yacht-racing circles.

•**ISLAND BEACH**, Barrier island, SE New Jersey; Extends from Point Pleasant S to Barnegat Inlet, protecting Barnegat Bay from the Atlantic Ocean. Much of the thin island is protected as a state park.

•**ISLAND HEIGHTS**, Borough; Ocean County; Pop. 1,575; Area Code 201; Zip Code 08732; Elev. 17'; located in E New Jersey; is named for location.

•**JACKSON**, Township; Ocean County; Pop. 25,644; Area Code 201; Zip Code 08527; located in E New Jersey; is named for *President Andrew Jackson* .

•**JAMESBURG**, Borough; Middlesex County; Pop. 4,114; Area Code 201; Zip Code 08831; Elev. 65'; located in Central New Jersey; is named for *James Buckelew* , miller, stage owner.

•**JERSEY CITY**, See special article.

•**JERSEYVILLE**, Monmouth County; Pop. 70; Area Code 201; Zip Code 07728; Elev. 50'; located in Central Eastern New Jersey on Hwy. 33; known until 1854 as Green Grove, is in the midst of almost denuded timberland.

•**JOHNSONBURG**, included in Frelinghuysen; Warren County; Pop. est. 200; Area Code 201; Zip Code 07846; located in NW New Jersey; from 1753 to 1765 the village was the seat of Sussex County. There were only a few log houses then; one of them, the jail, gave to the settlement its early name of Log Gaol.

•**KEANSBURG**, Borough; Monmouth County; Pop. 10,613; Area Code 201; Zip Code 07734; Elev. 13'; located in E New Jersey; is named after *John Kean* , U.S. Senator 1899-1911.

•**KEARNY**, Town; Hudson County; Pop. 35,735; Area Code 201; Zip Code 07032; Elev. 104; located in NE New Jersey just NE of Newark; is known for a large proportion of Scottish residents and for its shipbuilding and other industries. Lying between the Passaic and Hackensack Rivers, the town is fortunately placed for commercial development.

Kearny was named for *Maj. Gen. Philip Kearny* , brilliant cavalry officer who lived in the town when he was not fighting. He lost his left arm in the Mexican War, served with France against the Austrians in 1859, and returned to lead the first New Jersey troops into the Civil War. He was killed at Chantilly in 1862.

•**KENILWORTH**, Borough; Union County; Pop. 8,221; Area Code 201; Zip Code 07033; Elev. 91'; located in NE New Jersey; is named for Kenilworth Castle, England.

•**KENVIL**, included Roxbury; Morris County; Pop. 1,700; Area Code 201; Zip Code 07847; Elev. 720'; located in N New Jersey; formerly known as McCainville, advertises itself as the "Home of America's Oldest Continuously Operating Dynamite Plant" -the Hercules Powder Co. Plant, founded 1871. Two major explosions brought the plant into the headlines in 1934.

•**KEYPORT**, Borough; Monmouth County; Pop. 7,413; Area Code 201; Zip Code 07735; Elev. 25'; located in E New Jersey.

•**KINGSTON**, included Franklin; Somerset County; Pop. est. 900; Area Code 201; Zip Code 08528; Elev. 110'; located in N New Jersey; was settled about 1700. *Joseph Hewes*, a signer of the Declaration of Independence, was born here in 1730.

It was at Kingston that *Washington* and his army eluded the pursuing British under *Cornwallis*, Jan. 3, 1777, immediately after the Battle of Princeton, by filing off to the north along the narrow road leading to Rocky Hill. The enemy, believing he had pushed on to New Brunswick to destroy the British army's winter stores, kept on the main road. *Washington* had actually planned to move as *Cornwallis* imagined against New Brunswick, but at a horseback conference with his aides as he approached Kingston it was decided that the men were too weary. The army rested two days at Rocky Hill and then marched to Morristown. Named for *King William II*.

•**KINNELON**, Borough; Morris County; Pop. 7,770; Area Code 201; Zip Code 07405; Elev. 760; located in N New Jersey; is named after *Francis S. Kinney*, founder.

•**KITTATINNY LAKE**, Lake; Sussex County; Pop. est. 300; is one mile long; a mountain, shaped like an inverted cap, rises boldly from the lake's shore.

•**KITTATTINNY MOUNTAINS**, Mountain range, NW New Jersey; Extends as a ridge from NW border with New York to W Pennsylvania boundary, parallel to the Delaware River. Highest point in New Jersey, High Point (Elev. 1,803), is at N end of range. The Appalachian trail traverses these peaks.

•**LAFAYETTE**, Township; Sussex County; Pop. 1,614; Area Code 201; Zip Code 07848; located in N New Jersey; is named for *Marquis de la Fayette*.

•**LAKE CARASALJO**, Lake; Ocean County; with its borders of pines, cedars, and laurel, elaborate cottages and grounds were built by the Astors, Vanderbilts, Goulds, Rockefellers, Tilfords, Kipps, Rhinelanders, and other socially prominent New Yorkers of the '90's. The name of the lake is a combination of Carrie, Sally, and Josephine, daughters of *James W. Bride*, the ironmaster.

•**LAKE HOPATCONG**, Lake; Sussex and Monmouth Counties; located in northern New Jersey, is a summer resort. It is a Indian for honey pond of the many coves. It is the largest inland body of water in New Jersey. Rugged hills hem in its 40-mile shoreline, reflected in the clear lake surface. Hopatcong is second only to New Jersey's seacoast resorts in popularity as a playground.

•**LAKEHURST**, Borough; Ocean County; Pop. 2,908; Area Code 201; Zip Code 08733; Elev. 72'; located in E New Jersey on Hwy. 40; there are tall elms along the streets, planted in the Civil War period when real estate men tried to put new life into the old settlement of Manchester after the iron and charcoal industries died. The town was almost wiped out, but in 1860 the "new railroad," the Jersey CENTRAL, placed its repair shops here and Manchester again flourished. The shops have been closed since 1932; there is no industrial plant in the village now and little farming around it.

Into a tavern here early in September, 1937, came a local blueberry picker, *John Henry Titus*, 91, with a kerosene-soaked rag in his shoe to ward off mosquitoes. According to *Time* magazine, "he sank to one knee, and, with gestures, once more recited his famous poem, "The Face on the Barroom Floor." Scholars, however, generally give *H.H. D'Arcy* credit for the poem.

Nearby is the United States Naval Air Station. After World War I, Camp Kendrick, as it was called, was allocated to the Navy as a base for lighter than-air craft. In 1923 the first American-built, rigid, lighter-than-air ship, the Shenandoah, made here initial flight from Lakehurst. The ZR-3 arrived from Germany on October. 15, 1924, and became the *Los Angeles*, now decommissioned. The *Akron* left this station and fell into the ocean off Barnegat in 1933. The *Macon*, which crashed in the Pacific, made test flights from here before proceeding to her base in California. Four small airships were stationed here in 1938: the K-1, the J-4, the G-1 and the ZMC-2, plus three airplanes for aerological observations. In 1936 and 1937 this station was used as the landing field for the commercial flights of the German airship *Hindenburg*, destroyed here by fire on May 6, 1937, in the space of 4 minutes with the loss of 36 lives. The tragedy occurred as the ship was 250 feet above the ground, maneuvering toward the mooring mast. The crowd, gathered to watch the landing, stood helplessly as travelers leaped flaming from the gondola or were burned alive. The cause of the spectacular airship disaster has never been completely determined. With the passing of the Hindenburg, Lakehurst lost its importance as a base for commercial lighter-than-air craft.

•**LAKEWOOD**, Township; Ocean County; Pop. 38,464; Area Code 201; Zip Code 08701; located in eastern New Jersey at the junction of Hwy. 9 and 88; once a small settlement built around an iron works, is dependent on a winter resort business promoted by the dry, temperate climate of the pine district. *John D. Rockefeller Sr.* had an estate here and there were other costly houses along the shores of Lake Carasaljo.

Establishment of a smelter in 1812, to utilize bog-iron deposits, gave the town the name of Washington Furnace. Later the community became known as Bergen Works and next as Bricksburg, in honor of *James W. Brick*, the ironmaster. Two New York Stock Exchange brokers bought 19,000 acres of pine woods in 1879 and built the Laurel House, which entertained *Rudyard Kipling, Oliver Wendell Holmes, Mark Twain, William Faversham, Emma Calve'*, and other celebrities. It was torn down many years ago.

After the Depression, many new people moved into Lakewood from the congested cities. Also, refugees from Central and Eastern Europe poured in to the town and many of them helped begin the large egg and poultry business here. When World war II was over, these farms began to be sold to real estate developers, who accomodated the growing demand for suburban housing. Many older people also came to the town to retire. In 1967, the Laurel Hotel was completely destroyed by fire, however, and many tourists passed up this former resort town for sunnier climates to the south.

Lakewood became a well-known retirement community when *Robert Schmertz* brought his "Leisure Village" in 1963. By the mid 1970s, city officials estimated that one of every seven people in Ocean County lived in Schmertz-constructed homes or apartments.

In recent years, more than 30 manufacturers moved their plants into Lakewood, providing thousands of jobs. However, unemployment continued to climb to 12 percent levels in the late 1970s and early 1980s. Municipal Manager *Thomas LaPointe* hopes for more industry and retail growth in the largely undeveloped (50 percent) acreage of Lakewood.

•**LAMBERTVILLE**, City; Hunterdon County; Pop. 4,044; Area Code 201; Zip Code 08530; Elev. 76'; located in NW New Jersey; perches by the Delaware River on a narrow, hill-bound shelf opposite New Hope, Pa.

The Belvidere Delaware R.R., built through Lambertville in 1851, gave it the lead over Phillipsburg and prodded its industries into activity: paper, rubber footwear, iron works, railroad machine shops. When the Pennsylvania R.R. took over the Belvidere, however, the machine shops were abandoned.

Known first as Coryel's Ferry and then as Georgetown, Lambertville received its present name when *John Lambert* opened the first post office shortly after the War of 1812. In 1732 *Samuel Coryel* has started his ferry service, establishing at the New Jersey end an inn of good repute. His ferries came into play in the Revolution when *Cornwallis* tried to capture the boats because they were providing a crossing for the Continental troops. *Washington's* men occupied the town at one time.

•**LANDING**, (Shore Hills); included Roxbury; Morris County; Pop. 3,064; Area Code 201; Zip Code 07850; located in N New Jersey.

•**LANDISVILLE**, part of Buena; Atlantic County; Area Code 609; Zip Code 08326; Elev. 113'; located in SE New Jersey; was settled soon after the Civil War as a part of the colonizing efforts of *Charles K. Landis*. The village is a vegetable-producing and canning center.

•**LANOKA HARBOR**, included Lacey; Ocean County; Pop. est. 700; Area Code 201; Zip Code 08734; Elev. 20'; located in central E New Jersey; was originally Good Luck, then Cedar Creek, and next Lanes Oaks in honor of *George Oaks*, an old resident. Because the snug little port is hidden from the highway, the publicity-minded townspeople appended the word "Harbor" to the name. A final stage of evolution converted the jerky "Lanes Oaks Harbor" into streamlined "Lanoka Harbor."

•**LARISON'S CORNER**, Hunterdon County; is also known as Pleasant Corner, is the abandoned old brownstone Amwell Academy, founded in 1811 as a school appendage to St. Andrew's Church, discontinued in 1828 and reopened as a seminary in 1870 by *Cornelius, Andres, Katherine* and *Mary Jane Larison*. The tide of the nineteenth-century controversy between conservatism and science seems to have swirled to the doors of the little seminary at Larison's Corner and engulfed the family; in 1876 *Cornelius* and *Mary Jane Larison*, unable to convince *Katherine* of science's importance in the modern world, withdrew and set up their own school in the rear of their home. They called it the Ringoes Academy of Arts and Sciences.

The *Rockefeller* Family Burial Ground is at Larison's Corner. About 50 feet from the highway, it is enclosed by a low stone wall set into the United Presbyterian Church Cemetery. Some of the gravestones carry the name "ROCKEFELLER." A granite monument, 10 feet square, is inscribed: "In memory of Johann Peter Rockefeller, who came from Germany about the year 1723. Died in 1763. He gave this land for a burial place for his family, its descendants, and his neighbors. This monument erected in the year 1906 by *John Davidson Rockefeller*, a direct descendant." But according to *George W. Tine*, Rockefeller family historian, Johann was not buried here, but on a farm in the vicinity. In this county there are more living and dead Rockefellers than in any other locality in the country.

•**LAUREL SPRINGS**, Borough; Camden County; Pop. 2,249; Area Code 609; Zip Code 08021; Elev. 82'; located in SW New Jersey; descriptive name meaning "Medical Springs in laurel grove."

•**LAVALLETTE**, Borough; Ocean County; Pop. 2,072; Area Code 201; Zip Code 08735; Elev. 5'; located in E New Jersey; is named for *Admiral Lavallette* of the U.S. Navy.

•**LAWNSIDE**, Borough; Camden County; Pop. 3,042; Area Code 609; Zip Code 08045; Elev. 112'; located in SW New Jersey; was one of the first Black-owned and Black-governed boroughs in New Jersey, and one of the few such towns in the United States. It was founded during the antislavery agitation of a century ago. Purchased for the Blacks in 1840, the tract was sold on long-term payments and appropriately named Free Haven. The place grew between 1850 and 1860, when neighboring Quakers were operating the New Jersey division of the Underground Railway. After the Emancipation Proclamation more Blacks arrived from Snow Hill, Maryland, and the community became known as Snow Hill.

Since incorporation in 1926, Lawnside has had Black officials exclusively, from mayor to dog catcher.

•**LAWRENCEVILLE**, Township; Mercer County; Pop. 19,724; Area Code 609; Zip Code 08648; Elev. 130'; located in Central New Jersey on Hwy. 206, 10 miles SW of Princeton; was a post village incorporated in 1798 as Maidenhead, the name being changed in 1816 to honor *Capt. James Lawrence* ("Don't give up the ship!"). An iron fence with brick posts marks the grounds of Lawrenceville School, founded in 1810, an outstanding preparatory school for boys. *Thornton Wilder*, the novelist, was a member of the faculty from 1921 to 1928.

•**LEBANON**, Borough; Hunterdon County; Pop. 820; Area Code 201; Zip Code 08833; located in NW New Jersey; lying on a ridge, was founded in 1731 by German immigrants. Local historians relate that a group of Palatines bound for New York were greatly perturbed to find themselves in Philadelphia. They started overland with babes and baggage; when they came to this fertile, rolling country they decided to remain. Other Germans drifted down from New York State and soon the whole valley northward was known as German Valley. Named for Mt. Lebanon, Palestine.

•**LEDGEWOOD**, included Roxburg; Morris County; Pop. est. 100; Area Code 201; Zip Code 07852; Elev. 296; located in N New Jersey.

•**LEONIA**, Borough; Bergen County; Pop. 8,027; Area Code 201; Zip Code 07605; Elev. 31'; located in NE New Jersey; named was taken from Fort Lee.

•**LINCOLN PARK**, Borough; Morris County; Pop. 8,806; Area Code 201; Zip Code 07035; Elev. 200'; located in N New Jersey; is named after *President Abraham Lincoln*.

•**LINCROFT**, included in Middletown Township; Monmouth County; Pop. est. 4,100; Area Code 201; Zip Code 07738; located in E New Jersey on Hwy. 520; is a village dating back to 1680. Here are the famous Whitney Stables, with an indoor race track, where well-known race horses have been trained. Named for Anglo-Saxon description, "Small Field of Flax."

•**LINDEN**, City; Union County; Pop. 37,836; Area Code 201; Zip Code 07036; Elev. 37'; located in NE New Jersey; named for trees brought from Germany.

•**LINDENWOLD**, Borough; Camden County; Pop. 18,196; Area Code 609; Zip Code 08021; Elev. 50'; located in SW New Jersey.

•**LINWOOD**, City; Atlantic County; Pop. 6,144; Area Code 609; Zip Code 08221; Elev. 28'; located in SE New Jersey.

•**LITTLE FALLS**, Township; Passaic County; Pop. 11,496; Area Code 201; Zip Code 07424; located in N New Jersey; named for lesser falls of Passaic River.

•**LITTLE FERRY**, Borough; Bergen County; Pop. 9,399; Area Code 201; Zip Code 07643; Elev. 10'; located in NE New Jersey; named for colonial ferry.

•**LITTLE EGG HARBOR**, Bay, SE New Jersey; Extends along coastline approx. 10 mi. between Great and Barnegat Bays. Protected from Atlantic Ocean by Long Beach barrier island. Part of Intracoastal Waterway.

•**LITTLE SILVER**, Borough; Monmouth County; Pop. 5,548; Area Code 201; Zip Code 07739; Elev. 38'; located in E New Jersey; named for payment to Indians, or appearance of quiet water.

•**LITTLE YORK**, included in Alexandria and York; Hunterdon County; Pop. est. 125; Area Code 201; Zip Code 08834; located in NW New Jersey.

•**LIVINGSTON**, Township; Essex County; Pop. 28,040; Area Code 201; Zip Code 07039; Elev. 410'; located in NE New Jersey, 5 miles West of Newark; is named for *William Livingston*, New Jersey's Revolutionary Governor and one of the signers of the Constitution.

•**LODI**, Borough; Bergen County; Pop. 23,956; Area Code 201; Zip Code 07644; Elev. 43'; located in NE New Jersey; named after Lodi, Italy.

•**LONG BEACH**, Township; Ocean County; Pop. 3,488; Area Code 201; Zip Code 08008; located in E New Jersey; named for strip of beach bounding Barnegat Bay. Also, the barrier island itself, upon which are miles of bathing beaches and resort villages.

•**LONG BRANCH**, City; Monmouth County; Pop. 29,819; Area Code 201; Zip Code 07740; Elev. 19'; located in E New Jersey; is on the New Jersey coast, is an all year residential community as well as a summer resort.

The resort began in 1788 with a boarding house for Philadelphians who brought with them blue laws and religious meetings. By 1819 ocean bathing had become somewhat popularized but promiscuous bathing was taboo. When the white flag was run up, it was ladies' hour; the men had their turn when the red flag was hoisted. Later, in the 80's, however, a belle could not bathe without a male escort. The first gigolos in America were introduced at Long Branch, not as dancing partners but as bathing companions. Low-necked, spangled evening gowns were cut to knee length for the beach parade.

Before 1839, New Yorkers arrived in search of seashore homes, and a boom came with them. Hotels and cottages were built, blue laws were displaced by dancing, drinking, gambling, and fast driving along the hard Blue Drive, now Ocean Avenue. In the 1850's another boom brought impressive hotels and the resort became a rival of Saratoga. A popular race track, Monmouth Park, was opened in 1870, and a railroad, connecting the town with New York in 1874, brought a peak of prosperity.

Long Branch, decked out in the cast-iron trimmings of the U.S. Grant era and the fretwork of early Pullman art, became the playground for all the vivid personalities of the flamboyant 80's and 90's. *Phil Daly* ran his gambling club in a blaze of glitter even on Sundays while his wife played hymns in her chapel in the *Daly* garden. When *Daly* died, his wife decided to carry on his clubhouse, but her hymns got the best of her. *Dr. Helmbold* , a patent-medicine millionaire, bought old hotels to tear down and a city block to rebuild as he strove to make Long Branch a fit place in which to drive his showy tallyho. He died a hopeless lunatic trying to sweep the sunshine from his front porch.

Here *Lillie Langtry* kept here private car for an entire summer on a railroad siding adjoining the home of her current protector; there *Diamond Jim Brady* drove *Lillian Russell* in an electric coupe brightly illuminated on the interior rather than with headlights, so that all might see and enjoy; and here *Josie Mansfield* and *Ed Stokes* admired *Col. Jim Fisk* and his regiment in their gold braid as they played at drilling on the Bluff Parade Grounds. Named for Long Branch of Shrewsbury River.

•**LONGPORT**, Borough; Atlantic County; Pop. 1,275; Area Code 609; Zip Code 08403; Elev. 6'; located in SE New Jersey; named after *John Long* , landowner.

•**LONG VALLEY**, included in Washington; Morris County; Pop. 1,645; Area Code 201; Zip Code 07853; located in North Central New Jersey on Hwy. 24; settled by Germans at the turn of the 18th Century, was known as German Valley for more than 200 years; after the United States entered World War I, the name was changed. It is a tightly built little village in the center of a dairy and truck-farming section. Named for ten-mile length.

•**LUDLAM BEACH**, Barrier Island, SE New Jersey; Protects Ludlam Bay from Atlantic Ocean. Extends approx. 8 mi. between Peck and Seven Mile beaches, Cape May County.

•**LYNDHURST**, Township; Bergen County; Pop. 20,326; Area Code 201; Zip Code 07071; Elev. 60'; located in NE New Jersey; is an industrial town with a commuting population. First called New Barbados Neck by an early settler from Barbados, its name was changed in honor of *Lord Lyndhurst* , a frequent visitor.

•**MADISON**, Borough; Morris County; Pop. 15,357; Area Code 201; Zip Code 07940; Elev. 261'; located in N New Jersey; West of Newark - 10 miles - on Hwy. 24; was the home of *Mrs. Marcelus Hartley Dodge* , who is the former *Geraldine Rockefeller* , daughter of *William Rockefeller* and a niece of the late *John D. Rockefeller* . The Municipal Building is a memorial to her son, *Marcellus Hartley Dodge* ; its interior is finished in colored marbles and its rest rooms for policemen and firemen rival those of exclusive clubs. Madison is known as the "Rose City" because of its many greenhouses. Before 1834 it went by the plainer name of Bottle Hill. Some residents contend that the name was Battle Hill since the town site is said to have been the scene of two Indian skirmishes; but historians agree that the town took its first name from the nearby tavern. Named after *President James Madison* .

•**MAGNOLIA**, Borough; Camden County; Pop. 4,881; Area Code 609; Zip Code 08049; Elev. 79'; located in SW New Jersey on Hwy. 544, 10 miles SW of Camden; an agricultural center, was known in Civil War days as Greenland, not from the climate but because of the greenish tinge of the soil The town was renamed for the blossoms of magnolia trees in this area.

•**MAHWAH**, Township; Bergen County; Pop. 12,127; Area Code 201; Zip Code 07430; located in NE New Jersey; descriptive name meaning "meeting place." Birthplace of *Ernest P. Longerich*, prominent engineer.

•**MANAHAWKIN**, Unincorporated village, Ocean County; Pop. 2,300; Area Code 201; Zip Code 08050; Elev. 25'; located in E New Jersey on Hwy. 180; is on the site of an Indian village of the same name (Ind. good corn land). Manahawkin Lake is a cheerful foreground for this pleasant village, gateway to Long Beach Island on the ocean. The old Baptist Church, built in 1758, has served many denominations; the small plain white wooden building has had Victorian additions of two narrow gothic windows, a circular window in the gable, and a new wide vestibule with a narrow glass door to belie its actual age. The small steeple is surrounded by a plain low balustrade. The village was the boyhood home of *William Newell* , Governor of New Jersey (1857-60) and of the Indian Territory (1880). *Newell* was also the originator of the U.S. Life Saving Service. Named after Menach'hen meaning "island" and hawken meaning "place."

•**MANASQUAN**, Borough; Monmouth County; Pop. 5,354; Area Code 201; Zip Code 08736; Elev. 28'; located in E New Jersey; on the Manasquan River, a summer community. *Robert Louis Stevenson* lived here for six weeks in 1888 while preparing for his migration to the South Seas, where he died of tuberculosis. He spent most of the time in bed; part of the *Master of Ballantrae* was written at the Union House, later burned. On bright days he went out with his stepson, *Lloyd Osborne* , walking along the river or sailing. Saint Gaudens, the sculptor, visited Stevenson here to make impressions of the author's hands for the medallion now hanging in the Metropolitan Museum of Art in New York.

The Indian name of there place means "an enclosure with a house," the braves parking their wives here for safety while they went hunting and fishing. Descriptive name from Menach'hen meaning "island" and esquand meaning "door."

•**MANTOLOKING**, Borough; Ocean County; Pop. 433; Area Code 201; Zip Code 07838; Elev. 7'; located in E New Jersey; named for sub-tribe, Mantua, Iekau, "sand" and ink, "place."

•**MANTUA**, Township; Gloucester County; Pop. Town; 9,193; Area Code 609; Zip Code 08051; located in SW New Jersey; named for sub-tribe, Mantua.

•**MANVILLE**, Borough; Somerset County; Pop. 11,278; Area Code 201; Zip Code 08835; Elev. 44'; located in N New Jersey.

•**MAPLECREST**, Village, Essex County; Pop. included with Maplewood. Area Code 201; Zip Code 07040; located in NE New Jersey.

•**MAPLE SHADE**, Township; Burlington County; Pop. 20,525; Area Code 609; Zip Code 08052; located in S New Jersey.

•**MAPLEWOOD**, Township; Essex County; Pop. 22,950; Area Code 201; Zip Code 07040; Elev. 140'; located in NE New Jersey; lies immediately south of South Orange and some four miles west of Newark's business center. Incorporated in 1922, Maplewood is the youngest and in many ways the most progressive member of the Orange family.

•**MARGATE CITY**, City; Atlantic County; Pop. 9,179; Area Code 609; Zip Code 08402; Elev. 8'; located in SE New Jersey; Named after Margate, England.

•**MARLBORO**, Township; Monmouth County; Pop. 17,560; Area Code 201; Zip Code 07746; Elev. 190'; located in central eastern New Jersey on Hwy. 79; was first used as fertilizer, following the discovery of its properties in 1768 by an Irish settler. Named for marl beds.

•**MARLTON**, Burlington County; Area Code 609; Zip Code 08053; Elev. 100'; located in SW New Jersey, 15 miles SW of Camden on Hwy. 70; its name to an industry that has dwindled in recent years-the mining of marl from pits in this area. This fertilizer added greatly to the produce of Burlington County farms in the last century. Marl is now used to soften water in industry and to mix with sand for molding steel.

•**MARMORA**, included in Upper; Cape May County; Pop. est. 500; Area Code 609; Zip Code 08223; located in S New Jersey.

•**MARTINSVILLE**, included in Bridgewater; Somerset County; Pop. est. 900; Area Code 201; Zip Code 08836; located in N New Jersey.

•**MATAWAN**, Borough; Monmouth County; Pop. 8,837; Area Code 201; Zip Code 07747; Elev. 55'; located in E New Jersey;

descriptive name meaning "where two rivers come together" or mechawanienk, "ancient path."

•**MAURICE RIVER**, River; SE New Jersey; Flows SE approx. 40 mi. from source in Gloucester County to widened mouth at Maurice River Cove, at the Atlantic Ocean. Dammed to form Union Lake near Millville.

•**MAYS LANDING**, included in Hamilton; Atlantic County; Pop. 1,272; Area Code 609; Zip Code 08330; Elev. 20'; located in S central New Jersey; is the seat of Atlantic County. It is also the national capital of the nudists, who in 1937 designated the community as their headquarters. Along the bank of Great Egg Harbor River, 2 miles south of the village, a 500-acre tract known as Sunshine Park has been developed by this sun-loving cult. Named after *George May* , dock builder.

•**MAYWOOD**, Borough; Bergen County; Pop. 9,895; Area Code 201; Zip Code 07607; Elev. 94'; located in NE New Jersey.

•**MEDFORD**, Township; Burlington County; Pop. 17,471; Area Code 609; Zip Code 08055; Elev. 80'; located in S central New Jersey on Hwy. 541, S of 70; founded by Quakers before 1759, is a quiet village on the edge of the pines, at the crossing of two old stage roads. Orthodox Friends Meeting House, built in 1814, is in a widespread grove of maples, elms, and sycamores.

The South Branch of the Rancocas brought Quaker settlers here before 1759. The village was known by various names until *Mark Reeve* visited Medford, Mass., and was so much impressed with the place that he induced his neighbors in 1828 to name their town for it.

•**MEDFORD LAKES**, Borough; Burlington County; Pop. 4.958; Area Code 609; Zip Code 08055; Elev. 57'; located in S New Jersey.

•**MENDHAM**, Borough; Morris County; Pop. 4,883; Area Code 201; Zip Code 07945; Elev. 648'; located in North central New Jersey on Hwy. 24; a sign outside the Black Horse fixes the date of its establishment at 1743. In the barroom, however, is a framed card that advertises the birth year as 1735. According to those inhabitants who have wondered about the discrepancy themselves, 1735 was the estimate of a former proprietor. He had the card made, and then commissioned a local sign painter to emblazon the date outside. That sign painter seems to have been a man of considerable historiographic conscience. The true date, he said, was 1743. He thought the sign was a good idea; but it would go up right or not at all. The sign went up. Named after Myndham, England.

•MENLO PARK, Included with West Orange, Essex County, New Jersey; is known for the Site of Edison's Laboratory, marked by a rough-hewn granite boulder. In a hillside park behind the boulder stands the 129-foot Memorial Tower, topped by a huge electric light bulb about 14 feet high and 9 feet in diameter. The eight-sided tower is built of reinforced colored concrete. The great bulb is made of prismatic pyrex glass and illuminated by 12 lights inside. Bronze tablets placed on seven of the eight sides tell of Edison's inventions. A bronze and glass door gives a view of the perpetual light at the base, burning since 1929. The tower stands on the spot where the first incandescent bulb was made. Edison's home is gone; his workshop and many relics have been removed by *Henry Ford* to his museum in Dearborn, Michigan. Named after Menlo Park, California.

•MERCER COUNTY, Western New Jersey; Area 228 sq. miles; Pop. 307,863; Seat Trenton; Established Feb. 22, 1838; Named for *Hugh Mercer* .

•MERCERVILLE, included in Hamilton; Mercer County; Pop. 15,000; Area Code 609; Zip Code 08619; located in central W New Jersey, 5 miles NE of Trenton; was once known as Sandtown and later as Five Roads. The present name honors *Gen. Hugh Mercer* , fatally wounded in the Battle of Princeton.

•MERCHANTVILLE, Borough; Camden County; Pop. 3,972; Area Code 609; Zip Code 08109; Elev. 82'; located in SW New Jersey.

•METUCHEN, Borough; Middlesex County; Pop. 13,762; Area Code 201; Zip Code 08840; Elev. 117'; located in central New Jersey; has long been known, half seriously, as the "Brainy Borough." Its residents, including many New York businessmen, take pride not only in fine dwellings and shaded streets but also in cultural pursuits. Outstanding literary and artistic figures have made their homes here. Named after *Chief Matochshegan* .

•MICKLETON, included in East Greenwich; Gloucester County; Area Code 609; Zip Code 08056; located in SW New Jersey.

•**MIDDLEBUSH**, included in Franklin; Somerset County; Pop. est. 700; Area Code 201; Zip Code 08873; located in N New Jersey.

•**MIDDLESEX**, Borough; Middlesex County; Pop. 13,480; Area Code 201; Zip Code 08846; Elev. 63'; located in N central New Jersey; during the Revolution the New Jersey militia in this section carried on guerilla warfare against the British and Hessian garrison of New Brunswick, to protect the flank of *Washington's* position in the Watchung Mountains to the west.   *Middlesex has a number of green-houses which parallel Green Brook. They rank as one of the world's largest producers of orchids and gardenias. Named after Middlesex, England.*

•*MIDDLESEX COUNTY, Central Eastern New Jersey; Area 312 sq. miles; Pop. 595,893; Seat New Brunswick; Established March 1, 1683; Named for Middlesex, England.*

•*MIDDLETOWN, Township; Monmouth County; Pop. 62,574; Area Code 201; Zip Code 07748; located in E New Jersey.*

•*MIDDLEVILLE, included Stillwater; Sussex County; Pop. est. 150; Area Code 201; Zip Code 07855; located in N New Jersey.*

•*MIDLAND PARK, Borough; Bergen County; Pop. 7,381; Area Code 201; Zip Code 07432; Elev. 347'; located in NE New Jersey; named for location "amid Bergen hills."*

•*MIDTOWN, part of Newark; Essex County; Area Code 201; Zip Code 071 + zone; located in NE New Jersey.*

•*MILFORD, Borough; Hunterdon County; Pop. 1,368; Area Code 201; Zip Code 08848; located in NW New Jersey.*

•*MILLBURN, Township; Essex County; Pop. 19,543; Area Code 201; Zip Code 07041; located in NE New Jersey; named for Burn which supplied power for paper and other mills.*

•*MILLTOWN, Borough; Middlesex County; Pop. 7,136; Area Code 201; Zip Code 08850; Elev. 65'; located in central New Jersey; named for early gristmills.*

•*MILLVILLE, City; Cumberland County; Pop. 25,281; Area Code 609; Zip Code 08332; Elev. 37'; located in SW New Jersey on Hwy. 49, N of Maurice River; was originally Shingle Landing, later*

Maurice River Bridge and The Bridge. Settled as a shipping center in 1720, Millville's future was determined when German glassmakers learned of the vast deposits of silica that underlie most of south New Jersey and are near the surface here. This sand was the foundation of the glass industry in America. Name derived because of proposed establishment of a mill town.

•**MINDOWASKIN PARK**, Union County; is named for one of three Indians who sold the site to Gawen Lawrie, Scottish deputy governor, in 1684. In an old Indian Burial Ground, Broad St. and Springfield Ave., many relics have been recovered, and a few mounds remain.

•**MONMOUTH BEACH**, Borough; Monmouth County; Pop. 3,318; Area Code 201; Zip Code 07750; Elev. 12'; located in E New Jersey.

•**MONMOUTH COUNTY**, Eastern Coastal New Jersey; Area 477 sq. miles; Pop. 503,173; Seat Freehold; Established March 1, 1683; Named for Monmouth County, England; James Scott, (1649-1685), Duke of Monmouth.

•**MONTCLAIR**, Town; Essex County; Pop. 38,321; Area Code 201; Zip Code 070+zone; Elev. 337'; located in NE New Jersey; formerly a part of Bloomfield, broke off when the parent community refused to cooperate in building a railroad to run from Jersey City to the New York State Line. That was in 1868. The township's history can be traced to 1666, year of a town meeting convened in Milford, Conn., to consider inducements proffered by *Gov. Philip Carteret* of New Jersey to establish a settlement on the banks of the Passaic River. It was at first divided into two parts, Cranetown and Speertown, for two early settlers; *Stephen Crane* (1871-1900), the writer, was a descendant of the first *Crane* . Name derived from French meaning "bright mountain."

•**MONTVALE**, Borough; Bergen County; Pop. 7,318; Area Code 201; Zip Code 07645; Elev. 187'; located in NE New Jersey; named for topography of area.

•**MONTVILLE**, Township; Morris County; Pop. 14,290; Area Code 201; Zip Code 07045; located in N New Jersey; named for location - mountainous terrain.

•**MOORESTOWN**, Township; Burlington County; Pop. 15,596; Area Code 609; Zip Code 08057; Elev. 76'; located in S New Jersey; named after *Thomas Moore* , poet.

•**MORGANVILLE**, included in Marlboro; Monmouth County; Pop. est. 900; Area Code 201; Zip Code 07751; Elev. 140'; located in E New Jersey; is in the market garden belt.

•**MORRIS COUNTY**, North Central New Jersey; Area 468 sq. miles; Pop. 407,630; Seat Morristown; Established March 15, 1739; Named for *Lewis Morris* (1671-1746), first Governor of New Jersey.

•**MORRIS PLAINS**, Borough; Morris County; Pop. 5,305; Zip Code 07950; Elev. 399'; located in N New Jersey; named for *Lewis Morris*, Governor 1738-1746.

•**MORRISTOWN**, Town; Morris County; Pop. 16,614; Area Code 201; Zip Code 07960; Elev. 327'; located in N New Jersey when, about 1710, word came to the settlement at Newark that iron ore was plentiful beyond the Watchung Mountains, a small number of pioneers struck out on a wilderness road to engage in a new industry. One group selected a site at the foot of the present Water Street in Morristown, in the small valley (now known as The Hollow), and named their new village West Hanover. Newcomers spread to the tablelands above and formed a ring of improved properties around a central green which later became Morristown Green.

In 1739 a new county was laid out within the bounds of Hunterdon and named in honor of Lewis Morris, the first governor of New Jersey. The first session of the Morris County court was held in the tavern of *Jacob Ford*, the appointed justice. At this convening, the township of Morris was legally defined. Within two years the population was large enough to support a log church. A courthouse was built in 1755.

During the Revolution, when the demand for munitions tested the young industrial resources of the Colonies, no fewer than forty-five forges were operated in Morris County. In addition there were sawmills and gristmills on every sizable stream. The iron industry became the most important factor in the development of Morristown and neighboring communities.

No Briton or Hessian set foot in Morris County except as a prisoner, for the town was relentlessly defended as a key point in the theater of war. *General Washington* was aware of the natural advantage of Morristown's site on the frontier of the highlands. Good roads provided quick communication with Philadelphia and Congress, and made it easy to concentrate military supplies within striking distance of the British.

Washington led his exhausted army here in January 1777 for winter encampment in the Loantaka Valley after the victories at Trenton and Princeton. He returned with his troops to pass the winter of 1779-80. The men were quartered in crude huts in Jockey Hollow, while *Washington* made the Ford House his headquarters. With his army's condition even worse than it had been at Valley Forge, the commander-in-chief established a quota system for levying supplies upon the various counties. He wrote to a friend that the men sometimes went "five or six days together without bread" and that at one time "the soldiers ate every kind of horse food but hay."

Count Pulaski helped to maintain morale by exercising his cavalry corps before the Ford House. His special stunt was to fire his pistol while at full gallop, toss it into the air, catch it, and hurl it at an imaginary enemy ahead. With one foot in the stirrup, and his horse still galloping, *Pulaski* would then swing to the ground and pick up the gun. Some of the best Virginia horsemen suffered bad falls in attempts to duplicate this feat.

During this winter occurred the court martial of *Gen. Benedict Arnold*, requested by the officer himself after the Supreme Executive Council of Pennsylvania had accused him of partiality to Tories and rudeness to American Civil authorities when he was in command of Philadelphia. The trial was staged in the old Dickerson Tavern (no longer standing) with *Maj. Gen. Robert Howe* as presiding officer. The verdict was a recommendation for a reprimand by *General Washington*, a comparatively mild punishment, but one that stung the young officer. Arnold remained in the service only at the insistence of *Washington*, who placed him in command of West Point. There he entered into a plot with *Major Andre's* men to deliver the fortification to the British. It is said that *Washington* laughed heartily only once during his stay in Morristown--and that was when he was describing *Arnold's* ludicrous appearance as he galloped from the Robinson house near West Point to seek safety on a British vessel.

From 1780 until the fall of 1781 Continental troops were in and about the north New Jersey area. The Pennsylvania Line was quartered at Jockey Hollow in the winter of 1780-81 and from there went north to meet the troops that *Washington* was assembling at Newburgh for the final march to Yorktown.

When the iron industry diminished before Western competition during the nineteenth century, Morristown became largely a residential and shopping town. *Thomas Nast*, the cartoonist who created the Tammany tiger and pilloried Boss Tweed, made his home here. *Bret Harte* and *Frank R. Stockton* lived in Morristown for a time.

Rail connections between Morristown and Newark, over the tracks of the Morris and Essex Railroad, were established in January 1838. Today, approximately 1,200 persons commute daily to clerical jobs and executive positions in the cities of the metropolitan district, while a number of outsiders come to Morristown for work.

Tallyhos were characteristic of the recent decades when Morristown was peopled by millionaires and horse lovers. On any bright Sunday morning a walker along the tree-lined roads leading into the town might have been startled by the blast of a horn in the distance, then the fast beating of horses' hoofs, a flash of color from gaily liveried footmen--a cloud of dust and the bright equipage would be lost to sight. Famous were the annual parties given by the late *Otto Kahn* for his staff of servants and caretakers, numbering upwards of one hundred, on his forested estate in the Normandy Park section. The entire house was turned over to his employees, with continuous music and the best of refreshments provided.

•**MOUNTAIN LAKES**, Borough; Morris County; Pop. 4,153; Area Code 201; Zip Code 07046; Elev. 513'; located in N New Jersey; name given for twin lakes.

•**MOUNTAINSIDE**, Borough; Union County; Pop. 7,118; Area Code 201; Zip Code 07092; located in NE New Jersey.

•**MOUNT ARLINGTON**, Borough; Morris County; Pop. 4,251; Area Code 201; Zip Code 07856; Elev. 142'; located in N New Jersey; named after *Henry Bennet* , Earl of Arlington.

•**MOUNT EPHRAIM**, Borough; Camden County; Pop. 4,863; Area Code 609; Zip Code 08059; Elev. 70'; located in SW New Jersey at the junctions of 42 and 130; was a Colonial settlement. Stagecoach companies operating between Camden, Philadelphia, and the coast chose *Ephraim Albertson's* tavern here as a station. *Albertson* supplied fresh horses for the stages, and maintained a large stable and carriage shed in addition to the inn. Modern business structures now stand on the site of the tavern.

•**MOUNT HOLLY**, Township; Burlington County; Pop. 10,818; Area Code 609; Zip Code 08060; Elev. 52'; located in S New

Jersey; in 1676 *Thomas Rudyard* and *John Ridges* purchased a share of land from *Edward Byllynge* and the trustees of West Jersey. In 1701 *Edward Gaskill* and *Josiah Southwick* bought Ridges' 871 acres, on part of which the town now stands. In 1723 the North Branch of Rancocas Creek was dammed for a sawmill and, later for a gristmill. An iron works was established about 1730 by *Isaac Pearson*, *Mahlon Stacy* and *John Burr*; British raiders later destroyed the works, which had been supplying cannon and shot for the continental army.

During the Revolution Mount Holly was occupied at times by British troops, who converted the old Friends Meeting House into a commissary. In 1779 the same building was used for sessions of the legislature when, during November and December, the town was the temporary capital of the state. *Gov. William Livingston* at that time named Thursday, December 9, 1779, as the first Thanksgiving Day to be officially observed in the state, in accordance with a Congressional resolution.

An act of the legislature transferred the county seat from Burlington to Mount Holly in 1796, and the courthouse was erected in that year. Construction of the Burlington and Mount Holly Railroad half a century later strengthened industrial enterprise. By then the town had five mills, a woolen factory, nine stores, a bank, two newspapers and a boarding school.

In 1865 the population of Mount Holly was 3,878, and the town enjoyed steady progress as a small manufacturing and trading center. Some years later *Hezekiah Smith* built his locally famous bicycle railway, a monorail line, to Mount Holly from nearby Smithville. Name is descriptive of hill covered with holly trees.

•MOUNT LAUREL, Township; Burlington County; Pop. 17,614; Area Code 609; Zip Code 08054; located in S New Jersey; descriptive name for hill covered with laurel.

•MULLICA RIVER, River; SE New Jersey; Flows SE from source in Camden County to Atlantic Ocean, N of Atlantic city; was famous for its oysters. It was named for *Eric Mullica*, who led a Swedish colony across the state from Delaware in 1697. The River runs into the Great Bay. River flows through much of Wharton State Forest.

•MURRAY GROVE, Ocean Grove; is the birthplace of the Universalist Church of America. Named after *Rev. John Murray*, founder of Universalist Church.

•**MYSTIC ISLANDS**, Ocean County; Area Code 201; Zip Code 08087; located in E New Jersey.

•**NATIONAL PARK**, Borough; Gloucester County; Pop. 3,552; Area Code 609; Zip Code 08063; Elev. 20'; located in SW New Jersey; name derived from Red Bank Battlefield National Park.

•**NAVESINK RIVER (ESTUARY)**, River; Monmouth County; is an inlet that is approximately 10 miles in length. The river flows into Raritan Bay. It would flow directly into the Atlantic Ocean but it is blocked by the Sandy Hook peninsula.

•**NEPTUNE CITY**, Borough; Monmouth County; Pop. 5,276; Area Code 201; Zip Code 07753; Elev. 15'; located in E New Jersey; named for Roman god of the ocean.

•**NETCONG**, Borough; Morris County; Pop. 3,557; Area Code 201; Zip Code 07857; Elev. 882'; located in N New Jersey; is the center of a large summer resort area. The town was first settled by workers in the nearby iron works and mines. Descriptive name after Moschakgere meaning "clear," hannek, "stream" and onk "place."

•**NEWARK**, See special article.

•**NEWARK BAY**, Bay, NE New Jersey; Protected from Atlantic Ocean by peninsula of Jersey City and Staten Island, New York. Newark and Elizabeth front on this bay, which has been polluted by intense industrial wastes in recent years. Major port facilities.

•**NEW BRUNSWICK**, City; Middlesex County; Pop. 41,442; Area Code 201; Zip Code 089+zone; Elev. 42'; located in Central New Jersey; situated on the south bank of Raritan River, combines the attributes of a manufacturing center, a college town, a market place and a county seat.

   The area around New Brunswick was occupied by the Lenni Lenape Indians and one or two white settlers when *John Indian* and 10 associates from Long Island bought about 10,000 acres in 1681. *Indian* and his associates were English. They established an English hegemony which was not threatened until 1730 when Dutch settlers from Albany began to change the national character of the community.

   In 1686 *Indian* established a ferry, for which he received exclusive rights in 1697, and built a new road to Delaware Falls

(Trenton). The locality, previously known as Prigmore's Swamp, was called Indian's Ferry in 1713. On the water front were built the first homes, and taverns for wayfarers.

For a time it seemed that the Landing, 1.5 miles upstream at the head of navigation, would eclipse Indian's Ferry as a townsite. But the fact that ships could reach the Landing only when the tide was favorable, while Indian's Ferry was accessible at all times, spoiled the Landing's chances. Now it is little more than a bridge with a background of meadow lands populated chiefly by cows.

The name Brunswick, in honor of *King George I* , also Duke of Brunswick, first appears in court records of 1724. In 1730, when the settlement consisted of 125 families, it received a charter from *King George II* . The Dutch Reformed Church, which is known to have been in existence in New Brunswick as early as 1717, subsequently became a strong influence in civic life. Methodism made a start in 1740 when the evangelist, *George Whitefield* , preached to an immense crowd from the tail end of a wagon before the Reformed Church.

New Brunswick soon became one of the great agricultural depots of the Colony. Every stream that could turn a wheel had its mill. Warehouses and inns were erected, and the river front was lined with vessels.

Construction of the barracks in 1759 and their occupation by British troops after 1767 strengthened Tory sentiment among the wealthier citizens. Two years before, however, patriots had burned in effigy a delegate to the Stamp Act Congress for refusing to oppose the unpopular act. The crisis reached a head in 1774 when the Provincial Congress met here and chose delegates to the Continental Congress. Subsequent prohibition of trade with the enemy seriously injured commerce in New Brunswick, then a town of about 150 families.

Washington and his defeated army, retreating from New York, entered New Brunswick on November 28, 1776. Later, the general wrote, "In short, the conduct of the Jerseys has been most infamous. Instead of turning out to defend their country, and affording aid to our army, they are making their submissions as fast as can. If the Jerseys had given us any support we might have made a good stand at Hackensack, and after that at Brunswick..." On December 1, *Sir William Howe* led the British into the city for a destructive occupation of seven months.

Compensating for the unsoldierly conduct of the local troops New Brunswick rivermen turned their whaleboats into fighting ships. They did so much damage in nightly raids upon

British vessels around New York Bay that an expedition of 300 men was sent here to destroy the fleet of *Capt. Adam Hyler*, best known of the privateers. The burning of his boats and a skirmish with American militia was the last fight in or around the town.

Washington again brought his army to New Brunswick after the inconclusive battle at nearby Monmouth (Freehold) in the summer of 1778. And it was here that the Commander in Chief issued his unexpected order in 1781 for the march south that resulted in the British capitulation at Yorktown.

Trade revived after the war, and in 1784 the growing town was incorporated as a city. The first American railroad charter was granted in 1815 to *John Stevens* for a line from "near Trenton, to ...near New Brunswick" but the road was never started. Rail service came with the building of the New Jersey Railroad, whose passengers were shuttled by stagecoach across Raritan River to the New York connection until 1838 when through service was made possible by a new railroad bridge.

The busy port attracted *Cornelius Vanderbilt*, who had begun to amass his fortune with the steamship *Bellona*. However, New Brunswick's importance as a shipping terminal began to wane in 1834 when the Delaware and Raritan Canal, 42-mile waterway to Bordentown, was opened. For a time, though, the city benefited from the through traffic. The canal boom was short-lived; railroad competition and domination put the canal boats out of business, although nominal operation continued to 1933.

By the middle of the nineteenth century the city had grown to 8,693. There were 120 stores, 1 bank, 8 churches, and 2 schools for girls. Rutgers College, after weathering financial crises and suspensions, was an established institution. In addition to a carriage factory, a cotton mill and several shipyards. New Brunswick had three units of the newly developed rubber industry, producing rubberized sheets, carriage tops and boots. Other products of the period were machinery, wallpaper, shoes and hosiery.

The manufacture of pharmaceuticals was begun in 1886 by Johnson and Johnson. In 1916 the pharmaceutical industry was augmented by the arrival of E.R. Squibb and Sons. The National Musical String Company, founded in 1897, produced the first harmonicas in America, and has since become the world's largest maker of steel strings.

After 1900 the city's industrial pattern changed. The promising rubber industry moved westward to get more room for expansion, but the empty factories were quickly occupied by the needle trades and other newcomers. The old carriage factories were succeeded by an automobile plant in 1910 when the Simplex Automobile Company began operations. During the World War the Wright-Martin Aircraft Corporation made Hispano-Suiza and Liberty motors in the Simplex factory, which is now used by the International Motor Company for the production of automotive parts.

Steady industrial growth has been the main stream of New Brunswick's history since 1850. But political controversies, revival movements, and a celebrated murder case have rippled the current. In the early nineties, when the city council was deadlocked on the choice of a president, a coin was tossed, it is said, to decide the vote. The Democrats charged that the Republicans had used a double-headed coin. The city's saloons once enjoyed such excellent patronage both downstairs and up that reformers declared, "It would be an injustice to the devil to condemn him to live in New Brunswick." Crusading evangelists moved in, set up their tents on Livingston Avenue and "converted" hundreds.

•NEW EGYPT, Village, included in Plumsted township; Ocean County; Pop. 1,769; Area Code 201; Zip Code 08533; located in Central New Jersey, Junction 528 and 537 Hwys.; Crosswicks Creek here has been dammed to form Oakford Lake, a vacation spot with woodlands on the shore. The creek was the route followed by the first Quaker colonists soon after their arrival on the Delaware in 1675.

At the time of the Revolution the village was known as Timmons Mills. After the victory at Trenton in December, 1776, *Washington* needed grain for his army. *Benjamin Jones* , one of the General's New Jersey advisors, had a large quantity of buckwheat flour and cornmeal stored at the mills; he sent his secretary, *Joseph Curtis* , to bring the milled grain to Trenton. Hailing the welcome arrival, *Washington* said: "*Joseph* has been in Egypt and gotten the corn." The village was Egypt until 1845, when the prefix "New" was added to avoid confusion with other Egypts. Center of a fine farm and dairy section, New Egypt still has a never failing corn crop.

•NEWFIELD, Borough; Gloucester County; Pop. 1,563; Area Code 609; Zip Code 08344; Elev. 110'; located in SW New Jersey; descriptive name for new field development for a town.

•**NEWFOUNDLAND**, included in West Milford; Passaic County; Pop. est. 550; Area Code 201; Zip Code 07435; Elev. 760'; located in N New Jersey; bases its principal claim to distinction on the local belief that it was the birthplace of *William H. Seward*, Secretary of State in President Lincoln's cabinet and a general thorn in Lincoln's side. Historians are agreed that *Seward* was born in Florida, N.Y. Few Newfoundlanders seem worried about the dispute; they simply have not changed their minds. The site of the alleged birthplace is not known. Name derived from Pioneer's report, "The only land we found."

•**NEW MILFORD**, Borough; Bergen County; Pop. 16,876; Area Code 201; Zip Code 07646; located in NE New Jersey; named after Milford, Pa.

•**NEW PROVIDENCE**, Borough; Union County; Pop. 12,426; Area Code 201; Zip Code 07974; Elev. 220'; located in NE New Jersey.

•**NEWTON**, Town; Sussex County; Pop. 7,748; Area Code 201; Zip Code 07860; Elev. 636'; located in N New Jersey; called by the Indians Chinchewunska (side hill town), is the county seat of Sussex County and largest dairy center of northern New Jersey. Newton was settled prior to 1761 by *Henry Harelocker*, a Dutch colonist and tavern keeper.

The old Courthouse facing the square was built in 1847 and is a graceful example of late Classic Revival architecture with a severely plain pediment and Doric columns. The most famous building in Newton is the old Cochran House, also facing the square, at Main and Spring Sts. The inn has been rebuilt and modernized until now none of the original Colonial tavern of 1753 remains. *General Washington* and his staff were entertained here July 26, 1782, on their way to Newburgh, New York. Descriptive name meaning a "new town."

•**NORMA**, Village, included in Pittsgrove township; Salem County; Pop. est. 800; Area Code 609; Zip Code 08347; Elev. 90'; located in SW New Jersey; its neighboring Jewish communities of Brotmanville and Alliance to the north and Rosehayn and Carmel to the southwest, form essentially a single community with a common historical background. These communities represent a successful experiment in social service undertaken by the Hebrew Immigrant Society of New York City. In 1881 many Jewish refugees from Russia and Poland arrived in New York

without funds, relatives, or friends in this country to provide for
their immediate needs. The Hebrew Immigrant Society planned
agricultural communities for the newcomers and founded the colony of Alliance. Settlers turned to garment making and hand-
crafts to supplement their income from farming and their aid
from philanthropic sources. The soil, however, proved favorable
for growing vegetables and berries, and second and third generation descendants of the original settlers are farming successfully.
While few bearded elders with earlocks and long gabardines remain, many of the old Talmudic laws and Biblical customs are
still retained, though some have been altered by the accelerated
pace of modern living and the influx of other nationalities.

•**NORMANOCK**, Village, Sussex County; Pop. rural; located in N
New Jersey; is the office of the State Forest warden and his
aides, who are in charge of Stokes State Forest, one of the largest
in New Jersey maintained for recreation, with an area of 12, 428
acres. The forest was given to the state by *Gov. Edward Stokes* .
Named for *Chief Normanock* .

•**NORTH ARLINGTON**, Borough; Bergen County; Pop. 16,587;
Area Code 201; Zip Code 07032; Elev. 122'; located in NE New
Jersey; where the first steam engine in America was brought
here from England in 1753 by *John Schuyler* to pump water out of
his copper mine, and was set up by *Joshua Hornblower* . The once
profitable copper mine was discovered prior to 1719 by a black
slave on the *Schuyler* plantation. While plowing he turned up an
unusually heavy stone and took it to his master, a Dutch trader
and Indian agent of the Province. An assay showed it was 80 percent pure copper.

•**NORTH BERGEN**, Township; Hudson County; Pop. 47,019;
Area Code 201; Zip Code 07047; Elev. 43'; located in NE New
Jersey.

•**NORTH BRANCH**, Village, included in Branchburg township;
Somerset County; Pop. 2,500; Area Code 201; Zip Code 08876;
Elev. 70'; located in N New Jersey; on the North Branch of the
Raritan River, was laid out in 1884. Fine pastures and farm land
surround the town.

•**NORTH BRUNSWICK**, Township; Middlesex County; Pop.
22,220; Area Code 201; Zip Code 08902; located in Central New
Jersey.

•**NORTHFIELD**, City; Atlantic County; Pop. 7,795; Area Code 609; Zip Code 08225; Elev. 33'; located in SE New Jersey.

•**NORTH PLAINFIELD**, Borough; Somerset County; Pop. 19,108; Area Code 201; Zip Code 07060; Elev. 17'; located in N New Jersey.

•**NORTHVALE**, Borough; Bergen County; Pop. 5,046; Area Code 201; Zip Code 07647; Elev. 82'; located in NE New Jersey; named for location and topography.

•**NORTH WILDWOOD**, City; Cape May County; Pop. 4,714; Area Code 609; Zip Code 08260; Elev. 6'; located in S New Jersey.

•**NORWOOD**, Borough; Bergen County; Pop. 4,413; Area Code 201; Zip Code 07648; Elev. 90'; located in NE New Jersey; named for location; north woods of county.

•**NUTLEY**, Town; Essex County; Pop. 28,998; Area Code 201; Zip Code 07110; Elev. 91'; located in NE New Jersey; occupies part of the borderland of 1776-three low foothills of the Watchung Ridge that reach the Passaic River where "river guards" kept constant watch for enemy raiders during the Revolution. Its main business street still bears the name of *William Franklin*, last Royal Governor of New Jersey, though the town long ago dropped the name of Franklinville. Named for a resident's estate.

•**OAKHURST**, included in Ocean Township; Monmouth County; Pop. est. 4,600; Area Code 201; Zip Code 07755; located in NE New Jersey.

•**OAKLAND**, Borough; Bergen County; Pop. 13,443; Area Code 201; Zip Code 07436; Elev. 282'; located in NE New Jersey; is one of the oldest communities in Bergen County. It was known successively as Yawpaw (ind., wild plum), The Ponds, Scrub Oaks, Bushville and now Oakland. Once hanging from a bracket in the public square was a sign announcing "Oakland, Bergen County, New Jersey Established 1869." The legend is topped by a portrait of one *Chief Iaopogh* and the words, "Once There Was Indians all Over This Place." Named for white oak trees.

•**OAKLYN**, Borough; Camden County; Pop. 4,223; Area Code 609; Zip Code 08107; Elev. 28'; located in SW New Jersey.

•**OCEAN**, Township, Monmouth County; Pop. 23,570; Area Code 201; Zip Code 07712; located in E New Jersey; named for location on the Atlantic Ocean.

•**OCEAN CITY**, City; Cape May County; Pop. 13,949; Area Code 609; Zip Code 08226; Elev. 4'; located in S New Jersey; named for location on the Atlantic Ocean.

•**OCEAN COUNTY**, Eastern Coastal New Jersey; Area 639 sq. miles; Pop. 346,038; Seat Toms River; Established Feb. 15, 1850; Named for Atlantic Ocean.   *Since the middle of the 1800's, Ocean County has grown from a rural farming, fishing and boat-building area with a population of 14,000 to a booming region with urbanized towns, naval and army training centers, increasing industry and the states first nuclear plant. By the end of 1978 the population had passed the 320,000 mark.*

The lands south of the Manasquan River were part of Monmouth County until February 15, 1850, when Ocean County was created by an act of the state legislature. The area was settled by squatters around 1690 when property along Barnegat Bay was divided among the Board of Proprietors of the Province of East Jersey.

Whalers and smugglers werre the first to live in the coves along the shore, while settlements around sawmills began to appear by 1740 along the rivers and streams.

Two hundred years ago, Ocean County privateers were sweeping the Atlantic coast free of British shipping, slowing supplies to British headquarters in New York and aiding the American cause for freedom.

From 1776 to 1783 these privateers engaged in 77 naval battles off the coast of Ocean County, while British and Loyalist troops led 23 skirmishes against the local militia.

The clearing of trees in the early 1800's for the charcoal industry led to the cultivation of cranberries in the cedar swamps by 1850. As uplands were cleared for farming, the poultry industry started early in this century.

In the 1960's and 70's, however, many farms made way for residential development as Ocean County became the fastest-growing county in the U.S. Many of the new residents were senior citizens and the county claimed the greatest concentration of retirement communities in the Northeast.

The shorefront along Barnegat Bay and the Atlantic Ocean has continued to play a central role in the county's history. The resort trade and marine industries have traditionally been the backbone of the county's economy.

There are still vast open areas across the county. The Pine Barrens, sparsely populated and biologically unique, spread westward from the southwestern third of the county.

Ocean County is the fastest growing county in New Jersey, with a population increase of 90 percent in each of the last two decades. Most live in the Lakewood area.

•OCEAN GATE, Borough; Ocean County; Pop. 1,385; Area Code 201; Zip Code 08740; Elev. 7'; located in E New Jersey; named for location on the Atlantic Ocean Coast.

•OCEAN GROVE, included in Neptune; Monmouth County; Pop. est. 4,200; Area Code 201; Zip Code 07756; Elev. 20'; located in NE New Jersey, S of Asbury Park; belongs to the Reconstruction Era and Queen Victoria. The resort was developed in the period of Eastlake architecture, with odd half-houses to which tent fronts are added, with fretwork villas, and with neo-Swiss chalets of the Centennial Exposition type, ornamented with tiers of narrow porches and turrets.

Founded in 1869 for Methodist camp meetings, Ocean Grove strictly observed the religious ideals of the founders.

•OCEANPORT, Borough; Monmouth County; Pop. 5,888; Area Code 201; Zip Code 07757; Elev. 12'; located in E New Jersey.

•OGDENSBURG, Borough; Sussex County; Pop. 2,737; Area Code 201; Zip Code 07439; Elev. 677'; located in N New Jersey; named for Robert Ogden , distiller and mine owner.

•OLD BRIDGE, Township; Middlesex County; Pop. 51,515; Area Code 201; Zip Code 08857; located in Central New Jersey.

•OLD TAPPAN, Borough; Bergen County; Pop. 4,168; Area Code 201; Zip Code 07675; Elev. 50'; located in NE New Jersey; named for sub-tribe, Tappans.

•OLDWICK, Village, included in Tewksburg township; Hunterdon County; Pop. est. 450; Area Code 201; Zip Code 08858; Elev. 240'; located in NW New Jersey; is an old settlement known as Smithfield in Colonial days and later as New Germantown. Anglo-Saxon name meaning "old town."

•**ORADELL**, Borough; Bergen County; Pop. 8,658; Area Code 201; Zip Code 07649; Elev. 110'; located in NE New Jersey; named derived from Latin language ora, meaning "edge" and dell.

•**ORANGE**, City; Essex County; Pop. 31,136; Area Code 201; Zip Code 070 + zone; Elev. 204'; located in NE New Jersey; adjoins East Orange to the west, mother of all the other Oranges.

Orange was settled in 1678 with the aristocratic name of the Mountain Plantations. It is believed to have been afterward renamed in honor of *William* , Prince of Orange, who became *William III* of England. Up to the Revolution, Orange farmers were noted for their resistance to the Colonial government and were quick in 1776 to come down from the mountains to fight the British. After the war the governing Presbyterians characteristically turned to education, founding an academy in 1785 and a public library in 1793.

The industrial revolution brought the shoe industry to Orange, where it flourished as the leading manufacture until a decade after the Civil War. When it began to wane under competition from New England, it was replaced by hat manufacturing, for which the town was renowned until the turn of the century.

•**OXFORD**, Township; Warren County; Pop. 1,659; Area Code 201; Zip Code 07863; Elev. 500'; located in NW New Jersey on Hwy. 31; on the slope of Scotts Mt. is an iron-mining center. The village sprang up more than two centuries ago around Oxford Furnace, one of *Washington's* sources of military supplies. Named after *John Axford* , settler.

•**PACKANACK LAKE**, Lake; Passaic County; Pop. included in Wayne; Area Code 201; Zip Code 07470; located in N New Jersey; named after sub-tribe, Pequannuc.

•**PALISADES PARK**, Borough; Bergen County; Pop. 13,372; Area Code 201; Zip Code 07650; Elev. 150'; located in NE New Jersey; named for palisades of Hudson River.

•**PALMYRA**, Borough; Burlington County; Pop. 7,085; Area Code 609; Zip Code 08065; Elev. 20'; located in S New Jersey; named after Palmyra, Syria, meaning "palm trees."

•**PARAMUS**, Borough; Bergen County; Pop. 26,474; Area Code 201; Zip Code 07652; Elev. 58'; located in NE New Jersey; is an old Dutch farm community. A wide area is covered with a black muck, especially suited to celery growing, giving Paramus the local name of Celery Town. Dutch colonists first settled here in 1666. Name derived from peram-sepus, meaning "pleasant stream."

•**PARK RIDGE**, Borough; Bergen County; Pop. 8,515; Area Code 201; Zip Code 07656; Elev. 226'; located in NE New Jersey; named for location, on a ridge.

•**PARSIPPANY** (Troy Hills), Township; Morris County; Pop. 49,868; Area Code 201; Zip Code 07054; Elev. 300'; located in N New Jersey; lies at the southern tip of Parsippany Reservoir. The vine-run red brick Presbyterian Church dates back to 1718, when *John Richards* local schoolmaster, deeded three and a half acres to the township of Whippanong for a meeting house. The present building, with Gothic windows and Gothic panels in the doors near the pulpit, was erected in 1828. Named for *Parlin* family.

•**PASSAIC**, City; Passaic County; Pop. 52,463; Area Code 201; Zip Code 07055; Elev. 102'; located in N New Jersey; bounded on one side by Passaic River, 15 miles upstream from Newark Bay, the city is bordered on the other three sides by the semicircular area of residential Clifton.

Dutch traders were the first settlers of Passaic (Ind., *peaceful valley*). In 1678 *Hartman Michielsen* sailed up Passaic River from Manhattan, purchased Menehenicke Island, now Pulaski Park, from the Lenni Lenape Indians, and established a fur trading post. In 1685 Mickielsen, together with his three brothers and ten others from Communipaw (Jersey City), acqired the extensive Acquackanonk Patent. Other Dutch adventurers followed the "Fourteen Farmers of the Acquackanonk."

During the Revolutionary War, Passaic, then known as Acquackanonk Bridge, was occupied by Washington's troops, retreating from the British. *Lord Cornwallis* and the British Army later entered the village. After the war Passaic continued its slow, steady growth as an important river port and agricultural center.

When the railroads began after 1830 to push their way through the Passaic valley, shipping and farming gradually gave way before industrial undertakings. The Dutch, Irish, and tne few German families that had settled the area as farmers were followed by Slavic immigrants, attracted by the rising industry. In 1854 its name was changed to Passaic after the river around which its life centered. Six years after Passaic was chartered as a city (1873), the first trickle of immigrants from Central Europe began. *George B. Waterhouse*, head of a concern of manufacturers of shoddy, brought seven Hungarian immigrants to Passaic from Castle Garden, the Ellis Island of that day. In 1890, the year the Botany Worsted Mills were established, Polish families started to arrive in a steady stream that eventually made them the predominant national group in the city's population.

What newspapers called the first labor riot in the city's history took place on May 5, 1906, during construction of the Passaic *Herald* building. The police and fire departments, aided by citizens fought with striking members of an excavators' union. About one-third of the strikers were wounded, and many were arrested.

Organization of textile labor was long delayed by the Wool Council, official employment agency for the five largest manufacturers, and by a city ordinance that prohibited meetings without a permit. January 1926, however, saw the beginning of a textile workers' strike, destined to attain national importance because of the issue of civil liberties involved. It was precipitated by the discharge of a workers' committee that was asking the restoration of a 10 percent pay cut at the Botany Mills and spread to other mills until some 15,000 workers were out.

A year of strife followed, marked at times by police attempts to suppress public meetings as illegal. This brought liberal and radical leaders from all over the country to the scene to pretest the restrictions on free speech. Several arrests followed. *Norman Thomas*, later Socialist candidate for President of the United States, was hauled down from the crotch of a tree from where he had attempted to address a meeting. He was arrested, but the case was never prosecuted. Ultimately the United Textile Workers took over the strike. The mill owners finally agreed to union recognition, and to arbitration. The union did not hold its strength during the ensuing decade, but under the Textile Workers Organizing Committee (formed 1936) a new unionization drive began.

During Prohibition bootleggers and hijackers battled constantly for control of the Passaic area. So extensive were the operations that it was only mildly exciting to the citizenry when a pipe line was discovered under Passaic River conveying molasses from Wallington, on the opposite shore. In Passaic, the molasses was manufactured into alcohol and then pumped back to Wallington.

•**PASSAIC COUNTY**, Northern New Jersey; Area 194 sq. miles; Pop. 447,585; Seat Paterson; Established Feb. 7, 1837; Named for Indian word for "peace."

•**PASSAIC RIVER**, River; Morris County; in northeastern New Jersey about 80 miles long. The river starts at Morristown and runs along the county line and into Passaic County. South of Paterson is where the Great Falls of the Passaic occur. The river runs into the Newark Bay.

•**PATERSON**, See special article.

•**PAULSBORO**, Borough; Gloucester County; Pop. 6,944; Area Code 609; Zip Code 08066; Elev. 9'; located in SW New Jersey on Hwy. 44; lies west of Mantua Creek, and 2 miles west of the Delaware River. The town dates back to 1681, when 250 colonists settled in the section. *Phillip Paul*, for whom the settlement was named, arrived in 1685.

•**PEAPACK**, Borough; Somerset County; Pop. 2,038; Area Code 201; Zip Code 07977; Elev. 300'; located in N New Jersey; descriptive name meaning Pe "water" and pack "roots."

•**PECK BEACH**, Barrier Island, SE New Jersey; Protects Great Egg Harbor and Ludlam Bay from Atlantic Ocean; Ocean City, with its boardwalk, highlights this resort area.

•**PEMBERTON**, Borough; Burlington County; Pop. 1.198; Area Code 609; Zip Code 08068; Elev. 46'; located in S New Jersey; named after *James Pemberton*, landowner.

•**PENNINGTON**, Borough; Mercer County; Pop. 19,724; Area Code 609; Zip Code 08534; Elev. 211'; located in Central New Jersey, 10 miles N of Trenton on Hwy. 31; dates from 1697 when *Johannes Lawrenson* purchased the land. At first the village was called Queenstown, in honor of *Queen Anne*, but because of its insignificance people began to refer to it derisively as Penny Town. About 1747 it became permanently known as Pennington. Name derived from Corruption. of Pennytown, named for its size.

•**PENNSAUKEN**, Township; Camden County; Pop. 33,775; Area Code 609; Zip Code 081+zone; located in SW New Jersey; named after *William Penn* and sauk meaning "water inlet or outlet."

•**PENNS GROVE**, Borough; Salem County; Pop. 5.760; Area Code 609; Zip Code 08069; Elev. 12'; located in SW New Jersey; named after *William Penn* .

•**PENNSVILLE**, Township; Salem County; Pop. 13,848; Area Code 609; Zip Code 08070; located in SW New Jersey; named for *William Penn* .

•**PEQUANNOCK**, Township; Morris County; Pop. 13,776; Area Code 201; Zip Code 07440; located in N New Jersey; named after sub-tribe, Pequannuc.

•**PERTH AMBOY**, City; Middlesex County; Pop. 38,951; Area Code 201; Zip Code 088 + zone; Elev. 155'; located in Central New Jersey; was part of a large tract purchased from the Indians in 1651 by *Augustine Herman* , a Staten Island Dutchman. After the English took possession of New Jersey, the charter to Wood-bridge in 1669 stipulated "that Amboy Point be reserved...to be disposed of by the lords proprietors." Political difficulties during the next decade probably hindred settlement. In 1682 the twelve new proprietors described the point as "a sweet, wholesome, and delightful place," a view evidently long held by the Indians, who used it as a camp ground and for fishing excursions in the bay. The proprietors announced their "purpose by the help of Almighty God, with all convenient speed, to build a convenient town for merchandise, trade and fishery, on Amboy Point." They contributed 1,200 to build a house for each, and by August 1683 three buildings had been completed.

Two years later the population took a sudden spurt when the Earl of Perth permitted the immigration of nearly 200 oppressed Scots, many of whom were in prison as dissenters. These were soon joined by other Scots, English merchants, and French Huguenots. In 1686 the steadily growing commercial and shipping center was designated capital of East New Jersey. In 1718 Perth Amboy was granted the charter that makes it the oldest incorporated city in New Jersey. Five years later in Perth Amboy, *William Bradford* , official state printer, printed the Session Laws of 1723, the first printing in New Jersey.

The Indians had called this point of land Ompoge (large level piece of ground). Through a series of corruptions it became Amboy and then Amboy Point. This name persisted even though the community was dubbed New Perth in Honor of the Earl; finally the two were blended into Perth Amboy. There is a story that the name arose when Indians, unfamiliar with the Scottish kilts, referred to the Earl of Perth as a squaw. "No! Not squaw!" the Scot is supposed to have answered. "Perth am boy!" The nobleman, however, never crossed the Atlantic.

Tories were active in Perth Amboy at the outbreak of the Revolution, but several of the town's Royalist families fled when Revolutionists arrested *Governor William Franklin* and occupied the Governor's House in June 1776. Six months later the British jailed *Richard Stockton*, one of the five New Jersey signers of the Declaration of Independence.

During the war, Perth Amboy's tactical position at the mouth of Raritan River--highway for the whaleboats raids of Revolutionaries upstream--made it a goal for the contending armies. The town was occupied successively by the Americans under *General Mercer* and by the British under *General Howe*. *Benjamin Franklin*, *Edward Rutledge*, and *John Adams* stopped at Perth Amboy Inn in 1776 on their way to the conference on Staten Island, at which they refused *Sir William Howe's* offer of amnesty in exchange for surrender.

For twenty years after the Revolution, Perth Amboy was poor and barren, but from about the turn of the century until the Civil War the town enjoyed some vogue as a summer resort. The Governor's House was transformed into the Brighton House, a fashionable hotel, which became the social center for the hypochondriac rich utilizing the waters at the nearby spa. The city's industrial development began during the 1860's; its clay deposits were exploited, and steamboats replaced the sailing vessels. In 1832 South Amboy was made the terminal of the Camden and Amboy, the state's first railroad.

During this period, Eagleswood Military Academy was built as a school for young men. Eagleswood was also the home of *Sarah Grimke*, here sister *Angelina Weld*, and *Angelina's* husband, *Theodore D. Weld*, who were pioneers in the woman-suffrage movement and ardent Abolitionists. The school and home became the visiting place for many of the Abolitionists of the day, including *William Lloyd Garrison* and *Wendell Phillips*, and served as an important station of the Underground Railroad. One of the buildings is now part of a ceramics works.

Rebecca Spring, wife of the owner of Eagleswood, was also an abolitionist. When *John Brown* and his companions were taken at Harper's Ferry and condemned to death, *Mrs. Spring* wrote to *Aaron Dwight Stevens*, one of the condemned men, and asked that she might bring his body for burial to Eagleswood. He replied that he was indifferent to what happened to his body after the spirit had left it, but agreed that she might bury him if his poverty-stricken father did not claim his body. *Albert Hazlett*, friend and conspirator with *Stevens*, also wrote to *Mrs. Spring* asking her to bury him by the side of his comrade. She visited the two men in the Baltimore jail and supplied them with food and clothing. After the execution the bodies were brought to Eagleswood and buried. In the 1890s the bodies were disinterred and sent to North Elba, N.Y., to lie with that of *John Brown* on his old farm.

The Lehigh Valley Railroad, which came to Perth Amboy in 1859, forecast the town's industrialization. After the Civil War, Perth Amboy gave itself wholeheartedly to the wave of industrial expansion that rolled over the land. With the establishment of new factories, foreign workers moved into the city, and the descendants of early residents gradually withdrew.

Among the factories that followed the already firmly established ceramic industry was the refinery of M. Guggenheim Sons, a most important link in the chain of mines and smelters that in 1900 acquired control of the American Smelting and Refining Company. In 1912 the workers at the refineries struck against the 12-hour shift. Armed guards and strikebreakers broke the strike after a number of bloody street battles that resulted in the death of four strikers.

•**PHILLIPSBURG**, Town; Warren County; Pop. 16,647; Area Code 201; Zip Code 08865; Elev. 314'; located in North central New Jersey on the Delaware River; was long ago the site of an Indian Village called Chintewink. The city is built on a series of hills dropping down to the Delaware River. Named for *William Phillips*, settler.

•**PINE BEACH**, Borough; Ocean County; Pop. 796; Area Code 201; Zip Code 08741; Elev. 17'; located in E New Jersey.

•**PINE BROOK**, included in Montville; Morris County; Pop. est. 600; Area Code 201; Zip Code 07058; Elev. 200'; located in N New Jersey; is on an island-like hill in the floodlands of the confluence of three rivers: Rockaway, Passaic, and Whippany.

•**PINE HILL**, Borough; Camden County; Pop. 8,684; Area Code 609; Zip Code 08021; Elev. 170'; located in SW New Jersey.

•**PISCATAWAY**, Township; Middlesex County; Pop. 42,223; Area Code 201; Zip Code 08854; Elev. 120'; located in Central New Jersey; named for Piscataqua, Me.

•**PITMAN**, Borough; Gloucester County; Pop. 9,744; Area Code 609; Zip Code 08071; Elev. 132'; located in SW New Jersey; named for *Rev. Charles Pitman* .

•**PLAINFIELD**, City; Union County; Pop. 45,555; Area Code 201; Zip Code 070+zone; located in NE New Jersey on Hwy. 28; SW of Newark; is where the Quaker Meeting House, a plain brick structure with a small burial ground adjoining was built in 1788. At the Martine Homestead, the banker-poet, *Edmund Clarence Stedman* (1833-1908), lived as a child.

Washington Headquarters, built 1746, was the dwelling of *Deacon Nathaniel Drake* , a staunch patriot. *Washington* stopped here while on reconnoitering expeditions into the plains E. of the town is located here.

Green Brook Park was the site of Blue Hills military post, a large earthworks fort guarding the paths to the American Stronghold in the Watchung Mts. during the Revolution is a historical spot.

•**PLAINSBORO**, Township; Middlesex County; Pop. 5,605; Area Code 201; Zip Code 08536; located in Central New Jersey.

•**PLEASANTVILLE**, City; Atlantic County; Pop. 13,435; Area Code 609; Zip Code 08232; Elev. 22'; located in SE New Jersey; named for its surroundings, by *Dr. Daniel Ingersoll* .

•**PLUCKEMIN**, included in Bedminster; Somerset.County; Pop. est. 400; Area Code 201; Zip Code 07978; Elev. 180'; located in N New Jersey; a long-standing dispute revolves about the origin of its name. One school has it that the name is rooted in the custom of a local innkeeper who, anxious for trade, would stand in the road and simply "pluck 'em in." But the other authority leans to the belief that Pluckemin is an Indian word meaning "persimmon." At any rate, local residents pronounce the name Pl-kemin, with accent on the second syllable and the "kem" flattened out almost to "Kam." Named for Pluckemin, Scotland.

•**POHATCONG MOUNTAINS**, Mountain range, NW New Jersey; Ridgelike chain (part of Appalachians) runs SW to NE, parallel to Musconetcong River near Washington. Several recreational areas nearby.

•**POINT PLEASANT**, Borough; Ocean County; Pop. 17,747; Area Code 201; Zip Code 08742; Elev. 18'; located in E New Jersey; named for location, on Atlantic Ocean and Manasquan Inlet.

•**POINT PLEASANT BEACH**, Borough; Ocean County; Pop. 5,415; Area Code 201; Zip Code 08742; Elev. 14'; located in E New Jersey; named for location on Atlantic.

•**POMONA**, included in Galloway; Atlantic County; Area Code 609; Zip Code 08240; located in SE New Jersey; named after Roman goddess of fruits.

•**POMPTON PLAINS**, included in Pequanock; Morris County; Pop. est. 8,000; Area Code 201; Zip Code 07444; Elev. 190'; located in N New Jersey; was for many years the home of *Dan Voorhees*, Tammany sachem, who continued his political activities until he was more than 100 years old. Named for subtribe.

•**PORT ELIZABETH**, included in Maurice River; Cumberland County; Pop. est. 500; Area Code 609; Zip Code 08348; Elev. 10'; located in S New Jersey on Hwy. 47 just W of the Maurice River; was settled probably in the late 1600's. It was named for *Elizabeth Bodely*, who in 1790 purchased the property of the Swedish and English farming community. Philanthropists assembled many freed New Jersey slaves in Port Elizabeth. A schooner carried them to Haiti as farm colonists, but most of them came back discouraged.

•**PORT REPUBLIC**, City; Atlantic County; Pop. 837; Area Code 609; Zip Code 08241; Elev. 17'; located in SE New Jersey; named for U.S. Republic.

•**PRINCETON**, Borough; Mercer County; Pop. 12,035; Area Code 609; Zip Code 08540; Elev. 215'; located in W New Jersey; the half-dozen Quaker families who settled in the Princeton area in 1696 were not the first in this region. Predating them by 15 years was *Capt. Henry Greenland*, the irascible insurgent who was instrumental in dissolving the Colonial legislature in 1681. His plantation, established the same year, occupied most of what is now the town. One of the Quaker settlers was *Richard Stockton II*, whose descendants played an important part in national affairs. At first the settlement was called Stony Brook after the small stream that borders two sides of Princeton, but in 1724 the residents chose the name of Prince's Town (later shortened to Princeton) supposedly because of the proximity to King's Town (Kingston). Princeton was an important coaching center then: sometimes as many as 15 coaches would start off each way on Nassau Street, part of the New York-Philadelphia highway.

The town was slow to build until the middle of the eighteenth century when Princeton University was moved here from Newark and a Presbyterian Church was formed. During the years prior to the Revolution both the students and townspeople were active in the cause for independence. The state government was organized in Princeton under the new constitution in 1776, and the Council of Safety, a wartime tribunal with official power, met in Princeton several times. The village became a target for Tory hatred; farms were plundered and families destroyed by the marauding British.

Toward sunrise of January 3, 1777, *Washington* and his main army of a scant 2,500 men approached Princeton after an all-night march over an ice-covered back road from Trenton, where *Cornwallis* and his superior main army slept in the belief that they would crush the Americans at sunrise. In Princeton were three British regiments under *Colonel Mawhood* , and three troops of dragoons.

Washington divided his troops at first, but then led the Pennsylvania militia to support the troops of *General Mercer* who had been bayonetted in an advance action. The British, in the face of the entire American Army, prepared for a heavy assault. *Washington* made several futile attempts to rally his tired troops. Finally he reined his horse facing the enemy and sat motionless. With *Washington* still between the lines, both sides leveled their rifles. A roar of musketry was followed by a shout from the Americans as the British lines gave way. When the smoke cleared, *Washington* --unharmed--urged his men on in pursuit.

The battle ended in Nassau Hall (where two of the British regiments had taken refuge) when a daring militia captain with a handful of men charged into the hall. About 100 of the enemy had been killed and nearly 300 were made prisoners. Although the American loss did not exceed 30, the brief fighting took a heavy toll of officers. *General Mercer* died of his wounds nine days later.

Washington led his tired men off on the Rocky Hill road, just in time to escape the pursuing forces of *Cornwallis* , and headed for winter encampment. The victory at Princeton, coming on the heels of the maneuver at Trenton a week earlier, went far toward establishing new confidence throughout the Colonies in *Washington's* tatterdemalion troops. *Frederick the Great* went so far as to characterize *Washington's* strategy as the most brilliant operation in all military history.

In the summer of 1777 the first state legislature met at Princeton, and was addressed by *William Livingston*, first governor of the state. At these sessions the original state seal, first in the new nation, was adopted.

From June to November of 1783 the town was the nation's capital. Threatened in Philadelphia by unpaid soldiers who were imitating the Pennsylvania Line mutineers, the Continental Congress, "one by one, hurriedly in the night, fearing abduction by their threateners," left Pennsylvania and established offices at Princeton. To be close to the proceedings, *Washington* was summoned to Princeton. He moved with his family to Rocky Hill, where he lived for three months and wrote his historic farewell address to the army.

After the Revolution the quiet stability of Princeton was undisturbed except by occasional student riots and, to a less extent, by the War of 1812, in which a number of Princeton men fought. In 1813 the borough of Princeton was reincorporated with added territory.

Princeton men were mainly responsible for drawing the town out of the stream of New York-Philadelphia traffic. It was largely their money that financed construction of th. Camden and Amboy Railroad (1834) and the Delaware and Rari n Canal (1832), neither of which passed through the town.

Before and during the Civil War, Princeton was di d on the slave question. But when the many southern students not return after their holidays in 1863, sympathy grew for the n r-thern cause. Feeling was not unanimous, however, and even during the course of the war two pro-northern students were expelled for dousing a southern sympathizer under the town pump. More than 100 Princeton students served with commissions in the two armies.

After the Civil War the town had an abortive industrial boom. The New Jersey Iron Clad Roofing, Paint and Mastic Company, incorporated in 1868, evidently borrowed its name from Civil War naval vessels. Another company was formed in the same year to exploit a patented process for seasoning wood and preventing mold in fabrics, but the business was hampered by a series of fires and explosions.

The borough obtained a new 49-section charter in 1873, which drew the following comment from a contemporary historian: "It is like a garment cut much too large for the person who is to wear it, but the town may grow up to the dimensions of this charter in time."

Princeton University, mellowed by the traditions of more than two centuries of student life, is the product of a continued liberalization of the educational concept upon which it was founded. It was a wave of practical frontier students that first jolted the college from its narrow position as a Presbyterian school; it was a group of forward-looking educators who attracted other men of international distinction to Princeton's service; and it was the liberal spirit generated by both these forces that has directed the continued growth and widening influence of the nation's fourth oldest university.

The 800-acre campus, separated only by Nassau Street from the town, slopes gradually to Lake Carnegie. With Nassau Hall as a nucleus, the campus reflects the varying architectural tastes and styles of the 230 years during which the buildings were erected. But the lawns, the trees and the spreading ivy give a feeling of harmony. Nassau Hall and the older dormitories nearby sound a frank note of the determined righteousness of the Presbyterian founders. The College of New Jersey (as Princeton was first called) was opened at Elizabeth in 1747, as the result of a movement, begun in 1739 by the Synod of Philadelphia, to meet a need for Presbyterian educators. The original faculty consisted of one man, *President Jonathan Dickinson*, who was assisted by a tutor in instructing the six students. Upon the death of *Dickinson*, the college was moved to the Newark parsonage of the new president, the *Rev. Aaron Burr* (father of the Vice President). There the first commencement was held November 9, 1748.

•QUINTON, Township; Salem County; Pop. 2,887; Area Code 609; Zip Code 08072; Elev. 20'; located in SW New Jersey on Hwy. 49; was held by the county militia in the skirmish at Quinton Bridge, scene of the battle March 18, 1778, when *Maj. John Simcoe* and a British battalion marched here from Salem. The bridge was guarded by Colonial militia under *Col. Benjamin Holmes*. Concealing most of their troops in and around the Smith house, the British first led the Revolutionary militia into ambush, killing many. Then the invaders tried to cross the bridge, but *Andrew Bacon* seized an axe and, under fire, cut away the draw section, dropping it into the creek. Arrival of the Cumberland County militia with artillery compelled the British to retreat to Salem. Named after *Tobias Quinton*, settler.

•RAHWAY, City; Union County; Pop. 26,723; Area Code 201; Zip Code 070+zone; Elev. 25'; located in NE New Jersey; descriptive name derived from Rechouwakie meaning "place of sands."

•**RAMSEY**, Borough; Bergen County; Pop. 12,899; Area Code 201; Zip Code 07446; Elev. 373'; located in NE New Jersey.

•**RANDOLPH**, Township; Morris County; Pop. 17,828; Area Code 201; Zip Code 07869; located in N New Jersey.

•**RARITAN**, Borough; Somerset County; Pop. 6,128; Area Code 201; Zip Code 08869; Elev. 76'; located in N New Jersey; named after sub-tribe, Naraticong.

•**RARITAN BAY**, Bay, E New Jersey; Protected from Atlantic Ocean by Sandy Hook and Long Island, New York; Port of entry for cities of Perth Amboy and others up Arthur Kill. Staten Island, New York, is to N.

•**RARITAN RIVER**, River; Somerset County; located in North Central New Jersey approximately 75 miles in length. The river is formed by several branches of water in west Somerset County.

•**READINGTON**, Township; Hunterdon County; Pop. 10,855; Area Code 201; Zip Code 08870; located in NW New Jersey; named for *John Reading*, Governor, 1717, 1757-1758.

•**RED BANK**, Borough; Monmouth County; Pop. 12,031; Area Code 201; Zip Code 07701; Elev. 53'; located in E New Jersey; owes its importance largely to its site on the Navesink River, and its name to the river's clay banks. For more than 100 years the river has been the ice-boating center of the New York area. In summer the town is the shopping center for outlying estates. Descriptive name for red soil on the river bank.

•**RIDGEFIELD**, Borough; Bergen County; Pop. 10,294; Area Code 201; Zip Code 07657; Elev. 150'; located in NE New Jersey.

•**RIDGEFIELD PARK**, Village; Bergen County; Pop. 12,738; Area Code 201; Zip Code 07660; Elev. 96'; located in NE New Jersey.

•**RIDGEWOOD**, Village; Bergen County; Pop. 25,208; Area Code 201; Zip Code 074+zone; Elev. 144'; located in NE New Jersey; named for location.

•**RINGOES**, included in East Amwell; Hunterdon County; Pop. est. 650; Area Code 201; Zip Code 08551; Elev. 220'; located in NW

New Jersey; the community developed around Ringo's Old
Tavern, established by *John Ringo* in 1720.

•**RINGWOOD**, Borough; Passaic County; Pop. 12,625; Area Code
201; Zip Code 07456; Elev. 508'; located in NE New Jersey at the
top of Wanague Reservoir, 5 miles S of New York border; the
story of Ringwood stretches back over 200 years of New Jersey
history; the reputation of its iron mines, its forges, and the men
who governed this 15,000-acre domain is unparalleled in a state
that has known many forges and many large landowners. For
miles around the influence of the old company is still felt, even
though the mines have been closed for many years and the great
house is deserted. When a Ringwood resident speaks of The Company it is in capital letters.
        The company was founded as the American Iron Co. in 1763
when *Baron Peter Hasenclever*, a German, got wind of copper
and iron ore discoveries in the Ramapos.

•**RIVERDALE**, Borough; Morris County; Pop. 2,530; Area Code
201; Zip Code 07457; Elev. 232'; located in N New Jersey; is built
on a left bend in a hill-rimmed cup of flat land. The New Jersey
Historical Commission has allotted to it a share in the state's
Revolutionary history, and placed a marker asserting that
"Washington quartered at the Schuyler House July 12, 1777, and
visited Van Cortlandt here March 28, 1782."

•**RIVERSIDE**, Township; Burlington County; Pop. 7,941; Area
Code 609; Zip Code 08075; located in S New Jersey; named for loc-
tion on the Delaware.

•**RIVERTON**, Borough; Burlington County; Pop. 3,068; Area
Code 609; Zip Code 08077; Elev. 60'; located in S New Jersey.

•**RIVER EDGE**, Borough; Bergen County; Pop. 11,111; Area
Code 201; Zip Code 07661; Elev. 35'; located in NE New Jersey;
named for location on the Hackensack River.

•**RIVER VALE**, Township; Bergen County; Pop. 9,489; Area
Code 201; Zip Code 07675; located in NE New Jersey; named for
location on the Hackensack River.

•**ROBBINSVILLE**, included in Washington; Mercer County;
Pop. est. 550; Area Code 609; Zip Code 08691; located in W New
Jersey; was once known as Hungry Hill because wayfarers found

it hard to obtain food there. English Quakers settled the land in 1750; the village took its name from *George Robbins*, an early resident.

•**ROCHELLE PARK**, Township; Bergen County; Pop. 5,603201; Zip Code 07662; located in NE New Jersey; named after La Rochelle, France.

•**ROCKAWAY**, Borough/Township; Morris County; Pop. 6,852/19,850; Area Code 201; Zip Code 07866; Elev. 534'; located in N New Jersey; is a mountain village cupped in the narrow valley of Rockaway River. Descriptive name derived from Rechouwakie meaning "place of sands."

•**ROCKY HILL**, Borough; Somerset County; Pop. 717; Area Code 201; Zip Code 08553; Elev. 120'; located in N New Jersey.

•**ROEBLING**, included in Florence; Burlington County; Pop. est. 3,600; Area Code 609; Zip Code 08554; located on the Delaware River, 15 miles South of Trenton in S New Jersey; is a company town established by *John A. Roebling*, founder of the large steel-cable factory known to engineers all over the world for its part in building the Brooklyn Bridge and in supplying cables for the George Washington Bridge, the Golden Gate Bridge and other big suspension bridges.

•**ROOSEVELT**, Borough; Monmouth County; Pop. 835; Area Code 201; Zip Code 08555; Elev. 152'; located in E New Jersey; named for *President Theodore Roosevelt*.

•**ROSELAND**, Borough; Essex County; Pop. 5,330; Zip Code 07068; Elev. 356'; located in NE New Jersey.

•**ROSELLE**, Borough; Union County; Pop. 20,641; Area Code 201; Zip Code 072+zone; Elev. 51'; located in NE New Jersey; *Thomas Edison* for a time had a Laboratory here in which he installed the first electric lighting plant in the world.

Roselle was the first community in the world to have its streets lighted by incandescent bulbs. The Birthplace of *Abraham Clark* (1725-1794), one of the New Jersey signers of the Declaration of Independence is here.

•**ROSELLE PARK**, Borough; Union County; Pop. 13,377; Area Code 201; Zip Code 072+zone; Elev. 85'; located in NE New Jersey.

•**ROUND VALLEY RESERVOIR**, Reservoir, Hunterdon County; N Central New Jersey; In a valley between the Musconetcong and Watchung Mountain ranges; Formed by a damming of the South Branch of the Raritan River. A state recreational area is at E shore.

•**RUMSON**, Borough; Monmouth County; Pop. 7,623; Zip Code 07760; Elev. 15'; located in E New Jersey; named after *Chief Alumson*.

•**RUNNEMEDE**, Borough; Camden County; Pop. 9,461; Area Code 609; Zip Code 08078; Elev. 64'; located in SW New Jersey, S of Camden City; is a suburban residential section that has had a succession of names during a history that dates back to 1683, when Quaker settlers named their community New Hope. They operated gristmills and other small industrial plants. The name was changed to Marlboro in honor of the British military leader over the objection of some residents opposed to England. In 1844 the name Runnemede was adapted from the meadow near London where *King John* signed the Magna Carta.

•**RUTHERFORD**, Borough; Bergen County; Pop. 19,068; Area Code 201; Zip Code 070+zone; Elev. 98'; located in NE New Jersey; the name was taken from *John Rutherford*, son of a retired British officer but an active patriot and personal friend of *Washington*. The town was laid out on his land in 1862.

•**SADDLE BROOK**, Township; Bergen County; Pop. 14,084; Area Code 201; Zip Code 07662; located in NE New Jersey.

•**SADDLE RIVER**, Borough; Bergen County; Pop. 2,763; Area Code 201; Zip Code 07458; Elev. 175'; located in NE New Jersey; named for stream and valley in Argyleshire, Scotland.

•**SALEM**, City; Salem County; Pop. 6,959; Area Code 609; Zip Code 08079; Elev. 19'; located in SW New Jersey; in 1675, just seven years before *William Penn came to the opposite shore of the Delaware*, *John Fenwick* and a group of English Quakers settled the region and founded the city of New Salem, the first permanent English-speaking settlement on the Delaware. Previous settlements had been made by both the Dutch and the Swedes, many of whom subsequently moved farther inland.

The settlers who came with *Fenwick* were imbued with ideals of religious freedom and self-government. Others of like mind were soon attracted. Within two years the land had been bought from the Indians and divided into lots. By Royal Commission in 1682 the city of New Salem became a port of entry for vessels. Trade and industry prospered in the 100 years before the Revolution and new towns sprang up about the original village.

The early Quaker settlement was swathed in litigation. For the sum of 1,000 pounds the undivided half of New Jersey, later known as West Jersey, was conveyed to *Fenwick* by *Lord Berkeley*, who had received it as a grant from the *Duke of York*. Later, in a trial umpired by *William Penn*, *Fenwick* lost title to nine-tenths of the property on the ground that it had been purchased with funds advanced by *Edward Byllynge*. On the remaiing one-tenth, which included the site of Salem, *Fenwick* had given a mortgage. The mortgagees and *William Penn* deprived *Fenwick* of his title to this land, too. The fact that *Fenwick* had been a major in Cromwell's army may have had something to do with his frequent troubles with Royal favorites.

Early records name *Thomas Lutherland*, as the only known Salemite tested by the medieval Ordeal of the Bier, by which a suspected murderer was judged guilty if the corpse flowed or spouted blood when the suspect's hand was extended toward the body. After a jury trial, *Lutherland* was hanged in Salem, February 23, 1691. More cruel was the execution of a black woman named *Hager*. She was burned at the stake in 1717 for the hatchet murder of her master, *James Sherron*, high sheriff. It was customary for the courtroom crowd to vote as to whether the death penalty should be invoked.

Salem saw fighting, plundering and murder during the Revolutionary War. In February 1777 *Washington* at Valley Forge sent a force of about 300 men under *Anthony Wayne* to obtain supplies from southern New Jersey. *Wayne* collected 150 head of cattle and brought them to Valley Forge. Salem beef saved the starving army. While *Wayne* was driving his bawling bulls, *Howe*, stationed in Philadelphia, sent *Colonel Abercrombie* with 2,000 men in a vain effort to stop him.

Another detachment of 1,000 British troops under *Colonel Mawhood* and about 500 Tories (the Queen's Rangers) under *Maj. John Simcoe* came to Salem the following month to forage. The Colonial troops formed a line of defense at Alloways Creek, 3 miles south. It was along this front that the ambushing of the Americans, the repulse of the British at Quinton's Bridge, and the Hancock House massacre occurred.

The Revolution started Salem's decline as a river port. British war vessels in the Delaware River throttled shipping, while the British occupation of Philadelphia drew attention to that city's superior advantages as a deepwater port.

At the end of the century the soil turned sour after 150 years of unscientific planting, and many Salemites moved west. *Zadock Street* left Salem in 1803, founded Salem, Ohio, and then Salem, Indiana, a few years later. His son, *Aaron*, established Salem, Iowa; the parade ended at the Pacific Ocean with Salem, Oregon. The exodus stopped with the discovery of marl, present in the region in unlimited quantities, as fertilizer.

By 1840 the general appearance of Salem was "thriving and pleasant," according to the contemporary historians, *Barber and Howe*. The town had a bank, a market, 8 churches, 2 fire engines, 2 libraries, a newspaper printing office, 3 hotels and about 250 homes.

During this period the office of high sheriff was still an important position. Salem County's sheriff was especially proud of his work in hanging *Samuel T. Treadway*, who had shot his estranged wife and was convicted in a much publicized trial. Shortly afterward the sheriff went to Philadelphia, it is said, and applied for a hotel room. The clerk informed him that all rooms were taken, whereupon the sheriff leaned over the desk and said: "I am the high sheriff of Salem County, I hung Treadway, and I want a room in this hotel."

"Sir," the clerk answered coolly, "if you were sheriff of hell and hung the devil it wouldn't make any difference to me. There are no rooms in this hotel."

The reputation of the Quakers as Abolitionist spead throughout the South by grapevine telegraph just before the Civil War, and many escaped black slaves made Salem a stop on the Underground Railroad.

Industry became more firmly established in 1863 when a railroad reached the city, which had lost its status as a village by incorporation in 1858. The city is named for a Hebrew name meaning "peace."

•**SALEM COUNTY**, Southwest New Jersey; Area 350 sq. miles; Pop. 64,676; Established May 17, 1694; Named for Hebrew word "Shalom" meaning "peace."

•**SAYREVILLE**, Borough; Middlesex County; Pop. 29,969; Area Code 201; Zip Code 08872; Elev. 41'; located in Central New Jersey.

•**SCHOOLEYS MOUNTAIN**, Mountain; Morris County; Area Code 201; Zip Code 07870; located in N New Jersey; sometimes known locally as Hackettstown Mt. Neatly partitioned farm lands rolling over the hills are reminiscent of New England.

•**SCOTCH PLAINS**, Township; Union County; Pop. 20,744; Area Code 201; Zip Code 07076; Elev. 150'; located in NE New Jersey; is where a group of Scottish Presbyterian and Quaker immigrants came here in 1684 after refusing to swear allegiance to the British Crown. Named after *George Scott*, leader of the Scottish settlers.

•**SEA BRIGHT**, Borough; Monmouth County; Pop. 1,812; Area Code 201; Zip Code 07760; Elev. 4'; located in E New Jersey; named for Sea Bright, England.

•**SEA GIRT**, Borough; Monmouth County; Pop. 2,650; Area Code 201; Zip Code 08750; Elev. 19'; located in E New Jersey; named for Estate of Commander *Robert F. Stockton* .

•**SEA ISLE CITY**, City; Cape May County; Pop. 2,644; Area Code 609; Zip Code 08243; Elev. 6'; located in S New Jersey; is a family resort that long ago was labeled "The City With A Smile" and "The Island Of Contentment."

For several generations this island resort with five miles of seashore bathing beach has provided seashore living not only for the local year 'round residents, but also for the countless summer visitors who enjoy boating, fishing, bathing, dancing, concerts, art exhibits, and family entertainment. One of the highlights is a unique Skimmer Weekend--a three-day summer event which is filled with many activities, providing fun and festivities for all. Skimmer Weekend is reunion time for many long-time Sea Isle City visitors.

Sea Isle City is located on an island and the Atlantic Ocean and the inland waters of the back bays provide a picturesque setting for vacation pleasure.

The warm, gentle surf is patrolled in season by a crew of well-trained lifeguards who offer maximum protection to the bathers.

There are new motels, family vacation cottages, apartments and rooms available for the short-term or seasonal visitor.

•**SEASIDE HEIGHTS**, Borough; Ocean County; Pop. 1,802; Area Code 201; Zip Code 08751; Elev. 7'; located in E New Jersey; named for location on strip of beach.

•**SEASIDE PARK**, Borough; Ocean County; Pop. 1,795; Area Code 201; Zip Code 08752; Elev. 6'; located in E New Jersey; named for location on strip of beach.

•**SECAUCUS**, Town; Hudson County; Pop. 13,719; Area Code 201; Zip Code 07094; Elev. 12'; located in NE New Jersey; descriptive name from Sukit meaning "black snake."

•**SEVEN MILE BEACH**, Barrier Island; SE tip, New Jersey; Extends seven miles, protecting the Great Sound and rugged coastline from the Atlantic Ocean. Resort/fishing towns of Avalon and Stone Harbor lie on island.

•**SHILOH**, Borough; Cumberland County; Pop. 604; Area Code 609; Zip Code 08353; Elev. 118'; located in SW New Jersey on Hwy. 49; founded by Seventh-Day Baptists fleeing from persecution in England in 1705, was first known as Cohansey, an extensive settlement along the Cohansey Creek, named for an Indian Chief. In 1771, when the Baptists were moving an old frame church 2 miles to Cohansey, they reached Six Corners here at sundown on a Friday. Work ceased and religious services were begun. Their pastor used as his text, "The Ark of the Lord resteth at Shiloh," and by common consent the name of the community was changed to Shiloh.

•**SHIP BOTTOM**, Borough; Ocean County; Pop. 1,427; Area Code 201; Zip Code 08008; Elev. 10'; located in E New Jersey; is on Long Beach Island which lies on the Atlantic Coast; it's odd name is the center of controversy of date and detail rather than event. One tradition is that in 1817 *Capt. Stephen Willits* during a storm came upon a ship aground, bottom up. His men heard tapping inside and chopped a hole with an axe. Out stepped a beautiful young girl, whom they carried to shore, where she thanked them in a strange tongue, sank to her knees, and drew the sign of the cross on the sand. She was sent to New York and never heard from again.

The second version, dated 1846, duplicates the story of the capsized ship, the tapping, and the appearance of the beautiful young girl. Less adventurous, however, this maiden remained in the village, was properly wed, and ultimately became the ancestor of a Sandy Hook pilot.

•**SHREWSBURY**, Borough; Monmouth County; Pop. 2,962; Area Code 201; Zip Code 07701; Elev. 25'; located in E New Jersey; named after Shrewsbury, England.

•**SHREWSBURY RIVER**, River; Monmouth County; is an inlet 5 miles south of the Navesink River; which joins together and flows to the Raritan Bay.

•**SILVER BAY**, Bay, E New Jersey; at N reaches of Barnegat Bay, protected from Atlantic Ocean by barrier Island Beach. Part of Intracoastal Waterway.

•**SOMERDALE**, Borough; Camden County; Pop. 5,900; Area Code 609; Zip Code 08083; Elev. 83'; located in SW New Jersey.

•**SOMERSET**, Village, included in Franklin township; Somerset County; Area Code 201; Zip Code 08873; Elev. 60'; located in N New Jersey; was once a Colonial village. The Jedediah Scudder House, an old-fashioned rambling stone and frame structure, is said to have sheltered several of Washington's soldiers who, fatigued or nearly frozen were unable to march to Trenton. Named after Somersetshire, England.

•**SOMERSET COUNTY**, Central New Jersey; Area 307 sq. miles; Pop. 203,129; Seat Somerville; Established May, 1688; Named for Somersetshire, England.

•**SOMERS POINT**, City; Atlantic County; Pop. 10,330; Area Code 609; Zip Code 08244; Elev. 31'; located SE New Jersey; named for *John Somers*, landowner.

•**SOMERVILLE**, Borough; Somerset County; Pop. 11,973; Area Code 201; Zip Code 08876; Elev. 54'; located in N Central New Jersey on I-287; is the county seat. Its broad main street lined with stores and offices was used nearly 300 years ago by Dutch traders, and, before that, by Indians. In 1846 the first telegraph line between New York and Philadelphia was built along this route.

Somerville was the western terminus of the Elizabethtown and Somerville R.R. In 1842 the first train was put into operation with much pomp and ceremony, including a luncheon of cake and lemonade for the distinguished passengers who hazarded the trip from faraway Elizabethtown at 4 miles per hour. Named after Somersetshire, England.

•**SOUTH AMBOY**, City; Middlesex County; Pop. 8,322; Area Code 201; Zip Code 08879; Elev. 54'; located in Central New Jersey on the eastern coast, overlooking Raritan Bay; is impor-

tant in the clay industry. Claypits were dug here as early as 1807.
The town has been one of the largest railroad terminals for shipment of Pennsylvania hard coal, which is dumped into barges to
be towed to New York and New England. Named after the Earl of
Perth.

•**SOUTH BOUND BROOK**, Borough; Somerset County; Pop.
4,331; Area Code 201; Zip Code 08880; Elev. 45'; located in N Central New Jersey; an industrial town that has grown from a
village in which *Baron von Steuben* was stationed in 1778-1779.

•**SOUTH HACKENSACK**, Township; Bergen County; Pop. 2,229;
Area Code 201; Zip Code 076+zone; located in NE New Jersey.

•**SOUTH ORANGE**, Township; Essex County; Pop. 15,864; Area
Code 201; Zip Code 07079; Elev. 141'; located in NE New Jersey;
lies due south of Orange and was known originally as the Orange
Dale section of Orange, South Orange and was established as a
village in 1869. Its few manufactures include toilet preparations,
bituminous products, and cement blocks. The village has pooled
its educational resources with those of Maplewood to achieve a
first-class school system. It has been a leader in the crusade to
exterminate the Jersey mosquito. It's the home of Seton Hall College, founded in 1856 by the Catholic clergy of Newark Diocese.

•**SOUTH PLAINFIELD**, Borough; Middlesex County; Pop.
20,521; Area Code 201; Zip Code 07080; Elev. 67'; located in Central New Jersey.

•**SOUTH RIVER**, Borough; Middlesex County; Pop. 14,361; Area
Code 201; Zip Code 08882; Elev. 50'; located in E New Jersey, 5
miles W of Raritan Bay; is a port for small craft on South River,
a twisting arm of the Raritan. Named for tributary of Raritan,
from S.

•**SOUTH TOMS RIVER**, Borough; Ocean County; Pop. 3,954;
Area Code 201; Zip Code 08757; Elev. 31'; located in E New
Jersey.

•**SPARTA**, Township; Sussex County; Pop. 13,333; Area Code
201; Zip Code 07871; located in N New Jersey; descriptive Greek
name.

•**SPOTSWOOD**, Borough; Middlesex County; Pop. 7,840; Area
Code 201; Zip Code 08884; Elev. 30'; located in Central New
Jersey; named for Spottswoode, Scotland.

•**SPRINGFIELD**, Township; Union County; Pop. 13,955; Area Code 201; Zip Code 07081; Elev. 100'; located in NE New Jersey; was the center of important Revolutionary fighting on June 23, 1780; a good part of the battle took place along the main street of the village. The white-shingled First Presbyterian Church had an honorable part in it. When the Revolutionaries ran short of gun wadding the *Rev. James Caldwell*, Elizabeth pastor and chaplain of *Colonel Dayton's* New Jersey regiment, broke open the church doors and seized an armful of Watts' hymnbooks. The preacher threw them to the soldiers and shouted, "Give 'em Watts, boys-give 'em Watts!" Caldwell's wife, *Hannah*, had been killed two weeks before in the battle that razed Connecticut Farms. The Tories scornfully called him the "high priest of the Revolution," but to the patriots he was known as the "fighting parson." A marker commemorates *Parson Caldwell's* Revolutionary initiative. On the church lawn is the statue of a militiaman with the inscription: "Of what avail the plow or sail or land or life if Freedom fail!" Named because of abundant springs and brooks.

•**SPRING LAKE**, Borough; Monmouth County; Pop. 4,215; Area Code 201; Zip Code 07762; Elev. 25'; located in E New Jersey; descriptive name meaning "fresh water stream."

•**SPRUCE RUN RESERVOIR**, Reservoir, N Central New Jersey; Formed by a damming of the South Branch, Raritan River, in Hunterdon County. A state recreation area and park surround the lake.

•**STANHOPE**, Borough; Sussex County; Pop. 3,638; Area Code 201; Zip Code 07874; Elev. 882'; located in N New Jersey; in Revolutionary years the village was the home of the Sussex Iron Co.; a few of the workers' one-story houses, resembling French peasant cottages, remain. The first anthracite furnace in the United States was built at Stanhope.

On the Morris Canal are Ruins Of An Inclined Plane, where the boats were carried 75 feet up a railway run by water power to reach a higher level.

•**STILLWATER**, Township; Sussex County; Pop. 3,887; Area Code 201; Zip Code 07875; located in N New Jersey.

•**STIRLING**, included in Passaic; Morris County; Area Code 201; Zip Code 07980; named after *Gen. William. Alexander*, Lord Stirling, Revolution.

•**STOCKTON**, Borough; Hunterdon County; Pop. 643; Area Code 201; Zip Code 08559; Elev. 85'; located in NW New Jersey; named after *Stockton* family.

•**STONE HARBOR**, Borough; Cape May County; Pop. 1,187; Area Code 609; Zip Code 08247; Elev. 5'; located in S New Jersey; is "The Seashore At Its Best" and its bathing beach, shops, boating and fishing facilities, and Bird Sanctuary all combine to make it so.

Stone Harbor is a community of homes for summer vacationers and for many, a place to enjoy their retirement years. There are several motels and apartment houses and numerous cottages available for vacation rental.

Playground areas for children, a boat launching ramp and municipal boat dock, a bulkhead fishing area, municipal tennis and shuffleboard courts all are maintained.

Stone Harbor was miles of beach, several jetties and the shoreline along the inland waterway providing a place for surf casters. Party and charter boats sail daily for offshore waters.

•**STRATFORD**, Borough; Camden County; Pop. 8,005; Area Code 609; Zip Code 08084; Elev. 69'; located in SW New Jersey; named for Stratford-on-Avon, England.

•**SUCCASUNNA**, Village, Morris County; Pop. 7,400; Area Code 201; Zip Code 07876; Elev. 710'; located in N Central New Jersey on Hwy. 10; elms shade fine dwellings that have been enlarged and remodeled from the simple homes of "Old Suckysunny." The name in Lenape Indian language stands for black stone, or iron ore, which was once abundant here, and led to the discovery and exploitation of the vast magnetite and hematite deposits of the surrounding region. Descriptive name derived from sukit meaning "black" and assan meaning "stone."

•**SUMMIT**, City; Union County; Pop. 21,071; Area Code 201; Zip Code 07901; Elev. 388'; located in NE New Jersey; named for location on the Watchung Mountains.

•**SURF CITY**, Borough; Ocean County; Pop. 1,571; Area Code 201; Zip Code 08008; Elev. 6'; located in E New Jersey on Long Beach Island which is on the Atlantic Coast; is a resort that was built in 1873 around the site of the former Mansion of Health, oldest of the island hotels.

Old-time sailing masters and pilots lived here when Surf City was a port and a lumbering center. The earliest settlers on the island were whalers, who came to this spot after obtaining a grant of land in 1690. Two hundred years ago a whale watch pole, a post about 15 feet high topped with a railroad platform, stood on the beach. When a whale was sighted the boats put out to make the capture. The mammals were beached, stripped, and their blubber rendered on the sand.

•**SUSSEX**, Borough; Sussex County; Pop. 2,418; Area Code 201; Zip Code 07461; Elev. 464'; located in N New Jersey at the intersection at Hwys. 23 and 284; is one of the largest milk receiving stations in the state. It was originally known as Deckertown for *Peter Decker* , a Hollander who built himself a log cabin in 1734. Named after Sussex, England.

•**SUSSEX COUNTY**, Northern New Jersey; Area 528 sq. miles; Pop. 116,119; Seat Newton; Established May 16, 1753; Named for Sussex County, England.

•**SWEDESBORO**, Borough; Gloucester County; Pop. 2,031; Area Code 609; Zip Code 08085; Elev. 68'; located in SW New Jersey; named after Swedish settlers.

•**TEANECK**, Township; Bergen County; Pop. 39,007; Area Code 201; Zip Code 07666; located in NE New Jersey; Dutch name meaning "on a neck" of land.

•**TENAFLY**, Borough; Bergen County; Pop. 13,552; Area Code 201; Zip Code 07670; Elev. 52'; located in NE New Jersey; Dutch word meaning "on a meadow" or "garden meadow."

•**TENNENT**, included in Manalapan; Monmouth County; Pop. est. 300; Area Code 201; Zip Code 07763; Elev. 131'; located in Central New Jersey; it was along this route that *Gen. Charles Lee* advanced eastward in the Battle of Monmouth, only to fall back in confusion from a British attack.

•**THOROFARE**, included in West Deptford; Gloucester County; Pop. est. 1,400; Area Code 609; Zip Code 08086; located in SW New Jersey.

•**TINTON FALLS**, Borough; Monmouth County; Pop. 7,740; Area Code 201; Zip Code 07724; Elev. 88'; located in E New Jersey; named for Tintern Manor of *Col. Lewis Morris* .

•**TOMS RIVER**, Township; Ocean County; Pop. 7,303; Area Code 201; Zip Code 087 ; Elev. 20'; located in E New Jersey; county seat of Ocean County, is on the northern banks of Toms River, a waterway discovered in 1673 by the surveyor, *Capt. William Tom* . The town is widely known for its excellent clam chowder, served with ship's biscuit.

During the Revolution the settlement was a starting point for patriots' raids and its residents were described by the British as "a piratical set of banditti."

•**TOTOWA**, Borough; Passaic County; Pop. 11,448; Area Code 201; Zip Code 075 ; Elev. 260'; located in N New Jersey; is a residential extension of Paterson. During the Revolution, *Washington* and his men were encamped at Totowa, where they drilled on a vacant field. One of the early settlers, *Joshua Hott Smith* , was involved in *Benedict Arnold's* plot. He escaped execution after a summary court martial delivered the rather remarkable judgment that he was undoubtedly guilty of every charge but that the evidence, unfortunately, was insufficient to convict him. Dutch scholars translate Totowa, or Totua as it appears in some early records, as where you begin, suggesting that it was once the frontier to the wild west.

•**TOWACO**, included in Montrille; Morris County; Area Code 201; Zip Code 07082; Elev. 200'; located in N New Jersey; was formerly known as Whitehall. The land around Towaco is a rising plateau. Named for Sub-tribe, Towakan.

•**TRENTON**, See special article.

•**TUCKAHOE**, Cape May County; Pop. est. 650; Area Code 609; Zip Code 08250; Elev. 20'; located in SE New Jersey on Hwy. 55; name derived from Tawho-tuckah meaning "turnip."; lies on the south bank of Tuckahoe River. Nearly two centuries ago Tuckahoe was an important seaport, with busy shipyards. Quakers had settled this section prior to 1700 and had built a meeting house here, long vanished. Tuckahoe is the center of a fertile area raising early tomatoes. The woods around Tuckahoe (Ind., place where deer are shy) are known for wild deer.

•**TUCKERTON**, Borough; Ocean County; Pop. 2,472; Area Code 201; Zip Code 08087; Elev. 23'; located on the Eastern New Jersey coast; is on the Tuckerton River which runs into Pipers Cove. In Colonial days Tuckerton was a notable port of entry; flax and molasses formed a large part of the trade. Silkworms were cultivated here and the town is still studded with mulberry trees. British raiders in 1778 burned 30 prize ships here taken by the Americans. Named after *Ebenezer Tucker*, resident.

•UNION, Township; Union County; Pop. 50,184; Area Code 201; Zip Code 07083; located in NE New Jersey; descriptive name for union of several communities.

•UNION BEACH, Borough; Monmouth County; Pop. 6,354; Area Code 201; Zip Code 07735; Elev. 9'; located in E New Jersey.

•UNION CITY, City; Hudson County; Pop. 55,593; Area Code 201; Zip Code 07087; Elev. 189'; located in NE New Jersey.

•UNION COUNTY, Eastern New Jersey; Area 103 sq. miles; Pop. 504,094; Seat Elizabeth; Established March 19, 1857; Named for generic word "union."

Union County was part of an area explored and occupied by the earliest settlers of colonial America. *Henry Hudson*, sponsored by the Dutch, discovered Newark Bay (Arthur Kill), in September, 1609. Under Dutch control New Jersey was part of a region called New Netherlands. The Dutch occupied and actively traded furs in this area until the English conquest of 1664.

The area was originally occupied by the comparatively gentle Delaware Indians, or Lenni Lenape. By June, 1758, they had signed a treaty terminating all their land claims to New Jersey.

Governor Robert Nicolls of New York induced settlers to come to New Jersey. *Nicolls* approved the sale of land by Indians to the Elizabethtown Associates, a group of 80 English settlers from New England. This purchase in October, 1664, established the first English colony in New Jersey. Present day Union County is composed of communities sub-divided from colonial Elizabethtown.

Colonial *Governor Philip Carteret* held the first General Assembly in Elizabethtown in May, 1668. The college of New Jersey (now Princeton was founded here in 1746).

In the winter of 1776, the British occupied Elizabethtown and the townspeople retreated to the Short Hills area (near Springfield). The British again attacked during the severe winter of 1780, but were repelled by colonial troops. In their retreat the British burned the Presbyterian meeting house and courthouse in Elizabethtown. Present day buildings occupy the same ground.

Union County was part of Essex County for 175 years, from 1682 to 1857. For 21 years Elizabethtown was the port of entry, but the prominence of Elizabethtown was threatened when Newark became the seat of justice of Essex County and eventually pulled ahead of Elizabethtown in economic importance.

For 128 years the original township of Elizabeth remained undivided. Then the hamlets began agitating for sub-division. Springfield was established in 1793; New Providence (Turkey) in 1794; Westfield (West Fields) in 1794 Rahway (Spanktown) in 1804; Union (Connecticut Farms) in 1808; and Plainfield in 1847. The remaining townships of Union County as we know them today are sub-divisions of these original communities.

The discord between Newark and Elizabeth led to the eventual separation of Union County from Essex County. In 1807, the rivalry reached a high peak over the relocation of the Essex Court House. In spite of oppositions from Westfield and Plainfield, Elizabeth led the secession movement in 1855. The New Jersey legislature created Union County on March 19, 1857.

In the early days farming, whaling, tanning, and the export of leather were the means of livelihood. The gradual transition from agriculture to industry resulted from excellent transportation, harbor and banking facilities, close to major markets and skilled labor.

In 1831, The Elizabethtown and Somerville Railroad, predecessor to the Jersey Central, provided the first train service to Elizabeth. The county's oldest financial institution, The National State Bank of Elizabeth, was founded in 1812. Elizabethtown Gaslight Company was founded in 1855. Water service was made available in 1856. The first telephone in the county was used in Elizabeth in 1880. The first electric generating plant in the world was erected in 1882, in Roselle.

In the 1830's, Rahway became a carriage making center until the Civil War ruined its trade. One of the most important early industrial developments was the consolidation in 1873, of several Singer Sewing Machine Plants to form the Singer Manufacturing Company in Elizabeth Port. In 1903, Merck established its drug and chemical plant on the Rahway-Linden line. Humble Oil and Refining Company, now Exxon, located one of its largest refineries in Linden in 1908.

Union County, the youngest of New Jersey's 21 counties, is the second smallest. It occupies 103 square miles, less than 1.4 percent of the total area of the state.

Union County, begins at sea level along Newark Bay and Arthur Kill and rises to 550 feet in the Watchung Mountains. Most of the county is geologically known s New Jersey's Triassic Lowland area. Underlying formations are mostly red sandstone with volcanic traprock ridges forming the mountains. Two rivers - the Rahway and the Elizabeth run through the county. The Passaic River borders the western part of the county.

•**VENTNOR CITY**, City; Atlantic County; Pop. 11,704; Area Code 609; Zip Code 08406; Elev. 11'; located in SE New Jersey; named for Ventnor, England.

•**VERNON**, Township; Sussex County; Pop. 16,302; Area Code 201; Zip Code 07462; located in N New Jersey; named after *Edward Vernon*, English admiral; near Vernon is the Playboy "Great Gorge" Country Club, a favorite with golfers and tennis players.

•**VERONA**, Borough; Essex County; Pop. 14,166; Area Code 201; Zip Code 07044; Elev. 348'; located in NE New Jersey; is in the valley between the First and Second Watchungs. The Verona area was owned by *Caleb Hetfield*, a Tory who took no chances on the outcome of the struggle and sold his holdings before the Revolutionaries had the opportunity to confiscate them. They later became the property of *Christian Bone*, a Hessian who deserted German George to fight for the American uprising. Named for Verona, Italy.

•**VIENNA**, Village; Warren County; Area Code 201; Zip Code 07880; Elev. 580'; located in NW New Jersey; is a maple-shaded village that was once a thriving industrial community. At the eastern end of town is abandoned Vienna Foundry which, from 1860 to the end of the century, turned out double corn plows that made the reputation of the producer, *Simon Cummins*. Another abandoned plant, a sawmill north of the village, was owned by *Fisher Stedman*, inventor of wood-shaping machinery in use throughout the world. Named after Vienna Foundry.

•**VINCENTOWN**, included in Southampton; Burlington County; Pop. est. 800; Area Code 609; Zip Code 08088; Elev. 40'; located in S New Jersey; on the banks of Stop-the-Jade Run. Vincentown was known at one time as Quaky Town, because of a quivering of the soil at the edge of a millpond. Stop-the-Jade Run took its name from the troubles of *Thomas Budd*, an early settler, who founded Buddtown a few miles up the stream. When a young woman slave ran away, Budd posted notices in many villages offering a reward for her return. All closed with the appeal, "Stop the jade!."

•**VINELAND**, City; Cumberland County; Pop. 53,750; Area Code 609; Zip Code 08360; Elev. 106'; located in S Central New Jersey; *Charles K. Landis*, who came here in 1861, spent 20 years building the colony. He drew farm settlers largely from the Middle Atlantic States and induced many Italian peasants to immigrate to his farms. Vineland was so named by its founder. Grapes were grown in large quantities during its first 25 years, but grape diseases compelled the growers to abandon most of the vineyards. For several years semi-weekly auctions of eggs as wholesale and daily auctions of fruit and vegetables have been held in Vineland by two cooperatives with nearly 1,200 farmer members. Named Vineland as it was a 19th century vineyard development.

•**VOORHEES**, Township; Camden County; Pop. 12,919; Area Code 609; Zip Code 08043; located in SW New Jersey; named after *Van Voor Hees* family, Dutch settlers.

•**WALDWICK**, Borough; Bergen County; Pop. 10,802; Area Code 201; Zip Code 07463; Elev. 181'; located in NE New Jersey; Anglo-Saxon word meaning "village in a grove."

•**WALL**, Borough; Monmouth County; Pop. 18,952; Area Code 201; Zip Code 07719; located in E New Jersey; named after *Ganet D. Wall*, U.S. Senator 1835-1841.

•**WALLINGTON**, Borough; Bergen County; Pop. 10,741; Area Code 201; Zip Code 07057; Elev. 14'; located in NE New Jersey; named after *Walling Jackobs*.

•**WALPACK**, Township; Sussex County; Pop. 150; Area Code 201; Zip Code 07881; located in N New Jersey; derived from Walpekat meaning "very deep water."

•**WANAQUE**, Borough; Passaic County; Pop. 10,025; Area Code 201; Zip Code 07465; Elev. 240'; located in N New Jersey; descriptive name meaning "place wherre the sassafras tree grows."

•**WARETOWN**, included in Ocean; Ocean County; Pop. est. 900; Area Code 201; Zip Code 08758; Elev. 14'; located on Eastern coast of New Jersey on Hwy. 9; was named for *Abraham Waeir*, an early settler, who died in 1768. *Waeir* succeeded *John Colver* as the local leader of the Rogerenes a sect founded by *John*

Rogers . They came here in 1737, driven from Connecticut, where they haad stirred a commotion by heckling preachers at Sunday meetings. The Rogerenes opposed any Sabbath day observance. During the Revolutionary period they disbanded, but later they appeared in Morris County.

•**WARREN COUNTY**, Northwest New Jersey; Area 361 sq. miles; Pop. 84,429; Seat Belvidere; Established Nov. 20, 1824; Named for *Joseph Warren* .

•**WASHINGTON**, Borough; Warren County; Pop. 6,429; Area Code 201; Zip Code 07882; Elev. 463'; located in NW New Jersey on Hwy. 57 just W. of Hwy. 31; was a stop on the old Morris Canal. Its position on the Lackawanna R.R. helped to save it from paralysis when the canal died. Once an important center for the manufacture of pianos and organs. *Washington* was at one time called Mansfield Woodhouse, for a Presbyterian Church of the same name; the present name was taken from a tavern built in 1811 by *Col. William McCullough* , founder of the borough. Named after *President George Washington* .

•**WASHINGTON CROSSING**, Mercer County; Area Code 609; Elev. 60'; located in Central New Jersey on the Delaware River; is a quiet hamlet that won a name and fame in 1776. HEre, more than 200 years ago, *Washington* is said to have found shelter on the Christmas night when his troops were crossing the Delaware for the surprise attack on Trenton. Washington Crossing State Park, where the Continental troops landed their big flat-bottomed boats, poled through the ice-choked river. Many of *Washington's* men, disheartened by the defeats of Long Island and New York, had deserted. The term of service for others had nearly ended. Only 2,400 to 2,700 remained, the British holding New Jersey with three times their number. "I fear the hame is nearly up," *Washington* then wrote to his cousin, but as he wrote he planned the recrossing of the river and the blow at Trenton. Named for place where *Washington* crossed the Delaware.

•**WATCHUNG**, Borough; Somerset County; Pop. 5,290; Area Code 201; Zip Code 07060; Elev. 181'; located in N New Jersey; derived from Watschee meaning "hill."

•**WATERFORD**, Township; Camden County; Pop. 8,126; Area Code 609; Zip Code 08089; Elev. 125'; located in S Central New Jersey on Hwy. 536 W of 30; was named for a glassworks founded in 1824. Near here three brothers, *Sebastian* , *Ignatius* , and *Xavier Woos* , settled in 1760 after fleeing their native Germany to escape military services. They built a log house with walls so well chinked and joints so tight that settlers came from miles around to inspect it. The Woos brothers, unable to speak English, said in German that their home wa sschoen, meaning "beautiful." Their American neighbors corrupted the word into "shane" and named the place Shane's Castle. Named for Waterford, England.

•**WATER WITCH**, Monmouth County; located in E New Jersey; a section of Highlands, and scene of *James Fenimore Cooper's* novel of that name. The dwelling of 1762 in the story is gone, and its site lost. Near it stood the basswood tree from which the American patriot, *Capt. Joshua Huddy* , was hanged by Tories.

•**WAYNE**, Township; Passaic County; Pop. 46,474; Area Code 201; Zip Code 07470; located in N New Jersey; named after General "Mad Anthony" Wayne, Revolution.

•**WEEHAWKEN**, Township; Hudson County; Pop. 13,168; Area Code 201; Zip Code 07087; located in NE New Jersey; descriptive name meaning "place of gulls."

•**WENONAH**, Borough; Gloucester County; Pop. 2,303; Area Code 609; Zip Code 08090; Elev. 27'; located in SW New Jersey; named after Mother of Hiawatha.

•**WEST CALDWELL**, Borough; Essex County; Pop. 11,407; Area Code 201; Zip Code 07006; Elev. 240'; located in NE New Jersey.

•**WEST DEPTFORD**, Township; Gloucester County; Pop. 18,002; Area Code 609; Zip Code 08066; located in SW New Jersey.

•**WESTFIELD**, Town; Union County; Pop. 30,447; Area Code 201; Zip Code 070 ; Elev. 126'; located in NE New Jersey; named after undeveloped section, "the west fields"; many of its residents commute to jobs in nearby cities; others are employed in local industries. The Presbyterian Church is a white frame structure on the site of an earlier building that was the scene of the Revolutionary trial of *James Morgan* , who murdered the *Rev. James Caldwell* of Elizabeth. *Morgan* was hanged on Gallows Hill, Broad St. at the north-east side of the town.

•**WEST LONG BRANCH**, Borough; Monmouth County; Pop. 7,380; Area Code 201; Zip Code 07764; Elev. 27'; located in E New Jersey.

•**WEST MILFORD**, Township; Passaic County; Pop. 22,750; Area Code 201; Zip Code 07480; located in N New Jersey; named after Milford, Connecticut.

•**WEST NEW YORK**, Town; Hudson County; Pop. 39,194; Area Code 201; Zip Code 07093; Elev. 185'; located in NE New Jersey.

•**WEST ORANGE**, Town; Essex County; Pop. 39,510; Area Code 201; Zip Code 07052; Elev. 368'; located in NE New Jersey; immediately to the west of Orange. The spirit of *Thomas A. Edison* lives here. Rows of two-story frame houses, bordered by neatly kept lawns, are overshadowed by the steel-concrete buildings of the Edison Plant. To this site the inventor moved in 1887 from Menlo Park and here he experimented with and perfected the moving picture machine, the phonograph and the alkaline storage battery. Before the arrival of Edison, West Orange was but a small town which had separated from Orange in 1862. The establishment of the ploant, it developed into a well-run, modernized community, distinguished for its own suburb. Homne of the *Colgates* , the *Edisons* , and of *Maj. Gen. George B. McClellan* , Governor of New Jersey after the Civil War.

•**WEST PATERSON**, Borough; Passaic County; Pop. 11,293; Area Code 201; Zip Code 07424; Elev. 400'; located in N New Jersey.

•**WESTVILLE**, Borough; Gloucester County; Pop. 4,786; Area Code 609; Zip Code 08093; Elev. 16'; located in SW New Jersey; named after *Thomas West* .

•**WESTWOOD**, Borough; Bergen County; Pop. 10,714; Area Code 201; Zip Code 07675; Elev. 75'; located in NE New Jersey.

•**WHARTON**, Borough; Morris County; Pop. 5,485; Area Code 201; Zip Code 07885; Elev. 700'; located in N New Jersey; named for Wharton Steel Company.

•**WHIPPANY**, Morris County; Area Code 201; Zip Code 07981; located in N New Jersey; descriptive name derived from Winit meaning "tooth" and onk meaning "place."

•**WHITE HOUSE STATION**, included in Readington; Hunterdon County; Pop. est. 600; Area Code 201; Zip Code 08889; located in NW New Jersey.

•**WHITESBORO**, included in Pemberton; Cape May County; Pop. est. 50; Area Code 609; Zip Code 08252; Elev. 21'; located in the S tip of New Jersey; was founded by *Henry C. White*, a former Congressman from North Carolina. Named after Negro congressman, *Henry White*.

•**WICKATUNK**, included in Marlboro; Monmouth County; Pop. est. 400; Area Code 201; Zip Code 07765; Elev. 180'; located in E New Jersey on Hwy. 79; (Ind., place of an Indian house), was named by the Jersey Central R.R. when its station was placed here, as a shipping point for a large area in which potatoes are grown. Descriptive name derived from Wikwam meaning "house" and onk meaning "place."

•**WILDWOOD**, City; Cape May County; Pop. 4,913; Area Code 609; Zip Code 08260; Elev. 8'; located in S New Jersey; descriptive name meaning "abundance of wild flowers"; Wildwood-By-The-Sea is one of the East Coast's most famous resorts, blending a wide variety of housing accommodations, restaurants, stores, countless attractions of all kinds and a beautiful beach-boardwalk area into a place for everyone to come to vacation and play.

A wide beach combines clean, white sand, a gentle surf and warm ocean water. During the summer season, the surf warms up to a mild, comfortable temperature in the mid-70's.

The shallow surf, free from gullies, the refreshing water and little undertow draws the vacation visitor for a refreshing dip in the Atlantic Ocean.

An excellent view of Wildwood's bathing beach is afforded from the boardwalk where one has an unobstructed view of sea, surf and sand. The landside of the wooden promenade is lined with hundreds of souvenir shops, restaurants of all kinds, snack bars, fst-food parlors, amusement piers and other attractions. The boardwalk really comes alive at night when the lights go on, the people promenade and there is music.

While the beach and boardwalk have brought fame to Wildwood, it is equally as well known for its fine and wide choice of housing accommodations, and many restaurants.

Outdoor lovers can enjoy a full day, half day or even a night of exciting deep sea fishing, catcing bluefish, sea bass, weakfish, black drum, fluke and over 30 other kinds of exotic ocean and bay gamefish. There are party and charter boats which take visitors fishing or you can rent your own outboard powered boat for a day on the inland waterway.

•**WILDWOOD CREST**, Borough; Cape May County; Pop. 4,149; Area Code 609; Zip Code 08260; Elev. 9'; located in S New Jersey; descriptive name meaning "abundance of wild flowers."

•**WILLIAMSTOWN**, included in Monroe; Gloucester County; Pop. est. 4,075; Elev. 160'; located in S Central New Jersey on Hwy. 322; once a glass-making center, the town now depends largely on canneries, which preserve fruit and vegetables.

Williamstown has gradually lived down its early name of Squankum (Ind., place of the evil god). The name was brought here in 1772 from Squankum, Monmouth County, by *Deacon Israel Williams* ; 70 years later the town was named for the deacon himself. One historian recalls that in 1800 there were but four or five houses at Williamstown "within sound of the conch." This sea shell was brought to New Jersey in large quantities aboard sailing vessels trading with the WEst Indies and was used ashore as a dinner horn. At sea it served as a foghorn.

•**WILLINGBORO**, Township; Burlington County; Pop. 39,912; Area Code 609; Zip Code 08046; located in S New Jersey; named for Willingboro, England.

•**WINDSOR**, included in Washington; Mercer County; Pop. est. 400; Area Code 609; Zip Code 08561; Elev. 100'; located in Central New Jersey; 10 mile NE of Trenton; Windsor was named by the English who settled here about 1714.

•**WOODBINE**, Borough; Cape May County; Pop. 2,809; Area Code 609; Zip Code 08270; Elev. 40'; located in S New Jersey; the borough of Woodbine is the industrial hub of the Jersey Cape. This inland community had its beginnings in the latter part of the 19th century as a Jewish refugee community.

Woodbine is located in the northwest part of the county. It is a small community comprised mostly of single family homes.

Center-city Woodbine features a group of small, compact businesses nestled amid the residential clusters. Large amounts of woodland and farmland surround the developed areas. An airport and Industrial Park are near light industry.

Woodbine is close to bathing beaches, fine fishing and camping areas.

•**WINSLOW**, Township; Camden County; Pop. 20,034; Area Code 609; Zip Code 08095; located in SW New Jersey; named for glassworks.

•**WOODBRIDGE**, Township; Middlesex County; Pop. 90,074; Area Code 201; Zip Code 07095; Elev. 30'; located in Central New Jersey; has for over 100 years been sustained by the clay deposits of the surrounding area.

The community was settled by 1665 by Puritans from Massachusets Bay and New Hampshire. In 1751 *James Parker* established the first press in New Jersey. His periodical, the *American Magazine*, on sale seven years later, succumbed after two years because of lack of patronage. *Parker* was fined and even jailed for exercising his right to run a free press. Named after *Rev. John Woodbridge*, leader of settlers from Massachusetts.

•**WOODBURY**, City; Gloucester County; Pop. 10,353; Area Code 609; Zip Code 08096; Elev. 57'; located in SW New Jersey, on I-295, S of Camden; is the seat of Gloucester County; named after *John Wood*, settler.

•**WOODBURY**, Borough; Gloucester County; Pop. 3,460; Area Code 609; Zip Code 08097; Elev. 74'; located in SW New Jersey; named after *John Wood*, settler.

•**WOODCLIFF LAKE**, Borough; Bergen County; Pop. 5,644; Area Code 201; Zip Code 07675; Elev. 249'; located in NE New Jersey; named for location on lake in the woods under a cliff.

WOODLYNNE, Borough; Camden County; Pop. 2,578; Area Code 609; Zip Code 08017; Elev. 20'; located in SW New Jersey; is where Borough Hall sstands on the Site Of Mark Newbie's Bank, said to have been the first bank of issue in America. Newbie came here from Dublin in 1682 and in that year got a bank charter from the West Jersey Assembly. At a substantial discount he had purchased a quantity of farthings and halfpence struck in Ireland some 40 years earlier. These coins, known as Patrick's Pence, were not legal tender in Ireland. Newbie was forbidden by the legislature to mint money, but an exception was made for the use of his Irish pence. The bank did a thriving business, but less than year after its opening Newbie died and the coins were recalled or redemption. Coin collectors today value specimens. Named or Linden trees.

WOOD-RIDGE, Borough; Bergen County; Pop. 7,929; Area Code 201; Zip Code 070+zone; Elev. 188'; located in NE New Jersey; the first landowners here were the Brinerhoffs, who came late in the seventeenth century.

WOODSTOWN, Borough; Salem County; Pop. 3,250; Area Code 609; Zip Code 08098; Elev. 47'; located in SW New Jersey on Hwy. 40; has many old houses, including fine examples of Colonial architecture. It has been a Quaker center since *Jackanias Wood* built the first house early in the 1700's. During the Revolution, American and British troops marched through Woodstown and foraging parties made their headquarters here. Named after settler, *Jackanias Wood*.

•**WRIGHTSTOWN**, Borough; Burlington County; Pop. 3,031; Area Code 609; Zip Code 08562; Elev. 133'; located in S New Jersey; named for donor of street site, *John Wright*.

•**WYCKOFF**, Township; Bergen County; Pop. 15,500; Area Code 201; Zip Code 07481; located in NE New Jersey; named for Wicaugh, Malpas, England.

•**ZAREPHATH**, included in Franklin; Somerset County; Pop. est. 200; Area Code 201; Zip Code 08890; located in N New Jersey; name of a Biblical City; is a community founded by the Pillar of Fire, a religious sect. The society was formed in 1901 by *Mrs. Alma White*, a Methodist minister's wife, and named for the pillar of fire in Exodus that led the Israelites through the wilderness.

GUIDE TO HISTORICAL PLACES

Designations of Historical Places

Frequently the designations NHL, HABS, HAER, and/or G follow the ownership and accessibility. These are explained as follows:

NHL—A National Historic Landmark is a building, structure, site, district, or object declared eligible for recognition as a property of national significance by the Secretary of the Interior under the provisions of the Historic Sites Act of 1935. These properties are not administered by the National Park Service.

HABS—A Historic American Buildings Survey designation indicates that documentation by photographs, measured drawings, and/or data sheets has been made as evidence of a building's architectural or historical significance. The Historic American Buildings Survey is conducted by the National Park Service in cooperation with the American Institute of Architects and the Library of Congress where the records are deposited. A HABS designation is included in the description of historic districts when at least one property has been documented by the Historic American Buildings Survey.

HAER—A Historic American Engineering Record designation means that the property has been recognized and recorded as an important example of American engineering. The Historic American Engineering Record is conducted by the National Park Service in cooperation with the American Society of Civil Engineers. Records are kept at the Library of Congress.

G—A grant designation means that the property has received a National Park Service grant-in-aid under the National Historic Preservation Act of 1966.

GUIDE TO HISTORICAL PLACES

Atlantic City. **ABSECON LIGHTHOUSE,** Rhode Island and Pacific Aves., 1855–1857. Brick, 171' high, tapered cylindrical shape, 27' diameter at base, iron and glass lens chamber above, catwalk surrounding chamber, spiral iron staircase inside. Restored, 1964. Constructed under direction of Lt. George Meade, later commander of Union forces at Battle of Gettysburg. Operated from 1857 to 1933. Museum in adjacent building. *State:* HABS.

Margate City. **LUCY, THE MARGATE ELEPHANT,** Decatur and Atlantic Aves., 1881, James V. Lafferty, designer. Elephant-shaped frame building with terne metal sheathing, 65' high with an 80' circumference; rectangular side and rear windows, round windows in eyes; entrances and spiral stairs in rear legs, surmounted by howdah; interior divided into rooms; altered; moved; restored. Gothic Revival interior elements. Architectural folly built as real estate promotion scheme by James V. Lafferty, Philadelphia entrepreneur; later served as summer cottage, tavern, and tourist attraction. *Municipal:* HABS.

Somers Point. **SOMERS MANSION,** Shore Rd. and Somers Point Circle, c. 1725. Brick (Flemish bond with glazed headers), 2 1/2 stories, rectangular, gambrel roof, paneled end chimney, balcony around 3 sides at 2nd-floor level from 1930's restoration, shed roof crosses gable above balcony. Mostly original interior. Museum. *State:* HABS.

BERGEN COUNTY

PALISADES INTERSTATE PARK, W bank of the Hudson River (also in Orange and Rockland Counties, NY), 1899. Interstate park of 11 units, consisting of 53,320 acres over 24 mi. of the Hudson River shoreline; established in reaction against extensive quarrying of the cliffs; expanded with gifts in 1910 and later. Preserves large area of natural environment near NY metropolitan area. *State:* NHL.

Fair Lawn. **GARRETSON, PETER, HOUSE,** 4-02 River Rd., 18th C.. Stone, partially shingled; 1 1/2 stories, rectangular, bell-cast gambrel roof, 3 interior chimneys, gabled dormers, full-width front porch with center entrance, stone lintels; original 1720–1725 section enlarged, c. 1800; gambrel roof, shingling, and dormers, added, 1900. Dutch Colonial. *Private; not accessible to the public.*

Hohokus. **HERMITAGE, THE (WALDWIC COTTAGE),** 335 N. Franklin Tpke., Mid-18th C.. Rebuilding of original house in 1845 by architect William H. Ranlett: stone, 1 1/2 stories, irregular shape, steeply gabled roof sections, pierced bargeboards, pinnacles, dormers, label molds around windows, grouped chimney stacks, diamond-shaped window lights, few alterations. Fine example of Early Gothic Revival building and only known work in this style by the author of a popular architectural book on cottages. *State; not accessible to the public:* NHL; HABS.

Mahwah. **HOPPER-VAN HORN HOUSE,** 398 Ramapo Valley Rd., Late-18th C.. Uncoursed fieldstone and frame, clapboarding; 1 1/2 stories, modified rectangle, gambrel roof, 3 interior end chimneys, full-width shed veranda, center entrance with transom, clapboarding in gable end; older 1-story gabled stone ell with clapboarding in gable. *State; not accessible to the public:* HABS.

Oakland. **VAN ALLEN HOUSE,** Corner of U.S. 202 and Franklin Ave., 1777. Fieldstone, 2 sections: 1 1/2-story main structure, gambrel roof with shed dormers, entrance portico with broken pediment; 1-story small section, gabled roof replaced by gambrel roof, 2 additions. Built by Hendrick Van Allen. Site where Washington established temporary headquarters after Gen: Burgoyne's capture of Fort Ticonderoga (see also Fort Ticonderoga, NY). *Municipal.*

Paramus. **TERHUNE-GARDNER-LIN-DENMEYR HOUSE,** 218 Paramus Rd., c. 1730. Frame, clapboarding; 2 1/2 stories, modified rectangle, gambrel and gabled roof sections, interior and exterior end chimneys, round arched windows in gables; 2 1/2-story gambrel block added c. 1807 to original 2-story section; 20th C. porch. Federal elements. Example of evolution of residence reflecting changing tastes. *Private.*

Park Ridge. **WORTENDYKE BARN,** 13 Pascack Rd., c. 1770. Frame, clapboarding; 2 stories, rectangular, large gabled roof, front and rear carriage doors, small corner entrance; roof supported by H-shaped framing; windows added, 20th C. One of few remaining Dutch barns in NJ. *Private:* HABS.

River Edge. **STEUBEN HOUSE (ACKERMAN-ZABRISKIE-STEUBEN HOUSE),** Old New Bridge Rd., at the Hackensack River, c. 1720. Cut stone, brick gable ends; 1 1/2 stories, rectangular, gambrel roof, front veranda, 2 interior chimneys; expanded and altered, 18th and 19th C. Used by both Washington and Cornwallis during Revolution; owned briefly by Baron Friedrich von Steuben who received it in partial payment for war services. Museum. *State:* HABS.

Rutherford. **WILLIAMS, WILLIAM CARLOS, HOUSE,** 9 Ridge Rd., Late-19th or early-20th C.. Frame, clapboarding and shingling; 2 1/2 stories, modified rectangle, gabled roof, exterior end chimney, off-center gabled bay with imbricated shingling and lunette in gable, 2 rectangular windows in main gable, side wall dormer; rear extensions; interior substantially altered. Queen Anne elements. Home of Pulitzer Prize-winning author William Carlos Williams for most of his life. *Private; not accessible to the public.*

Westwood (Washington Township). **SEVEN CHIMNEYS (ZABRISKIE-VANEMBURGH HOUSE)** , 25 Chimney Ridge Ct., Mid-18th C.. Stone, frame with clapboarding; 2 stories, modified rectangle, gabled roof sections, numerous chimneys; later porch, 1812 frame 2nd story, and 1770 flanking frame wings; interior partitions filled with sand. Original stone house showing Dutch influence. Among owners was William Howland, publisher of magazines, *The Outlook*, in late-19th C., and *The Independent* in early-20th C. *Private.*

BURLINGTON COUNTY

Arney's Mount. **ARNEY'S MOUNT FRIENDS MEETINGHOUSE AND BURIAL GROUND,** Jct. of Mount Holly-Juliustown and Pemberton-Arney's Mount Rds., 1775, Samuel Smith, builder. Random ironstone, 2 stories, rectangular, gabled roof, interior chimney, box cornice, simple gabled entrance portico, irregularly placed windows; repaired after fires in 1800 and 1809. Grounds include cemetery with several graves older than building. *Private.*

Atsion. **ATSION VILLAGE,** U.S. 206, 18th–20th C.. Remains of early industrial community containing foundations of 18th C. gristmill and barn and several 18th C. house sites, restored store and 1824 Greek Revival house, L-shaped cotton factory, frame houses and a church, and a 20th C. schoolhouse. Settled as milling community along Atsion River; developed around early successful bog iron industry which failed in 1840's; economy temporarily revitalized by cotton industry (1860's) and a real estate development (1880's); last buildings constructed in 1920's; abandoned. Museum. *State:* NHL; HABS.

Batsto. **BATSTO VILLAGE,** 10 mi. E of Hammonton on CR 542, 18th–19th C.. District representing bog iron community, with frame workers' houses, grist and saw mills, blacksmith shop, barn complex, and mansion house; reflects several periods of growth and change through 19th C. Self-sufficient industrial community; produced glass and munitions used in Revolution and in War of 1812. Some restoration; museum. *State:* HABS.

Bordentown. **HOPKINSON, FRANCIS, HOUSE,** 101 Farnsworth Ave. at Park Ave., 1750. Brick (Flemish bond), 2 1/2 stories, L-shaped, mansard roof, 3 interior chimneys, pedimented dormers, bracketed cornice, segmental hood over center entrance with transom and side lights; 2-story rear ell; 19th C. alterations. Georgian elements. Home of Francis Hopkinson, pamphleteer, poet, America's first native composer, and signer of the Declaration of Independence. *Private:* NHL; HABS.

Brown's Mills vicinity. **HANOVER FURNACE,**
E of Browns Mills, 1792. Brick ruins of furnace
which supported early-19th C. industrial community of 200 residents; produced cannon and
cannonballs during War of 1812 and later
produced pipe for Philadelphia Water Works
and other commercial iron products until 1865.
Uninvestigated. *Federal/USA.*

Burlington. **QUAKER SCHOOL,** York and
Penn Sts., 1792. Brick, 1 1/2 stories, rectangu-
lar, gabled roof, dormer with triple windows; N,
S, and W gabled entrances; minor alterations.
Built as schoolhouse for Society of Friends.
Private.

Burlington. **ST. MARY'S EPISCOPAL**
CHURCH (ST. MARY'S COMPLEX) , N side
of Broad St. between Talbot and Wood Sts.,
1854, Richard Upjohn, architect (new St.
Mary's). Brownstone ashlar, 1 1/2 stories, Latin
cross shape, gabled roof; 160′ broached octagonal stone spire at crossing above square
base with louvered belfry and lancet windows;
pointed arched windows with stone label molds;
polychromatic interior. Earlier church and
graveyard on grounds. Gothic Revival. One of
most significant works by English-born
architect Richard Upjohn; among those buried
in churchyard is Elias Boudinot, president of
the Continental Congress. *Private:* HABS.

Medford vicinity (Medford Township).
KIRBY'S MILL (HAINES MILL) , NE of Medford at Church and Fostertown Rds., c. 1778.
Frame, clapboarding; 4 stories, rectangular, gabled roof, interior chimney, cross gable over
entrance, doors at each floor on gable end; altered 1890; converted to electricity, 1961.
Ground grain for local farmers until 1968;
served as social and commercial center of community. Museum. *Private.*

Mount Holly. **MOUNT HOLLY HISTORIC DISTRICT**, 18th–19th C.. Diverse district illustrating development of building styles and techniques over 2 centuries; features about 40 buildings, many of brick or frame, and some of stone or log construction, in styles ranging from Georgian through Gothic Revival and Queen Anne. Buildings include Burlington County Prison, by Robert Mills, and the 1723 Three Tuns Tavern. Area settled 1677; developed as trading and manufacturing center. *Multiple public/private:* HABS.

Mount Holly vicinity (Westampton Township). **PEACHFIELD,** N of Mount Holly on Burr Rd., 1725. Rubble, 2 stories, L-shaped, gabled roof, 4 large stone interior chimneys, shed veranda on portion of facade; extended 1731; rear ell; restored 1931 by Brognard Okie, after gutted by fire. Colonial elements. Property in Burr family for over 2 centuries. Museum. *Private.*

CAMDEN COUNTY

Camden. **COOPER, JOSEPH, HOUSE,** Head of 7th St. in Pine Point Park, c. 1695. Uncoursed stone and brick (Flemish bond), 1 1/2–2 1/2-story sections, modified rectangle, gabled roof sections, 3 interior chimneys, gabled dormers, pent roof on 18th C. brick addition above 1st story, 1st-and 2nd-story cove cornice on brick block. Colonial elements. Reputedly one of county's oldest extant structures. *Municipal; not accessible to the public* HABS.

Camden. **FAIRVIEW DISTRICT,** Roughly bounded by Newton Creek, Crescent Blvd., Mt. Ephraim Ave., Olympia and Hull Rds., 1917, Electus Litchfield, planner and architect. Predominantly residential area containing

1,000 brick row, detached, and duplex houses
and apartments and some commercial and
public structures, the majority of which feature
Colonial Revival detailing; designed on axial
street system. Built to house workers and families; conforms to neighborhood unit concept for
residential planning as developed by Clarence
Perry. *Public/private.*

Camden.   **NEWTON   FRIENDS'
MEETINGHOUSE,** 722 Cooper St., 1824.
Frame, random-width clapboarding; 1 story,
rectangular, gabled roof, interior end chimneys,
gabled entrance portico with classical elements;
simple interior with wainscoting and mahogany
pews; 1885 extension and semicircular side
vestibule addition. Oldest religious structure in
city. *Private.*

Camden. **POMONA HALL (COOPER HOUSE)**
, Park Blvd. and Euclid Ave., 1726. Brick
(Flemish bond with glazed headers and English
bond), 2 1/2 stories, rectangular, gabled roof, 4
interior end chimneys, pedimented dormers,
water table and string course, center pedimented entrance; builders' initials and dates in
gable ends; major extension, c. 1788; altered;
restored, 1935. Built for Joseph Cooper, Jr.,
local landholder and politician. Museum. *Municipal:* HABS.

Camden. **TAYLOR, DR. HENRY GENET,
HOUSE AND OFFICE,** 305 Cooper St., 1886,
Wilson Eyre, architect. Brick and limestone, 3
stories, rectangular, gambrel roof, 1 side and 1
front chimney with corbeled cap and brick
tumbling, off-center shed dormer; rock-faced
ashlar ground floor with off-center round arch
leading to entrance, small end basement entrance arch, oriel; Roman brick upper floors
with large Flemish gable, narrow window in
chimney, thin pilasters. Queen Anne. Early fine
work by Philadelphia architect Wilson Eyre, Jr.
Private.

Camden. **WHITMAN, WALT, HOUSE,** 330
Mickle St., c. 1848. Frame, clapboarding; 2 stories, rectangular, simply treated 3-bay facade.
Greek Revival elements. Home of Walt Whitman, poet best known for *Leaves of Grass*, from
1884 to his death in 1892. Museum. *State:* NHL;
HABS.

Cherry Hill. **COLES, SAMUEL, HOUSE,** 1743
Old Cuthbert Rd., 1743. Brick (Flemish bond),
2 stories, rectangular, gabled roof, 2 interior
end chimneys, box cornice, pent roof at 2nd-
floor level on facade, water table; builder's initials and date set in glazed headers in gable
end; altered late-19th C. Georgian. Built by
Samuel Coles, early area resident; used as jail
during 19th C. *Private.*

Cinnaminson vicinity. **MORGAN, GRIFFITH,
HOUSE,** 2 mi. W of Cinnaminson at confluence
of Delaware River and Pennsauken Creek,
1693. Stone and brick remains of house, 2 1/2
stories, L-shaped, originally with gambrel roof,
4 interior end chimneys; variety of brick and
stone work; expanded 18th C. County's oldest
extant house. *Private; not accessible to the
public.*

Haddonfield. **GREENFIELD HALL,** 343 Kings
Hwy. E, 1747. Brick, 2 1/2 stories, modified L,
gabled slate roof with balustraded deck, interi-
or end chimney pairs, dormers, center door-
way, regular fenestration, interior classical and
Chinese Chippendale designs; original 1747 E
wing expanded, 1841. Federal. Original section
built by early settler John Gill. Museum.
Private: HABS.

Haddonfield. **HADDON FORTNIGHTLY
CLUB HOUSE (THIRD METHODIST
CHURCH)** , 301 King's Hwy., 1857. Brick,
stuccoed; 2 stories, rectangular temple-form,
gabled roof, full plain entablature, 1930 colos-
sal tetrastyle Doric portico with lunette in pedi-

ment; 3 entrances with transoms in 3-bay facade, two 2nd-floor oculi; side pilasters; steeple removed and building extended, 20th C. Greek Revival. Originally a church; served as club since 1930. *Private.*

Haddonfield. **INDIAN KING TAVERN (CREIGHTON TAVERN)**, 233 Kings Hwy. E, c. 1750. Brick, stuccoed; 2 1/2- and 3-story halves, rectangular, gabled roof, shed porch across 7-bay front, gabled dormers, cornice with gable return. Georgian elements. Meeting-place of state legislature, including state's first assembly (1777), which created state's Council of Safety and adopted state's Great Seal; stopping point on road between Philadelphia and New York. Museum. *State:* HABS.

Pennsauken. **BURROUGH-DOVER HOUSE,** Off the Haddonfield Rd., 1710, 1793. Coursed fieldstone, 2 stories, square, gabled roof. Larger 2-story section added 1793, from which interior woodwork remains. Built by Samuel Burrough; addition built by descendants. Museum. *Private:* HABS.

CAPE MAY COUNTY

Cape May. **CAPE MAY HISTORIC DISTRICT,** c. 1850–1910. Oceanside resort town with about 600 19th and early-20th C. buildings of great variety and exuberance, including private residences, hotels, churches, and structures—the work of both builders and well-known architects. Area first settled by Dutch in 1630's; developed into internationally popular spa beginning in early-19th C. with regular steamboat traffic on the Delaware River; peak period, 1850–early-20th C., made town a showcase of late Victorian architecture. *Multiple public/private:* HABS.

Cape May vicinity. **CAPE MAY LIGHTHOUSE,** On Cape May Point W of Cape May off Sunset Blvd., 1859. Brick, 175' high, red brick lantern, interior spiral staircase. Fourth lighthouse commissioned on Cape May. *Federal/USCG.*

CUMBERLAND COUNTY

Bridgeton. **OLD BROAD STREET PRESBYTERIAN CHURCH AND CEME-TERY,** Broad and Lawrence Sts., 1792–1795. Brick (Flemish bond), 2 stories, rectangular, gabled roof, interior end chimney, center round arched entrance set in pedimented frame, round arched mullion windows, Palladian window, projecting string course; interior wainscoting, family pews; cemetery. Federal. Excellent example of post-Revolutionary church. *Private:* HABS.

Bridgeton. **POTTER'S TAVERN,** 49–51 Broad St., 18th C.. Frame with brick nogging, clapboarding; 2 stories, rectangular, gabled roof; double straight staircases to pedimented entrance above grade; rear shed addition. Saltbox type. Tavern known as "Bridgeton's Independence Hall" before the Revolution; radical newspaper, *The Plain Dealer,* published here late in 1775. *Municipal.*

Greenwich. **GREENWICH HISTORIC DISTRICT,** Main St. from Cohansey River N to Othello, Late-17th–19th C.. Pre-Revolutionary town consisting of about 18 structures, including brick, stone, and frame residences, store, school, and tavern. Town contributed to development of middle colonies through shipping and trade; scene of public burning of shipload of tea in repudiation of British authority, Dec. 1774. *Multiple public/private:* HABS.

ESSEX COUNTY

MORRIS CANAL, Irregular line beginning at Phillipsburg and ending at Jersey City (also in Hudson, Morris, Passaic, Sussex, and Warren counties), 1825–1836, Ephraim Beach, Ephraim Morris and others, engineers. Remains of canal (190 mi.); ran from E terminus in Jersey City, through summit (914' above sea level) at Lake Hopatcong (Landing), to the W terminus at Phillipsburg; originally contained 22 locks (approximately 90' x 12' each) and 23 inclined planes, averaging 63' of vertical lift in 8 minutes; accommodated boats and section boats up to 75 tons after enlargement. Constructed for promoter George P. McCulloch of the Morris Canal and Banking Co. to practically transport coal to NJ iron supplies; caused numerous area towns to develop around expanding iron industry and related businesses; served as training project for USA COE; disbanded and drained after unsuccessfully competing with railroad, 1920's. *Multiple public/private.*

Montclair. **CRANE, ISRAEL, HOUSE,** 110 Orange Rd., 1796. Frame, clapboarding; 2 1/2 stories, L-shaped, flat roof, 4 interior end chimneys, denticulated cornice, wide frieze with attic openings; recessed center entrance with transom, side lights, and pilasters; Ionic portico; alterations with classical details and ell added, 1838; moved, 1965. Greek Revival elements on earlier building. Built for Israel Crane, prominent businessman. Museum. *Private:* HABS.

Montclair. **MONTCLAIR RAILROAD STATION,** Lackawanna Plaza, 1913, William H. Botsford, architect. Brick, concrete trim; 1 story, irregular shape, gabled and flat roof sections, low parapet at gable ends; projecting entrance pavilion with parapet, entrance recessed within 1-story porch with 4 columns and flanking pilasters; large round arched window partially set within front gable, side clerestory windows; 4 tracks and 4 platforms. Neo-Classical Revival elements. City's railroad tracks laid 1872 after Montclair seceded from Bloomfield (1868) and issued a bond to help finance the tracks; station designed by William H. Botsford, chief architect for the Delaware, Lackawanna and Western RR. from 1910 to 1912. *Private*.

Newark. **BALLANTINE, JOHN, HOUSE,** 43 Washington St., 1884, George Edward Harney, architect; D. S. Hess & Co., interior decorators. Brick with sandstone trim, 3 1/2 stories, square, hipped roof with side dormers and front pediment, square entry porch with 3 trefoil arches, 20th C. alterations. Italian Renaissance Revival and Richardsonian Romanesque elements. Built in Washington Park, one of city's wealthiest sections in 19th C. when brewing was major industry. One of few remaining 19th C. structures in Newark. Museum. *Private*.

Newark. **CATEDRAL EVANGELICA REFORMADA (FIRST REFORMED CHURCH)** , 27 Lincoln Park and Halsey St., 1872, Thomas A. Roberts, architect. Stone, 2 stories, rectangular, gabled roof sections; projecting front center shed porch with center gable containing large pointed arch opening, flanked by a smaller opening on each side; 5-story front corner tower with louvered belfry and broach spire, smaller 2nd front tower, large front pointed arch tracery windows, lancet windows, buttresses. Gothic Revival and High Victorian Gothic Revival elements. *Private*.

Newark. **FIRST BAPTIST PEDDIE MEMORI-AL CHURCH,** Broad and Fulton Sts., 1890, William Halsey Wood, architect. Coursed granite ashlar, 1 1/2 stories, modified square, domed roof; 2 front and one rear corner towers, one with a pyramidal roof, one with one octagonal spire, and the other with conical cap; semielliptical corner entrance bay with domed roof, front ground-floor arcade beneath round arched windows, oculi. Eclectic. Built for city's oldest Baptist congregation by Thomas B. Peddie, Newark mayor and philanthropist. *Private:* HABS.

Newark. **FIRST UNITED METHODIST CHURCH (CENTRAL METHODIST EPISCOPAL CHURCH)** , 227 Market St., 1850–1851, Minard Lafever, architect. Stone, brick; 1 1/2 stories, rectangular, gabled roof, 200'-high center buttressed entrance tower with tall spire and compound pointed arched entrance, separate side aisle entrances, corner buttresses and pinnacles, pointed arched windows with tracery and label molds, string course, brick side walls; elaborate interior with gallery; rear addition. Gothic Revival. City's only remaining building by noted Newark architect and architectural writer, Minard Lafever. *Private.*

Newark. **GRACE CHURCH,** Broad and Walnut Sts., 1847, Richard Upjohn, architect. Brownstone rubble, 1 story, modified Latin cross shape, gabled roof, projecting front gabled entrance vestibule with pointed arch opening; front corner 3-stage tower with lancet windows, louvered belfry, and tall broach spire; front 2-story corner turret with conical roof; enlarged, 1872; parish house built, 1927. Designed by Gothic Revival leader Richard Upjohn; enlarged by his son Richard M. Upjohn. *Private.*

Newark. **HOUSE OF PRAYER EPISCOPAL CHURCH AND RECTORY (PLUME HOUSE)** , Broad and State Sts., 1849, Frank Wills, architect. Stone, 2 stories, modified rectangle, gabled roof sections; front corner tower with splayed arch entrance, louvered belfry, and broach spire with dormers; entrance at chancel end of nave preserves E–W orientation of church on lot; buttressed nave contains quatrefoil clerestory windows; rectory built c. 1710. Gothic Revival. Designed by Frank Wills, noted ecclesiastical architect; rectory was home of clergyman Hannibal Goodwin, inventor of celluloid film. *Private.*

Newark. **KRUEGER MANSION,** 601 High St., 1889. Brick, 2 1/2 stories, modified rectangle, hipped roof sections; projecting front corner 5-story turret with polygonal base, circular balcony around 5th story, and conical cap; projecting center hipped entrance bay with wall dormer, elaborately carved double doors, front and side porch with projecting entrance section with elaborate arch and circle motifs and balustraded deck, stained glass transom and segmental arched pediment over most windows, projections, porches; elaborate interior. Chateauesque. Home of Gottfried Krueger, founder of the famous G. Krueger Brewing Co. *Private; not accessible to the public.*

Newark. **NEW POINT BAPTIST CHURCH (SOUTH BAPTIST CHURCH)** , 17 E. Kinney St., 1850, John G. Hall, architect. Brick, brownstone-faced; 1 1/2 stories, rectangular, gabled roof, 3 entrances set in recessed center section of full-width pedimented porch with enclosed end bays; interior gallery; brownstone facing added, 1862–1863; porch enclosed and steeple removed, 20th C. Good city example of Greek Revival structure. *Private.*

Newark. **NEWARK ORPHAN ASYLUM,** High and Bleeker Sts., Newark College of Engineering, 1857, John Welch, architect. Brick, 3 1/2 stories, modified rectangle, gabled roof, 2 interior chimneys, triangular dormers, end Flemish cross gables, center battlemented turret and buttresses, battlemented balconies, painted and rowlock arches, brownstone trim; S wing built, 1874; interior altered, 1948. Gothic Revival. Served as orphan asylum until 1948. *Private.*

Newark. **NORTH REFORMED CHURCH,** 510 Broad St., 1857, William Kirk, architect. Coursed brownstone, 2 stories, rectangular, gabled roof; front center projecting square tower with pointed arch entrance, tracery window, oculus, clockfaces, and octagonal spire with dormers and pinnacles; rear auditorium and chapel; altered, 19th C. Gothic Revival. Reputedly derived from design by Richard Upjohn. *Private.*

Newark. **OLD FIRST PRESBYTERIAN CHURCH,** 820 Broad St., 1787–1791. Brick (Flemish bond), brownstone trim; 2 1/2 stories, rectangular, gambrel roof; front center projecting clock tower with 1st-story entrance with fanlight, pediment above 2nd story, clockfaces, octagonal 2-stage louvered belfry, and spire; modillion cornice: round arch windows, surrounds; rear chapel and parish house added, 1952. Federal. Built for one of America's earliest Presbyterian congregations. *Private:* HABS.

Newark. **PAN AMERICAN C.M.A. CHURCH (CHRIST CHURCH)** , 76 Prospect St., 1848, Frank Wills, architect. Coursed and random brownstone ashlar, 1 story, cross-shaped, gabled roof sections, gable end buttresses surmounted by gabled bell cote, pointed arched openings, buttresses; chancel and apse added.

Good example of early Gothic Revival church. Designed by Frank Wills, official architect of the New York Ecclesiological Society. *Private.*

Newark. **QUEEN OF ANGELS CHURCH (ST. PETER'S CHURCH)** , Belmont Ave. at Morton St., 1861, Otto Gsantner, architect. Brick, 2 1/2 stories, rectangular, gabled roof; slightly projecting front center tower with entrance in ogee surround, pointed arched 2nd-story window, louvered round arched belfry openings, and buttresses; pointed arched windows, bays articulated by buttresses; spire removed; adjoining school built, 1887; orphanage and chapel built, 1897. Gothic Revival. Built to serve German Roman Catholic congregation; presently serves black parish. *Private.*

Newark. **SOUTH PARK CALVARY UNITED PRESBYTERIAN CHURCH,** 1035 Broad St., 1853, John W. Welch, architect. Brownstone and brick, 1 story, rectangular, gabled roof, center tetrastyle pedimented Ionic portico; twin corner towers with octagonal upper sections, Ionic columns, and small domes; center entrance with transom, quoins; brick side walls with buttresses and round arched windows; towers altered, rear additions; iron fence on lot. Greek Revival. Designed by British-trained architect; considered among finer area examples of ecclesiastical buildings of this style. *Private.*

Newark. **ST. BARNABAS' EPISCOPAL CHURCH, W.** Market St. and Sussex and Roseville Aves., 1864, Thomas A. Roberts, architect. Stone, 1 story, Latin cross shape, gabled roof sections, crenelated side tower with louvered openings, center gabled vestibule beneath small rose window, lancet windows, angled corner buttresses; transepts added, 1869; porch added and tower heightened, 1913. Gothic Revival. *Private.*

Newark. **ST. COLUMBA'S CHURCH**, Pennsylvania Ave. and Brunswick St., 1898, Charles Edwards, architect. Rock-faced ashlar, 1 story, modified rectangle, pyramidal roof sections, front gabled dormer, bowed front Corinthian entrance portico surmounted by a buttressed recessed section, side bell tower, round arched openings; half-domed sanctuary, barrel-vaulted nave, Baroque details. Eclectic. Built for one of Newark's Roman Catholic parishes. *Private.*

Newark. **ST. JAMES' A. M. E. CHURCH (HIGH STREET PRESBYTERIAN CHURCH)**, High and Court Sts., 1850–1852, John W. Welch, architect. Ashlar, 1 story, L-shaped, gabled roof sections; center buttressed entrance tower with pierced crenelated parapet, pinnacles, and pointed arched openings; corner buttresses with pinnacles, aisle entrances beneath raking parapet pierced with trefoils, label molded openings; multistory 1890 rear addition with similar treatment by Carrere and Hastings. Gothic Revival. Landmark building overlooking city; one of several area buildings by John W. Welch, immigrant architect. *Private.*

Newark. **ST. JAMES' CHURCH**, Lafayette and Jefferson Sts., 1863–1866, Patrick C. Keeley, architect. Brownstone, 2 stories, rectangular, gabled roof, 224'-high corner tower with spire, large ornate rose window above gabled entrance with pointed compound arch, sculptural niche in gable end with statue of St. James, lancet windows, buttresses, pinnacles. Gothic Revival. Prominent landmark designed by Catholic ecclesiastical architect Patrick C. Keeley. *Private.*

Newark. **ST. JOHN'S CHURCH**, 22–26 Mulberry St., 19th C.. Brownstone ashlar, 1 1/2 stories, modified rectangle, gabled roof, twin corner towers with angled buttresses and pinna-

cles, center and end entrances, label molded
pointed arched openings, full-height turrets
flanking entrance; original 1827–1828 church
rebuilt 1838, added to c. 1847; altered; adjacent to convent and rectory. Gothic Revival
elements. Oldest Catholic parish in state;
developed architecturally during mid-19th C.
by Father Patrick Moran, pastor here for 33
years and artisan and designer. *Private.*

Newark. **ST. MARY'S ABBEY CHURCH,** High
and William Sts., 1856, Patrick C. Keeley,
architect. Brick, 2 stories, modified rectangle,
gabled and shed roof sections; corner tower
with bracketed cornice, round arched openings,
and recessed wall panels; center entrance
vestibule with gabled round arched entrance,
oculus in front gable, brick fretwork motif
beneath eaves, row of tall round arched windows above vestibule. Romanesque Revival elements. Built for German Catholic congregation
whose original frame church was damaged by
the Know-Nothing riots of 1854; designed by
Irish-trained architect who designed numerous
Catholic churches. *Private.*

Newark. **ST. PATRICK'S PRO CATHEDRAL,**
Washington St. and Central Ave., 1846–1850,
Patrick C. Keeley, architect. Brick, 1 story,
modified rectangle, gabled and shed roof sections; center tower with pointed arched
openings, corner buttresses, and crocketed
spire; small twin corner towers with buttresses
and pinnacles; altered, 1875; restored, 1950;
parish buildings and iron fence. Gothic Revival.
Church served as Roman Catholic Cathedral of
the Newark Archdiocese until 1954. *Private.*

Newark. **ST. STEPHAN'S CHURCH (UNITED
CHURCH OF CHRIST)** , Ferry St. and Wilson
Ave., 1874, G. Stahlin, architect. Brick, 2 sto-
ries, rectangular, gabled roof, center entrance

tower; 2-story recessed round arch with rose window, entrance with pediment form, pilasters, and quatrefoils in fanlight; round arched windows with tracery; interior includes German carved reredos and pulpit. Eclectic. Important visual landmark in area. *Private.*

Newark. **SYDENHAM HOUSE,** Old Road to Bloomfield, at Heller Pkwy., 18th C.. Fieldstone, frame, clapboarding; 2 stories, rectangular, gabled roof, stone cellar and lower story, expanded and altered over 19th C., one section slightly higher and wider than other, lunette window in end gable between interior end chimneys. Restored. Believed the oldest houses in Newark. *Private; not accessible to the public:* HABS.

Newark. **TRINITY CATHEDRAL,** Broad and Rector Sts., 1809, Josiah James, builder. Ashlar, 2 stories, rectangular, gabled roof, pedimented tetrastyle portico with giant columns, multistage tower with tall spire over portico, round arched center entrance and 2nd-floor windows with keystone in archivolts, end entrances with transoms, oculus in pediment; interior altered and rear extended under Richard Upjohn, 1860; some parts of original mid-18th C. church destroyed by fire remain. Federal with Gothic Revival elements. *Private:* HABS.

Nutley. **ENCLOSURE HISTORIC DISTRICT,** Enclosure and Calico Lane, Early-19th–early-20th C.. Section of village containing several artists' homes and studios, the majority of which are frame 2 1/2-story structures illustrating several 19th C. styles. Notable are the John Mason House (1812) and the studio (c. 1880) built for painter and art critic Frank Fowler. At the turn of the century, rural setting of community attracted large numbers of New York City

artists who commuted to the New York City art
market via nearby railroad. *Multiple
public/private*.

West Orange. **EDISON NATIONAL HISTOR-
IC SITE,** Main St. between Alden and Lakeside
Sts., 1880 (Glenmont), 1887 (laboratory).
House and laboratories of inventor and scientist
Thomas Alva Edison; includes the 23-room
Victorian dwelling, Glenmont, with barns,
sheds, greenhouses, and cottages on 13 acres,
and the laboratory complex which now includes
a full-sized replica of the tar-papered Black
Maria, the first motion picture studio, one of
numerous projects developed here by Edison
and his assistants. *Federal/NPS:* HABS.

GLOUCESTER COUNTY

Barnsboro. **BARNSBORO HOTEL,** Jct. of Pitman and Sewell Rds., 18th C.. Central log construction, frame, clapboarding covered by
asphalt siding; 2 1/2 stories, rectangular, gabled
roof, interior and interior end chimneys, corner
entrance, full-width front shed porch; original
(c. 1720) log structure enlarged and
remodeled, 18th–20th C. One of oldest taverns
in continuous operation in southern NJ.
Private.

Colonial Manor (West Deptford Township).
LADD'S CASTLE (CANDOR HALL) , 1337
Lafayette Ave., c. 1689. Brick (front Flemish
bond with glazed headers), 2 stories, modified
rectangle, gabled roof sections, interior end
chimneys, off-center entrance; W 2-story frame
addition faced with brick, roof replaced, and
other renovations, 1947–1948. Colonial elements. One of state's earliest brick structures;
built for John Ladd, who assisted William Penn
in planning Philadelphia. *Private*.

Glassboro. **WHITNEY MANSION (HOLLY BUSH)**, Whitney Ave., 1849, John Notman, architect. Coursed rubble, 2 stories, modified L shape, gabled roof sections; front 4-story square hipped tower with double-door entrance with fanlight, and gabled hood supported by stick work and decorative cast iron brackets; 1-story ornate front porch with bell-cast hipped roof, quoins; rear kitchen wing added later. Italianate. Built for Thomas H. Whitney, local glass manufacturer; scene of summit conference between President Lyndon B. Johnson and Soviet Premier Alexi Kosygin, June 1967. *State.*

National Park. **RED BANK BATTLEFIELD**, E bank of Delaware River and W end of Hessian Ave., 1777. Includes extensive remains of dry ditch and earthen ramparts of Fort Mercer, and adjacent Georgian Colonial house (1748). Fort built to defend Philadelphia; forced British general William Howe to take longer route to Philadelphia during his 1777 campaign, and later disrupted his supply lines by blocking his route to the sea; named for Gen. Hugh Mercer, killed at the Battle of Princeton, Jan. 1777. House used as Hessian hospital after battle of Red Bank, Oct. 1777. *County:* NHL; HABS.

National Park. **WHITALL, JAMES JR., HOUSE,** 100 Grove Ave., 1766. Brick (Flemish bond on front facade), 2 1/2 stories, rectangular, gabled roof, 3 interior end chimneys, modillion box cornice, S entrance with 6-light transom, construction date set in gable in glazed headers; 1-story wrap-around porch added. Georgian elements. Built by James Whitall, Jr., member of a prominent Quaker family. *Private:* HABS.

Oliphant's Mill (Medford Township). **MORAVIAN CHURCH,** Swedesboro-Sharp-town Rd., c. 1789. Brick (Flemish bond on front facade), ironstone foundation; 2 stories, rectangular, gabled roof; 2 front entrances, each with a 6-light transom; rear chimney partially demolished. Oldest and only surviving Moravian church building in southern NJ; design attributed to Francis Boehler, Moravian minister. *Private:* HABS.

Sewell (Mantua Township). **CHEW, JESSE, HOUSE,** 611 Mantua Blvd., 1772. Rubble, 2 1/2 stories, modified rectangle, gabled roof, interior end chimneys, 2 hipped dormers, front pent roof above 1st story, off-center entrance, 1772 date stone; 2-story side kitchen wing with frame porch added and entrance moved, 1912. Colonial elements. Home of Jesse Chew, early Methodist preacher. *Private.*

Swedesboro. **TRINITY CHURCH (OLD SWEDES CHURCH)** , NW corner of Church St. and King's Hwy., 1784–1786, Rev. Nicholas Collin, designer. Brick (Flemish bond), 2 stories, rectangular, gabled roof, center recessed entrance with fanlight set in broken pediment and surmounted by Palladian window and circular pediment date stone, rear center 5-story tower with belfry and cupola, round arched windows; tower added, 1836–1838; interior remodeled, 1854. Georgian. Built for early area Swedish Lutheran congregation; designed by congregation's minister, Nicholas Collin. *Private:* HABS.

Wenonah. **CLARK, BENJAMIN, HOUSE,** Glassboro Rd., c. 1796. Brick (Flemish and common bonds), 2 stories, rectangular, gabled roof sections, interior end chimneys, denticulated modillion cornice, projecting paired string courses above 1st story, 2 front pedimented entrances; original W section expanded and remodeled, 1801; frame kitchen section with bay window, c. 1940. Federal elements. Home of Benjamin Clark, Revolutionary patriot; frequently raided by British stationed at Billingsport. *Private.*

Woodbury. **HUNTER-LAWRENCE HOUSE,** 58 N. Broad St., c. 1765. Brick, 2 1/2 stories, L-shaped, mansard roof with some imbricated shingling and paired brackets; interior chimney; jerkinhead roof dormers with round arched windows, brackets, and decorative trim; center double-door entrance with transom and small, ornate porch; side bay window; late-18th and 19th C. interior woodwork; 18 alterations include the addition of mansard roof, dormers, entrance porch, bay window and bracketing and the remodeling of woodwork. Second Empire. Home of James Lawrence, whose dying words, "Don't give up the ship," became the motto of the U.S. Navy. *County.*

Woodbury. **WOODBURY FRIENDS' MEETINGHOUSE,** 120 N. Broad St., 1715. Brick (Flemish bond W facade), 2 1/2 stories, rectangular, gabled roof, interior end chimney; 2 double-door entrances with raised panels, similar panel treatment on shutters; original structure expanded, 1785; interior partitioned; 1-story shed porch and aluminum storm doors added. Served as British barracks and hospital during Revolutionary War; housed both Orthodox and Hicksite meetings after the 1821 controversy. *Private:* HABS.

Woolwich Township. **STRATTON, GOV. CHARLES C., HOUSE,** 0.5 mi. E of Swedesboro on King's Hwy., c. 1794. Brick (Flemish bond on front facade); 2 1/2 stories, rectangular, gabled roof, 4 interior end chimneys; 2 gabled dormers, each with round arched windows; center entrance with fanlight set in broken pediment, rear shed porch.

Federal. Birthplace and home of Charles C. Stratton, Congressman (1837–1839, 1841–1843) and first NJ governor elected under 1844 state constitution; died here, 1859. *Private:* HABS.

HUDSON COUNTY

MORRIS CANAL, *Reference—see Essex County*

STATUE OF LIBERTY NATIONAL MONU- MENT, *Reference—see New York County, NY*

Hoboken. **ERIE-LACKAWANNA RAILROAD TERMINAL AT HOBOKEN,** On the Hudson River at the foot of Hudson Pl., 1907, Kenneth Murchison, architect. Stone, copper, and wrought iron with concrete and steel foundation; separate gabled roof sections supported by elaborate pilasters over each train shed; 225′ tower removed and replaced by steel microwave tower. Replaced series of smaller structures. Expertly designed for position over water. *Private.*

Jersey City. **HUDSON COUNTY COURTHOUSE,** Newark and Baldwin Aves., 1910, Hugh Roberts, architect. Steel frame, granite; 4 stories, rectangular, hipped roof behind parapet and balustrade, central dome, coursed rusticated stonework over whole facade, heavy modillion cornice, projecting central pavilion with giant Corinthian columns in antis, arches below, belt course between ground and upper floors, giant columns or pilasters in center bays of each facade. Interior rotunda beneath stained glass dome, original murals by American artists including Frank D. Millet and Edwin Blashfield, giant marble columns and piers around rotunda. Beaux-Arts Classical. *County:* HABS.

Jersey City. **OLD BERGEN CHURCH,** Bergen and Highland Aves., 1842. Brownstone and brick, 1 story, modified rectangle, gabled roof, corner pilasters, clapboarded frieze, full-length Doric portico supported by 6 fluted columns, 2 entrances, square louvered belfry with 3 pilasters at each corner, interior balcony. Greek Revival. Third structure built for Bergen Church congregation. *Private:* HABS.

HUNTERDON COUNTY

Allerton vicinity. **FINK-TYPE TRUSS BRIDGE,** W of Allerton off NJ 31 over South Branch of Raritan River, 1857. Iron, Fink-type truss of 100' single span, 15' wide, stone abutments; constructed by the Trenton Locomotive and Machine Manufacturing Co. Design employing different systems of triangular bracings to distribute weight uniformly. Probably the oldest iron truss bridge in the U.S., designed after 1854 patent of Albert Fink, railroad engineer and later executive. *County:* HAER.

Annandale (Clinton Township). **BRAY-HOFFMAN HOUSE,** On Bray's Hill Rd., Early-19th C.. Brick, 2 1/2 stories, rectangular, gambrel roof, paired interior end chimneys, center entrance with small gabled porch, enclosed side shed porch; interior remodeled with Greek Revival details, 1830's. Federal elements. County's 3rd oldest brick structure; home of prominent area resident, John Bray. *Private; not accessible to the public.*

Clinton. **MCKINNEY, DAVID, MILL,** 56 Main St., c. 1763. Frame, clapboarding; 3 1/2 stories, rectangular, gambrel and gabled roof, late-18th or early-19th C. addition on W. Built by miller David McKinney; first operated as flax seed oil mill, later as a gristmill and salt mill. Mill wheel is restored and operating; much equipment intact. *Private.*

Clinton. **OLD GRANDIN LIBRARY,** 12 E. Main St., 1898. Brick, cast iron front with pressed metal 2nd-story elements; 2 stories, L-shaped, low pitched roof, front center gable with construction date in pediment, inset 1st-story front entrance with flanking windows set in cast iron decorative frame, 4 2nd-story windows separated by decorative pressed metal pilasters and surmounted by fancy cornice; concrete block rear and side addition. Excellent cast iron front building with Second Renaissance Revival elements. Built as public library, served in numerous public capacities. *Municipal; not accessible to the public.*

Lambertville. **MARSHALL, JAMES W., HOUSE,** 60 bridge St., c. 1816. Brick, 2 stories, rectangular, gabled roof, decorative frieze, small bracketed hood over door. House where James Marshall, discoverer of gold at Sutter's Mill, CA, 1848, spent his boyhood (see also Coloma, CA). *State.*

Lambertville vicinity. **DELAWARE AND RARITAN CANAL,** Follows the Delaware River to Trenton, then E to New Brunswick (also in Mercer, Middlesex, and Somerset counties), 1830–1834, Canvass White, engineer. 43-mile canal requiring a lockage of 116′, with 14 locks ranging 7–12′ high; includes 18 lock and bridge tender dwellings, generally small 2-story stone or frame buildings, and 2 tollhouses; principal feature was the navigable feeder, which provided the summit level at Trenton with water from 23 mi. upstream. Designed by one of principal engineers in charge of construction of the Erie Canal; linked the Delaware River, with its traffic of coal boats from the PA anthracite fields, to the port of New York; annual tonnage reached peak in 1866 with 2.3 million tons; operated until 1932; now serves recreational and industrial purposes. *State.*

Pittstown vicinity. **MECHLINS CORNER TAVERN,** NW of Pittstown, c. 1830. Frame, clapboarding; 1 1/2 stories, extended rectangle, gabled roof, interior chimneys, 2 front entrances framed by engaged square columns set under 1-story porch with flat roof, paneled corner pilasters, frieze with decorative iron grilles, denticulated cornice, 2-story W section with shed porch, 1 1/2-story W wing. Greek Revival. Site of tavern from mid-18th C. to 1934. *Private; not accessible to the public.*

Stockton vicinity. **GREEN SERGEANTS COVERED BRIDGE,** N of Stockton off Rosemont-Sergeantsville Rd., 1872, Charles Ogden Holcombe, engineer. Frame with vertical siding, Howe truss of 75' single span, 12' wide stone abutments; reconstructed, 1961. Built on site of 1750 bridge; named for local farmer; state's only extant covered bridge. *Private.*

Stockton vicinity. **LOCKTOWN BAPTIST CHURCH,** W of Stockton on Locktown-Stugeonville Rds., 1819. Fieldstone, 2 stories, rectangular, gabled roof, interior end chimney, 2 pedimented end entrances, shuttered windows, original woodwork. *Private; not accessible to the public.*

MERCER COUNTY

DELAWARE AND RARITAN CANAL, *Reference—see Hunterdon County*

WASHINGTON CROSSING STATE PARK, *Reference—see Bucks County, PA*

Ewing. **GREEN, WILLIAM, HOUSE,** Off NJ 69 on Green Lane, 18th–19th C.. Frame and brick, 2 1/2 stories, L-shaped, gabled roof.

Originally 1 room, 1 1/2-story frame house; 2-story, 3-bay brick addition, 1712; post-1776 clapboarded rear addition; pre-Civil War brick addition and destruction of original structure. Reflects growth of farming family. 1712 section considered earliest extant brick dwelling in Mercer County. *State; not accessible to the public.*

Harbourton (Hopewell Township). **HARBOURTON HISTORIC DISTRICT,** Jct. of Harbourton/Rocktown Rd. and Harbourton/Mt. Airy Rd., 18th-19th C.. District composed of rural crossroads settlement; contains 5 fieldstone and frame structures including church, residences, and former store/inn/post office. Example of vernacular construction and grouping of late-18th and early-19th C. agricultural community. *Multiple private.*

Hightstown. **SLOAN, SAMUEL, HOUSE,** 238 S. Main St., 1856–1859, Samuel Sloan, architect. Frame, clapboarding; 2 1/2 stories, Greek cross shape, flat roof, central cupola, paired bracketed cornice with octagonal windows, full-width front piazza, corner pilasters, off-center entrance. High Victorian Italianate. Built from a Sloan design that may have appeared in a popular building book. Also built in this manner was Sloan's Longwood (see also Longwood, MS). *Private; not accessible to the public.*

Hopewell vicinity. **STOUT, JOSEPH, HOUSE,** Province Line Rd., 1752. Fieldstone, 2 1/2 stories, modified rectangle, gabled roof, paired interior end chimneys, eyebrow dormer, center entrance with blind fanlight and louvered side lights, 1 1/2-story side wing, stone lintels; Greek Revival interior detailing; rear entrance originally the front entrance, 19th and 20th C. alterations. Georgian. Served as Hopewell area headquarters for George Washington; council of war meeting place for Washington and his generals, June 24, 1778. *Private:* HABS.

Lawrence (Lawrence Township). **ANDERSON-CAPNER HOUSE,** 700 Trumbull Ave., c. 1764. Brick, stuccoed; 3 stories, rectangular, hipped roof, paired interior end chimneys, center entrance; early-19th C. alterations included raising half-story and adding end lean-to. Federal elements. Purchased, 1829, by Thomas Capner, member of family that introduced new scientific methods of farming into the area. *Private; not accessible to the public.*

Lawrenceville (Lawrence Township). **LAWRENCE TOWNSHIP HISTORIC DISTRICT,** Lawrenceville and vicinity N, including both sides of U.S. 206, 18th–19th C.. Residential main street district of 2- and 2 1/2-story houses, with good examples of Georgian and mid-19th C. styles. Includes Lawrenceville School buildings by Peabody and Stearns, and campus landscaped by Frederick Law Olmsted. Well-preserved area in town inc. 1697. *Multiple public/private:* HABS.

Lawrenceville vicinity (Lawrence Township). **WHITE, JOHN, HOUSE,** 1 mi. N of Lawrenceville on Cold Soil Rd., c. 1800. Coursed rubble, 2 stories, L-shaped, gabled slate roof, paired interior end chimneys, center entrance with transom and classical frame, regular fenestration; interior retains much original detailing. Federal elements. Example of early-19th C. regional architecture. *Private; not accessible to the public.*

Pennington (Hopewell Township). **HART, JOHN D., HOUSE,** Curlis Ave., c. 1800. Frame, clapboarding; 2 1/2 stories, rectangular, gabled roof, interior end chimneys, molded cornice, off-center entrance with pent roof; interior woodwork similar to that of other area houses; 19th C. side addition. Colonial elements. *Private; not accessible to the public:* HABS.

Pennington (Hopewell Township). **PENNINGTON RAILROAD STATION,** Corner of Franklin and Green Ave., 1882. Stone, 3 stories, rectangular, mansard roof, interior chimneys, segmental arched dormers, bracketed cornice, decorative projecting center roof bay, 1st-floor center bay flanked by an entrance on each side, wide braced shed shelter between 1st and 2nd levels. Second Empire. Accommodated area train traffic; services declined after WWI; use discontinued, 1967. *Private; not accessible to the public.*

Pennington (Hopewell Township). **WELLING, JOHN, HOUSE,** Curlis Ave. at Birch St., Early-18th C.. Frame, clapboarding, round-butt shingling; 1 1/2 stories, rectangular, gabled roof, interior end chimneys; 2 front entrances, each with transom; some hand-wrought hardware and interior clay and horsehair remains; rear shed addition, probably mid-18th C. Dutch Colonial. Property purchased (1728) by John Welling, farmer who emigrated from NY; one of few examples of style in this part of state. *Private:* HABS.

Pennington vicinity (Hopewell Township). **HART-HOCH HOUSE,** SW of Pennington on NJ 546 and Scotch Rd., c. 1800. Brick (Flemish bond facade), 2 1/2 stories, L-shaped, gabled roof, interior end chimneys, off-center entrance with recent hipped porch; wooden lintels and horizontally paneled doors added, 1830's. Federal elements. *Private; not accessible to the public.*

Princeton. **CLEVELAND, GROVER, HOME (WESTLAND),** 15 Hodge Rd., 1854. Stone, stuccoed; 2 1/2 stories, rectangular, gabled roof, bracketed cornice, parapeted deck in center of roof, front Doric porch; later side addition in similar style. Italianate. Home of Grover Cleveland from 1897 to 1908, following the end of his 2nd term as President. *Private; not accessible to the public:* NHL.

Princeton. **HENRY, JOSEPH, HOUSE,** Princeton University campus, 1837. Brick, 2 1/2 stories, rectangular, gabled roof, 4 interior end chimneys, small Doric portico, decorated cornice, 1-story side dependencies. Moved. Greek Revival. Home of Joseph Henry, scientist who developed electromagnet, early electric motor, and electric telegraph, and became first secretary of the Smithsonian Institution (see also Smithsonian Building, DC). *Private; not accessible to the public:* HABS.

Princeton. **MAYBURY HILL (JOSEPH HEWES BIRTHPLACE AND BOYHOOD HOME)** , 346 Snowden Lane, c. 1730. Stone, stuccoed; 2 stories, L-shaped, gabled roof, paired interior end chimneys, denticulated cornice, slightly off-center entrance, 2nd-floor splayed lintels; enlarged and connected to kitchen building, mid-18th C.; stuccoed, c. 1900; outbuildings include large stone barn, probably built by Aaron Hewes, mason and father of Joseph Hewes. Georgian elements. Birthplace and boyhood home of Joseph Hewes, a signer of the Declaration of Independence for NC, merchant, and politician. *Private; not accessible to the public:* NHL.

Princeton. **MORVEN,** 55 Stockton St., 18th C.. Brick, painted; 2 1/2-story center block with 2-story wings, modified rectangle, gabled roof, modillion cornice, 19th C. Doric porches;

restored. Georgian. Home of Richard Stockton, signer of the Declaration of Independence; Cornwallis' headquarters during Battle of Princeton, Jan. 1777; now the official governor's residence. *State:* NHL; HABS.

Princeton. **NASSAU HALL, PRINCETON UNIVERSITY,** Princeton University campus, 1754–1756, Robert Smith, builder-architect. Stone, 3 stories, T-shaped, hipped roof, high central cupola; rusticated arched entranceway, similar opening above it in center pavilion; rebuilt by Benjamin H. Latrobe following fire, 1804; rebuilt and towering cupola added by John Notman following another fire, 1855. Georgian. First important college building of Middle Atlantic colonies, setting pattern for other early college buildings; first permanent building of Princeton University. Served as hospital and barracksduring Revolution; Continental Congress met here, 1783. *Private:* NHL.

Princeton. **PRESIDENT'S HOUSE (MACLEAN HOUSE)** , Nassau St., 1756, Robert Smith, builder-architect. Brick, 2 1/2 stories, L-shaped, gabled roof, interior end chimneys, center shed dormers, center entrance with fanlight set within classical frame, tetrastyle Ionic entrance portico with denticulated cornice, flat arched windows with slightly projecting keystones, 1-story side bay window; rear ell added, 1868. Georgian. Home (1768–1779) of John Witherspoon, early president of Princeton University, delegate to the Second Continental Congress, and signer of the Declaration of Independence. *Private:* NHL; HABS.

Princeton. **PRINCETON BATTLEFIELD,** Princeton Battlefield State Park, 1777. Memorial arch and 18th C. house on battlefield site where Washington defeated the British Army in an encounter on Jan. 3, 1777, following his surprise Christmas raid on Trenton (see also Old Barracks, NJ). These battles greatly restored American morale which had been lowered by a series of British victories in NY and NJ. Scene of Gen. Hugh Mercer's death. *State:* NHL; G.

Titusville vicinity. **SOMERSET ROLLER MILLS**, NJ 29, Early-18th C.. Mill complex containing simple stone house and mill, related outbuildings, and remains of miscellaneous equipment. Machinery here processed grain until Depression. Reflects development of 18th and 19th C. manufacturing process finally replaced by automation. *Private; not accessible to the public*.

Trenton. **BOW HILL (BARNT DE KLYN HOUSE)** , Jeremiah Ave. off Lalor St., 18th C.. Brick, 2 1/2 stories, modified rectangle, gambrel roof, paired interior end chimneys; pedimented front dormers, each with round arched window; front center recessed entrance with fanlight and flanking pilasters; elaborate interior trim; some Greek Revival molding added, 1830's. Excellent example of elaborate Federal dwelling. Built by Barnt de Klyn, wealthy area merchant and landowner. *Private; not accessible to the public:* HABS.

Trenton. **DICKINSON, GEN. PHILEMON, HOUSE (THE HERMITAGE)**, 46 Colonial Ave., 1784. Stone, stuccoed; 2 stories, hipped roof, 2 interior chimneys, off-center entrance, projecting pedimented hoods over far-right windows, cast iron attic window grilles in frieze; extensive remodeling, 1905, included demolition of the original 1705 section which made the rear facade the front, and divided the interior into apartments. Home of Revolutionary War general Philemon Dickinson, commander in chief of the NJ militia. *Private; not accessible to the public*.

Trenton. **DOUGLASS HOUSE,** Corner of Front and Montgomery Sts., 1766. Frame, clapboarding; 2 stories, L-shaped, 2 interior chimneys, cornice on front and rear facades, 1 1/2-story ell. Moved. Washington held a Council of War here on Jan. 2, 1777, after the 2nd Battle of Trenton. *Municipal:* HABS.

Trenton. **MANSION HOUSE (MCCALL HOUSE, ELLARSLIE)** , Cadwalader Park, 1845–1846, John Notman, architect. Brick, scored stucco; 2 stories, modified T shape, low gabled roof, interior chimneys, tower with triple round arched windows, belt course; original exterior details removed, 1935–1936. Italian Villa. Early example of work of Philadelphia architect John Notman, who introduced Italian Villa style to America. *Municipal.*

Trenton. **MERCER STREET FRIENDS CENTER (CHESTERFIELD FRIENDS MEETINGHOUSE)** , 151 Mercer St., 1858. Brick, 1 story, rectangular, gabled roof, interior end chimneys, porch with separate center entrances for men and women, side porch; 1-story shed addition, 1963–1964. Built for a faction from the Chesterfield Monthly Meeting of The Religious Society of Friends. *Private.*

Trenton. **OLD BARRACKS,** S. Willow St., 1758–1759. Fieldstone, 2 1/2 stories, U-shaped, gabled roof; 2 levels of galleries around inside of U, dormers, modillion cornice, pedimented doors; altered. Central wing reconstructed; building restored, 1917. Georgian. Built as barracks during French and Indian War; housed American, English, and Hessian soldiers during Revolution. Quartered Hessian troops during Washington's surprise Christmas night raid across the Delaware River, 1776. Museum. *State:* NHL; HABS.

Trenton. **OLD EAGLE TAVERN,** 431, 433 S. Broad St., c. 1765. Brick, 2 1/2 stories, rectangular, gabled roof; paired interior end chimneys connected by parapet, central and end chimney; molded cornice, gabled dormers, full-width front and rear hipped porches, 2 doorways; late-18th or early-19th C. extension; interior gutted mid-20th C. Georgian elements. Probably oldest commercial structure in vicinity. *Municipal; not accessible to the public.*

Trenton. **TRENT, WILLIAM, HOUSE,** 539 S. Warren St., 1719. Brick, 2 stories, rectangular, low hipped roof, large interior end chimneys, central hexagonal cupola, modillion cornice, segmental arches over 1st-floor openings, center door with transom. Restored, 1930's. Georgian. Constructed by merchant William Trent, on whose property the township of Trent Town was laid out, 1721. Museum. *Municipal;* NHL; HABS.

Trenton. **WATSON, ISAAC, HOUSE,** 151 Westcott St., 1708. Stone, 2 1/2 stories, rectangular, steeply gabled roof, interior end chimneys, extensively restored (mid-1960's). Built by pioneer Isaac Watson, farmer, surveyor, constable, and overseer of the highways. *County.*

Trenton (Ewing Township). **OLD RYAN FARM,** Federal City Rd., 18th–19th C.. Frame, clapboarding; 2 1/2 stories, rectangular, gabled roof, interior end chimneys, center entrance with small hipped porch; interior paneling and hardware c. 1750; original (c. 1710) 1 1/2-story structure with lean-to kitchen enlarged c. 1750; remodeled and raised one story, c. 1840. Area example of early frame farmhouse. *Private; not accessible to the public.*

MIDDLESEX COUNTY

DELAWARE AND RARITAN CANAL,
Reference—see Hunterdon County

Cranbury. **OLD CRANBURY SCHOOL,** 23 N.
Main St., 1896. Brick, 2 stories, rectangular,
gabled roof, central projecting pavilion
(original building) with front gable, bracketed
cornice with return on gable, square cupola,
segmental arched windows, corbeled arches;
20th C. wings, altered. Italianate. *Municipal.*

New Brunswick. **QUEEN'S CAMPUS, RUT-
GERS UNIVERSITY,** Bounded by College
Ave. and George, Hamilton, and Somerset Sts.,
18th–19th C.. Original Rutgers University campus; opened 1770's as Queen's College, named
for Queen Charlotte. First building (Old
Queen's) built 1809–1825, designed by John
McComb. Name changed for Col. Henry Rutgers, trustee. Expansion after state land grant,
1862. Site where Alexander Hamilton protected Washington's crossing of Raritan River
and where Hessian troops were stationed. Part
of present day Rutgers University. *Private:*
HABS.

Perth Amboy. **PROPRIETORY HOUSE (THE
WESTMINISTER),** 139–151 Kearny Ave.,
1764. Brick over stone basement, 3 1/2 stories,
L-shaped, gambrel roof, square cupola, slightly
projecting central pavilion beneath pediment,
round arched openings in center of pavilion on
1st and 2nd floors, brick string course, c. 1809
rear addition, front porch. Altered. Georgian.
Built as residence for provincial governor;
headquarters for Gen. Howe during British occupation of town, 1776; hotel for much of 19th
C. *State:* HABS.

Piscataway. **FITZ-RANDOLPH, EPHRAIM, HOUSE,** 430 S. Randolphville Rd., 1825. Frame, brick nogging, clapboarding; 2 1/2 stories, modified rectangle, gambrel and gabled roof sections, 2 interior chimneys, off-center entrance with 1-story hipped porch; side hall plan; 2-story gabled wing. Federal elements. Home of locally prominent Randolph family. *Private:* HABS.

Piscataway. **IVY HALL (CORNELIUS LOWE HOUSE),** 1225 River Rd., Sandstone (coursed front facade), 2 1/2 stories, rectangular, hipped roof, paired interior end chimneys, modillion cornice; jack arches over lower-floor windows in front, segmental in rear; later entrance porch and dormers. Georgian. Imposing 18th-C. home. *Private:* HABS.

Piscataway. **METLAR HOUSE (KNAPP HOUSE, BODINE HOUSE)** , 1281 River Rd., 1728. Frame, clapboarding; 1 1/2–2 1/2 stories, modified rectangle, gabled roof sections, interior chimneys, 1-story 4-bay entrance porch set on piers with centered entrance with fanlight and side lights, off-center Dutch-door entrance, lunette in front gable, side porch; original 1 1/2-story W section expanded by construction of a 2 1/2-story section with main entrance and porch, early-19th C., and a 2 1/2-story end section. Greek Revival elements. Original section built by Peter Bodine, 1728; one of 2 structures remaining from extensive 18th C. settlement at Raritan Landing. *Private; not accessible to the public.*

Piscataway. **ONDERDONK, ISAAC, HOUSE,** 685 River Rd., c. 1750. Frame, brick-filled, shingled; 2 1/2 stories, gabled roof. Original interior construction: exposed oak beams, wide pine floorboards, and mantels and hearths.

Originally 2-room central hall structure; later additions include 2 rooms, 2nd story, and shed-like extension. Built by the Onderdonks, a prominent Dutch family. *Private.*

Piscataway. **SMOCK, MATTHIAS, HOUSE,** Off River Rd. (NJ 18), c. 1720. Frame, clapboarding; 1 1/2 stories, gabled roof with front dormers; side addition with shed roof; original wide pine floorboards; restored and modernized, 1950–1971; 3 outbuildings. Dutch influence. County's earliest documented house. *Private:* HABS.

MONMOUTH COUNTY

Englishtown. **VILLAGE INN (DAVIS TAVERN)**, Water and Main Sts., 1732. Frame, shingling; 2 stories, modified T shape, gabled roof, interior end chimneys, center cross gable, full-width porch; wings and rear ell added, 19th C. Served as Gen. Washington's headquarters, June 1778, when he ordered the arrest of Gen. Charles Lee for failure to attack the enemy. *Private; not accessible to the public:* HABS.

Farmingdale. **ALLAIRE VILLAGE (HOWELL WORKS, MONMOUTH FURNACE)**, 3 mi. SE of Farmingdale on NJ 524, 18th–19th C.. Mostly brick, gabled industrial, commercial, and residential buildings, dating from 1822 to 1850 when complex was owned by James P. Allaire, a brass founder from NY. Earlier structures dating from period of Monmouth Furnace and Howell Works include 2 houses, iron furnace stack, and casting house wall. Bog iron industry of Allaire was significant in state's early industrial development. *State:* HABS.

Freehold. **HANKINSON-MOREAU-COVEN-HOVEN HOUSE (CLINTON'S HEADQUARTERS)**, 150 W. Main St., c. 1706. Frame, round-butt shingling, clapboarding; 2 1/2 stories, L-shaped, gabled roof, 2 interior chimneys, shed hood over off-center entrance framed by pilasters, 1 1/2-story kitchen wing, E lean-to; master bedroom contains decorative painted woodwork and a painting of ships on panel over fireplace; remodeled, c. 1750; restored. Colonial elements. Occupied by Sir Henry Clinton before the Battle of Monmouth, June 1778, the first engagement of Washington's troops after wintering at Valley Forge. *Private:* NHL; HABS.

Freehold (Manalapan Township). **MONMOUTH BATTLEFIELD,** NW of Freehold on NJ 522, W of Rte. 9, 1778. 1450-acre battlefield site in slightly altered condition, where Washington's army attacked the British under Gen. Clinton in the first action by the American forces after the winter at Valley Forge. Though the British continued onto the coast, the battle demonstrated the quality of the American army. Battle in which Mary Ludwig Hays earned the name "Molly Pitcher" by carrying water to the wounded and exhausted. Museum. *State:* NHL.

Highlands. **TWIN LIGHTS (NAVESINK LIGHTHOUSE),** S of NJ 36 on a promontory between the Navesink River and Sandy Hook Bay, 1826. Stone, octagonal and square lighthouse towers 73' high, one rebuilt and both connected in 1862 by crenelated ranges with central pavilion. First Fresnal lens used in U.S. installed, 1841; first electric arc lamp in U.S. lighthouse installed, 1898. Museum. *State.*

Holmdel   vicinity.   **KOVENHOVEN (KOUVENHOVEN)**, N of Holmdel off NJ 34, c. 1700. Frame, shingling; 1 1/2 stories, rectangular, gabled roof, irregular fenestration, numerous alterations, original E section enlarged before 1735. Colonial elements. Built by Cornelius Van Kowenhoven, one of area's earliest settlers. *Private:* HABS.

Holmdel vicinity. **OLD KENTUCK**, NW of Holmdel off NJ 34 on Pleasant Valley Rd., c. 1770. Two 2 1/2-story sections—main section and extension on lower level; frame, shingles, gabled roof, double gable end chimneys, side porch extension, some original interior woodwork. Early American and Dutch building elements. Home of Col. Asher Holmes, Revolutionary patriot. *Private; not accessible to the public.*

Manalapan vicinity (Manalapan Township). **ANDERSON HOUSE,** E of Manalapan on NJ 33, 18th–19th C.. Frame, clapboarding, round-butt shingling, flush siding, 1 1/2–2 stories, rectangular, gabled roof sections, 3 interior end chimneys; probable original W 1 1/2-story section has 2 gabled roof dormers, round-butt shingling, and attached 1-story shed; 2-story later frame sections with flush siding, clapboarding, cove cornice, 1-story shed porch on front facade; hand-hewn oak walls with brick nogging. Example of regional rural domestic architecture showing progression in construction. *Private; not accessible to the public.*

Matawan. **BURROWES, MAJ. JOHN, MANSION (ENCHANTED CASTLE)** , 94 Main St., 1723. Frame, round-butt shingling and clapboarding; 2 stories, modified rectangle, gambrel roof, interior end chimneys, modillion cornice, recessed entrance with double doors and transom; 2-story wing, possibly late-18th C. Colonial elements. Built for John Bowne, prominent provincial assemblyman; scene of Maj. John Burrowes' daring escape from Tories in 1778. *Private; not accessible to the public:* HABS.

Middleton. **KINGS HIGHWAY DISTRICT,** Irregular pattern—both sides of Kings Highway, S and W of NJ 35, 1664–20th C.. Heart of oldest NJ settlement, contains early colonial structures such as the Richard Hartshorne House (c. 1675) and later structures such as the Greek Revival Locustwood (1832). Located at jct. of 3 major Indian trails, one of which provided easy access to the sea and which later became part of the famed Kings Highway. *Multiple private.*

Middletown. **CHRIST CHURCH,** 92 Kings Hwy., 1835. Frame, clapboarding; 2 stories, L-shaped, gabled roof, square louvered belfry with 4 corner pinnacles, center pointed arched entrance beneath iron cross, louvered quatrefoil window in gable, pointed arched windows with louvered shutters. Gothic Revival. Built around walls of 1744 church. *Public/private:* HABS.

Middletown. **SEABROOK-WILSON HOUSE,** 119 Port Monmouth Rd., 1750. Frame, clapboarding with shingling on gable end; 2 1/2 stories, modified rectangle, gabled roof, interior end chimneys, off-center door, 1-story front entrance porch; side wing with shed addition is original; expanded, c. 1850 and c. 1880. Colonial elements. House shows a progression of 18th–19th C. construction. Museum. *Municipal.*

Navesink. **ALL SAINTS' MEMORIAL CHURCH COMPLEX,** Navesink Ave. and Locust Rd., 1864, Richard Upjohn, architect. Coursed fieldstone, 1 story, steeply pitched gabled roof, interior chimney, decorative bargeboards, round arched main entrance, 2 minor entrances, open belfry, pointed stained glass windows with Gothic tracery by Doremus and Sharp, ornately carved interior beams; parish house, rectory, and other outbuildings. Gothic Revival. *Private.*

New Shrewsbury. **OLD MILL AT TINTON FALLS,** 1205 Sycamore Ave., 1676. Stone and frame, shingling and flush siding; 3-story front, 7-story rear over hillside; rectangular, shed roof; rear lower stories of stone, extended with brick; roof altered; shed porch added; altered. Used as powder magazine by Americans during Revolutionary War, raided several times by British and sympathizers; used as gristmill into 20th C. *Private.*

Sandy Hook. **SANDY HOOK LIGHT,** 1764. Stone, tapered octagonal tower 85' high with lantern at top and walls 7' thick at base; rebuilt, 1857. Reputedly the oldest lighthouse in the U.S.; in continuous use with exception of interruptions during the Revolution and WWII. *Federal/USCG:* NHL.

Shrewsbury. **ALLEN HOUSE,** Broad St. and Sycamore Ave., c. 1670. Frame, round-butted shingling, clapboarding; 2 1/2 stories, rectangular, gambrel roof, interior and exterior end chimneys, off-center entrance, 1-story W wing, brick smokehouse. Colonial elements reflecting early Dutch and English construction. Restored, 1970. One of the county's earliest houses; part of historic Four Corners of Shrewsbury; 1779 scene of British capture of local troops. *Private; not accessible to the public:* HABS.

Shrewsbury. **WARDELL HOUSE,** 419 Sycamore Ave., 1764. Frame, clapboarding; 2 1/2 stories, rectangular, hipped roof, shed dormers; early-19th C. alterations included entrance pilasters, side lights, transom, and many interior decorative elements; 2 20th C. wings. 19th C. carriage house enclosing earlier building. Greek Revival elements. Built by prominent local citizen John Wardell, later exiled as Loyalist leader during Revolution. *Private; not accessible to the public.*

MORRIS COUNTY

MORRIS CANAL, *Reference—see Essex County*

Boonton. **BOONTON PUBLIC LIBRARY (JAMES HOLMES LIBRARY)** , 619 Main St., 1849. Frame, clapboarding; 3 stories, rectangular, low hipped roof; altered late-19th C. by addition of 3rd story with bracketed cornice and paneled frieze, and 3-story polygonal bay over entrance porch. Italianate elements. Owned by James Holmes from 1856 until his death in 1893; he bequeathed it to the Boonton Public Library Association. *Municipal.*

Boonton. **MILLER-KINGSLAND HOUSE,** Vreeland Ave., 900′ W of Montville Township boundary, c. 1740, 1808. W wing (1740): frame, stone fireplace wall, 1 1/2 stories, gabled roof with Dutch sweep. Main section (1808): 2 1/2-story frame dwelling, gambrel roof, front entrance porch, much original interior hardware and woodwork. Early American and Dutch elements. Earlier structure is Boonton's oldest house. *Private; not accessible to the public:* HABS.

Boonton vicinity. **SPLIT ROCK FURNACE,** NW of Boonton, 1862. Remains of iron-manufacturing community consisting of stone ruins of blast furnace, casting furnace, crushing mill, and numerous foundations. Industrial site since 1793; last charcoal furnaces built in the state. *Private; not accessible to the public:* HABS.

Chester. **CHESTER HOUSE INN,** Main St. and Hillside Rd., 1812. Brick and frame (clapboarding) sections, 3–3 1/2 stories, L-shaped, gabled roof sections, 1 set bridged interior end chimneys, 2-story balustraded porch with bracketed supports and cornice at 2nd story, recessed entrance with semielliptical fanlight; frame ell added, 1854. Federal. Nearly continuous use as an inn. *Private:* HABS.

Dover vicinity. **FORD-FAESCH HOUSE,** N of Dover at Mt. Hope Rd. and Mt. Hope Ave., 1768–1770. Stone, partially stuccoed; 2 1/2 stories, rectangular, gabled roof, interior and exterior end chimney, 1-bay pedimented center entrance porch, SW bay window, 2-story frame side addition. Extensive alterations. Georgian. Built for Jacob Ford, Jr., operator of local iron mine which supplied cannons and ammunition for Continental Army under direction of ironmaster John Jacob Faesch, prominent local official later elected to state convention ratifying the U.S. Constitution. *Private; not accessible to the public.*

Dover vicinity (Randolph Township). **FRIENDS MEETINGHOUSE,** S of Dover at Quaker Ave. and Quaker Church Rd., off NJ 18, 1758. Frame, clapboarding; 1 1/2 stories, rectangular, gabled roof, central chimney, center entrance; interior exposed framing, simple bench pews, and drop partition to separate congregation; clapboards and shingles replaced, chimney installed, 19th C. Built to house Quaker congregation founded 1740. *Private:* HABS.

Florham Park. **FORD, SAMUEL JR.'S, HAM-MOCK FARM**, 310 Columbia Tpke., 1766–1773. Stone, frame with clapboarding; 1/2–2 1/2 stories, modified rectangle, gabled and gambrel roof sections, interior end chimneys, modillion cornice section, bay window; original 1 1/2-story stone and clapboarded section has porch; 2-story frame section added, early-19th C. Federal elements. Home of Samuel Ford, Jr., state's most notorious colonial criminal and counterfeiter. *Private.*

Florham Park. **LITTLE RED SCHOOL-HOUSE**, Ridgedale Ave. at Columbia Tpke., 19th–20th C.. Brick, 1 story, rectangular, gabled roof, square bell tower, front gabled entry with double doors and segmental transom. Enlarged. Second structure on site of town's first public school. In use as 1-room schoolhouse until 1914. *Municipal.*

Mendham. **THOMPSON, DAVID, HOUSE**, 56 W. Main St., 1770's, Daniel Carey, master mason. Uncoursed stone, 2 1/2 stories, central hall, gabled roof, inset entrance with transom, 1 1/2-story kitchen wing with 19th C. frame addition. Original hardware, woodwork, doors, and mantels. Early American structure. Built for David Thompson, delegate to Provincial Congress and captain of local militia. *Private; not accessible to the public:* HABS.

Morristown. **ACORN HALL**, 68 Morris Ave., 1853. Frame, clapboarding; 2 1/2 stories, modified rectangle, gabled roof sections, cornice with paired scroll brackets, gabled dormers, center polygonal 3-story entrance tower with paired round arched windows and paneled frieze; front and rear verandas with intricate, curvilinear jigsawn work; bracketed hood over 2nd-floor center window, 1-story polygonal bay on side wing; fine interiors with original furnishings. Italian Villa. Ornate well-preserved house. Museum. *Private.*

Morristown. **CONDICT, DR. LEWIS, HOUSE,** 51 South St., 1797. Frame, clapboarding; 2 1/2 stories, modified rectangle, gambrel roof, center entrance with side lights and transom, 20th C. pedimented portico with modillion cornice; center gabled roof dormer with round arched window added, 1870; later rear additions. Federal. Built for prominent physiciar. Dr. Lewis Condict, who held state and national positions in the medical profession, and served in U.S. Congress. *Private.*

Morristown. **MORRISTOWN DISTRICT,** 19th–20th C.. Residential area of town which developed around Macculloch Hall, early-19th C. Federal style building built by George P. Macculloch and used for military, political, and educational activities. Settled by military veterans such as Christopher Raymond Perry Rodgers and Gen. Joseph W. Revere (see also Joseph W. Revere House, NJ) and other notables including political cartoonist and satirist Thomas Nast. Federal, Greek and Gothic Revival, and various Victorian styles represented. *Multiple public/private:* HABS.

Morristown. **MORRISTOWN NATIONAL HISTORICAL PARK,** At jct. of U.S. 202 and NJ 24 (also in Somerset County), 1777, 1779–1780. Site of winter quarters for Washington's Continental Army contains mansion and farmhouse which served as officers' headquarters, and reconstructions of log huts built 1779. First used Jan. 1777 after American victories at Trenton and Princeton (see also Washington Crossing State Park, PA, and Princeton Battlefield, NJ). Scene of unsuccessful mutiny after soldiers suffered worst hardships of war during winter of 1779–1780. *Federal/NPS/non-federal:* HABS.

Morristown. **NAST, THOMAS, HOME (VILLA FONTANA),** MacCulloch Ave. and Miller Rd., 1860–1861. Frame, 2 1/2 stories, square, mansard roof, modillion cornice, segmental arched dormers, flat window cornices, later Georgian elements, original porch removed. Originally Second Empire. From 1873 to 1902 the home of Thomas Nast, foremost political cartoonist employed by *Harper's Weekly* from 1862 to 1887, credited with major role in breaking up New York City's Tweed Ring. *Private:* HABS.

Morristown. **SPEEDWELL VILLAGE–THE FACTORY,** 333 Speedwell Ave., 1837–1838. Frame, stone foundation; 2 1/2 stories over basement, modified rectangle, gabled roof, corbeled interior end chimney; 1-story end extension; interior painted and sealed; originally functioned as gristmill, with millstones and other equipment intact; restored, 1972–1973. Site where Samuel F. B. Morse perfected electromagnetic telegraph in winter of 1837–1838. Museum. (See also Speedwell Village, NJ). *Private:* NHL.

Morristown. **SPEEDWELL VILLAGE,** 333 Speedwell Ave., 18th and 19th C.. Site of 19th C. ironworks complex operated by Vail family, including building originally on site and several moved here. Factory which manufactured engine and parts for S.S. *Savanna*, first vessel to cross Atlantic aided by steam, and where Samuel F. B. Morse and Alfred Vail perfected the electromagnetic telegraph, 1837. Area's iron ore deposits had attracted settlers in 18th C., iron forge in vicinity by 1776. Museum. *Private:* G.

Morristown vicinity. **REVERE, JOSEPH W., HOUSE,** NW of Morristown on Mendham Ave., 19th C.. Frame, clapboarding; 2 1/2 stories, L-shaped; front gabled overhang supported by open stick work of pointed arches, uprights and crossbeams; glassed center entrance vestibule, 2nd-story balcony extending to stickwork, label window molding, gabled wing, 4 outbuildings, much original interior decoration. Gothic Revival elements. Designed, 1854, by Gen. Joseph W. Revere, grandson of Paul Revere; occupied by Bret Harte, 1874–1875. *Private; not accessible to the public.*

Parsippany.   **BOWERS-LIVINGSTON-OSBORN HOUSE,** 25 Parsippany Rd., c. 1761. Frame, clapboarding; 2 1/2 stories, rectangular, gambrel roof, 3 interior end chimneys, center entrance with side lights and transom; full-width 1-story front and rear porches, partially enclosed rear sections; 2-story side bay window; basement partially paved with cobblestones, pegged hand-hewn timbers in attic; one chimney removed, c. 1890. Colonial elements. Possibly built as tavern by Lemuel Bowers; leased from 1777 to 1780 to William Livingston, first NJ governor after Independence. *Private;* HABS.

Parsippany vicinity. **CONDIT, STEPHEN, HOUSE,** NE of Parsippany on Beverwyck Rd. off U.S. 46, 1870. Frame, clapboarding; 2 1/2 stories, T-shaped, intersecting gabled roof with decorative bargeboards and finials, 2 interior chimneys, open entrance portico with decorative trim, full-width N porch, projecting rear porch, segmental arched windows with louvered shutters, wellhouse. Eastlake elements. Built for Stephen Hobart Condit, local businessman and official whose family remained influential in community affairs. *Private.*

Pompton Plains. **BERRY, MARTIN, HOUSE,** 581 NJ 23 at Jackson Ave., 18th C.. Rubble, partially stuccoed, and frame, clapboarding; 1

1/2 stories, modified rectangle, gambrel roof, paired interior end chimneys, front and rear gabled and hipped dormers; front center entrance with side lights, pediment, and front porch; attached gabled smokehouse. Dutch Colonial. Reputedly built 1720 by Martin Berry, member of early area family. *Private:* HABS.

Towaco. **DOREMUS HOUSE,** 490 Main Rd., Late-18th C.. Rubble and frame, clapboarding; 1 1/2 stories, modified rectangle, gabled roof, interior end chimneys, 2 front entrances; rear frame addition; 2-room interior with no hall. Dutch Colonial. Built by Henry Doremus in the settlement of Doremus Town; George Washington stayed here briefly in June 1780. *Private; not accessible to the public:* HABS.

Washington Valley. **WASHINGTON VALLEY SCHOOLHOUSE,** Washington Valley Rd. and Schoolhouse Lane, 1869. Brick (common bond), 1 1/2 stories, rectangular, gabled roof, square cupola, 2 entrances at gable end, 1 outbuilding. Replaced original schoolhouse; operated as 1-room schoolhouse until May 1913. *Municipal.*

OCEAN COUNTY

Barnegat Light. **BARNEGAT LIGHTHOUSE,** N end of Long Beach Island, off Broadway Ave., 1857, George Meade, engineer. Brick, tapering cylindrical shape, 163′ high, iron staircase inside. Built by Meade, later commander of Union forces at Gettysburg; operated as lighthouse from 1857–1927. Museum. *State:* HABS.

Manahawkin (Stafford Township). **MANAHAWKIN BAPTIST CHURCH,** N. Main St. (US 9) and Lehigh Ave., Mid-18th C..

Frame, clapboarding; 1 1/2 stories, modified rectangle, gabled roof sections, interior chimney, bracketed cornice with end returns; cupola with balustrade and rectangular and round arched openings, pyramidal roof; original interior woodwork; altered 1860's by construction of exterior walls and floor around earlier structure, repaired and altered 1870's; rear baptistry added later. Possibly oldest church in county; originally built as "free church" open to circuit riders of all denominations. *Private.*

Manchester Township. **HANGAR NO. 1, LAKEHURST NAVAL AIR STATION,** N of Lakehurst on CR 547, 1921. Steel, brick, and concrete; enormous rectangular building 966' long, 350' wide, and 224' high beneath a monitor roof; large motorized doors, one open space inside with exposed steel framing. Known as the American Airship Center, headquarters for lighter-than-air flight in the U.S.; housed the Navy's rigid airships in the 1920's and 1930's; international landing port where the German zeppelin *Hindenburg* crashed in 1937. (See also Goodyear Airdock, OH) *Federal/USN:* NHL.

PASSAIC COUNTY

Haledon. **BOTTO, PIETRO, HOUSE,** 83 Norwood St., 1907–1908. Stone, later aluminum siding on front; 2 stories, rectangular, flat roof, interior chimneys, 2 cross gables over 2-story bay windows flanking center porch and balcony; front porch and facade altered. During 1913 Paterson textile workers' strike, thousands gathered across from the Botto residence to hear speeches from the balcony; strike led by Industrial Workers of the World ended unsuccessfully after nearly 6 months. *Private.*

Mountain View (Wayne Township). **VAN DUYNE HOUSE**, Berdan Ave., Early-18th C.. Rubble, 1 1/2 stories, modified L shape, gabled roof sections, 3 interior chimneys, "1706" date stone, 2 entrances on facade, exterior cellar entrance; frame additions, 1750 and 1800; restored c. 1950. Dutch colonial structure built by Dominie Peter Van Duyne, minister from New Amsterdam; possibly used by Revolutionary couriers as way station. *Municipal:* HABS.

Paterson. **GREAT FALLS OF PATERSON (S.U.M.) HISTORIC DISTRICT**, Roughly that area along reservoir and Passaic River between Grand St. on the S and Ryle Ave. on the N, 1793–1912. Unique operating industrial district encompassing variety of brick and stone buildings from 1803 to 1912, still largely in use; and waterworks, including a mi.-long 3-tiered masonry raceway system and masonry, iron-reinforced dam from the late-18th and first half of the 19th C. First planned industrial development in U.S.; area initially laid out for the Society for Useful Manufactures in 1793 by Pierre Charles L'Enfant. *Multiple public/private:* HAER.

Paterson. **WESTSIDE PARK (VAN HOUTEN HOUSE)** , 114 Totowa Ave., Mid-18th C.. Brownstone ashlar, 1 1/2 stories, modified rectangle, gambrel and gabled roof sections, 2 interior chimneys; older wing with gabled roof and wide overhanging cornice; larger gambrel roof section with off-center entrance with fanlight, side lights, paired Ionic columns with broken entablature, and fluted archivolt; "1831" date stone in center of facade; larger section rebuilt 1831 following fire. Dutch Colonial with Greek Revival elements. Among few remaining pre-Revolutionary houses in NJ. *Municipal; not accessible to the public:* HABS.

Ringwood Borough. **RINGWOOD MANOR**, 3 mi. E of Hewitt, Ringwood Manor State Park, 18th and 19th C.. 758-acre park contains 78-room 19th C. manor house with eclectic elements; site of ironworks; and numerous outbuildings including dairy (originally stamp mill), waterwheel, and blacksmith shop. Associated with iron industry since 1739. Owned and operated by notable individuals such as Robert Erskine who served as George Washington's geographer during the Revolution; Peter Cooper, founder of Cooper Union (see also Cooper Union, NY); and statesman and philanthropist Abram S. Hewitt. *State:* NHL; HABS.

Wayne. **DEY MANSION**, 199 Totowa Rd., 1740. Stone, brick; 2 1/2 stories, rectangular, gambrel roof with kick at eaves, modillion cornice, brick front facade with stone quoining and window and door surrounds, stone belt courses and foundation; stone side and rear walls; center door with transom, tripartite 2nd-floor window above; small 1-story attached outbuilding. Georgian. Washington's headquarters during July, Oct. and Nov., 1780. Museum. *County:* HABS.

Wayne. **SCHUYLER-COLFAX HOUSE**, 2343 Paterson Hamburg Tpke., c. 1696. Random rubble, brick, and frame with clapboarding; 1 1/2 stories, rectangular, gambrel roof, 2 interior chimneys, large entablature on facade broken by 3 hipped wall dormers; full-width porch, center entrance with transom; "1696" carved in attic beam; porch and dormers added 1850. Dutch colonial elements. *Private:* HABS.

Wayne vicinity. **VAN RIPER-HOPPER HOUSE (WAYNE MUSEUM)** , 533 Berdan Ave., 1786. Rubble, frame with clapboarding; 1 1/2 stories, modified rectangle, gabled roof, interior chim-

neys, 19th C. gabled dormers, full-width porch,
Dutch door entrance and entrance with
transom; cross gable on frame and stone wing;
altered. Dutch colonial elements. Built by early
settler and miller, Uriah Van Riper; later occupied by Andrew Hopper, an active local citizen.
Museum. *Municipal.*

West Milford vicinity. **LONG POND IRON-
WORKS,** NE of West Milford on NJ 511, 1766,
19th C.. Site of 3 furnaces used to smelt high
grade magnetite and hematite ores. Contains
intact Westman Kiln, waterwheels, frame ironmaster's house, 2 dwellings, the ruins of 2 furnaces, and foundations of several structures; 1
furnace excavated, 1963. *State.*

SALEM COUNTY

Lower Alloways Creek Township. **HANCOCK
HOUSE,** Rte. 49 and Front St., 1728. Brick
(Flemish bond with glazed headers), rectangular, gabled roof, dormers, center door with
transom, shed hood across facade at 2nd-floor
level; gable end with "HWS" initials, "1734"
and vertical zigzag pattern in glazed headers;
enlarged to present state, 1734. Site of Mar. 21,
1778, ambush where British troops under Col.
John Simcoe killed a party of Patriots stationed
in the house. Museum. *State:* HABS.

SOMERSET COUNTY

DELAWARE AND RARITAN CANAL,
Reference—see Hunterdon County

**MORRISTOWN NATIONAL HISTORICAL
PARK,** *Reference—see Morris County*

Basking Ridge. **PRESBYTERIAN CHURCH IN
BASKING RIDGE,** 6 E. Oak St., 1839, William

Kirk and Thomas Kirkpatrick, builders. Brick, 1 story, rectangular, gabled roof, front square louvered belfry with gold-leafed dome, full-width tetrastyle entrance portico with pediment oculi, 2 front entrances; numerous NE additions; remodeled. Greek Revival. Built on site of 2 previous churches; visited by English evangelist George Whitfield; congregation's 5th pastor, Robert Finley, instigated organization of American Colonization Society, which sponsored a colony of emancipated American slaves in Africa. *Private:* HABS.

Franklin. **MEADOWS, THE,** 1289 Easton Ave., 1722. Frame, shingling in imbricated pattern; 1 1/2 stories, gabled roof with front overhang, entrance with transom bar, later kitchen addition, exposed interior post and beam construction. Typical early-18th C. vernacular style. One of county's oldest dwellings. *Private:* HABS.

Franklin Township. **ROCKINGHAM (OLD BERRIEN HOUSE),** E of Kingston on Old Rocky Hill Rd. (518), 1734. Frame, 2 stories, L-shaped, gabled roof, original block with large central chimney, later 2-story front verandas, side and rear additions. Colonial elements. Washington's headquarters from Aug. to Nov. 1783, while Congress met at Princeton. Museum. *State:* HABS.

Raritan. **FRELINGHUYSEN, GEN. JOHN, HOUSE,** Somerset St. and Wyckoff Ave., Early-19th C.. Main original block of extended L-shaped house: brick, 2 1/2 stories, rectangular, gambrel roof with small steps in gable ends at chimneys and eaves; belt course and water table, stone sills; later tetrastyle Doric portico; Adamesque mantel within. Federal. *Municipal:* HABS.

Somerville. **OLD DUTCH PARSONAGE,** 65 Washington Pl., 1751. Brick, 2 1/2 stories, rectangular, gabled roof, center entrance, clapboarded gable ends; moved, 1913; altered. Georgian. Built by Congregation of the First Reformed Dutch Church as parsonage and residence for theological students. Second owner, Rev. Jacobus Hardenbergh, was instrumental in establishing Queen's College (now Rutgers University) and served as its first president. *State:* HABS.

Somerville. **WALLACE HOUSE,** 38 Washington Pl., 1778. Frame, clapboarding; 2 1/2 stories, rectangular, interior chimneys, older 1 1/2-story wing, porches added. Headquarters for Gen. Washington, 1778–1779; he and his wife were house's first occupants. Museum. *State:* HABS.

SUSSEX COUNTY

MORRIS CANAL, *Reference—see Essex County*

Newton. **MERRIAM, HENRY W., HOUSE,** 131 Main St., c. 1883. Frame, clapboarding; 2 1/2 stories, modified rectangle; hipped and pyramid roof sections with gables and dormers, patterned roof shingling; corner tower surrounded by verandas, porte-cochere with room above; elaborate carved woodwork and spindlework on posts, balusters, fascias and brackets; rear addition, carriage house and cottage on site, all late-19th or early-20th C. Eastlake. Constructed for one of town's manufacturers, Henry W. Merriam. *Private.*

Sussex vicinity. **VAN BUNSCHOOTEN, ELIAS, HOUSE,** NW of Sussex on NJ 23, c. 1790. Frame, clapboarding; 2 1/2 stories over basement, modified rectangle, gabled roof, interior end chimneys, pedimented center entrance portico, front and rear shed porches, 2-story wing; outbuildings; renovated, mid-19th C. Federal. Home of Elias Van Bunschooten, area's first Reformed Dutch minister, who bequeathed large sum for theological study to Queen's College, which later split into Rutgers University and the Dutch Seminary (see also Queen's Campus, Rutgers University, NJ). Museum. *Private.*

UNION COUNTY

Cranford. **DROESCHERS MILL (RAHWAY RIVER MILL),** 347 Lincoln Ave. E., 18th C.. Frame, horizontal siding; 2 stories, rectangular, gambrel roof with dormers, 1 interior chimney. Last of 11 mills along Raritan River section extending from Cranford to Clark and then to Rahway. Produced blankets during Revolutionary War, Minie balls and cavalry spurs during Civil War; later used as an oil stone manufacturing works. *Private.*

Elizabeth. **BOXWOOD HALL (BOUDINOT MANSION),** 1073 E. Jersey St., c. 1750. Frame, shingling; 2 1/2 stories, rectangular, gabled roof, Palladian window above center door, originally had dependent wings; altered with additional floors, since removed. Restored. Home of Elias Boudinot, president of the Continental Congress, 1782, signer of Treaty of Paris, and superintendent of the U.S. Mint. *State:* HABS.

Elizabeth. **LIBERTY HALL (GOV. WILLIAM LIVINGSTON HOUSE)** , Morris and North

Aves., 1773. Frame, flush siding; 3 stories, modified rectangle, gabled roof, 2 interior end chimneys, bracketed cornice, small 1-story pedimented portico with balustrade, front center entrance with fanlight, rear wing and tower; original 2-story center section with 1-story side wings altered 1789 by addition of 2nd story over W wing; altered c. 1870 by addition of rear tower, 2nd story over 1 wing, and 3rd story on entire structure. Georgian elements. Home of William Livingston, first NJ governor; served as lodging for Martha Washington while attending husband's inauguration as President, 1789. *Private; not accessible to the public:* NHL; HABS.

Plainfield. **DRAKE, NATHANIEL, HOUSE,** 602 W. Front St., 1746. Frame, clapboarding, and board-and-batten siding; 1 1/2 stories, modified T shape; gambrel, mansard, and polygonal roof sections; 2 interior chimneys; altered 1865 by conversion of gabled roof to gambrel, and addition of rear 3-story mansard tower with cresting and roof dormers, board-and-batten siding, 2-story polygonal tower, and several porches. Stick Style elements. Served as George Washington's headquarters on June 26, 1777, during Battle of Short Hills. Museum. *Municipal.*

Rahway vicinity (Clark Township). **SEVEN-TEENTH CENTURY CLARK HOUSE,** 593 Madison Hill Rd., Late-17th C.. Frame, wide clapboarding; 1 1/2 stories, rectangular, gabled roof with gabled dormer on each side, central chimney, off-center entrance with shed hood, small windows beneath eaves, rear shed addition; interior features large summer beam, English post-medieval construction feature. One of state's only extant 17th C. buildings; reputedly a doctor's residence. *Municipal.*

Scotch Plains. **DE CAMP, JOHN, HOUSE,** 2101 Raritan Rd., 1739. Frame, clapboarding; 2 1/2 stories, 2-section gabled roof with saltbox overhang, front porch removed, restoration and alteration, 1931, by Howard E. Quimby. Built as farmhouse by John De Camp in 1739. *Private.*

Scotch Plains. **OLD BAPTIST PARSONAGE,** 547 Park Ave., 1786. Ashlar, clapboarded gable; 2 stories, rectangular, gabled roof, interior end chimneys, center entrance with 1-story pedimented portico; 2-story 1854 frame addition. Colonial elements. Built to replace frame parsonage that burned, 1786; uncommon use of stone in this part of state. *Private.*

Union. **FIRST PRESBYTERIAN CONGREGATION OF CONNECTICUT FARMS,** Stuyvesant Ave. at Chestnut St., 1782–1818. Brick and stone, clapboarded front gable; 2 stories, modified rectangle, gabled roof, front center octagonal wooden belfry with louvered lancet over square base with oculus, modillion cornice; rear and side additions. Federal. Replaced church built in 1740 and destroyed by British in 1780. *Private:* HABS.

Westfield. **MILLER-CORY HOUSE,** 614 Mountain Ave., Early-18th C.. Frame with brick nogging, clapboarding and flush siding; 1–2 1/2 stories, modified rectangle, gabled roof sections, interior and interior end chimneys, gabled dormer, off-center entrance with hood in main block, 2 entrances in side wing; original and duplicated interior stenciling; wing added late-18th C., alterations 1860's. Colonial elements. Home of Miller family, earliest settlers in area; later owned by Cory family. *Private.*

MORRIS CANAL, *Reference—see Essex County*

Hope. **HOPE DISTRICT,** 18th–19th C.. Settled by Moravians in 18th C. Includes numerous limestone Moravian structures and those of later settlers. Begun as experimental religious community with gristmill, sawmill, tannery, and distillery and brewery. Settlement failed, 1808. Area maintains 18th–19th C. character; no 20th C. structures. *Multiple private:* HABS.

Phillipsburg. **ROSEBERRY, JOHN, HOMESTEAD,** 540 Warren St., c. 1787. Coursed rubble, 2 1/2 stories over walk-in basement, modified rectangle, gabled roof sections, interior end chimneys, center front entrance with transom with 1-story full-width balustraded shed porch, 1 1/2-story kitchen side wing with front entrance. Colonial elements. Probably city's oldest structure. *Municipal.*

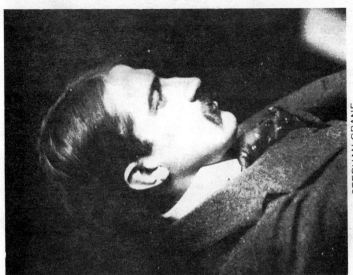

STEPHAN CRANE

AARON BURR

382

ALEXANDER HAMILTON

PHILLIP M. FRENEAU

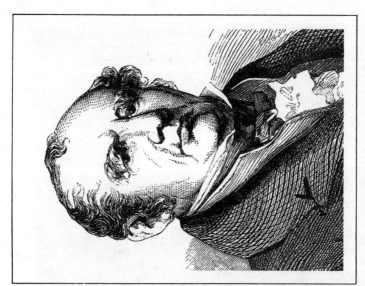

AARON OGDEN

WILLIAM LIVINGSTON

ZEBULUN M. PIKE

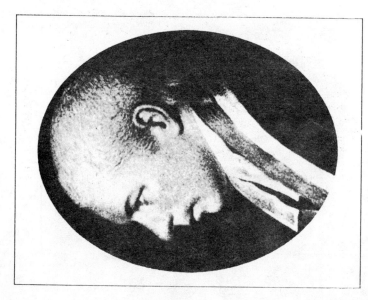

WILLIAM PATTERSON

385

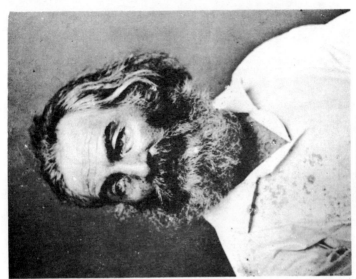

WALT WHITMAN

EDWARD WESTON

386

THOMAS WOODROW WILSON

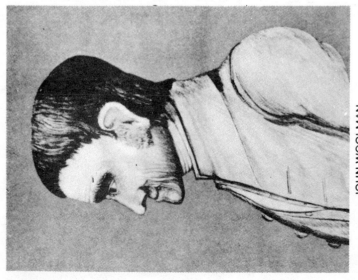

JOHN WOOLMAN

Glenmont, home of Thomas A. Edison

Thomas A. Edison's Library,
West Orange Laboratory

New Jersey Statehouse Complex

"Lucy", the Margate Elephant, Margate

390

State Museum, Cultural Center and
Planetarium, Trenton

Ford Mansion, Morristown Historical Park

Surfer at Seaside Heights

Hidden Valley Ski Area, Vernon

Atlantic City Boardwalk

Liberty State Park, Jersey City

Historic Gardner's Basin, Atlantic City

Sailing in Round Valley Reservoir

Victorian Cape May

Point Pleasant Beach

Old Salem Courthouse

Miss America Winners

Great Falls, Paterson

Main Street, Chester

Washington Crossing State Park

Constitution of the State
of New Jersey

As Amended to January 19, 1982

A Constitution agreed upon by the delegates of the people of New Jersey, in Convention, begun at Rutgers University, the State University of New Jersey, in New Brunswick, on the twelfth day of June, and continued to the tenth day of September, in the year of our Lord one thousand nine hundred and forty-seven.

We, the people of the State of New Jersey, grateful to Almighty God for the civil and religious liberty which He hath so long permitted us to enjoy, and looking to Him for a blessing upon our endeavors to secure and transmit the same unimpaired to succeeding generations, do ordain and establish this Constitution.

ARTICLE I

RIGHTS AND PRIVILEGES

1. All persons are by nature free and independent, and have certain natural and unalienable rights, among which are those of enjoying and defending life and liberty, of acquiring, possessing, and protecting property, and of pursuing and obtaining safety and happiness.

2. All political power is inherent in the people. Government is instituted for the protection, security, and benefit of the people, and they have the right at all times to alter or reform the same, whenever the public good may require it.

3. No person shall be deprived of the inestimable privilege of worshipping Almighty God in a manner agreeable to the dictates of his own conscience; nor under any pretense whatever be compelled to attend any place of worship contrary to his faith and judgment; nor shall any person be obliged to pay tithes, taxes, or other rates for building or repairing any church or churches, place or places of worship, or for the maintenance of any minister or ministry, contrary to what he believes to be right or has deliberately and voluntarily engaged to perform.

4. There shall be no establishment of one religious sect in preference to another; no religious or racial test shall be required as a qualification for any office or public trust.

5. No person shall be denied the enjoyment of any civil or military right, nor be discriminated against in the exercise of any civil or military right, nor be segregated in the militia or in the public schools, because of religious principles, race, color, ancestry or national origin.

6. Every person may freely speak, write and publish his sentiments on all subjects, being responsible for the abuse of that right. No law shall be passed to restrain or abridge the liberty of speech or of the press. In all prosecutions or indictments for libel, the truth may be given in evidence to the jury; and if it shall appear to the jury that the matter charged as libelous is true, and was published with good motives and for justifiable ends, the party shall be acquitted; and the jury shall have the right to determine the law and the fact.

7. The right of the people to be secure in their persons, houses, papers and effects, against unreasonable searches and seizures, shall not be violated; and no warrant shall issue except upon probable cause, supported by oath or affirmation, and particularly describing the place to be searched and the papers and things to be seized.

8. No personal shall be held to answer for a criminal offence, unless on the presentment or indictment of a grand jury, except in cases of impeachment, or in cases now prosecuted without indictment, or arising in the army or navy or in the militia, when in actual service in time of war or public danger.

9. The right of trial by jury shall remain inviolate; but the Legislature may authorize the trial of civil causes by a jury of six persons. The Legislature may provide that in any civil cause a verdict may be rendered by not less than five-sixths of the jury. The Legislature may authorize the trial of the issue of mental incompetency without a jury.

10. In all criminal prosecutions the accused shall have the right to a speedy and public trial by an impartial jury; to be informed of the nature and cause of the accusation; to be confronted with the witnesses against him; to have compulsory process for obtaining witnesses in his favor; and to have the assistance of counsel in his defense.

11. No person shall, after acquittal, be tried for the same offense. All persons shall, before conviction, be bailable by sufficient sureties, except for capital offenses when the proof is evident or presumption great.

12. Excessive bail shall not be required, excessive fines shall not be imposed, and cruel and unusual punishments shall not be inflicted.

13. No person shall be imprisoned for debt in any action, or on any judgment found upon contract, unless in cases of fraud; nor shall any person be imprisoned for a militia fine in time of peace.

14. The privilege of the writ of habeas corpus shall not be suspended, unless in case of rebellion or invasion the public safety may require it.

15. The military shall be in strict subordination to the civil power.

16. No soldier shall, in time of peace, be quartered in any house, without the consent of the owner; nor in time of war, except in a manner prescribed by law.

17. Treason against the State shall consist only in levying war against it, or in adhering to its enemies, giving them aid and comfort. No person shall be convicted of treason, unless on the testimony of two witnesses to the same overt act, or on confession in open court.

18. The people have the right freely to assemble together, to consult for the common good, to make known their opinions to their representatives, and to petition for redress of grievances.

19. Persons in private employment shall have the right to organize and bargain collectively. Persons in public employment shall have the right to organize, present to and make known to the State, or any of its political subdivisions or agencies, their grievances and proposals through representatives of their own choosing.

20. Private property shall not be taken for public use without just compensation. Individuals or private corporations shall not be authorized to take private property for public use without just compensation first made to the owners.

21. This enumeration of rights and privileges shall not be construed to impair or deny others retained by the people.

Article I, Paragraph 9 amended effective December 4, 1973.

ARTICLE II
ELECTIONS AND SUFFRAGE

1. General elections shall be held annually on the first Tuesday after the first Monday in November; but the time of holding such elections may be altered by law. The Governor shall be chosen at general elections or at such other times as shall be provided by law.

2. All questions submitted to the people of the entire State shall be voted upon at general elections.

3. (a) Every citizen of the United States, of the age of 18 years, who shall have been a resident of this State and of the county in which he claims his vote 30 days, next before the election, shall be entitled to vote for all officers that now are or hereafter may be elective by the people, and upon all questions which may be submitted to a vote of the people; and

(b) (Deleted by amendment, effective December 5, 1974.)

(c) Any person registered as a voter in any election district of this State who has removed or shall remove to another state or to another county within this State and is not able there to qualify to vote by reason of an insufficient period of residence in such state or county, shall, as a citizen of the United States, have the right to vote for electors for President and Vice President of the United States, only, by Presidential Elector Absentee Ballot, in the county from which he has removed, in such manner as the Legislature shall provide.

Article II, Paragraph 3 amended effective December 5, 1974.

4. In the time of war no elector in the military service of the State or in the armed forces of the United States shall be deprived of his vote by reason of absence from this election district. The Legislature may provide for absentee voting by members of the armed forces of the United States in time of peace. The Legislature may provide the manner in which and the time and place at which such absent electors may vote, and for the return and canvass of their votes in the election district in which they respectively reside.

5. No person in the military, naval or marine service of the United States shall be considered a resident of this State by being stationed in any garrison, barrack, or military or naval place or station within this State.

6. No idiot or insane person shall enjoy the right of suffrage.

7. The Legislature may pass laws to deprive persons of the right of suffrage who shall be convicted of such crimes as it may designate. Any person so deprived, when pardoned or otherwise restored by law to the right of suffrage, shall again enjoy that right.

Article III

DISTRIBUTION OF THE POWERS OF GOVERNMENT

1. The powers of the government shall be divided among three distinct branches, the legislative, executive, and judicial. No person or persons belonging to or constituting one branch shall exercise any of the powers properly belonging to either of the others, except as expressly provided in this Constitution.

Article IV

LEGISLATIVE

Section I

1. The legislative power shall be vested in a Senate and General Assembly.

2. No person shall be a member of the Senate who shall not have attained the age of thirty years, and have been a citizen and resident of the State for four years, and of the district for which he shall be elected one year, next before his election. No person shall be a member of the General Assembly who shall not have attained the age of twenty-one years and have been a citizen and resident of the State for two years, and of the district for which he shall be elected one year, next before his election. No person shall be eligible for membership in the Legislature unless he be entitled to the right of suffrage.

Article IV, Section I, paragraph 2 amended effective December 8, 1966.

3. Each Legislature shall be constituted for a term of 2 years beginning at noon on the second Tuesday in January in each even numbered year, at which time the Senate and General Assembly shall meet and organize separately and the first annual session of the Legislature shall commence. Said first annual session shall terminate at noon on the second Tuesday in January next following, at which time the second annual session shall commence and it shall terminate at noon on the second Tuesday in January then next following but either session may be sooner terminated by adjournment sine die. All business before either House or any of the committees thereof, at the end of the first annual session may be resumed in the second annual session. The legislative year shall commence at noon on the second Tuesday in January of each year.

(Applicable to the 1970 Legislature and thereafter.)

4.   Special sessions of the Legislature shall be called by the Governor upon petition of a majority of all the members of each house, and may be called by the Governor whenever in his opinion the public interest shall require.

Section II

1.   The Senate shall be composed of forty senators apportioned among Senate districts as nearly as may be according to the number of their inhabitants as reported in the last preceeding decennial census of the United States and according to the method of equal proportions. Each Senate district shall be composed, wherever practicable, of one single county, and, if not so practicable, of two or more contiguous whole counties.

2.   Each senator shall be elected by the legally qualified voters of the Senate district, except that if the Senate district is composed of two or more counties and two senators are apportioned to the district, one senator shall be elected by the legally qualified voters of each Assembly district. Each senator shall be elected for a term beginning at noon of the second Tuesday in January next following his election and ending at noon of the second Tuesday in January four years thereafter, except that each senator, to be elected for a term beginning in January of the second year following the year in which a decennial census of the United States is taken, shall be elected for a term of two years.

3.   The General Assembly shall be composed of eighty members. Each Senate district to which only one senator is apportioned shall constitute an Assembly district. Each of the remaining Senate districts shall be divided into Assembly districts equal in number to the number of senators apportioned to the Senate district. The Assembly districts shall be composed of contiguous territory, as nearly compact and equal in the number of their inhabitants as possible, and in no event shall each such district contain less than eighty per cent nor more than one hundred twenty per cent of one-fortieth of the total number of inhabitants of the State as reported in the last preceeding decennial census of the United States. Unless necessary to meet the foregoing requirements, no county or municipality shall be divided among Assembly districts unless it shall contain more than one-fortieth of the total number of inhabitants of the State, and no county or municipality shall be divided among a number of Assembly districts larger than one plus the whole number obtained by dividing the number of inhabitants in the county or municipality by one-fortieth of the total number of inhabitants of the State.

4.   Two members of the General Assembly shall be elected by the legally qualified voters of each Assembly district for terms beginning at noon of the second Tuesday in January next following their election and ending at noon of the second Tuesday in January two years thereafter.

SECTION III

1.   After the next and every subsequent decennial census of the United States, the Senate districts and Assembly districts shall be established, and the senators and members of the General Assembly shall be apportioned among them, by an Apportionment Commission consisting of ten members, five to be appointed by the chairman of the State committee of each of the two political parties whose candidates for Governor receive the largest number of votes at the most recent gubernatorial election. Each State chairman, in making such appointments, shall give due consideration to the representation of the various geographical areas of the State. Appoinments to the Commission shall be made on or before November 15 of the year in which such census is taken and shall be certified by the Secretary of State on or before December 1 of that year. The Commission, by a majority of the whole number of its members, shall certify the establishment of Senate and Assembly districts and the apportionment of senators and members of the General Assembly to the Secretary of State within one month of the receipt by the Govenor of the official deccenial census of the United States for New Jersey, or on or before February 1 of the year following the year in which the census is taken, whichever date is later.

2.   If the Apportionment Commission fails so to certify such establishment and apportionment to the Secretary of State on or before the date fixed or if prior thereto it

detemines that it will be unable so to do, it shall so certify to the Chief Justice of the Supreme Court of New Jersey and he shall appoint an eleventh member of the Commission. The Commission so constituted, by a majority of the whole number of its members, shall, within one month after the appointment of such eleventh member, certify to the Secretary of State the establishment of Senate and Assembly districts and the apportionment of senators and members of the General Assembly.

3. Such establishment and apportionment shall be used thereafter for the election of members of the Legislature and shall remain unaltered until the following decennial census of the United States for New Jersey shall have been received by the Governor.

Article IV, Section III, paragraphs 1,2,3, amended effective December 8, 1966.

SECTION IV

1. Any vacancy in the Legislature occasioned by death, resignation or otherwise shall be filled by election for the unexpired term only, as may be provided by law. Each house shall direct a writ of election to fill any vacancy in its membeship; but if the vacancy shall occur during a recess of the Legislature, the writ may be issued by the Governor, as may be provided by law.

2. Each house shall be the judge of elections, returns and qualifications of its own members, and a majority of all its members shall constitute a quorum to do business; but a smaller number may adjourn from day to day, and may be authorized to compel the attendance of absent members, in such manner, and under such penalties, as each house may provide.

3. Each house shall choose its own officers, determine the rules of its proceedings, and punish its members for disorderly behavior. It may expel a member with the concurrence of two-thirds of all its members.

4. Each house shall keep a journal of its proceedings, and from time to time publish the same. The yeas and nays of the members of either house on any question shall, on demand of one-fifth of those present, be entered on the journal.

5. Neither house, during the session of the Legislature, shall, without the consent of the other, adjourn for more than three days, or to any other place than that in which the two houses shall be sitting.

6. All bills and joint resolutions shall be read three times in each house before final passage. No bill or joint resolution shall be read a third time in either house until after the intervention of one full calendar day following the day of the second reading; but if either house shall resolve by vote of three-fourths of all its members, signified by yeas and nays entered on the journal, that a bill or joint resolution is an emergency measure, it may proceed forthwith from second to third reading. No bill or joint resolution shall pass. unless there be a majority of all the members of each body personally present and agreeing thereto, and the yeas and nays of the members voting on such final passage shall be entered on the journal.

7. Members of the Senate and General Assembly shall receive annually, during the term for which they shall have been elected and while they shall hold their office, such compensation as shall, from time to time, be fixed by law and no other allowance or emolument, directly or indirectly, for any purpose whatever. The President of the Senate and the Speaker of the General Assembly, each by virtue of his office, shall receive an additional allowance, equal to one-third of his compensation as a member.

8. The compensation of members of the Senate and General Assembly shall be fixed at the first session of the Legislature held after this Constitution takes effect, and may be increased or decreased by law from time to time thereafter, but no increase or decrease shall be effective until the legislative year following the next general election for members of the General Assembly.

9. Members of the Senate and General Assembly shall, in all cases except treason and high misdemeanor, be privileged from arrest during their attendance at the sitting of their respective houses, and in going to and returning from the same; and for any statement. speech or debate in either house or at any meeting of a legislative committee, they shall not be questioned in any other place.

SECTION V

1. No member of the Senate or General Assembly, during the term for which he shall have been elected, shall be nominated, elected or appointed to any State civil office or position, of profit, which shall have been created by law, or the emoluments whereof shall have been increased by law, during such term. The provisions of this paragraph shall not prohibit the election of any person as Governor or as a member of the Senate or General Assembly.

2. The Legislature may appoint any commission, committee or other body whose main purpose is to aid or assist it in performing its functions. Members of the Legislature may be appointed to serve on any such body.

3. If any member of the Legislature shall become a member of Congress or shall accept any Federal or State office or position, of profit, his seat shall thereupon become vacant.

4. No member of Congress, no person holding any Federal or State office or position, of profit, and no judge of any court shall be entitled to a seat in the Legislature.

5. Neither the Legislature nor either house thereof shall elect or appoint any executive, administrative or judicial officer except the State Auditor.

SECTION VI

1. All bills for raising revenue shall originate in the General Assembly; but the Senate may propose or concur with amendments, as on other bills.

2. The Legislature may enact general laws under which muncipalities, other than counties, may adopt zoning ordinances limiting and restricting to specified districts and regulating therein, buildings and structures, according to their construction, and the nature and extent of their use, and the nature and extent of the uses of land, and the exercise of such authority shall be deemed to be within the police power of the State. Such laws shall be subject to repeal or alteration by the Legislature.

3. Any agency or political subdivision of the State or any agency of a political subdivision thereof, which may be empowered to take or otherwise acquire private property for any public highway, parkway, airport, place, improvement, or use, may be authorized by law to take or otherwise acquire a fee simple absolute or any lesser interest, and may be authorized by law to take or otherwise acquire a fee simple absolute in, easements upon, or the benefit of restrictions upon, abutting property to preserve and protect the public highway, parkway, airport, place, improvement, or use; but such taking shall be with just compensation.

4. The Legislature, in order to insure continuity of State, county and local governmental operations in periods of emergency resulting from disasters caused by enemy attack, shall have the power and the immediate and continuing duty by legislation (1) to provide, prior to the occurrence of the emergency, for prompt and temporary succession to the powers and duties of public offices, of whatever nature and whether filled by election or appointment, the incumbents of which may become unavailable for carrying on the powers and duties of such offices, and (2) to adopt such other measures as may be necessary and proper for insuring the continuity of governmental operations. In the exercise of the powers hereby conferred the Legislature shall in all respects conform to the requirements of this Constitution except to the extent that in the judgment of the Legislature to do so would be impracticable or would admit of undue delay.

Article IV, Section VI, paragraph 4 added effective December 7, 1961.

SECTION VII

1. No divorce shall be granted by the Legislature.

2. No gambling of any kind shall be authorized by the Legislature unless the specific kind, restrictions and control thereof have been heretofore submitted to, and authorized by a majority of the votes cast by, the people at a special election or shall hereafter be submitted to, and authorized by a majority of votes cast thereon by, the legally qualified voters of the State voting at a general election, except that, without any such submission or authorization;

A. It shall be lawful for bona fide veterans, charitable, educational, religious or fraternal organizations, civic and service clubs, senior citizens associations or clubs, volunteer fire companies and first-aid or rescue squads to conduct, under such restrictions and control as shall from time to time be prescribed by the Legislature by law, games of chance of, and restricted to, the selling of rights to participate, the awarding of prizes, in the specific kind of game of chance sometimes known as bingo or lotto, played with cards bearing numbers or other designations, 5 or more in one line, the holder covering numbers as objects, similarly numbered, are drawn from a receptacle and the game being won by the person who first covers a previously designated arrangement of numbers on such a card, when the entire net proceeds of such games of chance are to be devoted to educational, charitable, patriotic, religious or public-spirited uses, and in the case of senior citizen associations or clubs to the support of such organizations, in any municipality, in which a majority of the qualified voters, voting thereon, at a general or special election as the submission thereof shall be prescribed by the Legislature by law, shall authorize the conduct of such games of chance therein.

B. It shall be lawful for the Legislature to authorize, by law, bona fide veterans, charitable, educational, religious or fraternal organizations, civic and service clubs, volunteer fire companies and first-aid or rescue squads to conduct games of chance of, and restricted to, the selling of rights to participate, and the awarding of prizes, in the specific kinds of games of chance sometimes known as raffles, conducted by the drawing for prizes or by the allotment of prizes by chance, when the entire net proceeds of such games of chance are to be devoted to educational, charitable, patriotic, religious or public-spirited uses, in any municipality, in which such law shall be adopted by a majority of the qualified voters, voting thereon, at a general or special election as the submission thereof shall be prescribed by law and for the Legislature, from time to time, to restrict and control, by law, the conduct of such games of chance and

C. It shall be lawful for the Legislature to authorize the conduct of State lotteries restricted to the selling of rights to participate therein and the awarding of prizes by drawings when the entire net proceeds of any such lottery shall be for State institutions, state aid for education.

D. It shall be lawful for the Legislature to authorize by law the establishment and operation, under regulation and control by the State, of gambling houses or casinos within the boundaries, as heretofore established, of the city of Atlantic City, county of Atlantic, and to license and tax such operations and equipment used in connection therewith. Any law authorizing the establishment and operation of such gambling establishments shall provide for the State revenues derived therefrom to be applied solely for the purpose of providing funding for reductions in property taxes, rental, telephone, gas, electric, and municipal utilities charges of eligible senior citizens and disabled residents of the State, and for additional or expanded health services or benefits or transportation services or benefits to eligible senior citizens and disabled residents, in accordance with such formulae as the Legislature shall by law provide. The type and number of such casinos or gambling houses and of the gambling games which may be conducted in any such establishment shall be determined by or pursuant to the terms of the law authorizing the establishment thereof.

Article IV, Section VII, paragraph 2 amended effective December 3, 1981.

3. The Legislature shall not pass any bill of attainder, ex post facto law, or law imparing the obligation of contracts, or depriving a party of any remedy for enforcing a contract which existed when the contract was made.

4. To avoid improper influences which may result from intermixing in one and the same act such things as have no proper relation to each other, every law shall embrace but one object, and that shall be expressed in the title. This paragraph shall not invalidate any law adopting or enacting a compilation, consolidation, revision, or rearrangement of all or parts of the statutory law.

5. No law shall be revived or amended by reference to its title only, but the act revived, or the section or sections amended, shall be inserted at length. No act shall be passed which shall provide that any existing law, or any part thereof, shall be made or deemed a part of the act or which shall enact that any existing law, or any part thereof, shall be applicable. except by inserting it in such act.

6. The laws of this State shall begin in the following style: "Be it enacted by the Senate and General Assembly of the State of New Jersey."

7. No general law shall embrace any provision of a private, special or local character.

8. No private, special or local law shall be passed unless public notice of the intention to apply therefor, and of the general object thereof, shall have been previously given. Such notice shall be given at such time and in such manner and shall be so evidenced and the evidence thereof shall be so preserved as may be provided by law.

9. The legislature shall not pass any private, special or local laws:

(1) Authorizing the sale of any lands belonging in whole or in part to a minor or minors or other persons who may at the time be under any legal disability to act for themselves.

(2) Changing the law of descent.

(3) Providing for change of venue in civil or criminal causes.

(4) Selecting, drawing, summoning or empaneling grand or petit jurors.

(5) Creating, increasing or decreasing the emoluments, term or tenure rights of any public officers or employees.

(6) Relating to taxation or exemption therefrom.

(7) Providing for the management and control of free public schools.

(8) Granting to any corporation, association or individual any exclusive privilege, immunity or franchise whatever.

(9) Granting to any corporation, association or individual the right to lay down railroad tracks.

(10) Laying out, opening, altering, constructing, maintaining and repairing roads or highways.

(11) Vacating any road, town plot, street, alley or public grounds.

(12) Appointing local officers or commissions to regulate municipal affairs.

(13) Regulating the internal affairs of municipalities formed for local government and counties, except as otherwise in this Constitution provided.

The Legislature shall pass general laws providing for the cases enumerated in this paragraph, and for all other cases which, in its judgment, may be provided for by general laws. The Legislature shall pass no special act conferring corporate powers, but shall pass general laws under which corporations may be organized and corporate powers of every nature obtained, subject, nevertheless, to repeal or alteration at the will of the Legislature.

10. Upon petition by the governing body of any municipal corporation formed for local government, or of any county, and by vote of two-thirds of all the members of each house, the Legislature may pass private, special or local laws regulating the internal affairs of the municipality or county. The petition shall be authorized in a manner to be prescribed by general law and shall specify the general nature of the law sought to be passed. Such law shall become operative only if it is adopted by ordinance of the governing body of he municipality or county or by vote of the legally qualified voters thereof. The Legislature shall prescribe in such law or by general law the method of adopting such law, and the manner in which the ordinance of adoption may be enacted or the vote taken, as the case may be.

11. The provisions of this Constitution and of any law concerning municipal corporations formed for local government, or concerning counties, shall be liberally construed in their favor. The powers of the counties and such municipal corporations shall include not only those granted in express terms but also those of necessary or fair implication, or incident to the powers expressly conferred, or essential thereto, and not inconsistent with or prohibited by this Constitution or by law.

1. Members of the Legislature shall, before they enter on the duties of their respective offices, take and subscribe the following oath or affirmation:"I do solemnly swear (or affirm) that I will support the Constitution of the United States and the Constitution of the State of New Jersey, and that I will faithfully discharge the duties of Senator (or member of the General Assembly) according to the best of my ability." Members-elect of the Senate or General Assembly are empowered to administer said oath or affirmation to each other.

2. Every officer of the Legislature shall, before he enters upon his duties, take and subscribe the following oath or affirmation: "I do solemnly promise and swear (or affirm) that I will faithfully, impartially and justly perform all the duties of the office of.................., to the best of my ability and understanding; that I will carefully preserve all records, papers, writings, or property entrusted to me for safekeeping by virtue of my office, and make such disposition of the same as may be required by law."

Article V

EXECUTIVE

Section I

1. The executive power shall be vested in a Governor.

2. The Governor shall not be less than thirty years of age, and shall have been for at least twenty years a citizen of the United States, and a resident of this State seven years next before his election, unless he shall have been absent during that time on the public business of the United States or of this State.

3. No member of Congress or person holding any office or position, of profit, under this State or the United States shall be Governor. If the Governor or person administering the office of Govenor shall accept any other office or position, of profit, under this State or the United States, his office of Governor shall thereby be vacated. No Governor shall be elected by the Legislature to any office during the term for which he shall have been elected Governor.

4. The Governor shall be elected by the legally qualified voters of this State. The person receiving the greatest number of votes shall be the Governor; but if two or more shall be equal and greatest in votes, one of them shall be elected Governor by the vote of a majority of all the members of both houses in joint meeting at the regular legislative session next following the election for Governor by the people. Contested elections for the office of Governor shall be determined in such manner as may be provided by law.

5. The term of office of the Governor shall be four years, beginning at noon of the third Tuesday in January next following his election, and ending at noon of the third Tuesday in January four years thereafter. No person who has been elected Governor for two successive terms, including an unexpired term, shall again be eligible for that office until the third Tuesday in January of the fourth year following the expiration of his second successive term.

6. In the event of a vacancy in the office of Governor resulting from the death, resignation or removal of a Governor in office, or the death of a Governor-elect, or from any other cause, the functions, powers, duties and emoluments of the office shall devolve upon the President of the Senate, for the time being, and in the event of his death, resignation or removal, then upon the Speaker of the General Assembly, for the time being; and in the event of his death, resignation or removal, then upon such officers and in such order of succession as may be provided by law; until a new Governor shall be elected and qualify.

7. In the event of the failure of the Governor-elect to qualify, or of the absence from the State of a Governor in office, or his inability to discharge the duties of his office, or his impeachment, the functions, powers, duties and emoluments of the office shall devolve upon the President of the Senate, for the time being; and in the event of his death, resignation, removal, absence, inability or impeachment, then upon the Speaker of the General Assembly, for the time being; and in the event of his death, resignation, removal, absence, inability or impeachment, then upon such officers and in such order of succession as may be provided by law; until the Governor-elect shall qualify, or the Governor in office shall return to the State, or shall no longer be unable to discharge the duties of the office, or shall be acquitted, as the case may be, or until a new Governor shall be elected and qualify.

8. Whenever a Governor-elect shall have failed to qualify within six months after the

beginning of his term of office, or whenever for a period of six months a Governor in office, or person administering the office, shall have remained continuously absent from the State, or shall have been continuously unable to discharge the duties of his office by reason of mental or physical disability, the office shall be deemed vacant. Such vacancy shall be determined by the Supreme Court upon presentment to it of a concurrent resolution declaring the ground of the vacancy, adopted by a vote of two-thirds of all the members of each house of the Legislature, and upon notice, hearing before the Court and proof of the existence of the vacancy.

9. In the event of a vacancy in the office of Governor, a Governor shall be elected to fill the unexpired term at the general election next succeeding the vacancy, unless the vacancy shall occur within sixty days immediately preceeding a general election, in which case he shall be elected at the second succeeding general election; but no election to fill an unexpired term shall be held in any year in which a Governor is to be elected for a full term. A Governor elected for an unexpired term shall assume his office immediately upon his election.

10. The Governor shall receive for his services a salary, which shall be neither increased nor diminished during the period for which he shall have been elected.

11. The Governor shall take care that the laws be faithfully executed. To this end he shall have power, by appropriate action or proceeding in the courts brought in the name of the State, to enforce compliance with any constitutional or legislative mandate, or to restrain violation of any constitution or legislative power or duty, by any officer, department or agency of the State; but this power shall not be construed to authorize any action or proceeding against the Legislature.

12. The Governor shall communicate to the Legislature, by message at the opening of each regular session and at such other times as he may deem necessary, the condition of the State, and shall in like manner recommend such measures as he may deem desirable. He may convene the Legislature, or the Senate alone, whenever in his opinion the public interest shall require. He shall be the Commander-in-Chief of all the military and naval forces of the State. He shall grant commissions to all officers elected or appointed pursuant to this Constitution. He shall nominate and appoint, with the advice and consent of the Senate, all officers for whose election or appointment provision is not otherwise made by this Constitution or by law.

13. The Governor may fill any vacancy occurring in any office during a recess of the Legislature, appointment to which may be made by the Governor with the advice and consent of the Senate, or by the Legislature in joint meeting. An ad interim appointment so made shall expire at the end of the next regular session of the Senate, unless a successor shall be sooner appointed and qualify; and after the end of the session no ad interim appointment to the same office shall be made unless the Governor shall have submitted to the Senate a nomination to the office during the session and the Senate shall have adjourned without confirming or rejecting it. No person nominated for any office shall be eligible for an ad interim appointment to such office if the nomination shall have failed of confirmation by the Senate.

14. (a) When a bill has finally passed both houses, the house in which final action was taken to complete its passage shall cause it to be presented to the Governor before the close of the calendar day next following the date of the session at which such final action was taken.

(b) A bill presented to the Governor shall become law:

   (1) if the Governor approves and signs it within the period allowed for his consideration; or,

   (2) if the Governor does not return it to the house of origin, with a statement of his objections, before the expiration of the period allowed for his consideration; or,

   (3) if, upon reconsideration of a bill objected to by the Governor, two-thirds of all the members of each house agree to pass the bill.

(c) The period allowed for the Governor's consideration of a passed bill shall be from the date of presentation until noon of the forty-fifth day next following or, if the house of origin be in temporary adjournment on that day, the first day subsequent upon which the house reconvenes; except that:

(1) if on the said forty-fifth day the Legislature is in adjournment sine die, any bill then pending the Governor's approval shall be returned, if he objects to it, at a special session held pursuant to subparagraph (d) of this paragraph;

(2) any bill passed between the forty-fifth day and the tenth day preceeding the expiration of the second legislative year shall be returned by the Governor, if he objects to it, not later than noon of the day next preceding the expiration of the second legislative year;

(3) any bill passed within 10 days preceding the expiration of the second legislative year shall become law only if the Governor signs it prior to such expiration, or the Governor returns it to the House of origin, with a statement of his objections, and two-thirds of all members of each House agree to pass the bill prior to such expiration.

(d) For the pupose of permitting the return of bills pursuant to this paragraph, a special session of the Legislature shall convene, without petition or call, for the sole purpose of acting upon bills returned by the Govenor, on the forty-fifth day next following adjournment sine die of the regular session; or, if the second legislative year of a 2-year Legislature will expire before said forty-fifth day, then the day next preceding the expiration of the legislative year.

(e) Upon receiving from the Governor a bill returned by him with his objections, the house in which it originated shall enter the objections at large in its journal and proceed to reconsider it. If, upon reconsideration, on or after the third day following its return, or the first day of a special session convened for the sole purpose of acting on such bills, two-thirds of all the members of the house of origin agree to pass the bill, it shall be sent, together with the objections of the Governor, to the other house; and if, upon reconsideration, it is approved by two-thirds of all the membes of the house, it shall become a law. In all such cases the votes of each house shall be detemined by yeas and nays, and the names of the persons voting for and against the bill shall be entered on the journals of the respective houses.

(f) The Governor, in returning with his objections a bill for reconsideration at any general or special session of the Legislature, may recommend that an amendment or amendments specified by him be made in the bill, and in such case the Legislature may amend and re-enact the bill. If a bill be so amended and re-enacted, it shall be presented again to the Governor, but shall become a law only if he shall sign it within 10 days after presentation; and no bill shall be returned by the Governor a second time.

Article V, Section I, paragraph 14 amended effective December 3, 1981.

15. If any bill presented to the Governor shall contain one or more items of appropriation of money, he may object in whole or in part to any such item or items while approving the other portions of the bill. In such case he shall append to the bill, at the time of signing it, a statement of each item or part thereof to which he objects, and each item or part so objected to shall not take effect. A copy of such statement shall be transmitted by him to the house in which the bill originated, and each item or part thereof objected to shall be separately reconsidered. If upon reconsideration, on or after the third day following said transmittal, one or more of such items or parts thereof be approved by two-thirds of all the members of each house, the same shall become a part of the law, notwithstanding the objections of the Governor. All the provisions of the preceding paragraph in relation to bills not approved by the Governor shall apply to cases in which he shall withhold his approval from any item or items or parts thereof contained in a bill appropriating money.

SECTION II

1. The Governor may grant pardons and reprieves in all cases other than impeachment and treason, and may suspend and remit fines and forfeitures. A commission or other body may be established by law to aid and advise the Governor in the exercise of executive clemency.

2. A system for the granting of parole shall be provided by law.

SECTION III

1. Provision for organizing, inducting, training, arming, disciplining and regulating a militia shall be made by law, which shall conform tb applicable standards established for the armed forces of the United States.

2. The Governor shall nominate and appoint all general and flag officers of the militia, with the advice and consent of the Senate. All other commissioned officers of the militia shall be appointed and commissioned by the Governor according to law.

SECTION IV

1. All executive and administrative offices, departments, and instrumentalities of the State government, including the offices of Secretary of State and Attorney General, and their respective functions, powers and duties, shall be allocated by law among and within not more than twenty principal departments, in such manner as to group the same according to major purposes so far as practicable. Temporary commissions for special purposes may, however, be established by law and such commissions need not be allocated within a principal department.

2. Each principal department shall be under the supervision of the Governor. The head of each principal department shall be a single executive unless otherwise provided by law. Such single executives shall be nominated and appointed by the Governor, with the advice and consent of the Senate, to serve at the pleasure of the Governor during his term of office and until the appointment and qualification of their successors, except as herein otherwise provided with respect to the Secretary of State and the Attorney General.

3. The Secretary of State and the Attorney General shall be nominated and appointed by the Governor with the advice and consent of the Senate to serve during the term of office of the Governor.

4. Whenever a board, commission or other body shall be the head of a principal department, the members thereof shall be nominated and appointed by the Governor with the advice and consent of the Senate, and may be removed in the manner provided by law. Such a board, commission or other body may appoint a principal executive officer when authorized by law, but the appointment shall be subject to the approval of the Govenor. Any principal executive officer so appointed shall be removable by the Governor, upon notice and an opportunity to be heard.

5. The Governor may cause an investigation to be made of the conduct in office of any officer or employee who receives his compensation from the State of New Jersey, except a member, officer or employee of the Legislature or an officer elected by the Senate and General Assembly in joint meeting, or a judicial officer. He may require such officers or employeês to submit to him a written statement or statements, under oath, of such information as he may call for relating to the conduct of their respective offices or employments. After notice, the service of charges and an opportunity to be heard at public hearing the Governor may remove any such officer or employee for cause. Such officer or employee shall have the right of judicial review, on both the law and the facts, in such manner as shall be provided by law.

6. No rule or regulation made by any department, officer agency or authority of this state, except such as relates to the organization or internal management of the State government or a part thereof, shall take effect until it is filed either with the Secretary of State or in such other manner as may be provided by law. The Legislature shall provide for the prompt publicaton of such rules and regulations.

Article VI

JUDICIAL

Section I

1. The judicial power shall be vested in a Supreme Court, a Superior Court, and other courts of limited jurisdiction. The other courts and their jurisdiction may from time to time be established, altered or abolished by law.

Article VI, Section I, paragraph 1 amended effective December 7, 1978.

Section II

1. The Supreme Court shall consist of a Chief Justice and six Associate Justices. Five members of the court shall constiute a quorum. When necessary, the Chief Justice shall assign the Judge or Judges of the Superior Court, senior in service, as provided by rules of the Supreme Court, to serve temporarily in the Supreme Court. In the case the Chief Justice is absent or unable to serve, a presiding Justice designated in accordance with rules of the Supreme Court shall serve temporarily in his stead.

2. The Supreme Court shall exercise appellate jurisdiction in the last resort in all causes provided in this Constitution.

3. The Supreme Court shall make rules governing the administration of all courts in the State and, subject to the law, the practice and procedure in all such courts. The Supreme Court shall have jurisdiction over the admission to the practice of law and the discipline of persons admitted.

SECTION III

1. The Superior Court shall consist of such number of judges as may be authorized by law, each of whom shall exercise the powes of the court subject to the rules of the Supreme Court. The Superior Court shall at all times consist of at least two judges who shall be assigned to sit in each of the counties of this State, and who are resident therein at the time of appointment and reappointment.

Article VI, Section III, paragraph 1 amended effective December 7, 1978.

2. The Superior Court shall have original general jurisdiction throughout the State in all causes.

3. The Superior Court shall be divided into an Appellate Division, a Law Division and a Chancery Division. Each division shall have such parts, consist of such number of judges, and hear such causes, as may be provided by rules of the Supreme Court. At least two judges of the Superior Court shall at all times be assigned to sit in each of the counties of the State, who at the time of their appointment and reappointment were residents of that county provided, however, that the number of judges required to reside in the county wherein they sit shall be at least equal in number to the number of judges of the county court sitting in each of the counties at the adoption of this amendment.

Article VI, Section III, paragraph 3 amended effective December 7, 1978.

4. Subject to rules of the Supreme Court, the Law Division and the Chancery Division shall each exercise the powers and functions of the other division when the ends of justice so require, and legal and equitable relief shall be granted in any cause so that all matters in controversy between the parties may be completely determined.

SECTION IV

Article VI, Section IV, repealed effective December 7, 1978.

SECTION V

1. Appeals may be taken to the Supreme Court:

(a) In causes determined by the appellate division of the Superior Court involving a question arising under the Constitution of the United States or this State;

(b) In causes where there is a dissent in the Appellate Division of the Superior Court;

(c) In capital causes;

(d) On certification by the Supreme Court to the Superior Court and, where provided by rules of the Supreme Court, to the inferior courts; and

(e) In such causes as may be provided by law.

2.   Appeals may be taken to the Appellate Division of the Superior Court from the law and chancery divisions of the Superior Court and in such other causes as may be provided by law.

Article VI, Section V, paragraphs 1 and 2 amended effective December 7, 1978.

3.   The Supreme Court and the Appellate Division of the Superior Court may exercise such original jurisdiction as may be necessary to the complete determination of any cause on review.

4.   Prerogative writs are superseded and, in lieu thereof, review, hearing and relief shall be afforded in the Superior Court, on terms and in the manner provided by rules of the Supreme Court, as of right, except in criminal causes where such review shall be discretionary.

SECTION VI

1. The Governor shall nominate and appoint, with the advice and consent of the Senate, the Chief Justice and Associate Justices of the Supreme Court, the judges of the Superior Court, and the judges of the inferior courts with jurisdiction extending to more than one municipality. No nomination to such an office shall be sent to the Senate for confirmation until after 7 days' public notice by the Governor.

2. The justices of the Supreme Court and the judges of the Superior Court shall each prior to his appointment have been admitted to the practice of law in this State for at least 10 years.

Article VI, Section VI, paragraphs 1 and 2 amended effective December 7, 1978.

3.   The Justices of the Supreme Court and the Judges of the Superior Court shall hold their offices for initial terms of seven years and upon reappointment shall hold their offices during good behavior. Such Justices and Judges shall be retired upon attaining the age of seventy years. Provisions for the pensioning of the Justices of the Supreme Court and the Judges of the Superior Court shall be made by law.

4. The Justices of the Supreme Court and the Judges of the Superior Court shall be subject to impeachment, and any judicial officer impeached shall not execise his office until acquitted. The Judges of the Superior Court shall also be subject to removal from office by the Supreme Court for such causes and in such manner as shall be provided by law.

5. Whenever the Supreme Court shall certify to the Governor that it appears that any Justice of the Supreme Court or Judge of the Superior Court is so incapacitated as substantially to prevent him from performing his judicial duties, the Governor shall appoint a commission of three persons to inquire into the circumstances; and, on their recommendation, the Governor may retire the justice or judge from office, on pension as may be provided by law.

Article VI, Section VI, paragraphs 4 and 5 amended effective December 7, 1978.

6.   The Justices of the Supreme Court and the Judges of the Superior Court shall receive for their services such salaries as may be provided by law, which shall not be diminished during the term of their appointment. They shall not, while in office, engage in the practice of law or other gainful pursuit.

7. The Justices of the Supreme Court and the Judges of the Superior shall hold no other office or position, of profit, under this State or the United States. Any such justice of judge who shall become a candidate for an elective public office shall thereby forfeit his judicial office.

Article VI, Section VI, paragraph 7 amended effective December 7, 1978.

1. The Chief Justice of the Supreme Court shall be the administrative head of all the courts in the State. He shall appoint an Administrative Director to serve at his pleasure.

2. The Chief Justice of the Supreme Court shall assign Judges of the Superior Court to the Divisions and Parts of the Superior Court, and may from time to time transfer Judges from one assignment to another, as need appears. Assignments to the Appellate Division shall be for terms fixed by rules of the Supreme Court.

3. The Clerk of the Supreme Court and the Clerk of the Superior Court shall be appointed by the Supreme Court for such terms and at such compensation as shall be provided by law.

ARTICLE VII

PUBLIC OFFICERS AND EMPLOYEES

SECTION I

1. Every State officer, before entering upon the duties of his office, shall take and subscribe an oath or affirmation to support the Constitution of this State and of the United States and to perform the duties of his office faithfully, impartially and justly to the best of his ability.

2. Appointments and promotions in the civil service of the State, and of such political subdivisions as may be provided by law, shall be made according to merit and fitness to be ascertained, as far as practicable, by examination, which, as far as practicable, shall be competitive; except that preference in appointments by reason of active service in any branch of the military or naval forces of the United States in time of war may be provided by law.

3. Any compensation for services or any fees received by any person by virtue of an appointive State office or position, in addition to the annual salary provided for the office or position, shall immediately upon receipt be paid into the treasury of the State, unless the compensation or fees shall be allowed or appropriated to him by law.

4. Any person before or after entering upon the duties of any public office, position or employment in this State may be required to give bond as may be provided by law.

5. The term of office of all officers elected or appointed pursuant to the provisions of this Constitution, except as herein otherwise provided, shall commence on the day of the date of their respective commissions; but no commission for any office shall bear date prior to the expiration of the term of the incumbent of said office.

6. The State Auditor shall be appointed by the Senate and General Assembly in joint meeting for a term of five years and until his successor shall be appointed and qualified. It shall be his duty to conduct post-audits of all transactions and accounts kept by or for all departments, offices and agencies of the State government, to report to the Legislature or to any committee thereof as shall be required by law, and to perform such other similar or related duties as shall, from time to time, be required of him by law.

SECTION II

1. County prosecutors shall be nominated and appointed by the Governor with the advice and consent of the Senate. Their term of office shall be five years, and they shall serve until the appointment and qualification of their respective successors.

2. County clerks, surrogates and sheriffs shall be elected by the people of their respective counties at general elections. The term of office of county clerks and surrogates shall be five years, and of sheriffs three years. Whenever a vacancy shall occur in any such office it shall be filled in the manner to be provided by law.

1. The Governor and all other State officers, while in office and for two years thereafter, shall be liable to impeachment for misdemeanor committed during their respective continuance in office.

2. The General Assembly shall have the sole power of impeachment by vote of a majority of all the members. All impeachments shall be tried by the Senate, and members, when sitting for that purpose, shall be on oath or affirmation "truly and impartially to try and determine the charge in question according to the evidence". No person shall be convicted without the concurrence of two-thirds of all the members of the Senate. When the Governor is tried, the Chief Justice of the Supreme Court shall preside and the President of the Senate shall not participate in the trial.

3. Judgment in cases of impeachment shall not extend further than to removal from office, and to disqualification to hold and enjoy any public office of honor, profit or trust in this State; but the person convicted shall nevertheless be liable to indictment, trial and punishment according to law.

ARTICLE VIII

TAXATION AND FINANCE

SECTION I

1. (a) Property shall be assessed for taxation under general laws and by uniform rules. All real property assessed and taxed locally or by the State for allotment and payment to taxing districts shall be assessed according to the same standard of value, except as otherwise permitted herein, and such real property shall be taxed at the general tax rate of the taxing district in which the property is situated, for the use of such taxing district.

(b) The Legislature shall enact laws to provide that the value of land, not less than 5 acres in area, which is determined by the assessing officer of the taxing jurisdiction to be actively devoted to agricultural or horticultural use and to have been so devoted for at least the 2 successive years immediately preceding the tax year in issue, shall, for local tax purposes, on application of the owner, be that value which such land has for agricultural or horticultural use.

Any such laws shall provide that when land which has been valued in this manner for local tax purposes is applied to a use other than for agriculture or horticulture it shall be subject to additional taxes in an amount equal to the difference, if any, between the taxes paid or payable on the basis of the valuation and the assessment authorized hereunder and the taxes that would have been paid or payable had the land been valued and assessed as otherwise provided in this Constitution, in the current year and in such of the tax years immediately preceding, not in excess of 2 such years in which the land was valued as herein authorized.

Such laws shall also provide for the equalization of assessments of land valued in accordance with the provisions hereof and for the assessment and collection of any additional taxes levied thereupon and shall include such other provisions as shall be necessary to carry out the provisions of this amendment.

Article VIII, Section I, paragraph 1 amended effective December 5, 1963.

2. Exemption from taxation may be granted only by general laws. Until otherwise provided by law all exemptions from taxation validly granted and now in existence shall be continued. Exemptions from taxation may be altered or repealed, except those exempting real and personal property used exclusively for religious, educational, charitable or cemetery purposes, as defined by law, and owned by any corporation or association organized and conducted exclusively for one or more of such purposes and not operating for profit.

3. Any citizen and resident of this State now or hereafter honorably discharged or released under honorable circumstances from active service, in time of war or of other emergency as, from time to time, defined by the Legislature, in any branch of the Armed Forces of the United States shall be entitled, annually, to a deduction from the amount of any tax bill for taxes on real and personal property, or both, in the sum of $50.00 or if the amount of any such tax bill shall be less than $50.00, to a cancellation thereof, which deduction or cancellation shall not be altered or repealed. Any person hereinabove

described who has been or shall be declared by the United States Veterans Administration, or its successor, to have a service-connected disability, shall be entitled to such further deduction from taxation as from time to time may be provided by law. The widow of any citizen and resident of this State who has met or shall meet his death on active duty in time of war or of other emergency as so defined in any such service shall be entitled, during her widowhood, and while a resident of this State, to the deduction or cancellation in this paragraph provided for honorably discharged veterans and to such further deduction as from time to time may be provided by law. The widow of any citizen and resident of this State who has had or shall hereafter have active service in time of war or of other emergency as so defined in any branch of the Armed Forces of the United States and who died or shall die while on active duty in any branch of the Armed Forces of the United States, or who has been or may hereafter be honorably discharged or released under honorable circumstances from active service in time of war or of other emergency as so defined in any branch of the Armed Forces of the United States shall be entitled, during her widowhood and while a resident of this State, to the deduction or cancellation in this paragraph provided for honorably discharged veterans and to such further deductions as from time to time may be provided by law.

Article VIII, Section I, paragraph 3 amended effective December 5, 1963.

4. The Legislature may, from time to time, enact laws granting an annual deduction from the amount of any tax bill for taxes on the real property of any citizen and resident of this State of the age of 65 or more years, or any citizen and resident of this State less than 65 years of age who is permanently and totally disabled according to the provisions of the Federal Social Security Act, residing in a dwelling house owned by him which is a constituent part of such real property or residing in a dwelling house owned by him which is assessed as real property but which is situated on land owned by another or others, but no such deduction shall be in excess of $160.00 with respect to any year prior to 1981, $200.00 per year in 1981, $225.00 per year in 1982, and $250.00 per year in 1983 and any year thereafter and such deduction shall be restricted to owners having an income not in excess of $5,000.00 per year with respect to any year prior to 1981, $8,000.00 per year in 1981, $9,000.00 per year in 1982, and $10,000.00 per year in 1983 and any year thereafter, exclusive of benefits under any one of the following:

a. The Federal Social Security Act and all amendments and supplements thereto;

b. Any other program of the Federal Government or pursuant to any other Federal law which provides benefits in whole or in part in lieu of benefits referred to in, or for persons excluded from coverage under, a. hereof including but not limited to the Federal Railroad Retirement Act and Federal pension, disability and retirement programs; or

c. Pension, disability or retirement programs of any state or its political subdivisions, or agencies thereof, for persons not covered under a. hereof; provided, however, that the total amount of benefits to be allowed exclusion by any owner under b. or c. hereof shall not be in excess of the maximum amount of benefits payable to, and allowable for exclusion by, an owner in similar circumstances under a. hereof.

The surviving spouse of a deceased citizen and resident of this State who during his or her life received a real property tax deduction pursuant to this paragraph shall be entitled, so long as he or she shall remain unmarried and a resident in the same dwelling house situated on the same land with respect to which said deduction was granted, to the same deduction, upon the same conditions, with respect to the same real property or with respect to the same dwelling house which is situated on land owned by another or others, notwithstanding that said surviving spouse is under the age of 65 and is not permanently and totally disabled, provided that said surviving spouse is 55 years of age or older.

Any such deduction when so granted by law shall be granted so that it will not be in addition to any other deduction or exemption to which the said citizen and resident may be entitled, but said citizen and resident may receive in addition any homestead rebate or credit provided by law. The State shall annually reimburse each taxing district in an amount equal to one-half of the tax loss to the district resulting from the allowance of tax deductions pursuant to this paragraph.

Article VIII,Section I,paragraph 4 amended effective December 4, 1980.

5. The Legislature may adopt a homestead statute which entitles homeowners, residential tenants and net lease residential tenants to a rebate or a credit of a sum of money related to property taxes paid by or allocable to them at such rates and subject to such limits as may be provided by law. Such rebates or credits may include a differential rebate or credit to citizens and residents who are of the age of 65 or more years, or less than 65 years of age who are permanently and totally disabled according to the provisions of the Federal Social Security Act, or are 55 years of age or more and the surviving spouse of a deceased citizen or resident of this State who during his lifetime received, or who, upon the adoption of this amendment and the enactment of implementing legislation, would have been entitled to receive a rebate or credit related to property taxes.

Article VIII, Section 1, paragraph 5 effective December 2, 1976.

6. The Legislature may enact general laws under which municipalities may adopt ordinances granting exemptions or abatements from taxation on buildings and structures in areas declared in need of rehabilitation in accordance with statutory criteria, whithin such municipalities and to the land comprising the premises upon which such buildings or structures are erected and which is necessary for the fair enjoyment thereof. Such exemptions shall be for limited periods of time as specified by law, but not in excess of 5 years.

Article VIII, Section I, paragraph 6 added effective December 4, 1975.

7. No tax shall be levied on personal incomes of individuals, estates and trusts of this State unless the entire net receipts therefrom shall be received into the treasury, placed in a perpetual fund and be annually appropriated, pursuant to formulas established from time to time by the Legislature, to the several counties, municipalities and school districts of this State exclusively for the purpose of reducing or offsetting property taxes.

Article VIII, Section I, paragraph 7 added effective December 2, 1976

SECTION II

1. The credit of the State shall not be directly or indirectly loaned in any case.

2. No money shall be drawn from the State treasury but for appropriations made by law. All moneys for the support of the State government and for all other State purposes as far as can be ascertained or reasonably foreseen, shall be provided for in one general appropriation law covering one and the same fiscal year; except that when a change in the fiscal year is made, necessary provision may be made to effect the transition. No general appropriation law or other law appropriating money for any State purpose shall be enacted if the appropriation contained therein, together with all prior appropriations made for the same fiscal period, shall exceed the total amount of revenue on hand and anticipated which will be available to meet such appropriations during such fiscal period, as certified by the Governor.

3. The Legislature shall not, in any manner, create in any fiscal year a debt or debts, liability of liabilities of the State, which together with any previous debts or liabilities shall exceed at any time one per centum of the total amount appropriated by the general appropriation law for that fiscal year, unless the same shall be authorized by a law for some single object or work distinctly specified therein. Regardless of any limitation relating to taxation in this Constitution, such law shall provide the ways and means, exclusive of loans, to pay the interest of such debt or liability as it falls due, and also to pay and discharge the principal thereof within thirty-five years from the time it is contracted; and the law shall not be repealed until such debt or liability and the interest thereon are fully paid and discharged. No such law shall take effect until it shall have been submitted to the people at a general election and approved by a majority of the legally qualified voters of the State voting thereon. All money to be raised by the authority of such law shall be applied only to the specific object stated therein, and to the payment of the debt thereby created. This paragraph shall not be construed to refer to any money that has been or may be deposited with this State by the government of the United States. Nor shall anything in this paragraph contained apply to the creation of any debts or liabilities for purposes of war, or to repel invasion, or to suppress insurrection or to meet an emergency caused by disaster or act of God.

SECTION III

1. The clearance, replanning, development or redevelopment of blighted areas shall be a public purpose and public use, for which private property may be taken or acquired. Municipal, public or private corporations may be authorized by law to undertake such clearance, replanning, development or redevelopment; and improvements made for these purposes and uses, or for any part of them, may be exempted from taxations, in whole or in part, for a limited period of time during which the profits of and dividends payable by any private corporation enjoying such tax exemption shall be limited by law. The conditions of use, ownership, management and control of such improvements shall be regulated by law.

2. No county, city, borough, town, township or village shall hereafter give any money or property, or loan its money or credit, to or in aid of any individual, association or corporation, or become security for, or be directly or indirectly the owner of, any stock or bonds of any association or corporation.

3. No donation of land or appropriation of money shall be made by the State of any county or municipal corporation to or for the use of any society, association or corporation whatever.

SECTION IV

1. The Legislature shall provide for the maintenance and support of a thorough and efficient system of free public schools for the instruction of all the children in the State between the ages of five and eighteen years.

2. The fund for the support of free public schools, and all money, stock and other property, which may hereafter be appropriated for that purpose, or received into the treasury under the provisions of any law heretofore passed to augment the said fund, shall be securely invested, and remain a perpetual fund; and the income thereof, except so much as it may be judged expedient to apply to an increase of the capital, shall be annually appropriated to the support of free public schools, and for the equal benefit of all the people of the State; and it shall not be competent, except as hereinafter provided, for the Legislature to borrow, appropriate or use the said fund or any part thereof for any other purpose, under any pretense whatever. The bonds of any school district of this State, issued according to law, shall be proper and secure investments for the said fund and, in addition, said fund, including the income therefrom and any other moneys duly appropriated to the support of free public schools may be used in such manner as the Legislature may provide by law to secure the payment of the principal of or interest on bonds or notes issued for school purposes by counties, municipalities or school districts or for the payment or purchase of any such bonds or notes or any claims for interest thereon.

Article VIII, Section IV, paragraph 2 amended effective December 4, 1958.

3. The Legislature may, within reasonable limitations as to distance to be prescribed, provide for the transportation of children within the ages of five to eighteen years inclusive to and from any school.

SECTION V

1. No lands that were formerly tidal flowed, but which have not been tidal flowed at any time for a period of 40 years, shall be deemed riparian lands, or lands subject to a riparian claim, and the passage of that period shall be a good and sufficient bar to any such claim, unless during that period the State has specifically defined and asserted such a claim pursuant to law. This section shall apply to lands which have not been tidal flowed at any time during the 40 years immediately preceding adoption of this amendment with respect to any claim not specifically defined and asserted by the State within 1 year of the adoption of this amendment.

Article VIII, Section V, paragraph 1 added effective December 3, 1981.

ARTICLE IX

AMENDMENTS

1. Any specific amendment or amendments to this Constitution may be proposed in the Senate or General Assembly. At least twenty calendar days prior to the first vote thereon in the house in which such amendment or amendments are first introduced, the same shall be printed and placed on the desks of the members of each house. Thereafter and

prior to such vote a public hearing shall be held thereon. If the proposed amendment or amendments or any of them shall be agreed to by three-fifths of all the members of each of the respective houses, the same shall be submitted to the people. If the same or any of them shall be agreed to by less than three-fifths but nevertheless by a majority of all the members of each of the respective houses, such proposed amendment or amendments shall be referred to the Legislature in the next legislative year; and if in that year the same or any of them shall be agreed to by a majority of all the members of each of the respective houses, then such amendment or amendments shall be submitted to the people.

2. The proposed amendment or amendments shall be entered on the journal of each house with the yeas and nays of the members voting thereon.

3. The Legislature shall cause the proposed amendment or amendments to be published at least once in one or more newspapers of each county, if any be published therein, not less than three months prior to submission to the people.

4. The proposed amendment or amendments shall then be submitted to the people at the next general election in the manner and form provided by the Legislature.

5. If more than one amendment be submitted, they shall be submitted in such manner and form that the people may vote for or against each amendment separately and distinctly.

6. If the proposed amendment or amendments or any of them shall be approved by a majority of the legally qualified voters of the State voting thereon, the same shall become part of the Constitution on the thirtieth day after the election, unless otherwise provided in the amendment or amendments.

7. If at the election a proposed amendment shall not be approved, neither such proposed amendment nor one to effect the same or substantially the same change in the Constitution shall be submitted to the people before the third general election thereafter.

ARTICLE X

GENERAL PROVISIONS

1. The seal of the State shall be kept by the Governor, or person administering the office of Governor, and used by him officially, and shall be called the Great Seal of the State of New Jersey.

2. All grants and commissions shall be in the name and by the authority of the State of New Jersey, sealed with the Great Seal, signed by the Governor, or person administering the office of Govenor, and countersigned by the Secretary of State, and shall run thus: "The State of New Jersey, to................................,Greeting".

3. All writs shall be in the name of the State. All indictments shall conclude: "against the peace of this State, the government and dignity of the same".

4. Wherever in this Constitution the term "person", "persons", "people" or any personal pronoun is used, the same shall be taken to include both sexes.

5. Except as herein otherwise provided, this Constitution shall take effect on the first day of January in the year of our Lord one thousand nine hundred and forty-eight.

ARTICLE XI

SCHEDULE

SECTION I

1. This Constitution shall supersede the Constitution of one thousand eight hundred and forty-four as amended.

2. The Legislature shall enact all laws necessary to make this Constitution fully effective.

3. All law, statutory and otherwise, all rules and regulations of administrative bodies and all rules of courts in force at the time this Constitution or any Article thereof takes effect shall remain in full force until they expire or are superseded, altered or repealed by this Constitution or otherwise.

4. Except as otherwise provided by this Constitution, all writs, actions, judgments, decrees, causes of action, prosecutions, contracts, claims and rights of individuals and of bodies corporate, and of the State, and all charters and franchises shall continue unaffected notwithstanding the taking effect of any Article of this Constitution.

5. All indictments found before the taking effect of this Constitution or any Article may be proceeded upon. After the taking effect thereof, indictments for crime and complaints for offenses committed prior thereto may be found, made and proceeded upon in the courts having jurisdiction thereof.

SECTION II

1. The first Legislature under this Constitution shall meet on the second Tuesday in January, in the year one thousand nine hundred and forty-eight.

2. Each member of the General Assembly, elected at the election in the year one thousand nine hundred and forty-seven, shall hold office for a term beginning at noon of the second Tuesday in January in the year one thousand nine hundred and forty-eight and ending at noon of the second Tuesday in January in the year one thousand nine hundred and fifty. Each member of the General Assembly elected thereafter shall hold office for the term provided by this Constitution.

3. Each member of the Senate elected in the years one thousand nine hundred and forty-five and one thousand nine hundred and forty-six shall hold office for the term for which he was elected. Each member of the Senate elected in the year one thousand nine hundred and forty-seven shall hold office for a term of four years beginning at noon of the second Tuesday in January following his election. The seats in the Senate which would have been filled in the years hereinafter designated had this Constitution not been adopted shall be filled by election as follows: of those seats which would have been filled by election in the year one thousand nine hundred and forty-eight, three seats, as chosen by the Senate in the year one thousand nine hundred and forty-eight, shall be filled by election in that year for terms of five years, and three, as so chosen, shall be filled by election in that year for terms of three years, and those seats which would have been filled by election in the year one thousand nine hundred and forty-nine shall be filled by election in that year for terms of four years, so that eleven seats in the Senate shall be filled by election in the year one thousand nine hundred and fifty-one and every fourth year thereafter for terms of four years, and the members of the Senate so elected and their successors shall constitute one class to be elected as prescribed in paragraph 2 of Section II of Article IV of this Constitution, and ten seats shall be filled by election in the year one thousand nine hundred and fifty-three and every fourth year thereafter for terms of four years, and the members of the Senate so elected and their successors shall constitute the other class to be elected as prescribed in said paragraph of this Constitution.

4. The provisions of Paragraph 1 of Section V of Article IV of this Constitution shall not prohibit the nomination, election or appointment of any member of the Senate or General Assembly first organized under this Constitution, to any State civil office or position created by this Constitution or created during his first term as such member.

SECTION III

1. A Governor shall be elected for a full term at the general election to be held in the year one thousand nine hundred and forty-nine and every fourth year thereafter.

2. The taking effect of this Constitution or any provision thereof shall not of itself affect the tenure, term, status or compensation of any person then holding any public office, position or employment in this State, except as provided in this Constitution. Unless otherwise specifically provided in this Constitution, all constitutional officers in office at the time of its adoption shall continue to exercise the authority of their respective offices during the term for which they shall have been elected or appointed and until the qualification of their successors respectively. Upon the taking effect of this Constitution all officers of the militia shall retain their commissions subject to the provisions of Article V, Section III.

3. The Legislature, in compliance with the provisions of this Constitution, shall prior to the first day of July, one thousand nine hundred and forty-nine, and may from time to time thereafter, allocate by law the executive and administrative offices, departments and instrumentalities of the State government among and within the principal departments. If such allocation shall not have been completed within the time limited, the Governor shall call a special session of the Legislature to which he shall submit a plan or plans for consideration to complete such allocation; and no other matters shall be considered at such session.

SECTION IV

1. Subsequent to the adoption of this Constitution the Governor shall nominate and appoint, with the advice and consent of the Senate, a Chief Justice and six Associate Justices of the new Supreme Court from among the persons then being the Chancellor, the Chief Justice and Associate Justices of the old Supreme Court, the Vice Chancellors and Circuit Court Judges. The remaining judicial officers enumerated and such Judges of the Court of Errors and Appeals as have been admitted to the practice of law in this State for at least ten years, and are in office on the adoption of the Constitution, shall constitute the Judges of the Superior Court. The Justices of the new Supreme Court and the Judges of the Superior Court so designated shall hold office each for the period of his term which remains unexpired at the time the Constitution is adopted; and if reappointed he shall hold office during good behavior. No Justice of the new Supreme Court or Judge of the Superior Court shall hold his office after attaining the age of seventy years, except, however, that such Justice or Judge may complete the period of his term which remains unexpired at the time the Constitution is adopted.

2. The Judges of the Courts of Common Pleas shall constitute the Judges of the County Courts, each for the period of his term which remains unexpired at the time the Judicial Article of this Constitution takes effect.

3. The Court of Errors and Appeals, the present Supreme Court, the Court of Chancery, the Prerogative Court and the Circuit Courts shall be abolished when the Judicial Article of this Constitution takes effect; and all their jurisdiction, functions, powers and duties shall be transferred to and divded between the new Supreme Court and the Superior Court according as jurisdiction is vested in each of them under this Constitution.

4. Except as otherwise provided in this Constitution and until otherwise provided by law, all courts now existing in this State, other than those abolished in paragraph 3 hereof, shall continue as if this Constitution had not been adopted, provided, however, that when the Judicial Article of this Constitution takes effect, the jurisdiction, powers and functions of the Court of Common Pleas, Orphans' Court, Court of Oyer and Terminer, Court of Quarter Sessions and Court of Special Sessions of each county, the judicial officers, clerks and employees thereof, and the causes pending therein and their files, shall be transferred to the County Court of the county. All statutory provisions relating to the county courts aforementioned of each county and to the Judge or Judges thereof shall apply to the new County Court of the county and the Judge or Judges thereof, unless otherwise provided by law. Until otherwise provided by law and except as aforestated, the judicial officers, surrogates and clerks of all courts now existing, other than those abolished in paragraph 3 hereof, and the employees of said officers, clerks, surrogates and courts shall continue in the exercise of their duties, as if this Constitution had not been adopted.

5. The Supreme Court shall make rules governing the administration and practice and procedure of the County Court; and the Chief Justice of the Supreme Court shall be the administrative head of these courts with power to assign any Judge thereof of any county to sit temporarily in the Superior Court or to sit temporarily without the county in a County Court.

6. The Advisory Masters appointed to hear matrimonial proceedings and in office on the adoption of this Constitution shall, each for the period of his term which remains unexpired at the time the Constitution is adopted, continue so to do as Advisory Masters to the Chancery Division of the Superior Court, unless otherwise provided by law.

7. All Special Masters in Chancery, Masters in Chancery, Supreme Court Commissioners and Supreme Court Examiners shall, until otherwise provided by rules of the Supreme Court, continue respectively as Special Masters, Masters, Commissioners and Examiners of the Superior Court, with appropriate similar functions and powers as if this Constituion had not been adopted.

8. When the Judicial Article of this Con_titution takes effect:

(a) All causes and proceedings of whatever character pending in the Court of Errors and Appeals shall be transferred to the new Supreme Court;

(b) All causes and proceedings of whatever character pending on appeal or writ of error in the present Supreme Court and in the Prerogative Court and all pending causes involving the prerogative writs shall be transferred to the Appellate Division of the Superior Court;

(c) All causes and proceedings of whatever character pending in the Supreme Court other than those stated shall be transferred to the Superior Court;

(d) All causes and proceedings of whatever character pending in the Prerogative Court other than those stated shall be transferred to the Chancery Division of the Superior Court;

(e) All causes and proceedings of whatever character pending in all other courts which are abolished shall be transferred to the Superior Court.

For the purposes of this paragraph, paragraph 4 and paragraph 9, a cause shall be deemed to be pending notwithstanding that an adjudication has been entered therein, provided the time limited for review has not expired or the adjudication reserves to any party the right to apply for further relief.

9. The files of all causes pending in the Court of Errors and Appeals shall be delivered to the Clerk of the new Supreme Court; and the files of all causes pending in the present Supreme Court, the Court of Chancery and the Prerogative Court shall be delivered to the Clerk of the Superior Court. All other files, books, papers, records and documents and all property of the Court of Errors and Appeals, the present Supreme Court, the Prerogative Court, the Chancellor and the Court of Chancery, or in their custody, shall be disposed of as shall be provided by law.

10. Upon the taking effect of the Judicial Article of this Constitution, all the functions, powers and duties conferred by statute, rules or otherwise upon the Chancellor, the Ordinary, and the Justices and Judges of the courts abolished by this Constitution, to the extent that such functions, powers and duties are not inconsistent with this Constitution, shall be transferred to and may be exercised by Judges of the Superior Court until otherwise provided by law or rules of the new Supreme Court; excepting that such statutory powers not related to the Administration of justice as are then vested in any such judicial officers shall, after the Judicial Article of this Constitution takes effect and until otherwise provided by law, be transferred to and exercised by the Chief Justice of the new Supreme Court.

11. Upon the taking effect of the Judicial Article of this Constitution, the Clerk of the Supreme Court shall become the Clerk of the new Supreme Court and shall serve as Clerk until the expiration of the term for which he was appointed as Clerk of the Supreme Court, and all employees of the Supreme Court as previously constituted, of the Clerk thereof and of the Chief Justice and the Justices thereof, of the Circuit Courts and the Judges thereof and of the Court of Errors and Appeals shall be transferred to appropriate similar positions with similar compensation and civil service status under the Clerk of the new Supreme Court or the new Supreme Court, or the Clerk of the Superior Court or the Superior Court, which shall be provided by law.

12. Upon the taking effect of the Judicial Article of this Constitution, the Clerk in Chancery shall become the Clerk of the Superior Court and shall serve as such Clerk until the expiration of the term for which he was appointed as Clerk in Chancery, and all employees of the Clerk in Chancery, the Court of Chancery, the Chancellor and the several Vice Chancellors shall be transferred to appropriate similar positions with similar compensation and civil service status under the Clerk of the Superior Court or the Superior Court, which shall be provided by law.

13. Appropriations made by law for judicial expenditures during the fiscal year one thousand nine hundred and forty-eight, one thousand nine hundred and forty-nine may be transferred to similar objects and purposes required by the Judicial Article.

14. The Judicial Article of this Constitution shall take effect on the fifteenth day of September, one thousand nine hundred and forty-eight, except that the Governor, with the advice and consent of the Senate, shall have the power to fill vacancies arising prior thereto in the new Supreme Court and the Superior Court; and except further that any provision of this Constitution which may require any act to be done prior thereto or in preparation therefor shall take effect immediately upon the adoption of this Constitution.

SECTION V

1. For the purpose of electing senators in 1967 and until the 1970 decennial census of the United States for New Jersey shall have been received by the Governor, the forty senators are hereby allocated among fifteen Senate districts, as follows:

First District—the counties of Gloucester, Atlantic and Cape May, two senators;

Second District—the counties of Salem and Cumberland, one senator;

Third District—the county of Camden, three senators;

Fourth District—the counties of Burlington and Ocean, two senators;

Fifth District—the county of Monmouth, two senators;

Sixth District—the county of Mercer, two senators;

Seventh District—the county of Middlesex, three senators;

Eighth District—the county of Somerset, one senator;

Ninth District—the county of Union, three senators;

Tenth District—the county of Morris, two senators;

Eleventh District—the county of Essex, six senators;

Twelfth District—the county of Hudson, four senators;

Thirteenth District—the county of Bergen, five senators;

Fourteenth District—the county of Passaic, three senators; and

Fifteenth District—the counties of Sussex, Warren, and Hunterdon, one senator.

2. For the purpose of electing members of the General Assembly and the senators from Assembly districts where so required in 1967 and until the 1970 census of the United States for New Jersey shall have been received by the Governor, the Assembly districts shall be established by an Apportionment Commission consisting of ten members, five to be appointe by the chairman of the State committee of each of the two political parties whose candidates for Governor receive the largest number of votes at the most recent gubernatorial election. Each State chairman, in making such appointments, shall give due consideraton to the representation of the various geographical areas of the State. Such Apportionment Commission shall be appointed no earlier than November 10 nor later than November 15, 1966, and their appointments shall be certified by the Secretary of State on or before December 1, 1966. The Commission, by a majority of the whole number of its members, shall certify the establishment of Assembly districts to the Secretary of State on or before February 1, 1967.

3. If such Apportionment Commission fails so to certify the establishment of Assembly districts to the Secretary of State on or before the date fixed or if prior thereto it determines that it will be unable to do so, it shall so certify to the Chief Justice of the Supreme Court of New Jersey, and he shall appoint an eleventh member of the Commission. Such Commission, by a majority of the whole number of its members, shall within one month after the appointment of such eleventh member certify to the Secretary of State the establishment of Assembly districts.

4. The Assembly districts so established shall be used thereafter for the election of members of the General Assembly and shall remain unaltered until the following decennial census of the United States for New Jersey shall have been received by the Governor.

Article XI, Section V, paragraphs 1, 2, 3, 4 added effective December 8, 1966.

SECTION VI

When this amendment to the Constitution providing for the abolition of the County Courts takes effect:

(a)   All the jurisdiction, functions, powers and duties of the County Court of each county, the judicial officers, clerks, employees thereof, and the causes pending therein, and their files, shall be transferred to the Superior Court. Until otherwise provided by law, the judicial officers, surrogates and clerks of the County Courts and the employees of said officers, clerks, surrogates and courts, shall continue in the exercise of their duties as if this amendment had not been adopted. For the purposes of this paragraph, a cause shall be deemed to be pending notwithstanding that an adjudication has been entered therein, provided the time limited for appeal has not expired or the adjudication reserves any party the right to apply for further relief.

(b)   All the functions, powers and duties conferred by the statute, rules or otherwise, upon the judges of the County Courts, shall be transferred to and may be exercised by judges of the Superior Court until otherwise provided by law or rules of the Supreme Court.

(c)   Until otherwise provided by law, all county clerks shall become clerks of the Law Division of the Superior Court and all surrogates shall become clerks of the Chancery Division (Probate Part) of the Superior Court for their respective counties and shall perform such duties and maintain such files and records on behalf of the Clerk of the Superior Court as may be required by law and rule of court; and all fees payable to the county clerks and surrogates prior to the effective date of this amendment shall continue to be so payable and be received for the use of their respective counties until otherwise provided by law.

(d)   The judges of the County Courts in office on the effective date of this amendment shall be judges of the Superior Court. All such judges who had acquired tenure on a County Court shall hold office as a judge of the Superior Court during good behavior, with all rights, and subject to all the provisions of the Constitution affecting a judge of the Superior Court, as though they were initially appointed to the Superior Court. All other judges of the County Courts shall hold office as judges of the Superior Court, each for the period of his term which remains unexpired on the effective date of this amendment; and if reappointed, he shall hold office during good behavior, with all the rights and subject to all the provisions of the Constitution affecting a judge of the Superior Court as though he were initially appointed to the Superior Court.

Article XI, Section VI, paragraphs (a), (b), (c), and (d) added by amendment effective December 7, 1978.

NEW JERSEY LEGISLATIVE DISTRICTS

1982

One Senator and two members of the General Assembly

elected from each legislative district

1st DISTRICT

All of CAPE MAY county; and

The following CUMBERLAND county municipalities: Bridgeton, Deerfield, Maurice River, Millville, Upper Deerfield, Vineland.

2nd District

The following ATLANTIC county municipalities: Absecon, Atlantic City, Brigantine, Corbin, Egg Harbor, Egg Harbor City, Estell Manor, Galloway, Hamilton, Hammonton, Linwood, Longport, Margate City, Mullica, Northfield, Pleasantville, Port Republic, Somers Point, Ventnor City, Weymouth.

3rd District

The following CUMBERLAND county municipalities: Commercial, Downe, Fairfield, Greenwich Hopewell, Lawrence, Shilohm, Stow Creek;

The following GLOUCESTER county municipalities: East Greenwich, Glassboro, Greenwich, Harrison, Logan, Mantua, National Park, Paulsboro, Pitman, South Harrison, Swedesboro, Wenonah, West Deptford, Westville, Woodbury, Woolwich; and

All of SALEM county.

4th DISTRICT

The following ATLANTIC county municipalities: Buena, Buena Vista, Folsom;

The following CAMDEN county municipalities: Chesihurst, Gloucester, Laurel Springs, Lindenwold, Magnolia, Waterford, Winslow; and

The following GLOUCESTER county municipalities: Clayton, Elk, Franklin, Monroe, Newfield, Washington.

5th DISTRICT

The following CAMDEN county municipalities: Barrington, Bellmawr, Brooklawn, Camden, Gloucester City, Hi-Nella, Lawnside, Mount Ephraim, Runnemede, Somerdale, Stratford, Woodlynne, and

The following GLOUCESTER county municipalities: Deptford, Woodbury Heights.

6th DISTRICT

The following CAMDEN county municipalities: Audubon, Audubon Park, Berlin boro, Berlin twp.,Cherry Hill, Clementon, Collingswood, Gibbsboro, Haddon, Haddonfield, Haddon Heights, Merchantville, Oaklyn, Pine Hill, Pine Valley, Tavistock, Voorhees.

7th DISTRICT

The following BURLINGTON county municipalities: Beverly, Burlington city, Burlington twp., Cinnaminson, Delanco, Delran, Edgewater Park, Maple Shade, Palmyra, Riverside, Riverton, Westampton, Willingboro; and

The following CAMDEN county municipality: Pennsauken.

8th DISTRICT

The following BURLINGTON county municipalities:Bordentown City, Bordentown twp., Chesterfield, Eastampton, Evesham, Fieldsboro, Florence, Hainesport, Lumberton, Mansfild, Medford, Medford Lakes, Moorestown, Mount Holly, Mount Laurel, Pemberton boro., Pemberton twp., Shamong, Southampton, Springfield, Tabernacle, Washington, Woodland.

9TH DISTRICT

The following BURLINGTON county municipalities: Bass River, New Hanover, North Hanover, Wrightstown; and

The following OCEAN county municipalities: Barnegat, Barnegat Light, Beach Haven, Beachwood, Berkeley, Eagleswood, Harvey Cedars, Island Heights, Jackson, Lacey, Lakehurst, Little Egg Harbor, Long Beach, Manchester, Ocean, Ocean Gate, Plumsted, Ship Bottom, South Toms River, Stafford, Surf City, Tuckerton.

10TH DISTRICT

The following OCEAN county municipalities: Bay Head, Brick, Dover, Lakewood, Lavallette, Mantoloking, Pine Beach, Point Pleasant, Point Pleasant Beach, Seaside Heights, Seaside Park.

11TH DISTRICT

The following MONMOUTH county municipalities: Allenhurst, Asbury Park, Atlantic Highlands, Avon-by-the-Sea, Belmar, Bradley Beach, Brielle, Deal, Highlands, Interlaken, Loch Arbour, Long Branch, Manasquan, Monmouth Beach, Neptune, Neptune City, Ocean, Oceanport, Sea Bright, Sea Girt, South Belmar, Spring Lake, Spring Lake Heights, Wall.

12TH DISTRICT

The following MONMOUTH county municipalities: Allentown, Colts Neck, Eatontown, Englishtown, Fair Haven, Farmingdale, Freehold boro., Freehold twp., Holmdel, Howell, Little Silver, Manalapan, Marlboro, Millstone, Red Bank, Roosevelt, Rumson, Shrewsbury boro., Shrewsbury twp., Tinton Falls, Upper Freehold, West Long Branch.

13TH DISTRICT

The following MIDDLESEX county municipality: Old Bridge; and

The following MONMOUTH county municipalities: Aberdeen, Hazlet, Keansburg, Keyport, Matawan, Middletown, Union Beach.

14TH DISTRICT

The following MERCER county municipalities: East Windsor, Hamilton, Hightstown, Washington; and

The following MIDDLESEX county municipalities: Cranbury, Plainsboro, South Brunswick; and

The following SOMERSET county municipalities: Franklin, Manville, Millstone, Rocky Hill.

15TH DISTRICT

The following MERCER county municipalities: Ewing, Lawrence, Princeton boro., Princeton twp., Trenton, West Windsor.

16TH DISTRICT

The following HUNTERDON county municipality: East Amwell; and

The following MORRIS county municipalities: Mendham boro., Mendham twp., Passaic; and

The following SOMERSET county municipalities: Bedminster, Bernards, Bernardsville, Bound Brook, Branchburg, Bridgewater, Far Hills, Green Brook, Hillsborough, Montgomery, North Plainfield, Peapack-Gladstone, Raritan, Somerville. South Bound Brook, Warren, Watchung.

17TH DISTRICT

The following MIDDLESEX county municipalities: Dunellen, Highland Park, Middlesex, New Brunswick, Piscataway, South Plainfield; and

The following UNION county municipality: Plainfield.

18TH DISTRICT

The following MIDDLESEX county municipalities: East Brunswick, Edison, Helmetta, Jamesburg, Metuchen, Milltown, Monroe, North Brunswick, Spots-wood.

19TH DISTRICT

The following MIDDLESEX county municipalities: Perth Amboy, Sayreville, South Amboy, South River, Woodbridge.

20TH DISTRICT

The following MIDDLESEX county municipality: Carteret; and

The following UNION county municipalities: Elizabeth, Linden, Rahway.

21ST DISTRICT

The following UNION county municipalities: Cranford, Garwood, Hillside, Kenilworth, Roselle, Roselle Park, Springfield, Union, Westfield.

22ND DISTRICT

The following ESSEX county municipalities: Caldwell, Essex Fells, Livingston, Maplewood, Millburn, Roseland; and

The following UNION county municipalities: Berkeley Heights, Clark, Fanwood, Mountainside, New Providence, Scotch Plains; Summit, Winfield.

23RD DISTRICT

The following HUNTERDON county municipalities: Alexandria, Bethlehem, Bloomsbury, Califon, Clinton town, Clinton twp., Delaware, Flemington, Franklin, Frenchtown, Glen Gardner, Hampton, High Bridge, Holland, Kingwood, Lambertville, Lebanon boro., Lebanon twp., Milford, Raritan, Readington, Stockton, Tewksbury, Union, West Amwell;

The following MERCER county municipalities: Hopewell boro., Hopewell twp.,Pennington;

The following MORRIS county municipalities: Chester boro., Chester twp., Mount Arlington, Mount Olive, Netcong, Roxbury, Washington;

The following SUSSEX county municipality: Stanhope, and;

The following WARREN county municipalities: Franklin, Greenwich, Washington boro., Washington twp.

24TH DISTRICT

The following SUSSEX county municipalities: Andover boro., Andover twp., Branchville, Byram, Frankford, Franklin, Fredon, Green, Hamburg, Hampton, Hardyston, Hopatcong, Lafayette, Montague, Newton, Ogdensburg, Sandyston, Sparta, Stillwater, Sussex, Vernon, Walpack, Wantage; and

The following WARREN county municipalities: Allamuchy, Alpha, Belvidere, Blairstown, Frelinghuysen, Hackettstown, Hardwick, Harmony, Hope, Independence, Knowlton, Liberty, Lopatcong, Mansfield, Oxford, Pahaquarry, Phillipsburg, Pohatcong, White.

25TH DISTRICT

The following MORRIS county municipalities: Boonton town,Boonton twp., Denville, Dover, Hanover, Harding, Jefferson, Madison, Mine Hill, Morris, Morristown, Mountain Lakes, Randolph, Rockaway boro., Rockaway twp., Victory Gardens, Wharton.

26TH DISTRICT

The following MORRIS county municipalities: Butler, Chatham boro., Chatham twp., East Hanover, Florham Park, Kinnelon, Lincoln Park, Montville, Morris Plains, Parsippany-Troy Hills, Pequannock, Riverdale; and

The following PASSAIC county municipalities: Ringwood, West Milford.

27TH DISTRICT

The following ESSEX county municipalities: East Orange, Orange, South Orange Village, West Orange, Part of Newark (North Ward Election Districts 3, 5, 28, 29, West Ward Election Districts 1, 3, 7, 9, 10, 42, 43, 44).

28TH DISTRICT

The following ESSEX county municipalities: Irvington, Part of Newark (North Ward Election Districts 1, 2, 4, 6 - 27, 31, 36 - 46, 48, West Ward Election Districts 2, 5, 6, 11, 13 - 41, 45).

29TH DISTRICT

The following ESSEX county municipality: Part of Newark (Central Ward, East Ward, South Ward).

30TH DISTRICT

The following ESSEX county municipalities: Belleville, Bloomfield, Cedar Grove, Glen Ridge, Montclair, Nutley, Verona.

31ST DISTRICT

The following HUDSON county municipalities: Bayonne, Part of Jersey City (Ward A, Ward B, Ward E Election Districts 1 - 8, 25, Ward F).

32ND DISTRICT

The following HUDSON county municipalities: East Newark, Harrison. Kearny, North Bergen, Secaucus, Part of Jersey City (Ward C, Ward D Election Districts 13, 14, 21 - 31, Ward E Election Districts 9 - 20).

33RD DISTRICT

The following HUDSON county municipalities: Guttenberg, Hoboken, Part of Jersey City (Ward D Election Districts 1 - 12, 15 - 20, 32, Ward E Election Districts 21 - 24), Union, Weehawken, West New York.

34TH DISTRICT

The following ESSEX county municipalities: Fairfield, North Caldwell, West Caldwell; and

The following PASSAIC county municipalities: Clifton, Little Falls, Totowa, Wayne, West Paterson.

35TH DISTRICT

The following BERGEN county municipalities: Elmwood Park; and

The following PASSAIC county municipalities: Haledon, Hawthorne, Paterson, Prospect Park.

36TH DISTRICT

The following BERGEN county municipalities: Carlstadt, East Rutherford, Garfield, Lyndhurst, Moonachie, North Arlington, Ridgefield, Rutherford, South Hackensack, Teterboro, Wallington, Wood-Ridge; and

The following PASSAIC county municipality: Passaic.

37TH DISTRICT

The following BERGEN county municipalities: Bergenfield, Cliffside Park, Edgewater, Englewood, Englewood Cliffs, Fairview, Fort Lee, Leonia, Teaneck, Tenafly.

38TH DISTRICT

The following BERGEN county municipalities: Bogota, Hackensack, Hasbrouck Heights, Haworth, Little Ferry, Lodi, Maywood, Oradell, Palisades Park, Paramus, Ridgefield Park, Rochelle Park, Saddle Brook.

39TH DISTRICT

The following BERGEN county municipalities: Allendale, Alpine, Closter, Cresskill, Demarest, Dumont, Emerson, Harrington Park, Hillsdale, Ho-ho-Kus, Montvale, New Milford, Northvale, Norwood, Old Tappan, Park Ridge, River Edge, River Vale, Rockleigh, Saddle River, Waldwick, Washington, Westwood, Woodcliff Lake.

40TH DISTRICT

The following BERGEN county municipalities: Fair Lawn, Franklin Lakes, Glen Rock, Mahwah, Midland Park, Oakland, Ramsey, Ridgewood, Upper Saddle River, Wyckoff; and

The following PASSAIC county municipalities: Bloomingdale, North Haledon, Pompton Lakes, Wanaque.

BIBLIOGRAPHY

Andrews, Charles M. *The Colonial Period of American History.* New Haven, Yale University Press, 1934-37.

Austin, Mary S. *Philip Freneau, the Poet of the Revolution: History of His Life and Times.* Ed. by Helen Kearny Vreeland. New York, 1901.

Baker, Ray Stannard. *Woodrow Wilson: Life and Letters:* Princeton, 1890-1910. Garden City, N.Y., Doubleday, Doran & Co., 1927.

Barber, John Warner, and Henry Howe. *Historical Collections of New Jersey.* Rev. ed. New Haven, J.W. Barber, 1868.

Barnes, Harry Elmer. *A History of the Penal, Reformatory and Correctional Institutions of the State of New Jersey.* Trenton, MacCrellish & Quigley Co., 1918.

Beck, Henry Charlton. *Forgotten Towns of Southern New Becker, Donald William, Indian place-names in New Jersey.* Cedar Grove, N.J., Phillips-Campbell Publishing Co., 1964.

Beer, Thomas. *Stephen Crane, a Study in American Letters.* New York, Knopf, 1923.

Boucher, Bertrand P. and H. Dunster Mead. *Pictorial New Jersey.* Cedar Grove, N.J., Phillips-Campbell Publishing Co., c.1964.

Boyd, Thomas Alexander. *Poor John Fitch, Inventor of the Steamboat.* New York, Putnam, 1935.

Boyer, Charles S. *Early Forges and Furnaces of New Jersey.* Philadelphia, University of Pennsylvania Press, 1931.
    -Rambles through old highways and byways of West Jersey. Edited by John D.B.Morgan. Camden,N.J., Camden Co

Burnaby, Rev. Andrew. *Burnaby's Travelsthrough North America.* Repr.from 3d ed. of 1798. New York, A. Wessels Co., 1904.

Chambers, Theodore Frelinghuysen. *The Early Germans of New Jersey: Their History, Churches and Genealogies.* Dover, N.J., Dover Printing C., 1895.

Collins, Varnum Lansing. *Princeton, Past and Present.* Princeton, University Press, 1931.

Cooley, Henry Scofield. *A Study of Slavery in New Jersey.* Baltimore, Johns Hopkins Press, 1896.

Carpenter, John Allan. *New Jersey (from its glorious past to the present).* Illus., Roger Herrington. Chicago, Childrens Press, 1965.

Cunningham, John T. *This is New Jersey.* Rev. ed. New Brunswick, N.J., Rutgers University Press, 1968.

Dana, John Cotton. *American Art: How It Can Be Made to Flourish.* Woodstock, Vt., Elm Tree Press, 1914.

Demarest, William Henry Steel. *History of Rutgers College, 1766-1924.* New Brunswick, Rutgers College, 1924.

Duer, William Alexander. *The Life of Wm. Alexander, Earl of Stirling; Major General in the Army of the United States during the Revolution.* New York, 1847.

Dyer, Frank Lewis, and Thomas Commerford Martin. *Edison, His Life and Inventions.* New York, Harper, 1929.

Erdman, Charles R., Jr. *The New Jersey Constitution: A Barrier to Governmental Efficiency and Economy.* Princeton, University Press, 1934.

Everson, A.R., comp. *Facts about New Jersey and the Cost of Government.* Trenton, N.J. Taxpayers Association, 1935.

Fisher, Edgar Jacob. *New Jersey as a Royal Province, 1738-1776.* New York, Columbia University Press, 1911.

Frothingham, Thomas Goddard. *Washington, Commander in Chief.* Boston, Houghton Mifflin. 1930.

Goldstein, Philip Reuben. *Social Aspects of the Jewish Colonies of South Jersey.* New York, League Printing Co., 1921.

Gordon, Thomas F. *Gazetteer of the State of New Jersey and History of New Jersey.* Trenton, D. Fenton, 1834.

Gummere, Amelia Mott, ed. *The Journal and Essays of John Woolman.* New York, Macmillan, 1922.

Hannau, Hans W. *New Jersey.* Doubleday, Garden City N.Y., 1968.

Hatfield, Edwin Francis. *History of Elizabeth, New Jersey: Including the Early History of Union County .* New York, Carlton & Lanahan, 1878.

Kalm, Peter. *The America of 1750: Peter Kalm's Travels in North America.* New York, Wilson-Erickson. 1937.

Knapp, C.M. *New Jersey Politics during the Period of the Civil War and Reconstruction.* N.Y., W.F. Humphrey, 1924.

Kobbe, Gustav. *The Jersey coast and pines; an illustrated guide-book with road maps.* Baltimore, Gateway Press, 1970.

Kull, Irving S., ed. *New Jersey: A History.* New York, American Historical Society. 1930.

Leaming, Aaron, and Jacob Spicer. *The Grants. Concessions and Original Constitutions of the Province of New Jersey.* Somerville, Somerset Gazette. 1881.

Lee, Francis Bazley. *New Jersey as a Colony and as a State.* New York, Publishing Society of New Jersey, 1902.

Lewis, Paul M. *Beautiful New Jersey.* Beaverton, OR., Beautiful America Publishing Co., 1980.

Lord, Beman. *On the banks of the Delaware; a view of its history and folklore.* Illus.,Allan Eitzen. New York, H.Z. Walck, 1971.

Meade, Emily Fogg. *The Italian on the Land: A Study in Immigration.* Washington, Government Printing Office. 1907.

Mellick, Andrew D., Jr. *The Story of an Old Farm, or, Life in New Jersey in the Eighteenth Century.* Somerville, Unionist-Gazette, 1889

Miers, Earl Schenck. *Down in Jersey: an affectionate narrative.* New Brunswick, N.J., Rutgers University Press, 1973.

Mills, Weymer Jay. *Through the Gates of Old Romance.* Philadelphia, Lippincott, 1903.

Milstead, Harley P. *New Jersey geography and history.* Philadelphia, Winston, 1960.

Monnette,Orra Eugene. *First Settlers of Ye Plantations of Piscataway & Woodbridge, Olde East New Jersey.1664-1714.* Los Angeles, Leroy Carman Press. 1930-35.

Morley, Christopher. *Seacoast of Bohemia.* Garden City, N.Y., Doubleday, Doran & Co., 1929.

Murray, David. *History of Education in New Jersey.* Washington, Government Printing Office, 1899.

Nelson, William. *The Indians of New Jersey with Some Notice of Indian Place Names.* Paterson. Press Publishing Co., 1894.

Nelson, William. *History of the City of Paterson and of the County of Passaic.* Paterson, Press Publishing Co., 1901.

New Jersey Historical Society. *Proceedings.* Published quarterly by the Society. Newark, 1845 to date.

New Jersey. *Geological Survey. Final Report Series of the State Geologist.* Trenton, Murphy, MacCrellish & Quigley, 1888-1917

Newark Museum Association. *The Work of the Potteries of New Jersey from 1685 to 1876*. Newark, Museum Association, 1914.

Parnes, Robert. *Canoeing the Jersey Pine Barrens*. Rev. ed. Charlotte, N.C., East Woods Press, c.1981.

Parsons, Floyd William. ed. *New Jersey: Life, Industries and Resources of a Great State*. Newark, State Chamber of Commerce, 1928.

Pepper, Adeline. *Tours of historic New Jersey*. Princeton, N.J., Van Nostrand, c.1965.

Port of New York Authority. *The Port of New York Authority: A Monograph*. New York, Port of New York Authority, 1936.

Resnick, Abraham. *New Jersey: its people and culture*. W.E.Rosenfelt, editorial consultant. Minneapolis, T.S.Denison, 1974.

Sackett, William Edgar. *Modern Battles of Trenton, v. 1: A History of Politics and Legislation, 1868-94*. Trenton, John L. Mur

Sedgwick, Theodore, Jr. *William Livingston: A Memoir*. New York, J. & J. Harper, 1833.

Sherman, Andrew M. Historic Morristown, *New Jersey: The Story of Its First Century*. Morristown, Howard Publishing Co., 1905.

Smith, Samuel. *History of the Colony Nova-Caesaria, or New Jersey*. Trenton State Reprint, William S. Sharp, 1890.

Steward, William, and Theophilus G. Steward. *Gouldtown: A Very Remarkable Settlement of Ancient Date*. Philadelphia, Lippincott, 1913.

Stockton, F.R. *Stories of New Jersey*. New York, American Book Co., 1896.

Storms, J.C. *Origin of the Jackson-Whites of the Ramapo Mountains*. Park Ridge, The Author, 1936.

Studley, Miriam V. *Historic New Jersey through visitors' eyes*. Princeton, N.J., Van Nostrand, 1964.

Tanner, Edwin P. *The Province of New Jersey, 1664-1738*. New York, Columbia University Press, 1908.

Trenton Historical Society. *A History of Trenton, 1679 1919*. Princeton, University Press, 1929.

Turnbull, Archibald Douglas. *John Stevens: An American Record*. New York, Century, 1928.

Urquhart, F.J. *History of the City of Newark, New Jersey, 1666-1913*. New York, Lewis Historical Publishing Co., 1913.

Van Deventer, Fred. *Cruising New Jersey tidewater, a boating and touring guide*. New Brunswick, N.J., Rutgers, c.1964.

Weiss, Harry Bischoff. *Life in early New Jersey*. Princeton, N.J., Van Nostrand, c.1964.

Wickes, Stephen. *History of Medicine in New Jersey and of Its Medical Men, from the Settlement of the Province to A.D.1800*. Newark, W. R. Dennis & Co., 1879.

Wilson, Edmund, Jr. *New Jersey, the Slave of Two Cities*. (In Gruening, Ernest, ed. These United States. 1st series.) New York, Boni & Liverright, 1923.

Wilson, Harold Fisher. *The story of the Jersey shore*. Princeton, N.J., Van Nostrand, 1964.

Worton, Stanley N. *New Jersey: past and present; a record of achievment*. New York, Hayden, c.1964.
  -*More Forgotten Towns of Southern New Jersey*. New York, Dutton, 1937.

INDEX

Italicized numbers indicate illustrations